Medical Group Management in Turbulent Times

How Physician Leadership
Can Optimize Health Plan, Hospital,
and Medical Group Performance

HAWORTH Marketing Resources
Innovations in Practice & Professional Services
William J. Winston, Senior Editor

New, Recent, and Forthcoming Titles:

Medical Group Management in Turbulent Times

How Physician Leadership Can Optimize Health Plan, Hospital, and Medical Group Performance

Paul A. Sommers, PhD

The Haworth Press
New York • London

The Haworth Press, Inc., 10 Alice Street, Binghamton, NY 13904-1580

Cover design by Monica L. Seifert.

Library of Congress Cataloging-in-Publication Data

Sommers, Paul A.
    Medical group management in turbulent times : how physician leadership can optimize health plan, hospital, and medical group performance / Paul A. Sommers.
        p.   cm.
    Includes bibliographical references and index.
    ISBN 0-7890-0487-9 (alk. paper)
    1. Hospital-physician relations. 2. Intergrated delivery of health care. 3. Health services administration. 4. Physician executives. [DNLM: 1. Delivery of Health Care, Integrated—organization & administration.   2. Practice Management, Medical—organization & administration. 3. Health Facility Administrators. 4. Physician Executives. W 84 S697m 1998]
    RA971.9.S65 1998
    362.1'068—dc21
    DNLM/DLC
    for Library of Congress   97-50421
                                                                                       CIP

CONTENTS

Chapter 9. Mission-Based Planning   299

Chapter 10. Financial Management   349

ABOUT THE AUTHOR

Paul Sommers has served in leadership capacities with physicians' groups and integrated health systems for the past twenty-one years. His initial health care experience includes work with the Marshfield Clinic and St. Joseph's Hospital (Marshfield, Wisconsin) and Gundersen Clinic and LaCrosse Lutheran Hospital (LaCrosse, Wisconsin). From 1985 to 1996 he served as Executive Vice President and Chief Administrative Officer of the Ramsey Clinic and Foundation, based in St. Paul, Minnesota. Ramsey includes St. Paul-Ramsey Medical Center and is part of HealthPartners' Care Delivery System of Minneapolis/St. Paul. In 1996 he joined the Allina Health System based in Minneapolis, Minnesota, to become Director of Health Measurement, Analysis, and Research. The Allina Health System supports more than 11,000 physicians, eighteen hospitals, and Medica Health Plans with more than one million members. In 1998, Sommers was appointed Vice President for United HealthCare to lead the development and implementation of data-based decision support services for its O'PIN Systems, a division of Applied Healthcare Informatics. O'PIN provides leading-edge managed care practice development and continuous improvement services in the health care industry. United HealthCare Corporation is based in Minneapolis and is the nation's second largest health insurer. More than 200,000 physicians compose its provider network.

Simultaneously, Dr. Sommers serves as Adjunct Professor at the University of Minnesota's Carlson School of Management, Division of Health Management and Policy, in Minneapolis. He has developed and teaches courses in medical group management and methods of practical problem solving for graduate students studying health care administration in programs leading to the MHA, MBA, and MPH degrees. He also serves as a preceptor to students in the MBA program in medical group management at the University of St. Thomas graduate school in Minneapolis.

He is author of more than eighty journal articles, textbook chapters, and related publications. In 1998, he wrote *Consumer Satisfaction in Medical Practice*, a book focused on the development of a detailed understanding of the role consumers play in the contemporary health care marketplace. His most recent book, *Alignment: A Practitioner's Guide to Managing Healthcare,* is forthcoming from The Haworth Press, Inc. *Alignment* shows how to convert the use of data from information to knowledge and subsequently to wisdom.

Preface

THE CONCEPTS BEHIND THIS TEXT

This text on managing medical practices is written from the orientation that leadership by and empowerment of physicians are essential to optimizing the integrated delivery of health care, now and into the future. Without clear and distinct leadership and proactive participation by physicians at each level within the universe of health care as it is defined today, there will be less effective health care, health products, and related services. The author's purpose is to enhance readers' understanding of and working relationship with practicing physicians, and enhance understanding of integration and the systems used to manage the delivery of effective medical practice. Defining attributes of and essential leadership characteristics in physicians in the contemporary practice of health care is a featured theme. Emphasis is placed upon the role of administrators in working as partners with practicing physicians toward the provision of effective, accessible, affordable services that provide excellence in health care.

The text is unique since it was developed with actual results acquired over the past twenty years of medical group management by the author. Specific statistics illustrate conditions present during the year the information was published or referenced. It is important to note that current yearly data can be acquired by contacting the source at the time plans are being reviewed to apply the information to physician and/or practice needs.

Each chapter has been established with defined goals and projected outcomes. Specific outcome-based objectives are outlined for each unit, and desired results are identified using examples as much as possible. Each unit is followed by a summary that highlights key points. Outcome analysis (analysis of how well targets were hit or goal[s] achieved) is considered by comparing one's understanding before and after the presentation of each unit. Upon successful analysis, understanding, and application of the material presented in this text, the reader will be able to:

1. Understand the physician's role in the management of a consumer-focused medical group.

2. Understand administration's role in the management of a medical group.
3. Understand the relationships and values among physicians, hospitals, and health plans working together.
4. Develop a positive philosophy of management concerning understanding and working with physicians in a medical group.
5. Understand the principles and value of integration that enable one to develop plans for joint operations among physicians, hospitals, and/or health plans that are predicated upon trust, common vision, and communicated mission.
6. Embrace change as a catalyst for the enhancement of medical practice, and establish processes to optimize the effectiveness of physicians that results from change.
7. Understand consumer satisfaction and the role it plays in the contemporary practice of health care. Incorporate consumer satisfaction as a way of doing business.
8. Develop an understanding of the outcome-based delivery of integrated service and of how to predict and achieve mutual success for the partners in the integration.
9. Understand and plan for (a) a shift in reimbursement of physicians, away from "fee-for-service" and toward "sum-certain," capitation, and other effective managed care methods of payment; (b) shifts in the practice of medicine away from "intervention" and toward "prevention"; and (c) "integration versus independence" in the development and implementation of systems for the delivery of care.
10. Create and understand jointly developed strategic plans and budgets predicated upon principles of continuous quality improvement.

Introduction

OVERVIEW: THE MANAGEMENT OF MEDICAL GROUPS IN TURBULENT TIMES

The attitude one takes to address a problem is oftentimes just as important as the technical and methodological skill used in its ultimate resolution. This text was written from a practical, "can-do" perspective. Timely and proven methods form the basis of each unit. Examples are frequently used to describe noteworthy activities and approaches.

Although administrators are trained to manage the delivery of medical care and service activities, simultaneously they must develop an effective working partnership with physicians, toward the desired outcome of implementing principles of practice management in operating systems. The administrator must become the eyes, ears, and heart of the organizational structure while understanding that results will depend upon how well administrators are able to empower physicians in leadership (and ownership) toward the achievement of planned results. The ability to function in this manner can be learned, and has been structured in the presentation of each unit, according to "can-do" principles of positive human interaction such as those taught by Pastor Robert H. Schuller on his series the *Hour of Power*[1] and others. There is no aspect of medical practice that cannot be accomplished through an effective practicing partnership among physicians and administrators. This text is predicated on a belief in empowerment of and leadership by physicians as essential building blocks in the long-term development of a successful medical group.

Encouraging the brightest minds toward healthy outcomes is within the grasp of every health care executive. Schuller speaks about developing relationships with others that lie within ourselves and start with a positive "can-do" attitude. It is incumbent upon each one of us to take responsibility for the development of positive relationship building. The following five-step sequence can be used to help guide activity:

> **Look**—Observe the written and the unwritten words (i.e., read between the lines).

1

Listen—Hear both verbal and nonverbal language (i.e., as in Stephen R. Covey's fifth habit, seek first to understand—then to be understood[2]).

Learn—We learn by making mistakes (e.g., it is always worth taking measured risks for the advancement of group rather than individual outcomes).

Lift—Build an organizational structure on a foundation of solid planning aimed at growth and enhancement while predicated upon quality, service, satisfaction, competitive price, and superior results.

Lead—Align targets for the medical practice with human and financial resources; measure and refine successes through continuous quality improvement.

Each chapter in this text has been developed with preset targets in mind for the reader. Understanding how various components interact with each other in the environment in which they exist is essential. Managing the elements of delivery of services in an organized manner is required to optimize effectiveness. Achievement of predictable results is a cardinal administrative responsibility that can be enhanced through application of continuous quality improvement.

Chapter 1

Changing Times, Trends, and the Business of Medicine

POINTS FOR FOCUS

Changes in health care and trends affecting contemporary medical practice are broadly reviewed in this chapter. Those responsible for the successful management of medical practice must first understand change and must learn to use the agents of change to enhance clinical and operating systems.

Targeted Goals

1. To understand what needs to be known about medical practice, in order to succeed by staying a little in advance of the times.
2. To define agents of change that affect both the clinical and administrative operations of a medical practice.

Objectives

1. Identify factors for potential success or failure within your practice or system.
2. Measure the effects of potential agents of change (positive and negative) upon accomplishment of targeted goals.
3. Align resources toward accomplishment of business targets determined to be influential predictors of success for your practice.

Content

Determine the current status and past trends of each component, activity, and/or measurement of importance in your practice or system that is associated with success of the organization.

Evaluation

An analysis is needed to determine the difference between what exists and what must be done to accommodate change. At this point it is most helpful to recognize and identify effects that need to be planned for in order to influence desired changes.

Continuous Quality Improvement (CQI)

Continuous quality improvement is a way of thinking about improvements in clinical practice and operating systems. At designated intervals of time, measure defined outcomes and/or progress toward the desired goals/targets, compared to expectations, and enhance or refine activity where needed.

CHANGING TIMES

Nothing is permanent except change.

—*Heraclitus*

To succeed in the marketplace, group practice leaders will have to master the art of managing change at both the organizational and individual levels.[1] Physicians are increasingly leading the way in shaping the future of health care. Health care in America is changing shape, size, and scope and will cease to exist in its present form throughout the United States early in the twenty-first century. As confirmed by Marion Merrell Dow Inc., in a 1995 review of health care in America, internally fueled health care reform is causing an unprecedented shift to managed care, resulting in lower health costs, as the private sector uses its economic clout to transform health care delivery in ways Congress can never hope to match.

After forcing a decrease in health insurance premiums for the first time in twenty years, employees continue to refine cost-cutting methods as they seek ways to improve quality of care and keep workers healthy. Hospitals and medical groups are feeling the effects of the price wars begun by health plans. Managed care is becoming a dominant model of delivery and must deliver on price, value, quality, performance, and consumer satisfaction. Integrated physician, hospital, and health plan-based organizations are forming large competitive networks. Physicians are changing management strategies to take advantage of the shift in payment away from fee-for-service medicine. Pharmaceutical manufacturers are leaving tradition behind to structure new alliances with health plans.[2]

Health care technology is positioning new product development to balance the promise of "state-of-the-art" with affordability. The rapid growth of home health care, which was originally developed to reduce hospital stays, may very well become the way many people have their health care needs met in the future. Telecommunication capabilities such as telemedicine are extending the practice of medicine to virtually the most remote, rural areas of the world. Finding itself in an unending fiscal dilemma, the federal government needs to restructure its health care business to effectively support consumers who qualify for Medicare, Medicaid, and other contracted/managed care services. Most state governments are seeking local opportunities but need flexibility to encourage innovation among interested providers. Change has been defined as the "new constant."[3]

Recognizing the importance of a strong "physician-hospital-health plan partnership," the Allina Health System, used as one example, structured a comprehensive approach to address tomorrow's issues in the extremely competitive Minneapolis-St. Paul, Minnesota marketplace. The top officers are a physician president and a nonphysician executive officer who jointly lead a team composed of more than 9,000 providers, more than 6,200 physicians affiliated by contract through the system's health plans, 19 owned or managed hospitals, over 1 million patient/members, and over $2 billion in annual revenues. The message and structural underpinning was clear: Allina was a level playing field where hospitals, physicians, and health plans have brought their respective talents to the table as equals.[4]

Another large, Minneapolis-St. Paul health system, HealthPartners, charted changing behaviors and demographics through environmental assessments. The following trends were observed:

- The expansion of metropolitan urban areas will slow: Service should be expanded toward residential areas and exurban centers.
- Core cities are declining, suburban resources are growing, and suburb-to-suburb commuting is increasing.
- Rural population is stabilizing after a long period of decline.
- People are "time-bankrupt" (except for seniors) because of time demands of work, family, day care, community, hobbies, commuting.
- Demand has increased for goods and services "anytime and anyplace."
- Baby boomers are entering a stage given to chronic disease. They have been accustomed to curative medicine for infectious diseases, which differ from chronic ones.
- Sequestration/individualism is an increasing factor, as seen in the physical, mental, or emotional separation of individuals from their greater community.
- Telecommuting/interconnectivity is an increasing factor; Internet connection is now available through personal computers.
- Temporary/part-time employment is an increasing factor.[5]

MARKET-DRIVEN REFORM

The health care system is evolving through the influence of market-forces. The functions of (insurance) carriers and (health care) providers are changing rapidly, and definitions are blurring as each vies for control of the premium dollar. Indemnity carriers (insurers and Blue Cross systems) are converting to network-based managed care. Companies providing managed care are developing advanced products, capitalizing on the leverage of twenty years of experience and superior informational systems.

A new category of companies is emerging that functions both as vendors of tools to carriers and as competitors for carriers' premiums. These companies will have great leverage, as indemnity carriers convert to managed care and as existing companies providing managed care seek new tools in order to remain competitive with leaders in the industry. This new class of companies has three main functions:[6]

1. organizing physicians;
2. developing new networks of managed care; and
3. developing managed care specialty products and networks (e.g., in disease management).

Companies in this emerging sector will likely market directly to government-mandated programs (e.g., Medicare) and to self-insured employers by focusing on treating high-cost areas of health care. At the same time, they can pursue markets for indirect sales to carriers and HMOs. We expect that these companies will be compensated by sharing in the health care premium in return for the risk they will bear. Although payers and consumers will likely be unaware of the changing environment, the function of carriers, HMOs, and providers will gradually change as risk is shifted to providers and to specialty companies that are compensated for the value they add.

RESEARCHING CONSUMERS

Consumers are well aware of the types of behaviors they engage in that are thought to contribute to poor health. They need something to spur them to active avoidance of such behaviors. This type of motivator is described by some as "something bad happening to you or someone you know." People are willing to have encouragement and information about leading a healthy lifestyle come from their health plans as well as from their physicians. People want incentives for living well and sanctions for people who raise the cost of everyone's health care by not doing so. They don't want to be in a pool with people who are not "eating their greens," if that raises their own payments. This attitude seems especially prevalent among people in their twenties and thirties.[5]

Choice among providers is decreasing as a factor in health care, but not because consumers wanted it to be less important. Consumers want to have a personal physician. They want their physician to show that he or she cares about them. Communication is the key to this relationship.

Consumers want to have better access to their physician, but people want the ability to get care without the trouble of going to see a physician. Do consumers in your area indicate willingness to use "remote access" to care, information, and prescriptions? Do they say, "Don't make me come in when I don't have to?" Having medical information centralized and available to any provider or on a "smart card" has been seen as a way of keeping valuable medical information accessible. The expectations of consumers concerning speed of service in their health care have not been increasing.

There is a lot of confusion and apathy among consumers about health plans. People are several name changes behind—"I don't know" is the leading health plan!

A SNAPSHOT OF MARKETPLACE REACTION TO REFORM

In 1995, more than 85 percent of metro-area residents in Minnesota participated in a plan offering managed care. The health plans compete for members with other insurers, self-insured companies, organizations served by preferred providers, and community-integrated service networks (CISNs). This results in a broader range of products being offered. Competitors offering health plans are working to reduce costs, competing on price to build market share (willing to take losses for several years to obtain business), and improving their risk pool.

The ten states with the fastest growth rates of capitated health plans are shown in Table 1.1.

Employers are starting to look at total cost per employee including costs for the health plan, sick leave, disability insurance, workers' compensation, and so on. In addition, they are taking a purchasing approach that includes competitive bidding and the creation of coalitions of buyers to increase their leverage. Other trends among key purchasers show (1) that employees are paying more of the cost of their insurance, (2) that employers are surveying employees on their opinions on health plans and are publishing results, and (3) that employers are demanding data and proof of

TABLE 1.1. Ten States with the Fastest Growth Rates of Capitated Health Plans

	Percentage of Population in Capitated Plans	Percentage of Increase 1990-1993
California	32.9	12.3
Massachusetts	32.7	21.8
Oregon	31.5	18.8
Colorado	21.6	12.5
Connecticut	19.5	14.4
Delaware	19.4	18.0
Maryland	19.4	16.4
New York	19.2	12.1
Pennsylvania	16.3	12.6
New Mexico	16.1	12.9

Source: Hamer, R. *The Competitive Edge,* InterStudy Publications, Minneapolis, MN, 1994. Reprinted with permission.

efficiency and effectiveness, are working toward longer-term partnerships with carriers, and are consolidating their offerings to one or two carriers.

Consumers are confused by the mergers and changes in networks;[6] there is opportunity for simplification. Consumers are being asked to pay a higher share of premiums along with higher co-pays and out-of-pocket costs.[7] This makes consumers demand more from their providers of health care. See Table 1.2 for an example of the growth of networks.

Some health plans are more aggressive with direct contracts to providers. Some are increasing the use of co-pays by the patient at the office visit, to reduce premiums. And there is a trend toward tighter networks to improve cost and manage quality. New bases of competition are developing among clinical systems within the same network of providers, and this competition (along with new products and forecasts of continued change) is producing benefits to consumers in service and in price.

The health program legislated by Minnesota is intensely relevant to the rest of the country. It serves in many ways as a prototype for impending federal proposals on health and for most states currently dealing with local efforts at reform.[8] While brainstorming to push his health reform plan in 1994, President Bill Clinton made Minnesota a frequent stop. He touted the

TABLE 1.2. Health Network Expansion—Expected Growth in Regional Networks by the Year 2000

Population of standard metro area	# of metro areas	Avg. networks/ metro area	Total networks
Fewer than 450,000	221	2	442
450,000 to 1.5 million	72	3.5	252
More than 1.5 million	28	5	140
Total	321	2.6	834

Source: Thomas P. Weil, Bedford Health Associates, Asheville, North Carolina, 1994. Reprinted with permission from Brown, A. *Research: Healthcare, Likely Trends as the Healthcare System Evolves.* A Brown and Sons, Baltimore, MD. January 3, 1995.

state's MinnesotaCare as a cutting-edge initiative for managed competition and inspiration for his own efforts. The comparison did neither him nor Minnesota's advocates for reform any good. The Clinton plan died. MinnesotaCare, like many other efforts, continues to face new scrutiny.

Preparing for Future Needs

Many of the changes we are witnessing in medicine today will lead to a system for health care tomorrow that provides for all Americans at a fair price. Among the most important of these changes are an increase in personal responsibility, the movement to measure and manage outcomes, and the effort to reform the system itself, according to C. Everett Koop, MD.[9] Few disagree that any reformed health system should provide access to health care for all Americans at a reasonable cost. That is what consumers want; that is what employers and other buyers of health care want; that is what politicians want; and that is what providers of health care want to deliver. But to get there, we must realize that reforming the health care system will not happen overnight. We must also realize that what we want as individuals and as institutions is not necessarily what is best for the country.

Many believe that health care is a right. But with that right comes a responsibility to use the system appropriately and prudently. Consideration of appropriate and prudent usage leads us to ask: How much health care should each person get? Asking that inevitably brings up the word no one wants to use—rationing. On this we should be perfectly clear: We have been rationing health care for decades. Just spend a few minutes in a hospital, in a doctor's office, in an HMO, or observe patients in a busy urban emergency room and you will see rationing firsthand. Take, for example, a typical family practitioner who has a waiting room so full of patients he cannot spend the time he would like with each one. That is why we have to find a way to communicate to all Americans that we cannot have every procedure and every test every time we want them and still control spending on health care.

To accomplish the goal of extending affordable and reasonable care to all Americans, we must curb the greed that is prevalent in the system—not just greed among some insurers, providers, and special interests, but also greed among some patients. The medical profession has taught patients to expect perfection from our system of health care

Patients who get anything less are quick to sue hospitals, doctors, and any provider they deem responsible. According to Donald M. Berwick, MD, President and CEO of the Institute of Health Care Improvement, Boston, Massachusetts, the mentality of health care providers is different now. Many health care institutions may be willing to consider approaches that are much more innovative than in the past. Once they begin to change, it is easier for them to make improvements in many areas.[10]

Payers

Annual increase in health insurance premiums are high compared to other indicators.[2] The payer system is not likely to change too dramatically over the next few years. Payment for health care is likely to remain largely employer-based, and government-run. Entitlement programs (Medicare and Medicaid) are not likely to expand. The most likely development is an increase in individual purchasers, particularly if a tax incentive is passed to encourage self-insurance.[7] Presently, corporations deduct the cost of health care benefits from taxable income, but individuals buying health insurance receive no tax benefit unless they are self-employed. See Figure 1.1.

Although the payer system is not likely to alter dramatically over the next few years, demands from the payer system are likely to change. Payers are beginning to expect from providers more information on quality and on outcomes; we believe those expectations will evolve into a demand. Today's rudimentary measures of quality and efficacy (e.g., accreditation by the National Committee for Quality Assurance [NCQA] and the standards/report cards of the Health Plan Employer Data and Information Set [HEDIS]) will develop into more sophisticated tools to help payers choose among their options.

FIGURE 1.1. Worker Earnings versus Health Care Costs

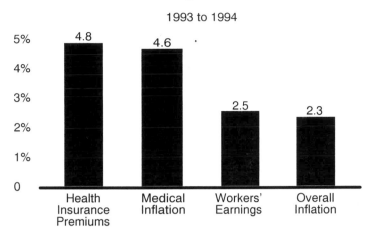

1993 to 1994

Source: *KPMG Survey of Employer-Sponsored Health Benefits,* KPMG Peat Marwick, Montvale, NJ, 1994, U.S. Bureau of Labor Statistics. Reprinted with permission from ALEX, Brown & Sons. Research: HealthCare, "Likely Trends as the Healthcare System Evolves," January 3, 1995.

The payer system is both direct and indirect. It includes carriers (indemnity, Blue Cross, and managed care companies); government entitlement programs (Medicare, Medicaid); employers that self-insure for their health care needs (or set aside a reserve for costs of health care rather than shift the risk to a carrier); and individuals. The dominance of a particular payer in a market depends on the type of population and level of employment in an area, whether large or small employers dominate there, and geographic location (innovations in health care, such as the HMO, generally develop and grow first in the West, in the United States). Although companies providing managed care have enjoyed robust enrollment, their total penetration among the United States population is only about 20 percent. Nearly 100 million people (about 40 percent of the total U.S. population and more than 90 percent of people on Medicare) are in Blue Cross systems.

In many markets, Blue Cross systems have greater than a 35 percent share of a market. Blue Cross and indemnity carriers dominate the small group market. It is believed that companies providing managed care will be able to continue to fuel growth by taking market share from indemnity carriers. However, even greater than expected conversion to managed care still leaves a considerable majority of the insured population in indemnity products.

IMPLICATIONS

Hospitals

Overcapacity and increased competition have put hospitals under intense financial pressure. To help ease that pressure and to make it easier to attract new patients, hospitals are joining with other hospitals and with physicians' groups as well. The one word that best describes what is happening throughout the hospital industry during the 1990s is: consolidation. Actions taken by the federal government in the 1980s were largely responsible for decreasing the number of occupied hospital beds. The rise in outpatient surgery also contributed to today's overcapacity. By forming alliances, hospitals hope to improve their profitability and become the accountable health plans of the postreform era—capable of providing comprehensive care to local or regional populations.[11]

Hospitals are struggling to retain power, as payers and carriers develop both sophisticated purchasing systems and more control in directing care. Of the three major players in the health care delivery system (carriers, physicians, and hospitals), hospitals have the least direct control of their revenue stream (the patient). Control is projected to diminish further, as payers and physicians become more organized and efficient.

Hospital costs represent the largest part of the nation's health care bill— about 37 percent of the total. Personal care (dental, home health, vision, durable medical equipment) represents 24 percent; physician service, 19 percent; administration, research, and construction, 12 percent; and nursing home care, 8 percent.[12] Jobs in hospitals account for more than half of all positions in health care. Of the 10.2 million men and women employed in health care facilities in the United States, 5.2 million work in hospitals.

While impending reforms in health care will present new challenges for the nation's hospitals, hospital administrators continue to struggle with the familiar problems of diminishing inpatient revenue and empty beds. According to the American Hospital Association (AHA), since 1989 inpatient procedures have declined steadily, while outpatient procedures have increased. The AHA says 310,000 of the nation's 925,000 community hospital beds are empty each night. The cost of each empty bed: $30,000 to $40,000 per year. Similar situations exist at other hospitals such as tertiary, or teaching, institutions. To help ensure their future, many hospitals are merging with other institutions. During fiscal 1993, the U.S. Department of Justice received fifty-six requests for approval from hospitals planning to merge. It had received twenty-one such filings in the previous year.[9]

Although many hospitals are interested in forming alliances with other hospitals, they fear that in trying to do so they may violate federal antitrust statutes. Both the Justice Department and the Federal Trade Commission (FTC) closely scrutinize proposed collaborations among hospitals. The government focuses mainly on the competitive impact of mergers of hospitals. Federal regulators presume that any reduction in the number of independent competitors—the necessary result of mergers or joint ventures involving existing hospital services—is likely to be associated with higher prices and lower quality, according to the AHA. Consequently, hospitals have attracted patients by offering the most advanced services, equipment, and facilities, the AHA maintains. This trend has resulted in extensive duplication without documented improvement. Perhaps most important, successful hospitals and physician-hospital alliances will have to prove their value by providing outcomes and other data that are comprehensive, accurate, and timely.[11] Results from 1997 show an 18 percent drop in merger and acquisition activity compared to 1996.[13]

Organizations Providing Managed Care

The functions of carriers and providers are blurring at a most rapid rate. Health plans are joining together, acquiring hospitals and groups of providers, and developing data to demonstrate quality and cost effectiveness. Health plans are forming alliances with hospitals, physicians' groups, and a variety of specialized organizations of providers, and merging all those into new entities called integrated service networks (ISNs), or integrated delivery systems, or integrated systems of care. The ISNs are structured to provide cradle-to-grave health care for entire populations. Most ISNs would receive a capitated, or fixed monthly per-person, fee for providing all necessary services related to health care for every participant.

The HMOs are struggling to find primary care physicians (PCPs). Moreover, they are working to meet employers' demands to demonstrate the quality and cost effectiveness of the care they deliver. Figures on enrollment in HMOs show that before 1980, fewer than 10 million Americans belonged to HMOs. By the end of 1994, 50 million Americans (16 percent of the population) had become members of an HMO, according to an estimate by the Group Health Association of America (GHAA), in Washington, an industry/trade group that represents more than 350 HMOs.

In 1992, fourteen of Minnesota's largest employers formed the Buyers Health Care Action Group (BHCAG) to address the rising costs of health care. The interest of BHCAG centers on working with providers to develop incentives to maximize quality at the lowest possible cost. Rather than simply buying an "off-the-shelf" product offered at a discounted price by a health plan anxious to serve the members of BHCAG, the action group issued a request for proposals, demanding an integrated and standard set of medical practices for delivering health care.[14] The declared aim of BHCAG is to restore the proper balance of power between systems for care, health plans, purchasers, and consumers, so that the health plans do not play the dominant role in the market. To put its money where its 100,000 mouths are, BHCAG is working with the Employers Association and the Minnesota Chamber of Commerce to develop a similar purchasing coalition for small businesses. All buyers should start sharing (the goal of high quality care at the lowest possible cost) to give providers a clear set of financial incentives.[15,16] By 1998, twenty-nine groups were part of the BHCAG representing 130,000 enrollees.[17,18]

Standard practices have been described in the past as "cookbook medicine." One advantage in this project, however, is that providers are enthusiastic about working together to develop the new standards rather than having outsiders impose standards upon them. It is the difference between creating incentives to get the system to control costs and quality on its own, on one hand, or hiring a consultant to try to control cost and quality after the fact, on the other. We want physicians to take control of their destiny. In exchange for restoring that discretion to the system—where the physician defines how to treat the patient—they will have to take some shared financial risk.

Part of the BHCAG solution that presents one of the greatest challenges concerns data. Providers are developing a clinical system that gathers data to help them understand variations in treatment—what works best and what does not. The system is very different from current payer-based systems used by government, HMOs, and insurance companies to review utilization for the purpose of reimbursement. Instead, BHCAG is working with providers on collecting data using an automated system of medical records that analyzes patterns in practice and help physicians define the highest quality, most cost-effective standards for treatment.

The BHCAG is looking toward the power of the market—not the mandate of government—for the solution. Says Steve Wetzell, Executive Director of BHCAG: "We're looking at what steps we can take and how we can structure our contracts to make sure the competition is at the level of the integrated delivery system."[14] Here, Wetzell disagrees with aspects of MinnesotaCare and with some of the work of the State Health Care Commission. As he puts it, "Although we agree conceptually with the concept of integrated service networks, we disagree with the amount of regulation they've created and the price controls they've overlaid on the system."[14] Other purchasing groups who have formed and are active in the regional marketplace include: State Employees Group Insurance Program, Minnesota Employees Insurance Program and Public Employers Insurance Program, and Employers Association Buyer's Coalition.[15]

BUYERS HEALTH CARE ACTION GROUP

"A focus on quality, not volume. Bigger is not better."[16]

1998 BHCAG member employers are:

American Express Co.	Minnegasco
AmerUs Group	3M Corp.
Barry-Wehmiller Group Inc.	Minnesota Mutual
Bemis Co. Inc.	Northern States Power Co.
B.F. Goodrich Rosemount Aerospace	Northwest Corp.
Cargill Inc.	Pfizer Inc.
Carlson Companies Inc.	Pillsbury Co.
CENEX Inc.	Rosemount Inc.
Ceridian Corp.	Sioux Empire Employers
Dayton Hudson Corp.	Health Care Group
General Mills Inc.	Supervalu Inc.
Honeywell Inc.	Target Stores
Jostens Inc.	Tennant Co.
Land O'Lakes Inc.	U.S. Bancorp
Mervyn's	U.S. West

Source: BHCAG.

Gambling on a new way of providing health care, a group of Minnesota's largest employers now has some sign that they are winning. With 1998 enrollment information in hand, the Buyers Health Care Action Group (BHCAG) has evidence supporting their efforts: When given a choice, employees opted for groups of providers that offer lower prices and have higher satisfaction survey results.[17]

BHCAG established itself as competition for health plans more than a year ago and is beginning to make some waves by charging its members who choose more expensive clinics a higher premium, while at the same time providing its members results of surveys ranking the quality of each group of clinics. Lower cost clinics groups experienced the most significant enrollment gains after last fall's open enrollment period, with increases ranging from 15 percent to 57 percent. High cost clinics, for the most part, saw enrollment shrink—except for one that also showed a high quality rating.[18]

BHCAG employers are excited about the enrollment information, but others question how big of a deal this really is. BHCAG enrollment grew by about 5,000 last year; its current 130,000 enrollees represent a small portion of the health care marketplace.

BHCAG's Choice Plus health plan offers enrollees the choice of sixteen care systems, or groups of providers. The care systems have three different prices, depending on the bids they gave BHCAG. Some employers absorb those differences themselves while others have fully implemented the model, with a price difference between the lowest and highest cost tiers of $19 per member per month.

The Price Differential

BHCAG employers charged their employees different premiums depending on the costs charged by each of sixteen health care systems that participate in the plan. Employees had to pay more if they chose to get their health care at more expensive clinics.

	Low Cost Clinics	Medium Cost Clinics	High Cost Clinics
Single coverage	no additional premium charge	plus $8.50 per month	plus $19 per month
Family coverage	no additional premium charge	plus $17 per month	plus $38 per month

Source: BHCAG.

Based on bids that each care systems submitted to BHCAG, the care systems are put into one of three cost groups; four are in the low cost group, eight in the medium cost group, and four in the high cost group. Employees who choose a low cost care system pay no additional premium. Choosing a medium cost care system adds about $8.50 per month for an individual and $17 for family coverage to the monthly premium. And choosing a high cost system boosts the premium by $19 for individuals and $38 for families.

Role of Consumer Satisfaction

Research on consumer satisfaction represents an unmet need. Although satisfaction scores may yield accurate rating estimates on a scale of 1 to 5 or excellent and poor, they do not necessarily report experiences. Follow-up work on BHCAG results to date seem to indicate that surveys based on the experience the patient had is much more highly valued by consumers than information derived from ratings alone. People seem to think about ratings as opinions, and the reporting of experiences more like facts. The key is to tie opinion and fact together for purposes of better meeting each consumer's need at the lowest level of expense. When it comes to having consumers switching providers based on cost and satisfaction information, the message to the provider community is that they are going to see more of that, not less, Wetzell said. The enrollment information shows that care systems with better than average patient satisfaction survey results saw higher enrollment gains and those with below average patient satisfaction survey results saw losses.

Next Steps

Besides quality information, the addition of more enrollees will be important in keeping and building provider interest as BHCAG moves ahead. The 130,000 current enrollees represent about 5 percent of the metro market, Wetzell said. They are the employees of some of the area's largest companies, such as Minneapolis-based Dayton Hudson Corp. and Maplewood-based 3M Co. New enrollees could come from newly recruited companies and from current employers who stop offering competing plans. BHCAG is holding its first-ever membership meeting in early 1998, telling nonmember employers what the group is and why they would want to join. BHCAG members all have at least 500 employees.

New Role for Health Plans

HealthPartners, Minnesota's second largest health plan, had been retained by BHCAG to provide administrative services such as enrollment, claims payment, members services, and certain plan-wide integration services through its subcontractor, Aetna. However, George Halvorson, CEO of HealthPartners, announced that they will not be bidding on the contract to administer the BHCAG plan after the year 2000.

Why? "They've become an HMO," said Halvorson. "We welcome the Action Group to the marketplace as a competitor." The Action Group, meanwhile, does not see itself as a competitor to HealthPartners, or any other HMO, said Steve Wetzell, the action Group's executive director. "We are not a competitor," Wetzell said. "Our employers disagree strongly with the charge that we are."[19]

The irony is that Buyers Health Care Action Group, a coalition of Minnesota's largest employers, came together in 1992 to counter the HMO's growing power and monthly premiums. The idea was that the largest employers—such as Dayton Hudson, 3M, and Honeywell—would pool their resources and ask doctors and hospitals to bid for the business of treating their employees, thus increasing competition in the marketplace. From the beginning, the Action Group drew a lot of national attention for its grand experiment in the health care marketplace. As recently as last month, *Fortune* magazine profiled the Action Group as an example of innovative thinkers.

When HealthPartners won the contract five years ago to administer the Action Group's business, HealthPartners hailed it as a huge win. But that was before the Action Group grew in numbers and sophistication and before it published the terms of the contract to administer the plan after 2000. An example of the type of evolving competition is reflected when BHCAG asks bidders to make its plan available to "new markets and populations, such as Medicare and Medicaid and consumers who do not currently have access." For an HMO such as HealthPartners, that would mean selling the Action Group's health plan and selling its own plans at the same time.

Also disconcerting to HealthPartners, the proposal asks whether the bidder would oppose expanded legislation to "level the playing field" with state regulated insurance products and health plans.

Because it is not legally an HMO, the Action Group is not regulated by the state or federal government. The advantage is that it does not pay the same taxes HMOs do, and is not required to set aside a reserve in case of unexpected costs, as HMOs are. There has been talk, however, about extending the HMO regulations to include programs such as the Action Group.

Numbers released by BHCAG demonstrated that when those care systems compete, and consumers have more choice based on price and satisfaction, a shift in the marketplace occurs. According to the Action Group, this year, the lowest cost care systems—doctors, clinics, and hospitals that have banded together—with average patient satisfaction survey results gained the largest percentage of members. Meanwhile, the highest cost care systems, with the lowest patient satisfaction, lost the highest percentage of members. The shift is a very early demonstration—based on a sampling of about 60,000 Minnesotans—that consumers make choices based on cost and satisfaction.

Physicians

As the number of Americans enrolled in health plans grows, so too does the influence of managed care on doctors' professional lives. As more doctors accept capitated, or fixed, payment for the care of patients, they are assuming responsibility for the cost of care as well as for its clinical results. Managed care is also affecting the way doctors are trained. Lawmakers and experts in issues concerning the workforce of physicians are calling for more medical students to receive residency training in HMOs and in ambulatory clinics, rather than in traditional teaching hospitals.

In general, physicians have formed a disjointed, unorganized system for delivery of health care. In some markets (particularly the northeastern United States), solo practice is still common. In most markets, physicians have at least begun to organize into group practices, but the size and power of the groups varies. In three areas (the West Coast, Minneapolis, and southern Florida), the organization of the delivery system is particularly advanced. In California, penetration of the market by HMOs was the catalyst that propelled the organization of physicians' systems into integrated networks of subcontractors. As membership in HMOs grew, physicians began to organize into groups to maximize leverage.

Ultimately, large multispecialty groups with solid alliances to hospital systems became subcontracting networks that managed risk (and patient care) for a percentage of premiums. A similar system developed in southern Florida as Medicare risk contractors subcontracted with physicians' groups rather than building their own systems, in order to enter the market quickly and accelerate gains in market share. In many markets, providers have aligned to form organized systems for delivery like the PHOs (physician/hospital organizations) that act as subcontracting units.[6,7] Physicians also understand that in a struggle among private and public buyers of health care to improve care and reduce costs, doctors will be held accountable for the number and types of services they deliver and for the ancillary expenses they generate.

In the late 1980s, many managed care organizations (MCOs) and indemnity insurers turned to utilization review (UR) to help them lower medical costs. Patients needed to obtain preauthorization for certain tests, as well as for some diagnostic procedures, admissions to a hospital, and surgeries. Doctors spent much of their time filling out forms and fielding requests for information from utilization reviewers asking them to justify their decisions concerning treatment. Many doctors objected to what they viewed as intrusions into their practices and to cost containment at the expense of patient care.

Although many health plans still rely on some form of UR, others have begun to switch to capitation, paying doctors a fixed amount every month for the total care of each patient. Capitation shifts responsibility for providing the best, most cost-effective care from the HMO to the physician. It minimizes the need to have outsiders question doctors' decisions concerning treatment. Moreover, doctors participating in plans providing managed care are answerable for their clinical outcomes and, increasingly, for patients' satisfaction. With capitation, doctors have every incentive to be efficient and to reduce waste.

Methods of payment used by HMOs vary widely. Capitation, however, is their most common form of payment, particularly to primary care providers (PCPs). A 1992 survey by the Group Health Association of America (GHAA) showed that 14 percent of HMOs paid straight salaries to PCPs; 42 percent used a method called payment per service unit, one of several variations of fee for service; and 44 percent relied on some type of capitation formula. Often, HMOs may add incentive payments based on prescribed measures such as high rates of immunization or high levels of patient satisfaction. Capitation will become more popular and widespread.[6]

The primary care provider will play an increasingly large role in the delivery of health care. Already, HMOs need more PCPs, and with more such physicians, all costs for health care should decline. Moreover, in their role as gatekeepers, PCPs coordinate patients' treatments, seeing that resources are used appropriately. Using the premise that there should be one PCP for every 1,200 to 1,500 people, the United States needs about 50,000 more PCPs.

Managed care organizations already need more PCPs than are available. A 1993 study by GHAA shows that about 60 percent of all HMOs find it difficult to recruit PCPs. Experts on policymaking in health care emphasize the importance of PCPs in coordinating medical treatment and ensuring that patients receive appropriate and necessary care. The gatekeeping activities of primary care physicians are critical to an optimal health care system and should be further developed to improve health care for all patients. Specialists, who have gained the reputation of ordering more tests, performing more procedures, and generally "practic[ing] a more expensive brand of medicine," are responsible for much of the continuing increase in the cost of health care. The current imbalance between specialists and generalists affects not only medical costs but also access to basic health care, a particular problem in rural areas and inner cities. Many areas have no physicians whatsoever, and there are counties where people have to travel for over an hour to receive any kind of health care.

In 1993, fewer than 20 percent of graduating medical students planned to become generalists, an increase from an all-time low of 14.6 percent the previous year, according to the Association of American Medical Colleges (AAMC) in Washington. The financial pressures of debts from attending medical school also shape students' choices of careers. Medical students owe an average of $50,000 each by the time they complete medical school. These debts hardly encourage students to choose careers in the lower paying disciplines such as primary care, despite estimates by health care analysts that if 50 percent of all physicians were PCPs, national expenditures for doctors' services would decrease by 39 percent. Even if one-half of all graduating medical students now chose to enter primary care, the desirable 50:50 ratio of generalists to specialists would not be achieved until the year 2040.

The federal government began a focused effort to help the shift toward development of primary care when it introduced Medicare's increase in fees for the provision of generalists' services in 1992. In redesigning its system for payments and introducing the resource-based relative-value scale (RBRVS), Medicare placed more value on medical care that requires a doctor's time and cognitive skills than on that involving the performing of procedures. Most doctors agree that the RBRVS has helped equalize selecting fees for PCPs, but critics argue that the schedule of payments has not gone far enough. By reimbursing doctors for invasive services at a rate that exceeds the actual costs, the system still favors specialty medicine.

Expectations Concerning Reporting

To ensure that providers are delivering the best care at the lowest cost, managed care groups are developing guidelines for practice and are requiring physicians to participate if they want to treat members in that plan. The development of guidelines, whether state or federal, has been an expectation of consumers. One step in that direction is the Health Plan Employer Data and Information Set (HEDIS), which defines a core set of measures of performance for health-plans and methodologies for deriving measures of performance. The National Committee for Quality Assurance (NCQA), in Washington, an accrediting organization, developed HEDIS with employers and with representatives of health plans.

The HEDIS helps employers develop standardized data with which to compare health plans. Health plans can also use HEDIS for self-evaluation. During 1998, NCQA will redefine the way the nation's health plans demonstrate quality in the years ahead. The release of the first true performance-based accreditation program for health plans—which does not take effect until July 1999—will formally integrate HEDIS and Accreditation, the two principal tools used by employers and consumers to help make health plan coverage decisions. The implications and the advantages for health plans, employers, and consumers are considerable. "Incorporating HEDIS measures into Accreditation will provide consumers and employers with better information to help guide choice," said NCQA president Margaret E. O'Kane. "For health plans that demonstrate excellent performance, that's a huge improvement over the status quo. It means widespread recognition of their achievements in the market."[20]

Over the past year, NCQA has worked with health plans, employers, and others to identify HEDIS measures that will be included alongside or in lieu of standards that look at related systems and processes. Thus, in the future, both clinical performance and a plan's systems and process will factor into their Accreditation decision. Development of the performance-based accreditation program was guided by input from NCQA's Committee on Performance Measurement and Standards, respectively responsible for evolving HEDIS and Accreditation. The two groups—both composed of representatives of employers, consumers, health plans, providers, and others—helped design the program to ensure that it would meet the needs of all groups with a stake in health care quality oversight.

Under the new program, a health plan's compliance with standards will still account for the majority of its overall score, but its HEDIS data will also count significantly toward its ultimate decision. NCQA is working with health plans and others to develop appropriate means of scoring HEDIS data in order to objectively incorporate these results into accreditation decisions. One issue of special concern is whether performance targets will be based on national or regional averages.

Incorporating HEDIS measures into Accreditation will also allow NCQA to create a new generation of information products, such as a revised Accreditation Status List and an updated version of the Accreditation Summary Report which will provide richer information for purchasers and consumers. In addition, NCQA expects to introduce new accreditation decision categories to better distinguish between plans. Over the past two years, NCQA has launched a number of programs designed to help streamline the oversight process and make it easier for health plans, providers, and administrators to focus on their core business—providing high quality care. A common theme running through these new programs has been the substitution of one review for many.

A variety of independent efforts were initiated to advance a common-sense approach toward the systematic management of medical problems. For example, in 1993, Group Health, Mayo Clinic, Park Nicollet Medical Center, and HealthPartners founded the Institute for Clinical Systems Integration (ICSI) in cooperation with BHCAG, which has grown from fourteen large businesses to a coalition of twenty-nine businesses in Minnesota in 1998. Their vision was for ICSI to be an organizational bridge in a new model for integrated delivery of health care. An independent, non-profit organization, ICSI provides quality improvement services to medical groups affiliated with HealthPartners in central and southern Minnesota and western Wisconsin.[21]

Measurements of health care are a fundamental part of the ICSI program. Data from records of claims, medical charts, and other sources are considered in all phases of the continuous process of quality improvement. Each guideline for health care includes a plan for measuring concordance (the match between the recommended and the actual practice) and/or short-term effects. Reports on measurements per guidelines are used by participating medical groups to target areas for continuous quality improvement, as well as by the ICSI to determine the need for changes in guidelines. Investigators at Group Health Foundation are collaborating with ICSI, HealthPartners, and the University of Minnesota on guideline impact studies. The studies evaluate whether the use of clinical guidelines is associated with improved care and reduced costs.[21] The accumulated experience in guideline evaluation will be used to improve strategies for guideline implementation.

Prevention versus Intervention

The establishment of guidelines or standards for practice is meant to lead to the development of best practices and, ultimately, to the use of less-intensive health care resources and the development of healthy lifestyles. The involvement of ICSI and of health care providers throughout HealthPartners' network is key to the success of Partners for Better Health. Partners for Better Health is a program designed to bring providers, employers, members, and the community together to prevent illness and improve the health status of the population.

ICSI will be very involved in identifying members of HealthPartners who are at risk, and then encouraging patients to access the information and tools available through Partners for Better Health. Providers can also benefit from the cumulative knowledge gained through working with a targeted population and measuring and analyzing the results of positive changes made in this population. Education about the prevention of disease and about development of healthy lifestyles is the major focus: determining how best to motivate people to change, which treatments and information are most effective, and how gradually to move an entire population to an improved state of health.

Allina's Community Health Improvement focus and Partners for Better Health are both aimed at disease prevention strategies to help reduce risk and improve health for members with disease conditions. Programs have been implemented to help members do what is necessary to promote prevention of disease by reducing existing risks for the disease, or help them actually make changes needed to recover from an illness and thereby improve their health.

Management of Disease

Management of disease is a relatively new concept being applied to a broad base of new medical protocols and systems. Managing disease represents a philosophical shift away from managing care through a focus on the primary care physician and other categories of input (e.g., on costs of prescriptions or on hospital days per thousand people in the population). The theory behind the new concept is to manage costs by focusing on costly diseases and shifting risk to a specialist or to a network handling a specialty. The basic tenet underlying the new focus is that since 5 percent of the population consumes 60 percent of dollars claimed in the provision of health care, it is most prudent to focus on the disease states of that 5 percent, rather than focusing on general primary care.

There are two primary approaches to managing a disease: the carve-out, and the carve-in. Carve-outs are generally single specialty, network-based programs designed to manage the care of a disease that can be segregated, such as mental health, substance abuse, or cancer. In those cases, companies specializing in the management of such a disease would carve out the costs of care for those high-cost patients on a shared-risk basis from a payer (a self-insured employer, an indemnity carrier, a managed care system, or an integrated delivery system).[6]

Some diseases, however, cannot be isolated from conditions of the patient's general health nor from the patterns of current practice by primary care physicians or multiple subspecialists. For those cases, specialists in management of the disease will create products that can be "carved into" the carrier's or provider's health care system. For example, diabetes causes complications so pervasive that the disease state cannot be managed separately from the patient's general health. In such a case, a company specializing in management of such a disease might design a product that could be "carved into" the managed care program of a self-insured employer, an indemnity carrier, a managed care program, or an integrated delivery system. Design of the product would include informational systems to identify high-risk patients, treatment protocols for managing the disease, and case managers and systems to measure outcomes and efficacy of treatment. Payment likely would be set at a percentage of total premiums or of costs saved, or by agreement on some other type of risk/profit sharing.

Wellness

In 1993-1994, the Levi Strauss Company began teaching its employees about preventive care through its program called Wellness Education Lowers Losses (WELL).[9] Workers are educated about common problems in health, and their health benefits and workers' compensational coverage are explained. The WELL program was instituted, in part, because the amount of money the company was spending on claims for workers' compensation had become astronomical. Many claims concerned carpal tunnel syndrome, a disorder of the wrist commonly associated with prolonged and improper positioning of the hands during repetitive work. In the case of the employees of Levi Strauss, many injuries resulted from improper use of sewing machines.

The WELL program was designed to teach employees how to recognize early symptoms of carpal tunnel syndrome so they could seek treatment immediately. It was most important, of course, to show workers how to prevent injuries. To monitor the effect of the plan on employee health, the company tracks visits to the emergency room and utilizations of the network for provision of care, and to compare those with claims against workers' compensation.

Quality Improvement

Donald Berwick, MD, President and CEO of the Institute for Health Care Improvement, believes that achievable improvements in cost and outcome can be enormous, but that they are not achievable within the current process of work. Many diseases are preventable, and many accidents do not have to happen. A lot of functional status is lost that could be recovered or restored and, most of all, a lot of money is spent without doing anybody any good.[10] Berwick sees management of quality as the method through which work can be changed in response to this social need.

Berwick notes that perhaps up to 50 percent of all deaths today occur from socially preventable causes: use of tobacco, accidents, sexually transmitted diseases, and so on. Even at the current level of integration of care and payers, it is not economically interesting for organizations to prevent disease. As we move toward capped systems or population-based payment, however, it becomes more and more financially interesting to keep people from getting sick. The question is how to do that.

Berwick's view is that it can only be done through integrating activities that currently are not well managed. For example, you cannot prevent sexually transmitted disease by confining your efforts to clinics that treat sexually transmitted disease; you prevent it by working on the entire system of transmission. Quality management, especially the "systems thinking" version, offers a chance to help people understand that they are part of a common aim. If that can be achieved, a lot of progress can be made. Many of the so-called integrated systems today have integration of finances without an integration of aims; quality management brings that issue forcefully to the table.

Brian Joiner, PhD, president of Joiner Associates, notes that many organizations focus on quality improvement by refocusing activities onto "what they should be doing" and then measuring and improving that.[23]

Joiner indicates that we need to improve what we are currently doing as well as changing operations or programs to what we should be doing, and measure outcomes and improve the new activity. He states that every improvement requires change, and every change requires an act of creation as well as an act of destruction.

Consumer Satisfaction

The role of the consumer in health care is rapidly becoming most important. Once service has been provided, it is imperative to measure clinical outcomes that reflect both the technical competence of the provider and the consumer's satisfaction. The latter may very well determine whether or not the patient and/or member of a health plan returns for regular care, however competent. More than general measures of satisfaction are needed to change processes in the delivery of care appropriately and to enhance the individual consumer's perceptions of the service received.[24]

Malpractice claims result from both real and perceived negligence. Three areas account for claims: (1) standard of care within a specialty, (2) legal obligations, and (3) relationships with the patient. Information from the risk-management service division of the St. Paul Fire and Marine Insurance Company shows that about one in one hundred hospitalized patients (10 percent) could legally bring an action for negligence against their provider of medical care for failing to act, or for acting improperly. Yet, less than 10 percent of them do. Why?

Often the answer lies with the type of relationship the patient has with his/her health care provider. The more positive the relationship, the less the risk of a suit for malpractice. The development of good relationships with patients occurs not by chance, but by prospective planning, systematic training, and ongoing evaluation. Furthermore, all staff functioning as part of the team that delivers service must become patient-oriented—not just the physician. Considerations for approaching the human aspect of patient care must be interfaced with its technical and operational aspects.[25]

Integration and Competition

The integration of systems relating to health care is a commonsense approach to comprehensive, seamless, consumer-oriented care.[26] Although current integrative efforts are at a very basic level of operation, the available information on outcomes shows significant promise for partners in such integrations. Integration resulting from the 1994 merger between Health-Partners and Ramsey, in Minneapolis and St. Paul, marked the first in Minnesota involving a health plan, physicians, and a hospital and created the first integrated service network exemplifying the kind of comprehensive health care system that will be warranted under the mandates of state and federal reforms.

Both the Allina Health System merger and the HealthPartners/Ramsey merger set the stage for rather strict control of expenses from their physicians, the hospitals, and contract providers and staff in the health plan networks. Such control of expenses will be accomplished, in large part, by redirecting the focus from care of inpatients to outpatients; emphasizing the "gatekeeping" approach by providers of primary care; hospitalizing patients only when necessary and case managing each patient carefully during hospitalization; using high-tech and specialty services only when needed; setting and sticking to targets for finances and utilization with a focus on enhanced outcomes; selective downsizing; and reengineering of operations as needed. It is incumbent upon the providers to manage care carefully, through an effective and efficient delivery system.[27]

The Allina Health System and HealthPartners/Ramsey health care partnerships are examples of vertical integration with a focus on quality, lower cost, and customer service. The mergers are one step further toward controlling the costs of health care, especially hospital expenses and referrals to specialists' services, by integrating inpatient and outpatient services and health plans within the same organization having a common structure of governance. This model enhances and very possibly augments the trend set in the Twin Cities from 1982 to 1992 in which hospital admissions and hospital days declined at about twice the national rate, as illustrated in Table 1.4.[28,29] Table 1.5 shows some of the decisions addressed when contemplating integration.

TABLE 1.4. Comparisons of Hospital Usage

	National/ U.S. 1992	Midwest Region 1992	Minneapolis/ St. Paul (7 county) 1992
Admissions per 1,000	78	91	71
Days per 1,000	454	549	276
Average length of stay (in days)	5.8	6.01	3.88
Average payment/ admission	$7,395	$9,023	$4,399

Reprinted with permission from Sommers, PA. Preparing for 2000 and beyond through physician group, hospital, and health plan integration. *Group Practice Journal,* 43(6): 38-43, 1994, November/December.

TABLE 1.5. Decision Matrix Used to Review Perceived Impact of Changes on Your Medical Practice

Your Medical Practice:	Less Reimbursements	Universal Change	Capitation	Prevention versus intervention	Need to expand primary care base	Shorter hospital stays	Integration with larger group	CQI	Outcome reporting	Etc.
Mission/Philosophy										
Image										
Academic Relationship										
Community Relationship										
MD Relationship(s):										
• Primary Care Sites										
• Specialty Care Sites										
Hospital Relationship										
Financial Condition:										
• Short term										
• Long term										
• Debt										
• Likelihood of Survival										
Insurance/HMO/PPO Affiliations										

TABLE 1.5 (continued)

	Less Reimbursements	Universal Change	Capitation	Prevention versus intervention	Need to expand primary care base	Shorter hospital stays	Integration with larger group	CQI	Outcome reporting	Etc.
Metro Presence										
• East										
• West										
Antitrust Implications										
Governance Structure										
Other Issues										
Current Relative Need										

Rating Key:

+ = Well positioned/maintain and enhance status where possible
0 = Will not affect practice
− = Will require significant change in practice

Although only a generalized picture of practice relationships can be obtained pending in-depth analysis, the findings will clearly determine the areas in need of attention by your group.

In 1992, the Minnesota Employers' Association Buyers Coalition (EABG) began its plan for group purchasing of health care for its members. The plan includes most of the approaches to improving quality and managing costs contained in proposals for reform of health care, including the use of guidelines for medical practice, measurement of clinical outcomes, surveys of patient satisfaction and functional status, and coverage of preventive procedures. Table 1.4 shows lower costs for hospital inpatient care; however, the belief held among many purchasers is that the "best is yet to come." Innovation and creative options to produce more and better is a current theme. The EABC joined forces with BHCAG in a venture to form a larger purchasing pool, further competition, and contain costs on a long-term basis.[15]

APPLICATIONS

Apply the effects that local, regional, and (potential) national changes will have on your practice. One way to document relative relationships quickly is to list what are defined as targets for success in your practice (individual and group) down one side of a matrix (see Table 1.5).

Targeted Goals

1. Can you determine what effects in your practice will reflect current trends within the contemporary practice of medicine? Now that you are aware of current trends/changes, how will your practice be enhanced by enabling its clinical and operating services to stay a little in advance of the times?
2. To what "agents of change" must you pay close attention this year? Next year? The next five to ten years? How will you monitor/enhance performance in your practice to optimize its ability to survive?

Objectives

1. Have factors for potential success or failure been identified easily? Can they be rank-ordered by their importance to the group?
2. Is more analysis needed to define specifically the critical status of key factors (determine their importance and their current status) relative to the group's success? Are the findings ready to be included in the group's planning efforts and development of follow-up plans of action?

Content

1. Have you determined any new opportunities that should be pursued by your group?

Evaluation

Evaluation of operations is a routine process. Reporting occurs monthly, with a comprehensive annual evaluation. Is the budget being met? Is/are the projection/s of revenue accurate? Have expenses been reduced? Are projections of activity and indicators of volume in line with actual activity and volume?

Continuous Quality Improvement

Have measures of performance been taken, to determine progress? Refinements related to clinical outcomes and operating systems are to be monitored annually. Have you documented what new elements your practice must address to enhance its market position and performance?

Chapter 2

Consumer-Focused Practices in Health Care

POINTS FOR FOCUS

Both clinical services and operating systems must be enhanced to meet consumers' needs and desires. Changes should be based upon what it will take to define and to meet expectations in clinical and other services.

Targeted Goals

To change the focus of practices in health care toward the consumer.

Objectives

1. Design clinical and operating services and systems to address consumers' needs (for high-quality care, good price, and satisfaction).
2. Assess the requirements for meeting those needs in ways that match care and service to consumers' expectations.
3. Align the resources of your system to attain high-quality service, good price, and satisfaction for the consumer.

Content

Determine the current status (and past trends) of quality of care, price, and satisfaction within the clinical and operating systems of the organization.

Evaluation

Monitor production in clinical and operating systems on the basis of consumers' needs and values as those relate to quality, price, and satisfaction.

Continuous Quality Improvement

Measure the differences between consumers' expectations and actual results of care and service. Eliminate duplicative activity that is not consumer focused.

SERVICE TO CONSUMERS

If the prices, outcomes, and quality of health care become similar, regardless of who provides them, what will be left for consumers to choose? The answer, in no small part, will reside in consumer satisfaction with the care they received and the services provided to them.

> In the past, medical professionals were able to function as a "service industry" without having to worry too much about addressing the issue of consumer satisfaction. The primary emphasis in medical care rested on the physician-patient relationship, with the physician generally held in high regard by the patient. Patients usually believed that a relatively equal—and high—standard of care could be received from almost all physicians. Very few patients gave much thought to comparative shopping.[1]

In recent years, however, patients have begun to ask for a greater voice in their own health care. They now see themselves as consumers of health care and, as consumers, have begun to question, along with their payers, both the quality of the care they receive and its cost. The result has been a growing demand for care of good quality at less cost. That, in turn, has led to increased competition among providers of health care.

In light of these trends, professionals in health care must change their old ways of doing business. Consumer satisfaction will play only a bigger and bigger role in medical practice, as patients and their families, referring physicians, and payer sources become more selective about determining which physicians will be getting their business. This chapter is intended to equip physicians and other decision makers in health care with the necessary tools to meet the growing demand for consumer satisfaction in medical practices. Using the tools described here must become a way of doing business if physicians, hospitals, and health plans are going to survive the economic changes projected for professions in health care.[1]

UNDERSTANDING THAT CONSUMER SATISFACTION IS THE ONLY WAY OF DOING BUSINESS SUCCESSFULLY

The practice of medicine has been confidential, with a privileged relationship between physician and patient. The nature of the physician-patient interaction is embodied in the Hippocratic Oath, which outlines the duties and obligations of physicians. When a physician enters the business of medical practice, therefore, he or she must run that business in association with high-quality medical care. Yet even high-quality care can be delivered without consumer satisfaction, as indeed it often has been in the past. More and more frequently, however, medical professionals are recognizing the importance of providing high-quality service as well as high-quality care to their patients. They have found that such a consumer-oriented approach makes good business sense. It also goes a long way toward assuring that the patient receives the very best care possible.[2]

Incorporating consumer satisfaction into a medical practice does not cost the typical physician any more than the old, less service-oriented approach. Consumer satisfaction is a style, a total approach, a complete way to deliver health care. Cost is a nonissue, because it does not cost any more to treat the consumer right the first time he or she comes into the hospital or clinic. In fact, *not* treating the consumer right can be very costly: first, all such complaints from patients must be documented and dealt with, which costs time and effort; and second, some of those complaints may develop into expensive lawsuits for malpractice.[3,4] In addition, the dissatisfied consumer may go elsewhere for care, another costly problem. Studies have found that it takes five times as much money to attract a new customer as it does to retain an existing one. By multiplying by five the annual value associated with *one* patient's outpatient and inpatient charges (including laboratory and X-ray charges), it is easy to see the loss of revenue from one unhappy consumer of health care.

Many providers of health care are unaware that their patients are dissatisfied with the care they are receiving, because patients seldom complain directly to providers. In fact, research has shown that 96 percent of unhappy customers never complain to the people providing them with a service. But they do tell their families and friends. Research has also shown that each dissatisfied customer tells nine other people about their concerns, and 13 percent tell as many as twenty other people. Word gets around.

Health care is primarily a physician-driven service. Without the commitment, leadership, and follow-through of physicians in the area of consumer satisfaction, little (if any) progress can be sustained. It is essential, therefore, that physicians take a leading and active role in identifying and implementing the changes that need to occur to make consumer satisfaction a way of doing business in hospitals and medical practices.[5,6] By caring enough about their patients to make these changes, physicians will find that their patients will remain loyal to them and will return to them whenever they have health problems.

MYTHS AND OTHER MISUNDERSTANDINGS ABOUT MEDICAL PRACTICE

For physicians to thrive instead of just survive in the contemporary marketplace for health care, traditional approaches to cost-effective medical practice will have to change. Like it or not, physicians are going to have to reexamine—and then discard—the following myths and outdated beliefs about what the practice of medicine is going to be like during the twenty-first century.

Myth #1: Solo practitioners and independent practices will dominate the practice of medicine.

With increasing frequency, independent physicians are going to find it advantageous to consider some form of affiliation with another physician, a group, or a consortium. Such affiliations will benefit independent physicians by helping them insure against potential suits for malpractice, negotiate with insurance carriers and HMOs, share patients within defined specialties, and reduce duplicative overhead costs, including those associated with incorporating consumer satisfaction into the practice.[7]

Myth #2: Medical practice will remain an entrepreneurial, small business.

In the past, many medical practices functioned as entrepreneurial small businesses, but that was before the government, the insurance industry, and other third-party payers declared the 1990s to be "the decade of containing physician costs," much as the 1980s were a watershed for significant cost-containing changes in hospitals. Payers and regulators of health care are fed up with uncontrolled costs and are doing something about it by directing patients to medical practices that are both quality oriented and cost conscious. As a result, reimbursement will decrease for all physicians, which in turn will force practices to de-escalate their costs while keeping standards for quality high. To hold down medical and administrative costs while enhancing revenues, physicians will need to think and act more collectively.

Myth #3: "Curing" patients is all that is needed for consumers to feel satisfied with the care they receive.

In the past, physicians had the luxury of practicing medicine without too much concern about how the service was perceived by the patient. In many cases, it was presumed that the patient was just grateful for whatever medicine or related care was received. Indeed, most people perceived service as something they received at a gas station, restaurant, or hotel, but not at a doctor's office.

Times have changed. The medical practices of physicians who have no other competition in their specialty in a particular geographic area may survive the changes forecast for the next ten years, but they will probably not thrive—unless those physicians make consumer satisfaction a way of doing business. Of course there will be always be exceptions—"one of a kind" medical practices such as those doing organ transplantations—but even those physicians will benefit (so will their patients) from offering consumer-oriented services. As a service industry, the practice of medicine is fast becoming as market-driven as those that serve travel, banking, hotels, and a myriad of other industries. Consumers expect high-quality service from all physicians. The perception of service received is predominant in swaying consumers when they evaluate a physician.[8]

Myth #4: Implementing a program to provide consumer satisfaction in a practice takes too much time and money.

Actually, it will be costly *not* to implement such a program, because patients will simply go elsewhere. The specific cost of a program for consumer satisfaction depends on how it is implemented—the number of personnel involved in surveying patients, for example, and how surveys will be conducted (by mail, telephone, focus groups, or a combination of these). Physicians whose practices are currently in an area without noteworthy competition would be wise to become consumer oriented now, before the competition arrives. Doing it now will be less expensive than doing it while dueling with other physicians for patients.

Myth #5: Once a physician has referred a patient to another physician, he or she will continue to refer patients to that physician.

A physician who receives a patient referred from another physician should not expect that he or she will receive further referrals from that source. Thus, referring physicians need to be treated as consumers. After being provided with a high-quality consultation, the referred patient should be returned to the referring physician in a timely fashion, along with a clear, concise report aimed at making it easy for the referring physician to incorporate the information into his or her planning for that patient's future needs for health care. Physicians should call referring physicians, a day or two after sending their report, to see whether they have any questions or concerns.

Myth #6: Consumer satisfaction is more important in some medical settings than in others.

Too often, less-than-satisfactory service is rationalized because of an erroneous belief that in some specific settings, meeting the consumers' high expectations for service is not all that important. This is not true. Consumer satisfaction should be the goal of all medical practices, no matter where nor under what circumstances the care is provided—whether inpatient or outpatient, for example, or in a hospital or private practice.[9] Physicians need to take the lead in being committed to consumer-oriented medical care, for it offers the greatest potential for attaining consumer satisfaction. Once physicians take the lead, other medical support staff will follow.[10]

Myth #7: A program for consumer satisfaction can replace programs for risk management and quality assurance.

Wrong. Through its emphasis on making patients and members of their families well-informed and active participants in their medical care, a consumer-oriented service can help minimize the risk of suits for malpractice. It does not, however, take the place of a carefully-thought-out program of risk management or quality assurance.

Some medical professionals worry that asking consumers to respond to any kind of questions about their medical care, even ones related only to service, will cause them to focus on what they did not like about the care, rather than what they did like. Some even worry that this may lead to more lawsuits for malpractice, as consumers begin to think that there must have been something wrong with the care, if the physician is quizzing them about it. This concern is unmerited. For medical practices to stay competitive, they must find out what their patients do not like, as well as what they do like. Only when problems have been clearly identified is it possible to design and implement modifications in service, to correct them. The goal is to find out what is wrong, not just what is right. When consumers are convinced that their input is really valued and that the goal in gathering that input is to improve medical services, they will become willing and generally supportive participants.

Myth #8: Attaining consumer satisfaction requires simple techniques such as "smile training."

Establishing a consumer-oriented approach to medical care requires more than superficial techniques. Physicians, support staff, and volunteers alike must be truly committed to improving their relationships with consumers. They must learn how to become good listeners and how to make sure each patient's needs are met. More often than not, these skills are not recognized as being important, even crucial, in health care.

Yet they are crucial. The St. Paul Fire and Marine Insurance Company has demonstrated that although about one of every hundred hospitalized patients could legally bring an action for negligence against their provider of medical care for failing to act or for acting improperly, less than 10 percent of those who could actually do. Why? The company reported that the answer can be found in the relationships patients have with their providers of health care. The more positive and satisfactory the patients perceived those relationships to be, the less likely they were to initiate a lawsuit.

Myth #9: Providing consumer satisfaction is outdated and too expensive.

Although it has been talked about for some time, consumer satisfaction has yet to be fully integrated into modern practices in health care as a way of doing business. Some physicians believe that they have enough to worry about—especially worries about shrinking reimbursement from Medicare and other payer sources—without spending time and money developing programs in consumer satisfaction for their practices. By putting all their efforts into counteracting government-initiated measures for cost containment, however, physicians are often overlooking the bottom-line benefits to their business of a program for customer satisfaction.

Physicians do not have to go overboard to become service oriented. Large expenditures are not needed, either for development of satisfaction surveys or for the purchase of systems to do the mailing, telephone calls, and collecting and analyzing of data. What is most needed in becoming consumer oriented is a commitment—a commitment to begin thinking about the consumer first. Whether a consumer arrives at a medical facility as a result of a marketing campaign, an ad in the Yellow Pages, or a referral from another professional, the fact remains that the care *and service* he or she receives at the facility will determine whether or not he or she returns. Furthermore, each satisfied consumer will tell at least five other people, one of whom is quite likely also to choose to use the facility.

LOOKING AT HEALTH CARE FROM THE PATIENT'S PERSPECTIVE

Good health is perhaps the most primary desire among humans, along with food, sleep, sex, and the need to feel important. Healthful living has been idolized and sought, from time immemorial. Kings, queens, and other luminaries have quested for perpetual life as far back in history as records have been kept. A belief in the importance of attaining and maintaining good health is almost universally shared by the world's societies. Thus, it is not surprising that efforts toward public health have been financially supported by government-run social, educational, and health-oriented agencies and by hundreds, possibly thousands, of volunteer and lay organizations throughout the world.

Annually, billions of dollars are spent on programs to promote health care and related services. In most cases, the consumer has had little to say in the evaluation of those services. That is now changing. Given the current climate of spiraling medical costs and the intense discussions now underway about a national program of health insurance in the United States, the need to involve those who benefit from health care—consumers—in the process of evaluating it has become more evident. Although the concept of asking consumers their opinions about the system for delivery of medical care is not new, it has not been addressed consistently by many providers of health care.

So what must be done to ensure that patients are more satisfied with their service in health care? To begin with, professionals in health care need to start examining the services they provide, from the patient's viewpoint. Take the office visit, as an example. Only 10 percent of the time a patient spends at a doctor's office is directly related to the health care sought. Most of the patient's time is spent waiting, filling out forms, or moving from one station to another. The amount of time actually spent with a doctor or nurse—whether it be for a physical evaluation, a laboratory test, or being informed about options for treatment—is usually quite limited. Patients have basically resigned themselves to the fact that most trips to the doctor are a waste of time, except for the few minutes they spend with the doctor or nurse.

Because patients have, for the most part, quietly endured long waits at their doctors' offices in the past, some practitioners have come to believe that it is now permissible to let patients sit in their waiting rooms well beyond the time for which their appointment was scheduled, without even giving them an explanation for the delay. Consumers are becoming increasingly intolerant of such treatment. Indeed, clinicians who fail to give patients and their families appropriate consideration will soon find themselves losing many of their patients to their competitors. Shopping for medical services is now commonplace, and people will not hesitate to travel an extra fifty to seventy-five miles for satisfactory services.

EXAMINING THE SYSTEM FOR DELIVERY OF SERVICE

Delivery of health care is designed around the doctor's schedule. Patients must fit their concerns—their working hours, the hours their children are in school, the distance they must travel from home or worksite to the doctor's office—into the doctor's schedule. Most medical practices try to assist the patient in finding a convenient time, but doing so is not considered a priority. If an appointment can be scheduled at a time that does not greatly inconvenience the patient, great. If not—well, perhaps the patient will have better luck next time. In the new competitive climate, however, this type of attitude is not going to be tolerated much longer.

Medical practices could learn a lot about meeting the needs of consumers from studying other businesses that count on consumer satisfaction for their livelihood—motels, hotels, and restaurants, for example. All these businesses are considered service industries, as are the providers of health care. These services, however, have routinely developed short checklists of questions to ask consumers when they call to make reservations—checklists that help the provider of the service better meet the needs of consumers. The business thus accommodates the consumer, rather than the other way around. Why cannot providers of health care do the same?

Hotels, restaurants, and other businesses conduct frequent and thorough surveys of consumers, to make sure their customers are happy with the services provided, while at the same time identifying accommodations to make their next trip even more enjoyable. Medical practices need to do the same. Although some medical organizations conduct periodic surveys to examine patient satisfaction, relatively few establish and maintain a routine system of such evaluations. The market for health services is highly competitive. To maintain ratings for accreditation, hospitals need a certain number of patients to occupy their beds and, to balance their budgets, all medical facilities need a certain number of patients walking through their doors. One would think, therefore, that providers of health care would place greater emphasis on the development of a complete consumer-oriented approach to the delivery of care.

ALIGNING SERVICES WITH PATIENTS' NEEDS

By placing oneself in the patient's shoes, it is possible to gain a better understanding of what leads a patient to feel frustrated and dissatisfied with the medical care he or she receives. Too often, for example, patients are expected to follow rigorous directions and procedures. Written orders and paperwork handed to them may be far too complex and detailed. Patients may be given pills for very good reasons, but some fail to understand adequately why they must strictly comply with the recommended dosage and schedule. Patients also frequently fail to understand the need for filling out a seemingly endless and often redundant stream of forms and applications.

All current activities and demands made of patients should be examined, and if one is found to impede favorable service, it should be eliminated if possible, or at least modified. These include not only activities at the nurses' station and the appointment desk, but also procedures in the physician's examining room and even paperwork aimed at patients that originates in offices doing billing or insurance processing. *Is medical service being provided with an eye on consumers' needs?* Such a question must be asked about all parts of the system.

Too many executive meetings aim discussions at one subject: the need to see a certain number of patients on a daily, weekly, monthly, or yearly basis. Yet it is often forgotten that office budgets, profits for practitioners, and the financial strength of progressive hospitals and physicians' service organizations (1) exist to provide better health, and (2) depend on consumer satisfaction, their view on whether services they receive are better. Few providers of health care manage to design services appropriately for the consumer. The organization that does will soon provide services truly appreciated by its patients.

One of the best ways to help employees in health care to see their services from a patient's viewpoint is through training, as well as volunteers. Employees, as well as volunteers, could be given training in such areas as "techniques in serving patients," "listening to patients' problems and then solving them," "turning patients' complaints into routine requests," and "developing a consumer satisfaction approach in your department." Only after the entire staff—doctors, nurses, medical assistants, administrators, nurse's aides, insurance clerks, financial counselors—everyone—makes a commitment to be consumer oriented, only then will the organization actually realize an increase in consumer satisfaction. Making such a commitment can also lead to higher morale among the staff itself, as employees begin to feel more appreciated by their satisfied customers (and as salaries increase to reflect the increase in business).

Some Points to Remember

- Everyone needs and deserves satisfactory services for their health— such services are more available now than ever.
- Health services would not be needed, without patients. Why don't producers of health care more carefully consider patients' needs in the planning, delivery, and evaluation of services provided to patients (consumers)?
- National health insurance has been supported for implementation by many. If enacted, it will cover charges incurred by consumers of health care, so that they may go just about anywhere to have their health needs met. Patients will eventually become very selective in seeking these services.
- Consumers have a tendency not to complain openly about problems or poor service. Instead, they leave the doctor's office without informing anyone of their concerns, making it impossible to correct the problem. (Of course, the patient's business is lost, along with the business of everyone else who comes in contact with that patient.)
- Both positive and negative information about one's practice should be sought from patients. It is extremely helpful to obtain negative information, since problems (or just poor service) can be improved after being identified.
- One way to influence a consumer is to talk in terms of what he or she wants. Patients seem to be developing an ever-increasing attitude favoring "shopping for health care" and are willing to drive past locally available doctors if they believe better care is available at another location.
- Examine the system for delivering services. Focus attention on those needs determined by the *patients* to be important.
- Implement a consumer-oriented approach to health care. Train members of your staff and volunteers to become consumer oriented.
- Satisfied patients will inform others about good services. Not only will new referrals increase but so will morale among your staff, because of appreciation shown them by these patients, and because of increases in their salaries related to increased profits in the practice as a business.

MAKING CONSUMER SATISFACTION
A WAY OF DOING BUSINESS

The Service Isn't Right Until the Consumer Says So[11]

Adopting a Consumers' Bill of Rights

To thrive rather than just survive in today's competitive marketplace for health care, every medical practice must acknowledge that the recipient of its services is a consumer, one whose rights must be observed. No matter how large or small a medical practice—whether it has one, or more than a thousand physicians—it must embrace the opportunity of assuring each consumer the following rights:[11]

Every consumer has the right to high-quality health care.

- The consumer deserves health care of the highest quality that money can buy.
- The consumer deserves the kind of care that will enable him or her to live a long, productive life.

Every consumer has the right to long-term protection of his or her health.

- The consumer deserves the security of knowing that he or she is receiving the best possible return on investment for his or her dollars spent for health care.
- The consumer deserves to receive health care consistent with the high standards required by the Hippocratic Oath.

Every consumer has the right to friendly evaluation and competent treatment.

- The consumer deserves to be treated as a person in need of health services, not just as a checkbook.
- The consumer deserves to do business with providers of health care who are interested in his or her needs, not just in the wants of the providers.

Every consumer has the right to information.

- The consumer deserves to understand clearly the condition of his or her health and how to maintain and/or improve it.

- The consumer deserves to know the truth about the status of his or her health.

Every consumer has a right to address grievances.

- The consumer deserves to be heard. Physicians cannot be expected to be perfect in their interactions with patients, but an uncaring response to a patient's concern is inexcusable.
- Consumers deserve to have their concerns listened to and addressed by the professionals in health care who serve them.

Every consumer has the right to satisfaction.

- The consumer deserves more than just a "thank you."
- The consumer deserves to feel totally satisfied with the treatment he or she receives. This includes feeling satisfied with the attitude of the health care provider during treatment, as well as with the quality of care.

Suggestion Box for Identifying and Following Up on Less-Than-Satisfactory Service

- Ask your consumers how satisfied they were with the services provided. You can do this in person, by telephone, or by mail, after the visit to the office.
- Invite groups of patients and/or their families to quarterly meetings to address complaints about less-than-satisfactory service and to offer suggestions that might help resolve the problems.
- Send a follow-up letter to each patient or the patient's family, after an evaluation or treatment, to let them know what is the status of the patient's health, what needs to be done to improve it, and what questions need to be answered before further treatment can proceed.
- Provide educational opportunities for patients and their families. These could include classes or support groups where they could learn more about their particular medical concerns or conditions and possible courses of treatment.
- Provide friendly, helpful assistance with insurance claims and billing.
- Encourage patients to call you at your expense—toll-free or collect—with questions or concerns about their treatment plan or if they need help with insurance claims.
- Establish a definition of consumer satisfaction that acknowledges that the consumer's needs and desires are to be fulfilled, concerning

quality of both clinical care and service. Make sure everyone in your practice understands the meaning of consumer satisfaction and understands his or her role in implementing it.

- Ensure that consumers receive appropriate and timely information regarding the status of their health.
- Design a process that promotes a continuing relationship between physicians and consumers. For example, send out periodic newsletters, announcements of changes in staff, or notices of new programs or expanded hours, to all consumers who use your medical facility.
- Give all consumers access to videotapes and libraries that provide medical information in lay terms.
- If practical, establish closed-circuit televised programming for consumers, so they can view special programs regarding their interests in health care.
- Draft a formal "Bill of Rights" for patients. This sets the stage for patients—and their families—to participate fully in their care and in follow-up treatment.[11]

BECOMING CONSUMER-ORIENTED

Health care is a competitive business and, as such, part of the free-enterprise system. Its product is service of high quality. The quality of service that a patient receives while under treatment by a professional in health care is what he or she will remember longest. It is also what will bring the patient back to the practice when further care is needed. Providers of health care must therefore emphasize individualized, patient-oriented service to keep their current patients, and to enjoy success in recruiting new ones.

Consumer satisfaction, in settings providing health care, can be measured objectively.[12,13] Medical practices already measure, either by time or by function, the services they provide. These measurements can be found in fee schedules and other accounting practices. Consumer satisfaction with the quality of service can be similarly measured at each stage of delivery of the service. For example, asking consumers to fill out a short questionnaire after a visit to your clinic or hospital can provide valuable tips on how to improve services. A suggestion box should be available for recommendations. By encouraging patients' feedback on services and then acting on those suggestions, providers of health care can give patients the opportunity to participate actively in planning their own health care. As service improvement recommendations are implemented, it is important to communicate results to the patients who made the recommendations.

Active participation by patients in planning care of their own health is the hallmark of a successful program for consumer satisfaction. Once the patient believes that a health care professional is sincerely interested in his or her opinion about the care being received, a visible change in the patient's attitude can be seen. Patients become much more open about their feelings and concerns. Most important, this information then helps the attending physician or other providers of health care to improve the ways they meet the patient's medical needs. Patients and clinicians alike benefit from these partnerships—patients receive care directly related to their individual needs, and providers watch their practices thrive and grow, as word gets around that they are patient oriented.

Without a strong partnership between those providing and those consuming health care, consumer satisfaction happens only randomly. Yet for too long, even in the most respected medical centers and physicians' offices, the patient's role in health care has been of secondary concern. Only recently have providers of health care realized the importance of attaining partnerships with patients and of including them in their own care.

Tips for Becoming Service Oriented

1. Remember that your medical practice is a competitive business; treat it accordingly.
2. Keep in mind that many patients consider the quality of service they receive to be as important as the end result of that service.
3. Devise ways to measure the quality of service in your practice.
4. Build partnerships with your patients. Their attitudes toward you will become more positive when they know that you value their opinions about the care they receive.
5. Remember that a patient-oriented practice grows and thrives.
6. Recognize patients whose suggestions for improving service have been implemented.

RECOMMENDATIONS FOR MAKING CONSUMER SATISFACTION A WAY OF DOING BUSINESS

In your medical practice, you can make consumer satisfaction a way of doing business by (1) establishing standards that define, measure, and monitor consumer satisfaction; (2) increasing support from the involvement of managers; (3) using tools for quality assurance; and (4) improving relations with patients, physicians, and employees in a manner acceptable to the patients, physicians, employees, administration, board of directors, and community. Here are some recommendations:[11,12,13]

Recommendation #1: Define consumer satisfaction.

Adopt a definition of consumer satisfaction that incorporates the views of physicians, employees, patients, and administrators.

A Sample Definition

> Consumer satisfaction is the perception held by consumers inside and outside of the organization that their needs and desires concerning health care have been fulfilled, and that a high quality of both treatment and services is being received.

Defining the consumers in your medical practice is essential. Considerations should include:

- Patients
- Regulatory agencies of compliance
- Families of patients
- Contracting parties such as groups that use your lab, radiology, and services of consulting physicians
- Physicians
- Nonphysician staff
- Payers (government, HMOs, other third parties)
- Other producers/users related to the medical practice

Recommendation #2: Develop written surveys of patient satisfaction.

The surveys can be mailed to patients either at or after their discharge from the hospital, or on completion of their treatment. Questions in the survey should cover such matters as the staff's concern for the patient, the quality and quantity of medical and nursing care, the quality of information supplied to the patient, the friendliness of the staff, the promptness of service, and prices and billing procedures. Be sure to encourage patients to request follow-up contact to clarify areas of low satisfaction. You should also ask for demographic information and ask about any other health care needs they may have that concern health care.

Recommendation #3: Develop scheduling procedures that recognize and value each patient's time.

Conduct studies to identify scheduling procedures that would maximize physicians' time yet not inconvenience patients.

Recommendation #4: Establish focus groups of consumers.

Invite five or six discharged patients and perhaps one member of each family to a meeting of a focus group, to discuss their perceptions of the service they received while at your medical practice. Be sure to provide all participants with a free lunch and parking. An experienced facilitator should lead the meeting, making sure that patients feel comfortable in expressing their opinions of the quality of service from your medical practice. The facilitator should write a summary of positive and negative comments that emerge from the focus group. These comments should then be organized according to the department they affect, and the complete summary should be sent to administrators and middle managers. To ensure that all points brought up in the meeting are thoroughly understood and acted upon, the meeting should be videotaped. Departmental representatives or representatives of physicians should be encouraged to view the video, and it should be discussed at departmental meetings. The confidentiality of testimonies from patients, of course, should always be honored.

Recommendation #5: Place consumer satisfaction on the agenda for meetings on planning.

Both physicians and managers need to make consumer satisfaction the "way of doing business." Thus, consumer satisfaction should be an item on the agenda at joint meetings of committees on planning for your hospital and medical clinic. It should be directly included in all plans for the medical practice.

Recommendation #6: Encourage top physicians and managers to have direct contact with patients.

Every member of top management should meet at least one consumer each week. The manager should ask the consumer about his or her visit to the medical practice. Administrators should also take turns assisting staff in areas where large numbers of patients wait for service. They should wear name tags at these sites, so that patients can clearly identify them.

Recommendation #7: Make consumer satisfaction part of all evaluations of employee performance.

Standards for consumer satisfaction should be incorporated into all evaluations of employee performance, including those of physicians. Such standards should also become part of the guidelines for the office, hand-books, and personnel policies for both physicians and other employees.

***Recommendation #8: Make consumer satisfaction
a routine subject for discussion at meetings
for your office or department.***

Physicians and managers should clarify the priority given to consumer satisfaction within your medical practice. Nurses and physicians should provide input, feedback, and follow-up. Routine reports on progress in resolving identified problems with consumer satisfaction should be sched-uled at subsequent meetings.

***Recommendation #9: Train head nurses and physicians
in management to serve as role models for appropriate
interpersonal and communicative skills.***

Leading physicians and managers must see to it that nurses and staff physicians are provided with the necessary education and training that will ensure consumer satisfaction within the medical practice. The development of interpersonal skills and the ability to communicate effectively among mem-bers of the staff is essential.

Recommendation #10: Solicit opinions from employees.

Employees should be asked for their perceptions about the working environment and about problems in performance of services.

***Recommendation #11: Recognize "heroes" in quality of service
with dramatic awards.***

To provide a meaningful incentive to change their behavior, award employees with days of vacation or cash bonuses for their efforts in improv-ing consumer satisfaction. Name a "Pro of the Month." Employees should be "caught being good" and should be rewarded for it!

***Recommendation #12: Make criteria for performance on consumer
satisfaction part of every employee's job description.***

These criteria should also be a substantial part of reviews of perfor-mance and of considerations for raises in pay for all employees.

Recommendation #13: Tailor sessions for training in consumer satisfaction specifically to each service unit and/or department.

Although all employees should receive such training, the sessions should focus on employees in positions with high levels of public contact, such as nurses, receptionists, and patient account representatives. Make participation in training sessions mandatory. Also, be sure to emphasize that the performance of skills learned in those sessions will be included in future job reviews. Nurses, chief technicians, and/or departmental managers should be trained first, so that they can encourage and reinforce a consumer-oriented attitude among other employees.

Recommendation #14: Implement a formal program of patient education.

Through a formal education program, both patients and their families can receive information about their condition and about options for its treatment. Special classes on common medical conditions should also be made available to all consumers of health care. Personal letters should be sent to all patients following treatment. The letters should explain what happened during the visit, answer all questions that might have arisen from the visit, and restate instructions given to the patient regarding medication or therapy.

Recommendation #15: Provide patients with assistance in processing bills and insurance claims.

Designate a person from the billing or insurance department to be available to answer questions from patients and families. Distribute to patients a telephone number where they can get quick and easy answers to their questions. Many medical practices have an 800 number for this purpose.

THE PHYSICIAN'S ROLE IN DEVELOPING A CONSUMER-ORIENTED INITIATIVE

Physicians must take steps now to improve the quality of service they provide their consumers. Because of the physician-oriented nature of the marketplace in health care, it is up to physicians to take positions of leadership in this effort. Such an initiative should be:

1. Integrated with current programs for improving quality, managing risk, and managing care
2. Consumer driven, with leadership by physicians
3. Designed as an ongoing process that will result in fundamental operational changes

The initiative must improve the quality of service in ways consistent with other key factors for success—quality of medical care and cost effectiveness.

When a program for consumer satisfaction is initiated, discrepancies can be anticipated between administrative goals for the program and physicians' acceptance of those goals. Physicians are usually more focused on patient outcomes, while administrators typically emphasize the process of delivery. Medical and administrative goals can be integrated, however, by having the two groups work together in the planning and implementation of the program. Issues that are likely to emerge between physicians and administrators include:

- Lack of information about the necessity for consumer satisfaction
- Lack of incentives for consumer satisfaction
- Lack of agreement on the meaning of consumer satisfaction
- Lack of agreement on the business value of consumer satisfaction.

Physicians must be specifically trained on the merits of incorporating consumer satisfaction into the conduct of their practices. Most physicians do not receive any formal training on this subject during medical school, residency, or experiences in fellowship. The process of convincing physicians to accept this idea begins with education. Here are some recommendations:

Recommendation #1: Get physicians to take leadership in the establishment of a program for consumer satisfaction.

Historically, the practice of medicine has been "physician driven" although, in response to measures aimed at cost containment in recent reforms, nonphysician medical professionals are increasingly being used to deliver certain services. Yet only physicians can admit patients to a hospital, and only physicians—or their appropriate designees—can prescribe medications. For a system for consumer satisfaction to work, therefore, it must be physician driven or physician directed. Physicians must take the lead in establishing a program for consumer satisfaction and, by their own example, set the standards for others to follow. Good administrative support is, however, necessary for physicians to take such a lead; it allows physicians to focus on physician-to-physician communication about consumer satisfaction, an essential element in making any program work.

Recommendation #2: Educate physicians by demonstrating the importance of consumer satisfaction to the successful operation of a medical practice.

The long-term economic success of a medical practice rests on a steady or slightly increasing number of patients. Due to the current trend of decreasing reimbursement from third-party payers, it has become more difficult to obtain revenues in excess of expenses without significantly increasing the number of paying consumers. This situation will be further tested, under the "capitation system" in which HMOs will pay providers a set amount for a certain number of patients. If providers find they need to spend more than that amount to take care of their designated patients, they will have to do so out of their own pockets. Thus, under the capitation system, providers must be able to attract and keep as many healthy patients as possible, to nullify the financial impact of those patients who need more care.

A practice built on consumer satisfaction is assured return appointments. Satisfied patients and their families also bring in new patients through word of mouth. Physicians, however, have been taught in their medical training that to satisfy consumers, all they need to do is provide competent patient care. Thus, they do not feel a need to be educated about consumer satisfaction—something they think they are already providing. Research shows otherwise. Studies have revealed that no significant connection exists between patient satisfaction and physicians' perception of patient satisfaction.

Physicians must therefore be educated on the importance of patient/physician interactions and on how such interactions relate directly to the economic success of their practice. Studies have found that the conduct of a physician, as perceived by patients and their families, is clearly the most important factor determining whether or not consumers feel satisfied with the care they have received. Other factors—accessibility, availability of other specialists, completeness of the facilities, and continuity of care—also contribute to consumer satisfaction, but not as much as the conduct of the physician. In one study that looked at why families change pediatricians, the determining factors that parents cited concerning their satisfaction with a particular pediatrician's care were all related to the personal qualities of the physician—communication skills, clinical competence, and apparent level of concern for the child.

Recommendation #3: Incorporate standards for consumer satisfaction into evaluations of physician performance.

Responses from surveys of patient satisfaction should be included in evaluations of each physician's performance—right along with indicators of the physician's productivity and ability to meet his or her obligations on the staff. Some medical groups encourage involvement of physicians in service to the community and activities in volunteer organizations such as serving as physician for a high school's athletic team or working for charitable organizations. Such outside involvement demonstrates a physician's interest in the community and is often considered by committees on compensation, when they evaluate salary adjustments. Surveys of patient satisfaction can be coded by specialty, by program, or by individual physician. The surveys would thus become a database for evaluating the performance of each physician. Once the first set of results has been collected and analyzed, they become a basic measurement against which it can be determined whether any progress has been made toward correcting less-than-favorable results.

Recommendation #4: Provide head nurses and physicians with education and hands-on training in management and budgeting, as well as in interpersonal and communication skills.

A broadened awareness of and involvement in the management of a medical practice will increase the probability that a physician will embrace a consumer-oriented approach to doing business. Each member of the medical and supporting staff needs to have a stake in the management of consumer satisfaction. A team approach to the issue will have a greater impact on the achievement of consumer satisfaction than will one or more members of the staff acting as individuals.

Recommendation #5: Measure physician satisfaction through questionnaires for employees.

If physicians are not satisfied with their working environment, it is unlikely that their supporting staff or their patients will be pleased, either. Harmony and disharmony are contagious. It is therefore important to identify and rectify less-than-harmonious relationships among staff before the negative side effects of those relationships detract from the quality of services being offered consumers. Employees, including physicians, should be given questionnaires periodically, to find out what they like or do not like about their working environment. Areas of dissatisfaction should be discussed at meetings of medical staff, and appropriate solutions or responses should be developed to increase physician satisfaction. Other steps that can be taken include:

- Telling physicians whenever positive comments about their care appear in the surveys of patient satisfaction
- Decreasing patients' rate of "no-shows" by instructing ancillary staff to make reminding telephone calls to patients twenty-four hours before their scheduled appointments
- Fostering good relationships between physicians and supporting staff by planning shared lunches, parties, and other get-togethers

Recommendation #6: Reward behavior by physicians that demonstrates competence, caring, and good use of communication skills.

Develop a special award such as "Pro of the Month," or other ways to recognize physicians for excellence in service to consumers. The "Pro of the Month" could be chosen from the entire pool of employees, or from separate groups for physicians and for other employees. Each year, award the physician who received the most positive responses in surveys of patient satisfaction with a meaningful memento such as a gold pin, a pen, a trophy, or an ornament for the desk. Develop a system of monetary rewards for physicians who exhibit excellence in enhancing consumer satisfaction, as demonstrated by the surveys. The system should be linked to basic compensation or to incentive/bonus pay.

Recommendation #7: Provide physicians with education on how to continue the emphasis on consumer-oriented service.

The results of each survey should routinely be shared with physicians and their supporting teams. Past performance should be compared to current trends, to determine the effects of any changes that have been made. This is the time to refocus efforts and to emphasize the changes called for by consumers. Successful strategies would include:

- Providing, for viewing at meetings of medical staff, videos of patients' focus groups in which patients are shown discussing problems and suggesting changes

- Involving physicians in activities for marketing and public relations—those aimed at referring physicians as well as patients
- Offering seminars for physicians, on the topic of enhancing consumer satisfaction, led by outside consultants
- Making the concept of consumer satisfaction part of the orientation of physicians new to the practice

HOW CONSUMERS SELECT AND EVALUATE PHYSICIANS

In order to develop an effective marketing message for their practice, providers of health care must first understand the factors and criteria that consumers use when selecting and evaluating their physicians. In March, 1987, Ramsey Clinic hired Nelson Research Services, Inc., to conduct a study on how people living in the area served by the clinic select their primary physicians. A scientific sample of 240 people was interviewed for the study, some in person, others on the telephone. Findings of the study offer some important information about consumers of health care and the factors they consider when selecting their physicians. Here is a summary of the findings of that study:[14]

- Three-fourths of consumers in the five-county area served by Ramsey Clinic have a personal physician. People living in rural areas and people sixty years of age or older were more likely to have a personal physician, while adults under thirty were less likely.
- Most primary care physicians are general practitioners. Very few specialists (other than family practitioners and internists) function as primary care physicians.
- About three of every ten consumers in the five-county area have been with their current primary care physicians for at least ten years. Long-term relationships with physicians are especially common in rural areas and among consumers sixty years of age or older. This suggests that these rural and older consumers are least likely to switch to a different primary care physician.
- The most important factors consumers use when choosing a primary care physician are qualities exhibited by his or her staff. In this survey, consumers cited the following specific factors as being most important:

  — The physician's skill at communicating—at listening, asking questions, and explaining medical matters in understandable language

— The physician's diagnostic and problem-solving skills
— The physician's willingness to refer the patient to another physician for services in a specialty or perhaps for a second opinion
— The physician's ability to project a kind, caring, and considerate manner to the patient
— The physician's willingness to involve the patient in making decisions about treatment and care
— The physician's availability for consultations by telephone
— The attitude and manner of the physician's staff

• On the other hand, many factors played little or no role in selection or evaluation of a primary care physician by a consumer. These included:

— The physician's gender, age, and mode of dress
— The medical school the physician attended
— The physician's affiliation with a teaching or research facility
— The size of the medical group
— Whether the patient was referred to the physician by a referral service
— The availability of parking at the physician's office or clinic
— The physician's fees

• Several other factors fell somewhere in the middle. They were of some importance to consumers when selecting a physician. These include (in order of importance):

— Length of lead time required to schedule an appointment with the physician
— Whether the physician expressed a friendly interest in the patient, beyond his or her immediate health problems
— Length of the wait in a waiting room (most consumers judge a twenty-minute wait to be acceptable, although men, consumers in upper-income brackets, and residents of the metropolitan area are less patient than others, but all consumers are agreeable to waiting longer than twenty minutes—if given a good reason)
— The reputation of the clinic
— The location of the office or clinic
— The physician's previous work experience
— The physician's practice of offering follow-up, by letter or telephone
— The availability in the clinic of a wide variety of specialists
— The hours the clinic is open

— The physician's affiliation with a large group of specialists
— Recommendation of the physician by a friend

- Interestingly, the overall ranking of factors used to pick a primary care physician was similar, for all segments of people surveyed, regardless of area (rural or metropolitan), gender, age, income, or insurance coverage.

From another perspective, analyses of findings of this study place consumers of health care in the area served by Ramsey Clinic in three basic categories:

1. Consumers to whom interpersonal skills are key factors in choosing and evaluating a physician; 89 percent fall into this group.
2. Consumers who are practical, oriented to convenience, and choose their physicians accordingly; 8 percent do this.
3. Consumers who assign a high value to technical considerations; only 2 percent of consumers are of this type.

Therefore, the technical competence that distinguishes Ramsey Clinic from its competition, its affiliation with a teaching and research facility, and its expansive multispecialty network of physicians influence only 2 percent of people in the area served by the clinic when it comes time to choose medical care (see Table 2.1). Furthermore, it is important to note that respondents to the survey indicated that they do not consider it particularly difficult to find physicians who offer the benefits they are looking for. This finding emphasizes how intensely competitive the health care industry has become, in this five-county metropolitan area.[14]

THE ROLE OF MANAGEMENT IN DEVELOPING A CONSUMER-ORIENTED INITIATIVE

Implementation of a program for consumer satisfaction will typically encounter some roadblocks among the nonphysician staff as well as from physicians. Although administrators are usually highly supportive of the concept, clinicians and members of the supporting and ancillary staffs frequently have had no consistent experience in making consumer satisfaction part of their day-to-day performance on the job. Furthermore, they are likely to perceive consumer satisfaction as a separate, compartmentalized function of the medical practice rather than as an integral aspect of the job of each staff member.

TABLE 2.1. Factors Considered by Consumers When Selecting a Physician

Major Factors	Principal Components
Personal relationships	Willing to talk on telephone
	Good communication skills
	Involves patient in decisions
	Spends time, doesn't rush
	Kind, considerate, caring
	Willing to refer patient
	Letter/phone follow-up
Convenience	Time spent in waiting room
Practicality	Length of time to schedule an appointment
	Hours
	Physician's fee
	Availability of parking
	Location
Technical	Affiliation with a teaching facility
	Affiliation with a research facility
	Physician's medical school
	Size of group (number of physicians)
	Referred by referral service
	Affiliated with large group of specialists
	Clinic has physicians with wide range of ages

Source: Nelson, A. Consumer Satisfaction Evaluation Study of Ramsey Clinic Services. Internal study conducted by Nelson Research Services, Inc., Minneapolis/St. Paul, Minnesota, 1987. Reprinted by permission.

Many factors appear to be responsible for these misconceptions. Consumer satisfaction may not have been made a priority within the practice. The practice may also lack clear guidelines and expectations for employee performance of services for consumers. A systematic procedure for rewarding excellence in service also may not be in place. So how can the leadership of a medical practice persuade its clinicians and supporting staff to participate actively, to support and implement effectively, a program for consumer satisfaction? The following are some recommendations:

Recommendation #1: Develop a practice-oriented mission statement that clearly defines service to consumers as a key element in the mission of the practice; then develop a campaign to publicize the statement.

A clear, concise, and highly visible statement of mission communicates a strong and focused message to employees as well as to consumers. Through such a statement, both groups will have an improved understanding of the expectations of the organization regarding service. A strong mission statement can also become a "guiding light" for the organization, defining the culture of the practice. The revision of a mission statement is, ultimately, the responsibility of the partners in the practice, its shareholders, or its board of directors. Administrators, however, can assist this process, ensuring that the concept of service to consumers becomes a clear and concise element of the statement.

After the statement is revised, the next challenge becomes increasing its visibility. One way of doing this is to publicize the mission statement itself. Posters can be placed at strategic locations throughout the organization. The statement can also be included on the letterhead and prominently featured on all the brochures and publications for the organization. To further increase the visibility of the mission statement—and the concept of consumer satisfaction as a way of doing business—a promotional campaign can be initiated within the organization. The campaign should have a theme or promotional slogan developed as an outgrowth of the statement, such as "You're Special at the Doctor's Clinic." The slogan could then be promoted through posters and publications. It could even be embossed on buttons worn by employees or included on their name tags.

The revised mission statement, the organizational emphasis on consumer satisfaction, and the promotional campaign can be presented to employees through a series of inservice programs. For these programs to be effective, all employees must be involved, no matter how much actual contact they have with patients. Employees must understand that it is important to treat each other, as well as patients, as consumers. Poor relationships among employees of an organization will spill over with negative consequences onto the relationships of employees with consumers. Be sure that all physicians and administrators take part in the inservice programs; their presence lends credibility to the endeavor and provides evidence of administrative support. But to avoid the perception of criticism, physicians and administrators must be sure to communicate to the rest of the staff that they believe the employees are already doing a good job. They must also stress the importance of incorporating the principle of consumer satisfaction into the very fabric of the medical practice.

Recommendation #2: Develop or revise job descriptions for nonphysicians on the staff, to state clearly the expectation by the organization that employees will incorporate the concept of high-quality service and consumer satisfaction into their day-to-day performance on the job.

Descriptions of jobs in medical practice typically emphasize the clinical aspects of care, almost to the exclusion of everything else. Descriptions should be revised to include expectations concerning service to consumers. To permit quantitative evaluation, these expectations should be specifically defined and stated in measurable terms. In addition, programs for orientation of employees should routinely devote time to the subject of consumer satisfaction. An employee's initial orientation should also be regularly followed by continuing on-the-job training that reinforces the updates, concepts, and techniques learned for consumer satisfaction. Once standards for performance have been established, supervisory and rank-and-file employees can more appropriately work on concerns aimed at attaining the desired results.

To incorporate into day-to-day performance on the job, consistently, the concept of high-quality service to consumers as well as other aspects of the mission statement, the organization should clearly outline its expectations of each employee in each job described. Rather than serving as a tool for pointing out poor performance, the job description should provide clear expectations of performance. It serves, therefore, as an instructional device and should specify the behaviors expected of the employee as concretely as possible. A focus group of supervisory and nonsupervisory personnel could be formed, to get this process started. The objective for such a group should be to specify at least three measurable key behaviors for each classification of jobs.

For a receptionist, for example, the key behaviors could include the following:

1. Answers the phone in two to three rings, using proper identification of the organization, the department, and its name
2. Acknowledges a patient's presence promptly with eye contact, a courteous hello, or, if on the phone, some nonverbal signal such as a nod or a smile
3. Gives the patient undivided attention and uses effective communication techniques—empathy, confirming information, eye contact—to allow the patient to express his or her concerns or questions
4. Returns to calls on hold within 30 to 60 seconds while assuring waiting patients of continued attention to their needs

***Recommendation #3: Use the criteria of consumer satisfaction
in evaluations of performance on the job.***

Key indicators developed for job descriptions can be incorporated into evaluations of performance. This sets the stage for open dialogue between the employee and supervisor concerning the concept of consumer satisfaction and how its measurable aspects will be considered in review of performance. The employee receives important feedback concerning definable outcomes in this area, while the supervisor reemphasizes that consumer satisfaction remains a top priority for the organization. The evaluation of performance also enables supervisors to identify substandard performance and to develop individual plans of action to correct the situation. Routine, ongoing monitoring of outcomes related to the plan for action enables employee and employer to chart results that will form bases for the next evaluation.

***Recommendation #4: Develop a "Pro of the Month" award,
to recognize employees for outstanding performance
in "living the mission statement."***

Programs for recognition of employees, such as a "Pro of the Month Award," are based on the proactive concept of "let's catch the employees doing it right." As noted in the section for physicians, "Pro of the Month" can include both physicians and nonphysicians, or a separate monthly designation can be made for each group. The award sends a clear message throughout the organization that efforts by employees are highly valued. As part of the award, the employee should receive personal notification by leaders of the organization, special recognition in the form of flowers and perhaps a lunch or dinner with the leaders, prominent coverage in in-house newsletters and on posters located in common areas throughout the organization, and the addition of the employee's name to a plaque honoring "Pros of the Month" in a central corridor of the organization. The award should provide recognition that is positive and highly visible. The committee selecting for these awards to both physicians and nonphysicians should be presented as a recognizable and respected group of physicians and nonphysicians. The purpose of the selecting committee is to establish the standards for qualification and then to solicit recommendations and applications for nominations each month from the staff at large, and then select the most worthy member of the staff from among those nominated.

The "Pro of the Month" award offers a systematic and positive way of reinforcing the mission of the organization to provide outstanding service to consumers. Thus, criteria for the award should clearly correspond to a mission statement. The award should send a nonambiguous message to all employees and to the community that the recipient of the reward is being acclaimed for "living the mission statement" of the practice.

Recommendation #5: Routinely monitor the results of surveys of consumer satisfaction.

Routinely administered surveys provide a basis for monitoring the quantitative effectiveness of the program for consumer satisfaction. The surveys should be longitudinally charted to assure that the program is doing what it was designed to do. When measuring outcomes, it is most important to focus on less-than-satisfactory performance. Although it is also important to acknowledge and reward employees for what is going right, it is extremely important to identify and correct less-than-satisfactory services. Routine review of the outcomes will identify the elements responsible for the problems that necessitate changes leading to an improvement of the service or services in question. Each plan for remediation that is implemented to correct a problem with service must be closely monitored, to ensure the desired outcomes.

THE ROLE OF NONPHYSICIAN STAFF IN MAKING A CONSUMER-ORIENTED INITIATIVE WORK

The managing staff of most medical practices is usually aware that a high level of consumer satisfaction is necessary for continued success. In some cases, however, managers who recognize the importance of high-quality service to consumers find themselves working with a staff who have not yet experienced the same recognition. Consumer satisfaction has not yet become the way of doing business in those practices. It has not yet become part of the culture of that organization.

Difficulty in communicating to staff the message about consumer satisfaction can be traced to two basic causes:

1. The widely diverse training and experience among individuals within a typical practice
2. Problems related to the structure of a medical practice

Recommendation #1: Treat physicians and nonphysician staff as consumers.

Experts say that cultural acceptance is essential for the successful implementation of any major initiative in an organization. Using education to develop that culture is not enough. Change in organizational values must also occur. One way of initiating change in organizational values is to expand the traditional definition of "consumer" to include fellow physicians and other staff. Satisfying these "internal customers" should be given the same priority as satisfying external ones, and it should occur on both the interpersonal and the interdepartmental levels. The manner in which one member of the staff treats another is contagious; it will influence how the staff treats patients and other outside customers. As one expert in management has suggested, "the employee's capacity to provide quality service to other employees and customers will be directly related to the quality of service they receive as internal customers of the organization's day-to-day management."[11] By improving employee satisfaction, an organization will likely see improvements in patient satisfaction, as well.

Both physicians and other leaders must become role models for the "ethic of consumer satisfaction." Managers may have little contact with external customers on a day-to-day basis, but they have many opportunities to show exemplary consumer-oriented behavior in their service to each other and to those they supervise, which they can demonstrate by "walking their talk." In fact, administrative job descriptions and incentive plans should be modified to include criteria that measure the level of consumer satisfaction they provide to intraorganizational consumers (other employees). Criteria should be included that measure how well they provide to the employees they supervise a role model for the "ethic of consumer satisfaction." Leadership is the key to initiating cultural change within organizations.

Recommendation #2: Change those organizational values that hinder the successful implementation of a program for consumer satisfaction.

The most important element of any attempt to make an organizational change is ensuring that the change becomes so internalized and so much a part of the everyday workings of the organization that it will last long after the initial incentives to implementing have gone. Consumer satisfaction must become a way that business is routinely conducted in the health care industry. Changing organizational norms is, however, extremely difficult. In *Management of Corporate Culture*, Ralph H. Kilmann suggests the following approach:[15]

- Work with groups of employees to elicit lists of the norms of the practice—both positive and negative (such as whether most people arrive at work on time). This process is designed to allow employees to see the counterproductive "directives" they have imposed on one another.

- Work with staff to establish new norms. This step in the process should include discussion of where the organization is headed—its mission, vision, core values, goals, and objectives. From these discussions, employees should be able to develop an acceptable list of norms that fit with the goals of the organization.

In the *Medical Group Management Journal*, J. Silversin and M.J. Kornacki have listed the following as values often found among employees working in organizations with a commitment to service:[16]

- Respect for each other
- Acknowledgment of the mission to service
- Universal accountability for behavior—everyone is expected to obey the rules
- Participation in decision-making and discussion
- Teamwork
- Superior quality of service to consumers

Identify gaps between existing norms in the practice and the new, desired norms. Close the gaps. Having a list of new organizational values is not enough. Those values must be put into practice. This can be accomplished in a variety of ways. Some of the most important include:

- Role modeling by physicians and other leaders
- Clear communication of the values through changes in job descriptions and mission statements
- Ceremonies to award recognition upon reaching certain milestones

By including members of the staff as active participants in the creation of the new norms, the staff will feel an important ownership of them. Members of the staff will be more likely to encourage each other to adhere to the new values and let go of the old.

Recommendation #3: Implement the program for consumer satisfaction on a service-by-service basis. Also, work to create a model program that can serve as an example to be replicated by others.

Individual leaders among physicians and other staff should be made responsible for implementation of the program in their own services. This recognizes that different services make changes at different rates. It will also allow leaders to focus on specific problems related to each of their services. The creation of a model service provides an example of other services to emulate and a chance for managers to demonstrate the benefits of a program in consumer satisfaction.

Using members of the staff from that service as trainers for other services will facilitate expansion of the program throughout the organization. They will have become the experts and will appear credible, when training people to do the same jobs they do themselves. Appropriate recognition should be given, as each service reaches designated milestones in the implementation of their program for consumer satisfaction.

Recommendation #4: Hold educational seminars on the subject of consumer satisfaction and/or include the topic as part of other presentations on service in the delivery of health care.

The goal of the educational process should be to inform staff of progress made toward the attainment of goals and objectives in consumer satisfaction, and of ways this information is related to the medical practice. Ideas that have proven beneficial for certain services should be discussed and adapted for implementation by other providers of service. The following are some general suggestions for which specific examples could be drawn and presented at educational sessions:

- Point out that, in order to survive, the practice must attract consumers and that a high level of consumer satisfaction is one way of doing that. Show the correlation between the number of returning visits made by patients, and their levels of satisfaction.
- Point out that consumer satisfaction is the life blood of most service industries. Service of high quality motivates us to shop at certain stores; why shouldn't it motivate us when selecting the place where we receive health care? Show examples where low levels of patient satisfaction led to an erosion of the patient base.
- Stress that it can make the medical practice a better place to work. A program for consumer satisfaction has very good potential to improve employee satisfaction on the job, once the staff begin to treat each other as they would like to be treated themselves.
- Note that it is already working. Allow past "Pros of the Month" and other employees who are pleased with the program to give testimonials and teach others about its merits.
- Show clips of taped comments, both critical and complimentary, from consumers' focus groups. These should show the significance consumers place on such things as having the staff answer phone calls promptly, and getting friendly help with questions about billing.

- Results from past and current surveys should be discussed, to demonstrate quantifiable outcomes and to associate key findings with patient activity and financial benchmarks.

Recommendation #5: Expand the definition of "consumer" to include employees as well as patients.

Staff should be required to serve internal consumers—fellow employees—with the same commitment as when serving external consumers. Studies confirm the positive, contagious nature of the "self-fulfilling prophecy" of treating others as you would like to be treated yourself. Once in motion, this aspect of behavior will be shared with all people with whom an employee comes in contact—staff and patients alike. Furthermore, such commitment should be recognized; staff should have a uniform way of rewarding those within the organization who serve each other well. Employees of Federal Express, for example, use special stickers that can be placed on memos or paperwork to recognize those who serve them well or who are doing a good job in general.

Recommendation #6: Develop a survey of satisfaction among the staff.

These should be similar to the surveys of satisfaction among external consumers that are given to patients. Through these internal surveys, satisfaction with service within the organization can be measured and evaluated. They should also be used in evaluation of employee performance and for setting new goals for service.

Recommendation #7: Modify administrative and managerial job descriptions and performance evaluations to include criteria on consumer satisfaction.

The criteria should be based on service to those whom managers supervise (internal consumers) as well as on their service to patients. Administrators should be evaluated for how well they serve as a role model for the "ethic of consumer satisfaction." Leading physicians and administrators should review the program at regular intervals. Routine review, at least annually, is required to make sure the program remains on course and is still applicable. Employee feedback from surveys should prove a useful tool in evaluating the program.

FROM INITIAL CALL FOR APPOINTMENT TO BILLING: TREATING THE PATIENT RIGHT

When patients arrive at a hospital or a physician's office, they are there for help. Whether they are merely seeking information about a new insurance plan, or checking in for surgery on their gallbladder, they have come for one reason: to get assistance with a problem.[11] The quickest way to create dissatisfied patients is to treat them poorly during this initial contact, but unfortunately it is done all too often. Instead of showing an interest in their patients' needs, medical facilities usually insist that patients deal first with the bureaucratic demands of the organization, asking them, for example, to fill out forms, or having them first check in at the desk that handles insurance, to make sure the bill will be paid, or embarrassing them by indicating they are too early or too late for their appointment.

Before the Appointment

In anticipation of the patient's visit, whether to a doctor's office or a hospital, several considerations should be made to make the visit satisfying and efficient. For some patients, it may be advantageous to schedule all appointments on the same day, ending with a meeting of the staff to summarize all findings. Other patients, to avoid exhaustion, may appreciate appointments coordinated over more than one day. In the past, many specialists accepted referrals only from other physicians, but most medical practices today are quite open to accepting appointments for patients who have demonstrated insurability, whether or not they were directly referred by another physician. It should be pointed out, however, that most plans from an HMO will limit and/or direct their referrals to specialists and will almost always permit such referrals only after the patient has been evaluated by a primary care physician viewed by the HMO as a "gatekeeper."

Many patients find it helpful to receive written brochures or other literature describing a particular program or service at a hospital or clinic. Such information can provide understanding as a background and, in many cases, can help set the patient and family at ease about going to a doctor whom they have never met before.

Service on questions of fees, insurance, and financial needs should be brought up, as the plan for evaluating satisfaction is developed. Too frequently, patients are not given clear answers to their questions about costs and, as a result, remain unaware of the financial impact of their care until a bill is received. Since patients are responsible for paying their bills, they should know approximately how much the charges are going to be before treatment begins. If the patient has insurance, staff should help verify the extent of their coverage prior to the service; every insurance policy is different, and the cost to be covered by the patient may vary considerably. This may require that the staff do some searching and perhaps telephoning to secure the information, but such duties are required of a consumer-oriented business. Patients who appear embarrassed about the matter of paying their bills should be quickly befriended by the staff, and an effort should be made to find out what outside financial resources might be considered in setting up an installment plan based on ability to pay, for low-income patients.

Establishing Rapport

If patients are treated poorly during the first few minutes after their arrival at a medical practice, chances are quite good they will not return. A more appropriate way of greeting newly arrived patients is to smile and welcome them into the setting with a cheerful "hello" or "good afternoon." Such common pleasantries establish a friendly and informal, yet business-like, attitude. Staff should also be encouraged to offer a kind compliment or two to the patient, if appropriate, on what he or she is wearing, or perhaps to make a comment about the weather or about parking difficulties. Such personalized pleasantries are easy to make and will help patients relax and feel that the staff is interested in them as people, rather than just "health cases."

Members of the staff should identify themselves to the patient by name, and briefly indicate who they are (nurse, doctor, receptionist). They should then describe to the patient how they plan to help. Here are two examples of beginnings for such a dialogue:

> Hello. My name is Sally Jones. I am a patient coordinator, and I am here to help you today. Do you have any questions, before we begin? First, I would like to outline what you can expect to happen at each of your appointments.

> Good morning. I am Doctor Smith. I am a pediatrician. My special training is in pediatric cardiology, and I will be giving your son a physical examination. This examination will be used to determine whether it will be necessary to do additional testing of his heart. My procedure will involve . . .

This open and easygoing communication pattern between the patient and members of the staff should continue throughout the appointment. Each dialogue sets in motion a clear, meaningful relationship with the patient. Briefly outlining what will be taking place during the appointment allows the patient to prepare, both physically and mentally, for what will follow.

Defining the Patient's Needs and Wants

Always talk in terms of what the patient wants. In a friendly way, convince the patient that you are going to do everything reasonably possible to make sure his or her needs are met, but that to accomplish this, you must have the patient's total, undivided cooperation. Ask yourself, "How can I encourage them to want to do it?" Demanding cooperation of people seldom works. Rather, you must plan an approach that encourages the patient to see that their needs can best be met by cooperating with you.

When confronted with an uncooperative patient, it is natural to recoil with defensiveness. All members of the staff must learn, however, that they must exert as much willpower as necessary to resist responding with the same kind of abrasiveness. The only way to come out ahead, in an argument, is to avoid the argument in the first place. So even if the patient is clearly wrong, avoid debating the point. One argument may lead to another, creating an even more uncooperative patient.

You also have the patient's health to consider. Arguing with patients who are ill, especially those with dangerously high blood pressure or other serious conditions, might exacerbate their problems. Remember Murphy's Law: "Anything that can go wrong, will go wrong." Instead of arguing, concede to the patient that you are wrong. It will do absolutely no good to lose control of your temper. A patient who believes he or she has been neglected or mistreated will never be won over by an out-of-control argument.

Instead of reacting defensively, train yourself to let the "hot air go in one ear and out the other," and listen for a comment from the patient or pause in the conversation that you can use to find common ground. The ability to listen quietly and stay focused on a patient is a difficult but essential skill. Openly acknowledge that the patient may be right and you may be wrong. Offer to reexamine the facts. Chances are quite good that some of the facts associated with the case may have been overstated, either by you or the patient. After the patient has finished describing the problem, politely ask questions rather than pointing out all the places where the patient's statement of the facts was in error. By gently asking questions, the patient will most likely be able to see the errors, on his or her own. This enables the patient to save face—and calm down.

Remember that the goal of a consumer-oriented approach requires you, as a provider of health care, to put yourself in the patient's place. When in doubt, the rule of thumb becomes one of treating the patient as you would want to be treated, if you exchanged roles.

Solving Problems

Complaints are inevitable. If a complaint does not surface from time to time, perhaps the service being provided is not worth complaining about. Remember, however, that each problem or issue between two or more individuals can be viewed from several different perspectives. Be prepared to search for these divergent points of view, as you receive and review complaints from patients.

Don't go looking for problems, but be alert for warning signs that indicate areas of potential conflict. Obvious complaints—such as an error in the billing statement—will surface quickly and will not be difficult to identify. Many patients, however, indicate their dissatisfaction much more subtly, in statements such as "I have obtained information from another doctor that may be worth considering," or "Here are some facts about my history that I trust you will not lose sight of," or "The other doctor said. . . ." When a patient criticizes or challenges you, it is important that you remain calm and refrain from taking the criticism personally. Avoid allowing patients to transfer their anger onto you. Becoming angry yourself may cause you to overlook important information that can help resolve the situation more quickly and quietly.

Angry patients often need a lot of time to express fully what is bothering them. Try not to interrupt. Let them continue until they have finished. Then tell them you appreciate their point of view and acknowledge that you know how important this issue is to them. Probe all aspects of the case, and assure them that all matters will be cleared up to their satisfaction. This technique will quickly remove the "wind from their sails," and angry patients will find themselves unable to continue their harassment. It is not important that the issue be totally resolved then and there. What is important is that patients feel they are being heard and listened to. Any disagreement, however, should be followed up with proper corrective action—and patients should always be notified of what has been done to resolve the problem.

Patients also often complain about the amount of time and attention they receive—or rather, do not receive—from medical professionals, particularly their physicians. Doctors should heed these complaints and change their behavior accordingly. The patient-doctor relationship may be the most crucial factor in determining a patient's satisfaction. Patients who feel that their physicians listen to their concerns and complaints tend to rate service in their health care higher than those patients who feel they have little say in their own care.

Turning Complaints into Routine Requests

Let the patient talk. Listen carefully with an open mind. Ask polite and meaningful questions about background essential to this history and related problems. When patients become convinced that you are genuinely interested in their welfare, they will also become convinced that the care they are receiving is highly satisfactory.

To make a lasting impression, go beyond just letting patients talk; engage them in meaningful conversation about their needs concerning health. You will soon learn how to judge the needs of each patient and thus when and how to end each conversation appropriately. Some people can talk and talk without saying too much, while others can provide a lot of information with only a few words. The ability to listen and subsequently to guide patients through these very important conversations will improve over time and with practice. Even if only a few minutes can be given to a patient, that time should be spent in a friendly, caring exchange of information, rather than in a brisk, one-sided rush that implies "I'm too busy and am only going to give you the facts about your health."

Possibly one in 100 patients will protest a correct bill. Perhaps the patient believes a second X ray or laboratory test was unnecessary. Or perhaps the patient did not fully understand the need for a certain procedure and, when billed for it, refused to pay. Most medical practices follow a standard procedure with an unpaid bill: They repeatedly send a bill to the patient over a period of months until, if the bill remains unpaid, it is turned over to a bonded collection agency or an attorney, for legal action. This process can be avoided, and a great deal of time and expense saved, if an effort is made simply to discuss unpaid bills with patients.

When entering into such a discussion, treat the patient with respect. It should be assumed that the patient is sincere, honest, and responsible, and that he or she would like to arrange payment, or to find an acceptable alternative, for a debt justly incurred. Begin by explaining why the particular service was provided and that no attempt was made to overcharge, double bill, or conceal charges. Then listen attentively to the patient's response. After exploring together all facets of the case, turn the focus to the specific charges listed in the bill. Give the patient a copy and explain each entry in detail. Acknowledge that, as the recipient of the services, the patient knows more about them than anyone else—and that he or she is likely to agree to a payment plan, out of a sense of fair play. Patients treated in a personal yet businesslike fashion will, in all likelihood, also return to the practice for future medical services.

Making the Job Easier for Providers of Health Care

A surefire way to make your job, as a provider of health care, easier is to find convenient methods of helping patients have their needs met. All aspects of the medical practice should be as streamlined as possible, while still providing comprehensive care. One place to start is with the avalanche of paperwork that often greets patients as soon as they arrive in a medical facility. Avoid duplicating similar bits of information on different forms. A review of most medical records and registration forms reveals much duplicated information. In hospitals, this problem is often compounded by having the patient fill out similar forms in each department. By consolidating a patient's history and the forms with associated information into one concise set, the burden on the patient—and on the staff—is greatly reduced.

When talking to patients, begin by discussing matters on which you agree. By emphasizing things that are mutually agreeable, you convey the idea that you are both interested in achieving the same outcome. As a result, you are more likely to have a positive conversation. If a difference of opinion arises later in the conversation, stress that the conflict is over the way things are being done, not over the purpose of doing them. Providers of health care need to take an adequate amount of time to explain why certain requirements exist and what has to happen to resolve the issues. When patients understand the need for doing something, whether filling out a form or taking a medication, most issues can be resolved to mutual satisfaction.

Make it your goal to alleviate the patient's immediate need, no matter how minor you believe it to be. If you treat a patient's problem on the basis of your perception of the importance of the issue, rather than on the patient's perception, you are headed for significant difficulties in communication. No one should have to prove their need for health care before receiving prompt and courteous service. Of ten typical patients seen in the doctor's office, at least eight will have average complaints, concerns, and expectations. All deserve the empathy of the medical staff. Patients should not need to justify why they have sought care. Instead, they should all be treated with an equal concern for the needs of their health and an understanding of their concern about the medical process.

Only through such appreciation and understanding of the reasons patients seek medical attention will it be possible to deliver consumer-oriented care. Although taking a few extra minutes to empathize with the patient will usually not significantly alter the provider's decisions on medical treatment, it will alter the patient's perception of that treatment. By approaching each individual who comes into their clinic first as a person and only then as a patient, physicians and other professionals in health care will find that such a person will then leave the clinic as a more satisfied, informed, and compliant patient who will then return as the need arises.

Helping the Referred Patient

All aspects of case processing and associated details should be handled by a member of the staff of the receiving physician, following the referral. This task should not be left to the patient nor to the referring physician. Forms to authorize the release of information should be signed by the patient, which permits the staff of the receiving physician to acquire previous records and reports that may be helpful to better understanding of the problem with that patient's health and may help avoid duplication of tests. Forms for collecting information on the patient's history should be sent directly to the patient's home, along with a telephone number (preferably toll-free or collect), so that the patient can call if there are questions. All forms and requests for information should be accompanied by a stamped, self-addressed envelope, to make them more convenient for a patient to return.

Be sure to include a form that gives your agency the right to share any information obtained with significant people such as other physicians, nurses, and school personnel. If a child is being seen by a doctor because of a learning problem, for example, it would be helpful if the child's school psychologist, teacher, or principal could receive a copy of the medical report. Vocational rehabilitative agencies or other regional, state, or federal groups may need a copy of a doctor's report for purposes of instituting financial, social, or training services on behalf of the patient. A patient may also be eligible for assistance to buy a motorized wheelchair through the Muscular Dystrophy Association or other agency. Before this can be determined, however, a copy of the medical report will need to be sent to that group. Once forms have been signed by the patient or his or her representative authorizing release of medical records, the staff providing health care can expedite the necessary follow-up services.

TIPS FOR PROVIDING SERVICE OF HIGH QUALITY

- Remember that each patient you see today is there because he or she needs help.
- Listen intently, pay attention to the patient, and be eager to help.
- Go out of your way to greet each patient in a friendly yet business-like way. Without being asked, identify who you are and what ser-

vices you will be providing. Remember: the first impression you make will set in motion an attitude about all the services that the patient can expect to receive.

- Talk to the patient about his or her needs. Convince the patient that you will be working to assure his or her satisfaction.
- Assume the position that the patient is never wrong. Whether this axiom is true is not important; what is important is that you evoke a patient-oriented attitude when trying to resolve problems.
- Remember that the only way to come out ahead, in an argument, is to avoid the argument in the first place. Even if you are clearly right and the patient is clearly wrong, do not argue! You will not change the patient's opinion by doing so.
- Do not go looking for problems, but do learn to be a good listener. Probe for all factors related to the patient's problem; most can be solved by identifying the issues and engaging the proper services and resources to lead to resolution.
- Keep a friendly attitude when confronted by an angry patient; strive to find common ground that will help you both resolve the problem.
- If a disagreement arises, convince the patient that you are both after the same results. Make sure the disagreement focuses on methods, not purpose. Methods can be renegotiated; purposes should stay intact.
- Find ways of making it easier for you to provide good service to patients.
- Before being seen by the physician, each patient should be instructed to develop a list of questions he or she would like the physician to answer. This process will assure that patients receive answers to their main concerns about health.
- Let patients talk about their problems and concerns and even vent their anger. Only then can you develop a complete picture of the problem and guide the patient ever so gently to resolution.
- Do not harass patients about their bills. Treat them as you would expect to be treated, with respect, patience, and understanding.

Follow Up on Good Service

Many cases requiring the attention of providers of health care are resolved at the time of the visit to the office. Others need long-term treatment. In both instances, it is important to make follow-up contact with the patient after the visit. Such contact will make it possible to continue to monitor that person's health. It will also promote a continuing linkage between the patient and the provider and will facilitate the consumer's satisfaction with the service.

Patient satisfaction is one aspect of health care that is frequently over-looked or taken for granted. A "halo effect" appears to be in place on providers of health care, particularly physicians: this involves a perception that the doctor can do no wrong, and that once care has been given, no questions need to be asked. Yet despite the extensive and excellent training and experience of physicians, they are human and, thus, fallible. Questions about the adequacy of services in health care must therefore be asked of patients as well as of doctors, if improvement in that care is to occur.

Medical services have generally been assumed by consumers to be of high quality, but this assumption has not been adequately tested.[1,13] Only recently has the Joint Commission on Hospital and Ambulatory Care Accreditation, for example, begun focusing its efforts on clinical outcomes and the development of parameters for a practice to judge appropriate quality.[17,18] Patient satisfaction is a very reliable indicator of successful medical practice. It needs to be continually assessed, if services perceived by patients as relevant and meaningful are to be offered.

Effective Forms of Follow-Up Service

Effective follow-up services for patients can take a variety of forms. Patients should be asked to write out questions they wish the doctor to answer about their health problems. For their convenience, a place to list these questions should be included on the forms used for obtaining a history that patients fill out upon their arrival at the medical facility. Personnel giving health care should still encourage patients to ask their questions orally, but putting questions in writing can provide added insight into the patient's expectations. In addition, the questions can serve as bench-marks to compare against, when a determination is being made about whether the patient's expectations of care were met.

If a patient is seen by more than one staff member during the process of evaluation, each person who sees the patient should review with the patient his or her findings from the evaluation. Every visit should also be followed up with a letter, telephone call, and/or report. Research has shown that such follow-up has a strong and positive influence on how patients feel about the care they received, yet it is all too often neglected. Providing a letter summarizing and explaining the physician's findings and recommendations for care is one of the most meaningful services that can be offered a patient. It gives "closure" to the patient's questions. It indicates problems that were either ruled out or confirmed, during the examination. The summary also provides a record of the current status and recommended direction of treatment. If the patient viewed service received as satisfactory, he or she will likely continue to seek care from that provider. The summarizing report should be sent to the patient within ten working days after an appointment.

Follow-up may also include telephoning the patient to check on his or her medical progress. This technique is especially valuable after surgery or in cases where medications have been prescribed; it can help determine whether the surgery or medications have had the desired results. Telephoned follow-up also establishes a personal link between the doctor and the patient. If the initial treatment does not appear to be working, the physician can prescribe an alternative treatment and/or request that the patient return for another appointment. Some practices ask the patient to call the doctor at specified intervals or whenever the need arises, but this approach to follow-up service has been found to have a low rate of compliance. At the very least, the organization should provide a toll-free or collect telephone number, to make calls more convenient for the patient.

Return appointments also fall into the category of service in follow-up. Many problems that require therapy or frequent checks on medication necessitate periodic appointments. Scheduling patients on a weekly, biweekly, monthly, quarterly, semiannual, or annual basis sets up a systematic avenue of communication between doctor and patient. Such scheduling should always be done with the patient's needs in mind. When patients believe their needs are being met, they will remain undaunted in their trust and support of the provider of their health care.

Monitoring how well follow-up services are provided will prove to be a valuable asset to management when called on to reflect organizational commitment to consumer satisfaction. When an administrator is asked, "How satisfied are your patients with the services provided?" it will be possible to refer to current outcomes and speak of specific changes made to enhance services to patients. Only through systematic participation of patients in the evaluative process can professionals in health care really know whether their patients are pleased with the services they have received.

Evaluators of health care often recognize the need to include information from consumers in their assessments: whether, for example, the consumer felt a physician answered all questions or whether the consumer received a follow-up report. But those same evaluators often fail to include in their assessments the consumer's specific likes and dislikes about the medical care and service received. Many doctors neglect to assess objectively any aspect of their patient's satisfaction with services. Others collect information so sweeping that it cannot be used except in the most general way. Still others ask the wrong questions, leading to the collection of useless information. One must:

Cast aside what is thought to be the patient's need and instead ask the patient about his or her expectations. Once the expectations have been defined, it is up to the physician and supporting staff to fulfill them.[5]

Only by focusing on those activities that patients state are important to them can a consumer-oriented system be built that will meet the needs of both patients and providers.

Involving Patients and Their Families in the Evaluative Process

Patient participation in the evaluative process is valuable on at least two levels: (1) it improves care for individual patients, and (2) it makes it possible to compile data on the opinions of large groups of patients, thus showing ways of improving care for all patients. Through such compilations of data, researchers have learned that what patients often remember best about their medical care is whether they were given opportunities to ask questions of their physician; how their appointments were scheduled, and what kind of follow-up care they received. Research and experience have also shown that several other steps can be taken to enhance patients' experiences at the physician's office.

A good index of patient satisfaction involves comparing what kinds of services the patient expected to receive with what he or she felt was actually received. This requires thinking about services from the consumer's point of view. For example, what could a patient expect to hear when calling for an appointment? Would the patient's schedule at work be considered? Could multiple appointments be scheduled for different services on the same day? This technique would not only save time and perhaps make the visit easier for the patient, but it would also reduce the risk of duplicating laboratory tests, X rays, and such, thus lowering costs.

Patient participation must continue far beyond the hospital or the doctor's office.[8] What happens to the patient after the appointment is all-important. Now the question becomes: Do the medical services resolve the patient's problems? If the answer is "no," or worse yet, if a medical facility does not know the answer, the potential for a lawsuit for malpractice is there, and for good reason.

The follow-up process may involve referring the patient to a specialist. Most patients are usually unaware of the services of specialists, so it is up to the examining physician, usually a primary care provider, to inform them of those services. In fact, most HMOs require authorized referral by a primary care provider before they pay for the services of the specialist. Matching a patient to the right specialist is an important part of providing service of high quality. Once the specialist has evaluated the referred patient, it is important that the results of the evaluation be sent back to the primary care physician. This assures a continuity of care that is in the patient's best interest.

Getting Consumers Actively Involved

Providers of health care often recognize the need to include information from consumers in an assessment of their service, yet they fail to conduct the systematic evaluations needed for such assessment. If an organization wants to provide patients with satisfactory services, then it must take the necessary steps to assess how well their needs are being met. Active participation of consumers in this process is essential, and there are a variety of ways to encourage this activity. For example, consumers can be placed on advisory boards, committees, or task forces considering health care.[8]

Such appointments make consumers full participants in the development of policies and procedures for the organization. Some health organizations have mandated that a certain number of appointments to or positions on a committee be reserved for members of the public. These organizations can clearly state that their services and methods have developed with full participation by consumers. Similarly, many federal, state, and private grant-giving agencies require the participation of consumers on governing bodies of all health care organizations applying to them for funds. The funding agencies believe such a requirement ensures that the public's opinions about health care and its delivery will be heard.

Unfortunately, what typically happens with this form of participation is that the organization appoints, elects, or recruits its own "friends." Such action defeats the purpose of seeking unbiased input to help assess patient satisfaction. Effective efforts toward participation by consumers must go far beyond the token involvement of friendly appointments. If a health care organization truly wants to get an accurate estimate of how satisfied are its consumers, it must involve its patients—and not necessarily just its "friendly" ones—in the evaluative process.

Assuming the organization does provide services that are capable of meeting the patient's needs, the first step in the process of assessment is rather routine: Just ask the patients what they thought of the services, either through questionnaires, follow-up phone calls, or focus groups. Some providers of health care believe that this form of participation by consumers actually places the patient in a position of judgment over the provider. It does, and rightly so. The patient should be the judge of how well his or her needs have been met, particularly since the patient is the one responsible for the final bill and the one who must live with the functional results in his/her personal health.

Only with direct participation by patients does the evaluation of services become a valid process. It is patients who are qualified to determine whether their doctors gave them enough time to ask questions, or whether their appointments occurred at the times scheduled, or whether they noticed any improvement after their visit. The people receiving medical services—the patients, not the providers—can assess these questions. What a provider can and should do is measure the results of the patients' evaluations and then modify their services to improve any weaknesses identified during the process.[1,13]

HINTS FOR FOLLOW-UP SERVICE

- We often recognize the need to involve patients in the delivery of services for their health, yet fail to conduct evaluations to determine how successful our efforts are.
- Many forms of patient involvement are possible. Search for those most meaningful to the goals and objectives of your organization.
- Are the actual services being provided perceived as adequate by your patients? If not, why not?
- Patient involvement in the delivery of services will help you identify where improvements need to be made.
- Do consumers want to participate? Ask them; this is the only way to find out.
- Anticipate what your consumers expect from their visit to the doctor's office, and then make sure they get it.
- Patient satisfaction is that aspect of health care that is often taken for granted or overlooked. Make sure each patient receives answers to all questions, and actively involve them in an evaluation of the system responsible for delivery of their care.
- Services to consumers go beyond their visit to your office. Follow-up communication, after the visit, is needed to ensure patient satisfaction.

CONSUMER SATISFACTION: A SUMMARY

- Everyone needs and deserves satisfactory service in caring for their health. That is available now more than ever.
- Providers of health care must be more careful in considering patients' needs in the planning, delivery, and evaluation of their services.

- Universal health insurance, or an equivalent result of current activity to reform health care, will make it possible for consumers to go just about anywhere to have their needs for health care met. Patients will eventually become very selective in seeking this service.
- Consumers have a tendency not to complain openly to their providers about problems or poor service. They usually leave the doctor's office without informing anyone there of their concerns, thus making it impossible for the physician to identify or correct the problem.
- Patients should be asked for both negative and positive comments about the service they received. Negative information is extremely helpful because a problem (or just poor service) can be improved only after it has been identified. Positive comments support the ongoing allocation of financial resources so that the organization can maintain and perhaps enhance those elements of the service-system noted to be positive.
- One way to provide good service is to think in terms of what the consumer wants. Patients are shopping around for health care more than ever before, and are quite willing to forsake local doctors if they believe better service is available elsewhere.
- Examine the system that delivers services; focus on those needs deemed important by the patient.
- Implement a consumer-oriented approach to health care. Train staff so that they become consumer oriented.
- Satisfied patients will inform others about the good service they received. This increases the number of new referrals to the practice and increases the staff's morale, as employees receive appreciation from patients, and higher salaries due to the increased business brought in.[11]

APPLICATIONS

Targeted Goals

Have all aspects of the practice (clinical and operational) been reviewed (redefined if necessary) to focus on consumers? Eliminate any element in the practice not essential for operations that does not relate to consumers' needs.

Objectives

1. What measures were used to determine consumer satisfaction with medical care and the delivery of services?

2. Were guidelines for practice used? Compare results by physician and/or by specialty.
3. What method did you use to assess consumer satisfaction? Could the results be used to differentiate between acceptable and nonacceptable levels of care and service? How was the lack of information from nonrespondents followed up on?
4. How were outcomes defined to focus on ways to improve less-than-satisfactory care and services? Can you identify which components of medical care and service were most important to consumers? Did you add staff and/or include dollars for expansion in the annual plan on the basis of needs defined by consumers?

Content

List results that represent measures of the quality of care, prices of service (fee schedule, Medicare, and/or contract with a health plan) and each measure of consumer satisfaction. How do these outcomes compare to those from the last evaluation (if one was done)? How do the results compare to benchmarks throughout the community and region and nationally?

Evaluation

Did the results meet preestablished expectations? What evidence can you point to that shows how well clinical services and functions in the operating system were received by consumers?

Continuous Quality Improvement

What aspects of care and service provided could be improved? Do you know which components account for the greatest growth in net revenues? How does consumer satisfaction relate to compensation and retention of physicians?

Chapter 3

Leadership by Physicians

POINTS FOR FOCUS

Leadership by and active participation of physicians in the processes of management is a requirement for the successful medical organization of the future. Very little practical guidance is available, however, to enable physicians to prepare for this important role.

Targeted Goals

To develop a strong, physician-led health care organization.

Objectives

1. Develop a basis for leadership by and active participation of physicians in the organization.
2. Create opportunities to promote training in leadership.
3. Encourage, guide, and support the involvement of physicians in all aspects of the practice or health care organization.

Content

Needs for internal and external training must be defined. Programs for training in medical leadership are more appropriate, due to unique needs of physicians and due to organizational mission and values.

Evaluation

It is important first to define needs for training on the basis of organizational expectations. Specific activities for internal and external training are designed to meet organizational needs and needs for leadership by physicians.

Continuous Quality Improvement

Training for leadership is an ongoing requirement for every successful practice and/or health care organization. Needs for training must be assessed and specific skills enhanced at least annually, enabling leadership by physicians to stay a little in advance of the times.

TRAINING

The role played by the involvement of physicians, particularly as leaders in the progressive management of medical groups, has been less than adequately addressed. Health care organizations, including physician-governed group practices, reluctantly seek out leadership from physicians among rank-and-file members of their groups, medical staffs, and/or networks of physicians. The involvement of physicians in the activities of medical groups and organizations varies considerably, although their roles and functions are typically defined in bylaws or related legal documents. Others in management seem to recognize the need to include physicians in leadership capacities but fail to maximize the effectiveness of significant contributions by physicians.

Success in guiding a medical group practice depends upon the leader's ability to create and integrate process change throughout the entire organization. Dr. Paul Batalden of Dartmouth Medical School developed a framework for understanding management theory related to the leadership role. The three-step process begins first with *building knowledge* (e.g., construct a view of the situation, formulate options, and select an alternative); second, *take action* (e.g., change the situation, elicit "back talk," and identify surprises); and third, *review and reflect* (e.g., identify "change concepts," work them through organization, monitor and measure, and continuously enhance quality improvement efforts).[1]

Physicians have economic clout. They control patient care and remain the key to admissions to hospitals, prescriptions of medicine, authorizations for essential adaptive equipment and necessary living aids for patients, and creation and authorization of documented evidence sufficient for the construction of a medical record. The medical record is the single most valued interactive source of information between the patient/member, the providers of health care, payers, and (when necessary) the legal system. It is important to recognize (and seek out) the untapped opportunities residing within the abilities of physicians and to channel their energy and creativity as a power source toward the most difficult problems and issues faced by a medical group.

Training to cultivate leadership by physicians can be both formal and informal. On the formal level, universities, colleges, and educational associations for physicians and executives offer endless courses virtually throughout the world—on interactive television, via telephone and other vehicles for telecommunication, on radio, in correspondence classes, and through computer systems such as the Internet available in the home. Trade associations in medical management have made opportunities to enroll in training and continuing education a *main* benefit of membership.

Less formal training is typically provided by the employing health care organization itself. As physicians are appointed or elected to its various offices or positions, a certain amount of in-house/in-service training is required to help the physician understand his/her expected role. In many cases physicians are expected to ask questions and basically to "learn the ropes" on their own. It is at this point that management typically misses an opportunity by not structuring and supporting the continuing learning experience for the developing physician leader.

CHANGING PHYSICIAN PRACTICE STYLE

This subject was introduced by Hoyt Skabelund in 1996. At the time, Skabelund was a student in the MHA program at the University of Minnesota. Physicians practice differently for many reasons.[2] Due to the complexity of medicine, there is no clearly defined *right way* to practice medicine. Lack of empirical evidence adds to the variations in practice patterns. Also, differences in training add to this variation. In attempts to assure and improve quality of care and increase cost efficiency, four general approaches have been used to change physician practice styles: education, feedback, administrative rules, and financial incentives and penalties.[3]

Education, the traditional and most common approach to changing physician behavior, is based on the assumption that if physicians are provided appropriate information backed by empirical study, they will change their practice accordingly. Educational approaches include dissemination of printed materials, group education, and one-on-one academic detailing.

Study of experimental literature reveals that mailed printed materials "failed to support the claim that they are effective when used alone in changing physician prescribing behavior. However, the low costs of printed materials indicate that they may be worth implementing."[4] Small-group education such as rounds and tutorials have proven more effective but more expensive than large group education such as conferences, lectures, and seminars.[5] Academic detailing, patterned after pharmaceutical sales efforts, is the most effective educational method, particularly when an opinion leader is involved in the detailing.[6] However, this method is also the most expensive of the three.[7]

Overall the effects of education in changing physician behavior have been marginal. Eisenberg emphasizes that the need for change must be established with physicians before education can be effective, and even then the longevity of those effects would be in question.[3] Education efforts maybe necessary to maintain appropriate practice styles, but this approach alone has not shown to be effective in changing physician practice.[8]

Feedback consists of providing physicians data regarding their practice and outcomes. This data can be provided individually, aggregated, or as an individual compared against peers. Studies have shown individual and peer feedback to be more effective than group feedback.[9] Quality improvement programs use peer feedback to encourage practice style changes. By providing individual physicians with data comparing their performance to that of their peers, Intermountain Health Care has been able to motivate change in physician practice patterns.[10]

Schroeder's review of empirical studies shows mixed results of the effectiveness of feedback approaches in changing physician behavior.[8] "Pre-admission certification and second opinion consultation programs have been shown effective in both changing behavior and decreasing costs."[5] Additionally, organizations can adopt a strategy of using alternative providers to eliminate the need for physicians to perform certain treatments. Although this approach appears successful, it shares the danger of compromising quality of care. Although utilization may be affected by these approaches, practice patterns may in fact remain the same.[3]

Simplification of documentation and computer reminder systems are methods to encourage physician compliance with standards and protocols. Due to convenience and timeliness, these approaches have been successful in changing physician behavior.[5,7]

Financial incentives and penalties are based in behavior psychology and aim to change practice style through positive and negative reinforcement. Financial incentives include payment systems such as fee-for-service, capitation and bonus plans. On a national level, Medicare's DRG payment system is an example of a very effective financial incentive, resulting in reduction in length of hospital stays.[6] Financial incentives have shown to be the most effective method of changing physician practice styles.[11] However, with the exception of financial penalties, "experience with financial incentive within institutions has been limited because of ethical and other constraints."[7]

In summary, education and feedback are less expensive approaches to implement and maintain compared to administrative rules and financial incentives. However, rules and incentives have shown to be more effective in changing physician practice styles. Eisenberg reminds us to consider timing in regard to determining the effectiveness of education and feedback:

In this setting, where physicians are presumably more aware of the need to reconsider the efficiency of their practice styles, methods of changing their utilization of services may be more successful. The limited success of education and feedback in the past may have been due to the resistance of practitioners who were not ready to change. In new era of medical practice . . . it may be that [these approaches] will induce changes in utilization that were not achieved in the past.[3]

Each of the approaches reviewed in this paper has been studied in isolation. The complexity of medicine requires more than a single view when determining successful methods of changing physician behavior.

Physicians' utilization of medical services is influenced by many diverse influences on clinical decision making. The black box of medical decision making does have windows through which we have come to understand some of the factors that shape this process. By understanding these influences, we can identify ways to alter them and change the decisions that govern the use of most medical care services.[3]

As future efforts are made to change physician practice patterns, leaders of these initiatives should consider combinations of the above-mentioned approaches. Different combinations may prove more effective in each unique setting. Careful measures should be made to track the success of each combination to determine the factors that contribute to successful change in practice behavior. If synergies can be identified and harnessed, effective change of physician practice style can more effectively be achieved.

UNDERSTANDING AND CULTIVATING LEADERSHIP BY PHYSICIANS

When physicians are appointed to positions of leadership, the job for management actually is just beginning, in cultivating that leadership—yet, many managerial structures seem based on a belief that the work is completed once the vacancy has been filled and/or an appointment has been made. In some cases, managers believe that the physician's role, although essential and often a requirement, is more like a "necessary evil" than a creative internal energy force to help the organization resolve its most significant problems, address contemporary issues, and plan proactively for a successful and thriving future. Understanding the nature and intent of programs for educating physicians is a first step.

MEDICAL EDUCATION

The health care system in this country will not be truly reformed until medical education is reformed. If our system is truly flawed, we must go back to the drawing board—back to what shapes the system and defines the way it works, according to C. Randall Nelms, MD, in his role as president of Minnesota Medicine in 1994.[12] Physicians have a societal responsibility to ensure the general welfare of people, and medical education will be judged on how well it teaches physicians to carry out this responsibility. The medical literature is filled with examples of how poorly medical education prepares physicians for their careers. Articles have been published on flawed standards for practice, inappropriate utilization of technology, and arbitrariness in practice. To prepare physicians properly, the educational system must admit the right students, give them the right skills, and equip them to function in our health care system.

What is a proper preparation for the practice of medicine? Most potential medical students think more college courses in science are the key to success, but there is no evidence that additional science provides greater insight into the practice of medicine. A background in the liberal arts may be equally appropriate as preparation for a medical career. Nelms notes that James M. McGreery, MD, Associate Professor of Medicine at the University of Utah Medical School, gives seven reasons why this should be considered:[12]

1. It enhances the enjoyment of a privileged occupation, one that allows the practitioner to intervene in persons' lives in a unique and profound way
2. It aids in the understanding of human nature and of the responses of individuals in crisis
3. It provides a framework for critical decision making in problems that cannot be predicted or rehearsed
4. It provides a refuge during life's disappointments and trials
5. It sharpens the ability to communicate
6. It provides an ability to recognize true quality in people
7. It engenders a moral fabric, an almost innate sense of what is right and wrong, that will foster correct decisions in dealing with human life and suffering

Medical education should also prepare students to practice in our communities' health care systems. President Clinton's plan proposes that the government support the programs for such training, rather than supporting educational institutions themselves. Programs for training in integrated networks or other community-based institutions could conceivably qualify for this type of support and compete successfully for funds to support research on outcomes and quality of care. Training physicians in this type of environment could equip them to function in the health care system. More medical education should be carried out in these community-based settings.

Medical education is typically supported by public funds and patients' fees, and society is demanding new, improved products in return for its support. The users of our health care system want educational institutions to produce more primary care practitioners and fewer specialists, and they want its researching organizations to generate more knowledge about improving outcomes and quality, and its providers to produce health care services with increased efficiency.

CUSTOMER-FOCUSED OPTIONS

Contemporary systems for the delivery of managed medical care and services are trying to differentiate their services from those of rivals by training physicians to offer friendlier service and a wider menu of customer-focused options to their patient members. As reported in the December 1, 1994 issue of *The Wall Street Journal,* Kaiser Permanente, one of the largest health plans in the world, is teaching its doctors to be nicer.[13] Something as simple as repeating a patient's own description of symptoms helps underscore attentiveness and can be part of a broader change in attitude, doctors say. Physician-to-physician training in customer service has been received quite well. Perhaps programs in medical education should focus on this attitude more formally and more frequently in their course offerings.

When Dr. Andrew J.K. Smith became president of the Minnesota Medical Association in September of 1994, he noted that physicians can take control of their future by restructuring medicine and developing physician-related organizations. According to Toubin, who interviewed Smith for *Minnesota Medicine* in 1994, physicians must continue to focus on putting patients' interests above all others:

> As we begin to look at the design and development of new systems of health care delivery, and we do that in a patient oriented fashion, we'll find that many of those efficiencies actually allow us to provide better health care. What we're talking about are such things as improved ways that doctors can communicate with each other about patient care.[14]

Physicians can help mold a new system for the delivery of health care because they are considered part of the solution—rather than an obstacle—to reform. The public continues to respect and trust physicians and expects them to take leadership roles in reform. Physicians need to take advantage of this public trust, and need to use their power and ability to get down to the business of building systems that are patient oriented. Physicians are in the best position to balance quality and cost, to do appropriate allocations of resources, and to put patients' needs first, all of which are necessary to compete in this evolving marketplace. Managers can help physicians see that they have alternatives, that they can be the ones managing the managed care.

Smith notes that as physicians enhance their role as leaders it is important to make sure not to lose sight of values that physicians hold most dear: the primacy of the doctor-patient relationship, the need to move as quickly as possible toward universal access and coverage, the ability of patients to choose their physician as well as the ability of physicians to choose the type of practice they want, the need for continuity of care, and (last but certainly not least) the importance of medical education and research:

> For most physicians the practice of medicine will always be rewarding. There will always be opportunities for young physicians. When it comes down to it, physicians get most excited about taking care of patients with as little external hassle as possible.[14]

Management's role in this regard is to unencumber physicians from the bureaucracy of practice while encouraging, training, and supporting activities for customer-oriented care and services as much as possible.

HELPING PHYSICIANS DEVELOP THE "CAN DO" ATTITUDE

Physicians can make the future work for them, as is described by Mike Mitka in the January 17, 1994 issue of *American Medical Association News*.[15] Mitka notes growing concern among physicians about the impact that reforms will have on the practice of medicine. Many physicians see an evolving change in practice, away from the reasons they entered the practice of medicine. Change offers opportunity, but physicians have to be willing to learn how to deliver health care in new ways.

Doctors need to become savvy businesspeople—because the old promises of a secure income are fading. They have generally assumed they were paid well as compensation for the time they devoted to learning highly sophisticated skills, and for the huge debts they ran up getting that education. The truth is that they are paid well because of basic economic principles: high demand for their services and short supply of those providing them. But while that once meant that physicians were able to dictate prices, now payers are banding together to control the costs of health care. So what can physicians do to survive—and even thrive—in this new environment? Mitka offers recommendations, which appear in the sections below.[15]

Assess Needs

The first step is an honest assessment of the practice the physician has now. Why do patients come to this practice? Is it because the quality of care is so good? Because the physician is popular, and friendly colleagues refer patients? Or because a major employer opened a plant across the street, and patients find the office convenient? Is the practice properly staffed? Is it computerized? What about its location?

Learn why insurers and employers are doing what they are doing and find out how you can fit your medical practice into the needs they have to meet. Perhaps the greatest skill a physician needs to learn is asking the right questions. It may be a cliché, but knowledge really is power. The right questions will elicit information about the characteristics of the market, the strengths and weaknesses of the competition, and how well the individual practice fits in.

Specialists need to court primary care physicians and adapt to their needs—especially in managed care settings, where gatekeeper physicians receive the capitation payments and must pay out of the capitation for specialists to whom they send their patients. The key is for physicians really to look at the practice as a business, one that either is now or probably soon will be part of managed care. If that is understood, then the strategy is to increase income by keeping people healthy in cost-effective ways.

Learn New Skills

There are a variety of sources for acquiring the skills to practice medicine profitably in this brave new world. Some physicians are returning to school. Others are seeking out lawyers, accountants, and consultants who are experts at maximizing physicians' income through managed care. Still others are turning to their specialty's societies and other professional organizations for advice.

Mitka's article refers to a survival guide published by Medical Marketing Inc. One aspect is aimed at helping physicians to focus on business skills such as the following:

- *Learn to negotiate:* You have economic clout because you control patient care. Do not be intimidated by lawyers or MBAs. Everything is negotiable, from contracts to compensation.
- *Do assessments of managed care:* Find out what companies offering managed care are looking for and do what it takes to join up—but do not sell yourself short.
- *Survey referring physicians:* Ask primary care and other physicians what they want, and make a commitment to provide it.
- *Identify key employers:* Companies are forming health care alliances. Let them know that you can deliver cost-effective care to their employees.

A second part of the survival guide suggests physicians, especially those dependent on referrals, consider these:

- *New skills for generalists:* Find out what HMOs and generalists think specialists must learn to do—and why.
- *Broadened competencies:* Specialists are now focused on specific organs or procedures, not their contexts.
- *Reinterpreting the initial complaint:* Specialists are used to seeing patients after a generalist has clarified the initial complaint.
- *Follow the patient:* Specialists tend to treat patients over the short term, for a specific condition.
- *Coordinate services:* Some may not know how to work in a team with other health professionals.
- *Do not waste services:* Specialists order more tests and more referrals than do generalists.
- *Promote prevention:* Some specialists see prevention as outside their purview.

Managers must find out what needs and gaps in knowledge exist among their physicians, prioritize those needs, and work with the physicians to meet those needs. This includes specific training and education for physicians as their organization becomes involved with managed care. Only after the needs have been defined is it possible to devise plans and align the required human and financial resources to meet those needs in an effective "can do" manner.

THE ROLE OF MANAGERS IN FACILITATING
LEADERSHIP BY PHYSICIANS

The successful health care organization of the future will have a rock-solid structure of physicians as its core. Such a structure must be built by and for its physicians who have been designated to lead in organizational development. The role of management is to facilitate leadership by its physicians through goal-directed participation.

As in the development of a specific program or service, an orderly planning process is required to achieve the desired culture among physicians and the accompanying leadership capacities that will mutually foster. Assessing the needs of individuals and the group provides a format by which to understand what is important to members now and in the future. The needs assessment can be used to determine available skills and technical capabilities, and what members would like to see in the future. Issues in planning related to this process could include:

- How to develop "vision"
- How to move from vision to strategic advantage
- Lateral and vertical thinking—creativity
- Viewing changes as threats or opportunities
- Anxiety associated with change
- Implementing changes and monitoring outcomes
- Time involved and difficulty of changing an organization

Making changes in an organization involves first obtaining knowledge, then changing attitudes, changing individual and group behavior, and, finally, changing organizational structures.[16]

CASE EXAMPLE

The following is one example of how two groups of physicians from extremely different cultures and practice environments developed plans for integrating duplicated services due to a merger. One group was a staff model HMO, the second a multispecialty group practice primarily based on fee-for-services. A needs assessment was completed by an equal number of physicians and administrative staff from each group, who agreed to become members of a joint long-range planning advisory body, on behalf of the merged corporation. The information was collected and assembled by an independent planning facilitator, who used the information to construct an interviewing instrument. The facilitator then proceeded to interview each member of the joint long-range planning body to determine initial strengths and weaknesses.

The lists of strengths and weaknesses from the interviews were used as the springboard for determining what to keep in the new organization. After some small group exchanges, the members identified a list of strengths to retain in the new system. There was a great deal of discussion among the members concerning what each strength "really meant," and, for several months, each attribute was discussed in detail by the combined group. The key strength attributes identified in this example as present in the practice then were:

- Customer focus
- Provision of care for diverse populations
- Inclusion of primary care providers
- Provision for continuity of care
- Use of a provider team approach
- Availability of a wide spectrum of care
- Provision for secondary care
- Inclusion of centers and programs for excellence
- Value—good quality and reasonable costs
- Good stewardship of resources
- Salaried physicians whose incentives are consistent with provision of high-quality care
- Community orientation
- Provision of teaching/education
- Academic affiliation
- Employee-mindedness
- Self-determination, leadership, and ownership by member physicians

The specific task relative to each strength attribute was to:

1. Discuss what each attribute meant to each member of the group
2. Come to an agreed-upon definition/understanding of it
3. Articulate why this attribute would be useful to retain as a part of a new system for delivering care.

As the combined group moved forward in its discussions, the following perspective on attributes was delineated:

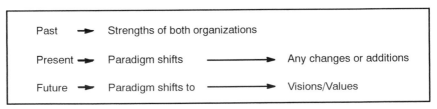

Moving from a "Yours/Mine" to an "Ours" Through Integration

Some discussions of the attributes took place with the entire combined group involved and others in small groups. If the primary discussion had begun in a small group, their definition was then presented to the larger group. The large group then modified, adopted, or rejected the work of the small group. As might be expected in any substantially changing situation, the first discussions were quite difficult, but as time went on they became somewhat easier. In an effort to continue its forward progress, the members of the group, at one point, suggested that they meet for longer periods of time. Two retreats were held to move the effort forward faster.

The attributes they discussed served as elements of a foundation upon which a new integrated group culture could be built. The facilitator outlined a framework of categories for the attributes that was accepted by the long-range planning group. These categories basically identified *who* is being served, *how* services are to be delivered, *what* services are to be delivered, within *what context*, by *whom*, and *how* they are to be paid for. The six categories were:

- Population Serviced
- Providers of Care
- Structure/Methods for Delivery of Care
- Financing of Care/Buyers
- Context of Care
- Organizational Issues

A long-range planning group was charged with the task of creating a vision for a new care delivery system. The group carried out their charge by first describing the basic framework for care delivery and then describing the key attributes of that system.

Shared Values and Vision

A vision was presented on the belief that leadership by physicians, based upon shared values, is essential to providing excellent health care and to creating the health care system of the future. This belief was crystallized through extensive discussion among the physicians participating in integration of the values important to physicians. One of the key results of this process was the understanding and appreciation the group gained for the talent, diversity, and dedication of each other in their new partnership.[17]

The attributes discussed on the previous pages served as building blocks in the formation of a new common vision. In developing the list of attributes, the focus remained on what was believed to be the most valuable qualities within the existing systems of the two physician groups. The integrating groups articulated the following principles to serve as a foundation to support a collective vision for their contemporary practice of medicine.

We envision a health care system that: Maintains customer focus by placing the primary emphasis on meeting the needs of our members and patients. At the same time, we will strengthen our ties to our community and provide care to diverse populations, especially to underserved groups.

We envision a health care system in which: The *primary care provider* is the one person who focuses on an individual patient and knows her or him best. Patient satisfaction will be achieved by *continuity of care* and a multidisciplinary *provider team approach.*

We envision a health care system that: Integrates primary and *secondary care* in a way that distinguishes it in the marketplace. Integration of care will be achieved by clear and seamless support of the primary care provider by specialists, but with direct access to specialists when appropriate.

We envision a health care system that: Provides a *spectrum of care* delivered in the most appropriate setting that matches the needs of individual patients. For certain defined areas, our physicians will establish *centers or programs for excellence* that will distinguish us in the community.

We envision a health care system that: Focuses on value by applying the best evidence-based medical practices at an affordable cost. This goal will be realized by providing to physicians and managers *incentives consistent with the promotion of quality of care and stewardship of resources.*

We envision a health care system that: Values intellectual inquiry. A commitment to *research* will be one of the ways in which we will serve and improve the health of our members and community. Formal *teaching/educational* programs will complement a patient-focused system for delivering care. We will foster the best teaching, research, and education by creating mutually fulfilling relationships with *academic institutions.*

We envision a health care system that is: Employee-minded and shows sustained mutual accountability and responsibility between the organization and its individual employees.

We envision a health care system whose: Physicians have a sense of, and command a substantial degree of, self-determination. This empowerment will extend from decisions about individual patient care to decisions about the development and management of programs, while being consistent with the mission and direction of the organization itself (*physicians' self-determination, leadership,* and *ownership*).

A Basis for Building Long-Term Relationships

Leadership and active participation of physicians is required for the development of long-term programs and relationships in health care systems. This integration of different cultures of physicians into new unified models moved forward by first establishing mutually agreed-upon attributes. Although not mutually exclusive, the attributes are illustrated to show the nature and intent of composite planning by physicians for the future of the new integrated group.

Population Served
Customer focus
Care for diverse populations

Providers of Care
Primary care providers
Continuity of care
Provider-team approach

Structure/Methods
  for Delivery of Care
Spectrum of care
Secondary care
Centers and programs
  for excellence

Buyers/Financing of Care
Value—quality and costs
Stewardship of resources
Salaried physicians with
  incentives consistent
  with quality care

Context of Care
Community orientation
Teaching/education
Research/education
Academic affiliation

Organizational Issues
Employee minded
Leadership by physicians

Population Served

Customer Focus. The agreed-upon definition/understanding of "customer focus" is that *focus needs to be on identifying and meeting customers' needs/ preferences*.

The following characteristics identify physician priorities:

Primary Focus	**Secondary Focus**
Members	Referring MDs
Patients	Employer groups
	Government
	Students/trainees
	Community
	University medical school (multiple roles)
	Other academic institutions

Reasons why this definition is useful to retain as part of the new system include:

- It provides benefits (value) to customers by making them our physicians' top priority
- The physicians' survival depends on having this type of customer focus

Care for Diverse Populations. The agreed-upon definition/understanding of "care for diverse populations" is that *physicians need to have a sense of openness, commitment, and the capability to provide care to all in our community, especially those in underserved groups.* This is an *ethical imperative* and *basic to the physicians' mission.* This value needs to be put into operation throughout the entire system delivering care.

Reasons why this definition is useful to retain as part of the physicians' system include that:

- It helps health care professionals to understand the needs of diverse populations;
- It can provide physicians with business opportunities;
- It is consistent with the physicians' objectives and mission;
- It is community responsive;
- It is critical to improving the health of our community/communities;
- It provides the opportunity to develop systems to care for underserved populations.

Providers of Care

Primary Care Providers. The agreed-upon definition/understanding of "primary care providers" is that *a primary care provider is the one person (doctor, midlevel) who is part of a small team of nurses, receptionists, and such who know the patient best and coordinate, oversee, and provide care for that patient over a continuous span of time.* Patients realize that the physician is not available twenty-four hours a day, as in our grandparents' time, but they still want a provider who (they feel) knows them well and to whom they can go when something is wrong.

The following details some of the importance of this provider relationship as it becomes operational in the system:

- The primary care provider is the person patients entrust with their care
- If the provider is not a physician, there needs to be some form of accountability to a specific physician
- Providers in either a subspecialty or primary care can be principal caregivers in certain areas such as HIV treatment, renal dialysis, and such
- Good communication between the patient and the provider is essential
- We need to work with individual patients to understand what they expect that the "span of care" should be from a primary care provider

Reasons why this definition is useful to retain as part of the physicians' system include that:

- It is a source of comfort to the patient, and potentially lowers their anxiety
- It can facilitate the distribution of patient care within the system and throughout the community
- It is a useful and effective way for people to gain access to the system delivering care
- Patients will be able to identify their primary provider
- It provides a way that patients can be educated about their care

Continuity of Care. The agreed-upon definition/understanding of "continuity of care" is *the integration and coordination of health services across the spectrum of care and over time. The result is that patients' needs are anticipated and patient satisfaction can be better ensured.*

The following details the importance of this concept as it becomes operational in the system. There needs to be:

- A primary person in charge of integrating and coordinating the care
- An efficient and rapid mechanism for transferring data, both within and between our sites
- A direct access to primary care providers for patients

Reasons why this definition is useful to retain as part of the physicians' system include:

- Benefit to consumers—the patient and family will know who is responsible for their care, and the interactions among patient, family, and physician will improve, both in communication and in quality.
- Benefit to the physicians' practice—care of higher quality will result from providing integration and coordination of care; and there will be less duplication of services and greater cost savings to the physicians' practice organization.

Provider-Team Approach. The agreed-upon definition/understanding of "provider-team approach" is that *the physicians will emphasize a multidisciplinary approach in the care of the organization's members/patients. (A multidisciplinary team includes MDs, midlevel, providers-in-training, nursing personnel, professionals in mental health, and paramedical personnel.)* The following details the importance of this concept as it becomes operational in the system: The multidisciplinary team needs to center/focus on a specific patient's needs for care.

Reasons why this definition is useful to retain as part of the physicians' system include:

- Benefits to consumers

    a. consumers get the benefit of multiple opinions, up-to-date and shared information
    b. consumers get improved access to services
    c. the multidisciplinary approach covers all aspects of an individual's needs for health care
    d. care and the outcomes of the care are best when physicians participate together across professional boundaries

- Benefits to the physicians' practice

    a. physicians and other health care professionals have access to colleagues, and lateral consultation is enhanced
    b. it provides for greater continuity of care

Structure/Methods for Delivery of Care

Spectrum of Care. The agreed-upon definition/understanding of "spectrum of care" is that *spectrum of care involves the provision of health services in the setting/site most appropriate for a patient's/member's needs.*

Some examples of the types of settings/sites that could be used to meet an individual patient's needs include:

- Centers developing wellness/healthy outcome
- Centers providing preventive care and education
- Offices
- Inpatient hospitals
- Schools
- Homes
- Nursing homes
- Hospices
- Surgical centers
- Prisons
- Care given over the telephone

Reasons why this definition is useful to retain as part of the new physicians' system include:

- Alternative settings/sites will enable providers to match the appropriate care to an individual patient's needs
- Providers' options to use alternative settings/sites in the provision of care will encourage innovative alternatives for the delivery of care
- A patient's independence and comfort will be maximized
- There are potential cost efficiencies in seeking and utilizing alternatives

Secondary Care. The agreed-upon definition/understanding of "secondary care" is that *secondary care involves medical services that are commonly required to support primary care providers. The manner in which the physicians' group organizes its integration of primary and secondary care will distinguish it in the marketplace.*

The following details the importance of this concept as it becomes operational in the system:

- In some cases, the physicians' group can best serve its members by providing direct access to specialized/secondary care
- In some cases, it makes sense for a given provider to function in both roles, i.e., as both secondary and primary care provider

Reasons why this definition is useful to retain as part of the physicians' system include:

- Benefits to consumers
  a. an integrated approach increases quality and members' satisfaction

    b. primary care and specialists will know each other well
    c. a connected system of health care provides synergy among providers' potentials, resulting in greater satisfaction to the consumer
    d. an integrated approach gives physicians a sustainable/competitive advantage in the marketplace
    e. contracting groups are supported by providing them an integrated, high quality, consistent, cost-effective system for delivery of care

Centers and Programs for Excellence. The agreed-upon definition/ understanding of "centers and programs for excellence" is that *centers and programs for excellence and defined components of the new physicians' organization require specific resources as well as commitment and expertise of medical professionals. These centers and programs need to be aligned, to ensure volume and to ensure that the care provider shows a measurable difference to customers and to the community.*

The following details the importance of this concept as it becomes operational in the system:

- Centers will be distinguished by *value*, not *where these centers/programs for excellence are located*
- A center/program that is developed will have to be unique or, if competition does exist, the nature of its unified physicians' services must distinguish itself from those of this competition

Reasons why this definition is useful to retain as part of the new physicians' system include:

- Benefits to consumers
    a. the availability of centers and programs for excellence, as defined above, will provide excellent care to the consumer and serve the community
    b. centers and programs for excellence will be financially attractive for the consumer
    c. the availability of centers and programs for excellence will equate, in the consumer's view, with excellence in the system and its care
    d. within the context of the centers and programs, a seamless system can be created for the consumer

- Benefits to the physicians' organization
  a. availability of centers and programs for excellence will attract patients and buyers
  b. centers and programs for excellence created within the context of the above definition will enable the physicians' group to control and acquire specific niches in the market
  c. the physicians' reputation for excellent patient care will be enhanced by the availability of the centers and programs

Buyers/Financing of Care

Value—Quality and Costs. The agreed-upon definition/understanding of "value—quality and costs" is that *the best value in terms of quality and costs will be obtained by the physicians focusing on providing the best possible outcomes of care to meet the needs of its members/patients and on utilizing resources efficiently. The best medical practice (evidence based), consistently applied, will result in care of high quality and in the best outcomes to our members at an affordable price.*

The following details the importance of this concept as it becomes operational in the system:

- Using health education and prevention will be important in the development and creation of the best outcomes for patients
- Insurance coverage needs to be consistent with best medical practice

Reasons why this definition is useful to retain as part of the physicians' practice include:

- Benefits to consumers
  a. the consumer will receive health care of high quality
  b. consumers' needs will be met at the lowest possible cost

- Benefits to the physicians' practice organization
  a. more members will be attracted to the group of physicians, by providing greater value to consumers
  b. more resources will be available to the community, if greater value in quality and costs is available to the consumer

Stewardship of Resources. The agreed-upon definition/understanding of "stewardship of resources" is that *physicians maximize the health status of the community through their stewardship of resources. Through appropriate conservation of resources, physicians will be able to provide more health services to meet members' needs.*

The following details the importance of this concept as it becomes operational in the system:

- Appropriate stewardship of resources will require alignment of incentives to providers so that they meet patients' needs in the best ways
- Appropriate stewardship of resources also will recognize the needs of both individual patient/members and of the community

Reasons why this definition is useful to retain as part of the physicians' practice include:

- Benefits to consumers—appropriate stewardship of resources will result in

    a. decreased variability in treatment
    b. measurable improvements in quality of care
    c. an emphasis on prevention
    d. improved accessibility of care to consumers
    e. improved coordination of care

- Benefits to the physicians' practice organization—appropriate stewardship of resources will result in

    a. decreased variability in costs and outcomes
    b. measurable improvements in quality
    c. better data on members' satisfaction, outcomes, and costs of care
    d. pooling of resources for innovations in health care

Salaried Physicians with Incentives Consistent with Quality Care. The agreed-upon definition/understanding of "salaried physicians with incentives consistent with quality care" is that *the physicians' practice organization needs to offer physicians appropriate financial, working ethical, and academic incentives that promote high-quality care. Working ethical incentives must establish expectations for each physician at each level of activity; these activities should include clinical, administrative, and academic (educational) responsibilities.*

The following details the importance of this concept as it becomes operational in the system:

In that the revenue for the group of physicians does not rely purely on revenues from providing acute care or on procedure-based billings, the system can focus more broadly on prevention, the use of midlevel providers, and alternatives in care delivery.

Reasons why this definition is useful to retain as part of the physicians' practice include:

- Benefits to consumers—proper incentives

    a. improve the willingness of providers of health care and of employees to provide service to the patient (consumer)
    b. should control costs and make the physicians' "package" attractive to patients/consumers

- Benefits to the physicians' practice organization—proper incentives

    a. make hiring and retention of health care professionals easier
    b. improve satisfaction with the working environment
    c. help control costs of delivering the health care product

Context of Care

Community Orientation. The agreed-upon definition/understanding of "community orientation" is that *the physicians' practice organization recognizes that there are many types of communities, and that they need to be sensitive to and recognize the needs of these different communities, and understand the changing nature of their communities.*
The following details the importance of this concept as it becomes operational in the system:

The physicians' practice will benefit by serving communities.

Reasons why this definition is useful to retain as part of the physicians' practice: by being sensitive to the community, the physicians' organization will:

- Be viewed as philanthropic
- Be able to create new products and unique services
- Be able to meet its public-health obligations
- Provide valuable training for their use as professionals
- Create new ways of delivering service

Teaching/Education. The agreed-upon definition/understanding of "teaching/education" is that *teaching/education is an important part of the physi-*

cians' system. The physicians need to create a different model for teaching/ education that combines the best characteristics of previous systems.

The following details the importance of this concept as it becomes operational in the system:

> Formal educational programs should be part of the physicians' practice. The educational program needs to complement a patient-focused system for care delivery and, wherever appropriate, be affiliated with a center of higher education.

Reasons why this definition is useful to retain as part of the physicians' practice include the following benefits:

- A focus on education will enable the physicians to recruit the best health care providers
- The physicians will be perceived as having excellent care providers with high-quality expertise
- A focus on education enables the physician to structure and deliver services that would otherwise be impossible; e.g., the burn treatment and trauma centers
- The physicians will develop and then retain other physicians who can complement the needs of the system
- A focus on education will provide opportunities for continuous quality improvement
- Training of future physicians will be possible

Research/Education. The agreed-upon definition/understanding of "research/education" is that *the physicians' group values intellectual inquiry. Research is one of the ways in which the physicians serve and improve the health of their members and their community.*

The following details the importance of this concept as it becomes operational in the system:

> Research is the systematic investigation of questions to discover new knowledge; it is the foundation for determining the best practices upon which to base the delivery of high-quality health care.

Reasons why this definition is useful to retain as part of the physicians' practice include:

- Benefits to consumers
    a. using the above definition, research will be applicable to patients' needs

b. patient care will be "on the cutting edge" of medical science
c. consumers will be able to participate in medical advancements
d. research conducted would be directly applicable to the consumers' health issues/problems
e. consumers often associate the best and brightest physicians with research

- Benefits to the physicians' practice organization—research/education

a. encourages and supports creative ideas and endeavors among providers
b. keeps caregivers active and apprised of the currently accepted methods and modes of treatment and prevention
c. allows the organization to play a role in developing new and innovative medical knowledge
d. enhances the reputation of these physicians in the community
e. attracts a wider variety of applicants for positions as physicians here
f. provides community service
g. stimulates providers to question current practices
h. enables the physicians to evaluate outcomes and delivery of health services
i. patient input on the effects of new and experimental treatments such as comfort levels, physical changes, and treatment effects
j. benefits physicians, patients, and future physicians through training

Academic Affiliation. The agreed-upon definition/understanding of "academic affiliation" is that *affiliation with academic institutions needs to result in mutually fulfilling relationships. There should be equal partnership (i.e., between the physicians' group and academic institutions) in educational decision making and planning.*

The following details the importance of this concept as it becomes operational in the system. The physicians need to:

- Develop a central coordinating structure
- Separate the business of education from the application and practice of education
- View a single affiliation as an advantage, but not preclude other relationships

Reasons why this definition is useful to retain as part of the physicians' organization include:

- Benefit to consumers

    a. good teaching provides good health care and good medicine

- Benefits to the physicians' organization academic affiliation

    a. creates access to new knowledge for providers of health care
    b. increases access to research protocols for providers of health care and for consumers
    c. provides prestige for the organization
    d. enables the organization to employ greater power in recruitment of staff
    e. ensures that physicians will have future health care workers

Organizational Issues

Being Employee Minded. The agreed-upon definition/understanding of "employee minded" is that *being employee minded means mutual accountability and responsibility among physicians and the individual employees of the organization. (This concept applies to all employees.)*

The following details the importance of this concept as it becomes operational in the system:

- There is a recognition that the physicians' organizational goals may be best met through flexibility in structuring work for individual employees
- Employee input into decision making is encouraged
- All employees should expect fair treatment
- Employees' professional growth is encouraged
- There will be fair compensation for effort
- Diversity and gender equity in the workforce will be promoted
- There will be recognition of the individual needs and lifestyles of employees

Reasons why this definition is useful to retain as part of the physicians' practice include:

- Benefits to consumers

    a. creates an environment that encourages good patient care
    b. maintains a service orientation
    c. by being more culturally sensitive to employees, employees become more culturally sensitive to members'/patients' needs

- Benefits to the physicians' organization
    a. potential growth in membership could be realized by fostering good employee/employer relationships
    b. stability of the organization can be maintained
    c. greater retention of employees can be achieved
    d. organizational *esprit de corps* can be realized

Leadership by Physicians. The agreed-upon definition/understanding of "leadership by physicians" is *physicians' self determination, leadership, and ownership in the organization.*

The following details the importance of this concept as it becomes operational in the system:

> The physicians' organization should have a culture in which its physicians sense and command a substantial degree of self-determination. This empowerment must extend from decisions about individual patient care to decisions about program development and management, while being consistent with the mission and direction of the organization itself.

Reasons why this definition is useful to retain as part of the physicians' practice:

- Leadership by physicians is of utmost importance; it results in high-quality medicine provided in the best possible way.
- Ownership by physicians is clearly different, in this era of integration. Although a physician may be salaried/employed rather than "an owner," ownership of the process of providing care is critical, for job satisfaction and medical responsibility; it results in commitment to good outcomes.
- Empowering physicians with self-determination and ownership will yield high dividends—owners are more productive, tolerate greater burdens, and better assure quality.

APPLICATIONS

Targeted Goals

Has the role and training of physicians been addressed by the practice/health care organization? Have physicians in positions of leadership received additional training in management? (If yes, specifically how much and of what nature for each position?) What evidence (or lack thereof) demonstrates that the practice/organization is physician led?

Objectives

Outline the new/continuing opportunities for physicians to train for leadership. What roles do physicians play throughout the practice/organization (include community events/activities)? Identify the amount of budget set aside for training in leadership (beyond continuing medical education).

Content

How many internal and external activities were provided toward training physicians in leadership? List participation by active medical staff. Review content presented across the courses in training, compare these with the evaluations of courses/activities given by the participating physicians, and then contrast that against the grades received (and/or other tangible results demonstrating increased proficiencies in leadership).

Evaluation

Are more physicians achieving leadership roles in the practice/organization? What areas continue to need further training/course enhancements? Have the physicians who received training in leadership achieved adequate proficiency/skills? How is this attribute being measured? Have measures of reliability and validity been adequately applied to the content of training courses to assure adequate statistical relevance?

Continuous Quality Improvement

Of what curricular guide or operating principles are your activities/coursework in leadership training a part? Annual review and enhancement of levels of skill and assessments of proficiency and course content are essential for CQI.

Chapter 4

Changes in Medical Practice: Prevention and Management of Disease

POINTS FOR FOCUS

The physician's role must change its focus from intervention to prevention through patient education and counseling. The ability to convey the elements required for enhancement of a patient's lifestyle will become a contemporary physician's "black bag."

Targeted Goals

Create a seamless system for delivery of medical care that is consumer focused and programmed for the development of healthy lifestyles.

Objectives

Design medical care and operational systems specifically to meet patients' needs. Clearly communicate, verbally and in writing, exactly what your patients need to know to correct current problems and to enhance status to prevent the occurrence of future problems. Participate in the process of curricular development with your local public and private schools. Provide health education and units on enhancement of lifestyle throughout the entire K-12 curriculum.

Content

Perhaps most respected among community leaders, physicians can have maximum and lasting impact as healers, educators, and counselors. Written and oral instruction will enhance the quality and style of the lives of members of their community.

Evaluation

Consumer satisfaction, disease-free lives, and enhanced lifestyles are desired outcomes.

Continuous Quality Improvement

Refinements to plans for individual care and annual upgrades to curricular materials are requirements.

The practice of medicine began as, and should remain, a close, confidential relationship between a physician and a patient. The preferred state of health aims at physical and mental well-being—to be disease free. Preventive advice and understanding given by a physician to patients have significant, positive, long-term effects, with mutual benefits to physicians and patients alike and the community in general:

- The physicians' practice can grow and prosper since fewer resources (or less of each) are needed to care for an increasing number of healthy patient members
- Patient-members are healthier, requiring less out-of-pocket expense associated with health services
- Consumer satisfaction with the advice received will help retain the patient member as a customer
- The community will benefit, as a healthier population grows and as programs and services enhance levels of healthy activity and decrease the amounts of time and money that businesses and other payers lose through illness and claims for workers' compensation

TURBULENT TIMES

Physicians must be more alert than ever before. Rapid changes are affecting virtually all areas of health care: hospitals, health plans, physicians' coalitions, for-profit and not-for-profit health organizations, academic centers, and more. At this point, there is no single faction controlling the reform of health care and its reorganization, reengineering, or horizontal or vertical integration. Instead, it appears that various combinations of health care providers and/or benefactors are forging new and sometimes unique alliances to address the factors causing change.

PHYSICIANS' SELF-ANALYSIS

- Watch your competitors. What are they up to?
- If you want to know what health plans are doing in your state, call the insurance commissioner to find out who is applying for licenses. (The federal government has also become a good source, along with the Group Health Association of America, a Washington, DC-based trade association for health plans.)

- Listen to the conversations in physicians' lounges: MDs everywhere are experiencing a drop in income, fewer visits from patients, and much more inclination to do procedures that they would not have done before.
- Understand your expenses from the perspective of what it costs you to enter the delivery system, as a solo practice or a group practice, as a health plan provider, in association with a hospital, as an owner, and/or in an integrated situation with one or more of the above included.

Benchmarks

How do your physicians compare to others in the same specialties? Include as broad a set of characteristics as possible, to provide the most comprehensive profile. An example of elements may include (if applicable):

- Financial indicators

    a. operating income (monthly and year to date)
    b. days' cash on hand
    c. days of net revenue available in net accounts receivable

- Indicators of volume serviced

    a. adult and pediatric patient days (monthly and year to date)
    b. adult and pediatric admissions (monthly and year to date)
    c. visits to the emergency room (monthly and year to date)
    d. cases served in the operating room (monthly and year to date)
    e. visits to your outpatient clinic (monthly and year to date)
    f. cases receiving same-day surgery (monthly and year to date)

- Human-resources indicators

    a. total FTEs employed
    b. rates of turnover among physicians
    c. rates of turnover among employees
    d. staff physicians, by year
    e. percentage of staff employed who are minorities

- Indicators in service and quality

    a. complaints from inpatients
    b. complaints from outpatients
    c. complaints from users of the emergency room

    d. rates of C-sections done

    e. mortality rates

OPTIMIZING THE PHYSICIAN'S ROLE

Some hospital organizations have tended to bypass physicians, operating a sort of "gotcha doctors" type of program where, if physicians (1) want the business and (2) want their patients to save dollars, they have to go to certain hospitals at a set dollar amount. This is a short-sighted approach that puts patients in the middle and sets hospitals against physicians. A partnership with hospitals that has physicians in active roles can meet the financial goals, maximize resources, and promote seamless' customer service. Integrated physician hospital models need to be developed on the basis of mutual benefit as patient members' needs are most effectively met. Focus must be on ways to capitalize on the physician's attributes and role/responsibility; for example, physicians admit patients to hospitals, write orders, and prescribe medications and special equipment. The physician is a most valuable resource in every health care environment. When given a choice, the patient will most often follow the doctor.

Those groups who understand these facts will succeed, and can integrate physicians into active, problem-solving teams within their organization/groups, and can encourage physicians' participation and leadership in a planned manner (e.g., strategic and operational leadership roles including positions on the board, as department heads, as committee chairs, etc.) in any reasonably planned and appropriately conducted activity in the health care business.

For more than a decade, Paul Ellwood, MD, and Leland Kaiser, PhD (considered two of the very best visionaries in health care) have been alerting physicians to the need for change. They predicate the need for change upon the presence of a cultural revolution—a revolution in technology, politics, and economics; and there is no stopping it. Growth of HMOs' managed care and managed competition has pushed the American medical economy into the sixth or seventh largest in the world. That is, the United States spends more on medical care than China spends on everything.[1]

Ellwood and Kaiser reflect on the emergence of super-med organizations and vertical integration, for example in organizations that would include doctors, hospitals, health plans, and nursing homes. Super-meds continue to grow by purchasing more. There are three tiers:

    a. Super-meds—national and regional networks such as Kaiser, Cigna, and more recently Humana, HCA, and Columbia

b. Regional combinations of A
c. Organizations that supply A and B

The costs associated with entering each of these tiers are extraordinary:

- To become a super-med takes $100 million or more for each of four or five years
- Establishing a regional combination system costs 25 to 50 million dollars for four or five years

THE NEW MEDICAL ECONOMICS

Up until now, the game has all been about trading off doctors' visits for days in the hospital. (Based upon the way expenditures for medical services were shaped: 68 percent for hospitals and 32 percent for physicians.) Super-meds have reversed the payment situation: 45 percent for hospitals, 55 percent for physicians, with overall total expenditures smaller. Remaining dollars are used to (1) attract patients (members) by giving more benefits to exchange for choice (2) provide incentives to physicians to hospitalize less, emphasizing outpatient care and (3) bring financial profit to the super-med.

Currently there is an oversupply of hospital beds, but more aggressive hospitals find margins positive despite rates of occupancy being at their lowest levels. To promote these positive margins they use cost containment, reengineering the system, and/or planned integrations among groups of physicians and hospitals to consolidate duplicate services. In addition, visits to physicians are declining, along with income from those. Systems for reimbursement are being changed to give incentives for use of less expensive outpatient-based primary care services and to eliminate, as much as possible, referrals to specialty services. Providers must first unite, and secondly must seek out opportunities where physicians, hospitals, health plans, and other related programs can more effectively meet defined needs for health care in a unified manner rather than as independent, competitive, and (quite possibly) redundant services.

MENTAL ATTITUDE, MIND-SET, AND CONSCIOUSNESS

To quote from Ellwood and Kaiser:

> The Universe is full of garbage and gold. Watch your bucket, because you collect just what you are looking for! What's out there is a set of building blocks. There is no determinism in those blocks. They are

just blocks—blocks to be used optimistically or to be viewed pessi-mistically.[1] (p. 17)

Your future is between the ears of the people who make up your group. *Your future . . . the future . . . is between the ears of the people who make up your group.* How long does it take you to change your future? Answer: As long as it takes to change your mind. How long does it take to change the future of a medical group? Answer: As long as it takes to change its collective mind. How do we change what's out there? Answer: The two most critical strategies for a medical group are the production of better ideas, and long-term acquisition of capital.

- Your group's ultimate limitation is the imagination available among its physicians.
- Capital is the single most important issue. In a capitalistic society, the one with the most capital "wins." One can buy into a market. One can also artificially lower prices.

Ways to position yourself—promotion of wellness, prevention, sensible policies regarding tobacco, alcohol, stress—all those are coming along very quickly, as we move toward improvements in lifestyles. The money in this business is in better lifestyles, not in medical care. The super-meds may buy up the schools—you have to educate the people in your own system: in residencies, internships, fellowships—the whole thing! This also means research: acquire the best minds to invent the devices, the implants, and the transplants (for example, an artificial heart), and commit maybe $2 million to it, and when the kinks are ironed out it may earn you $20 million annually! The medical group of the future will be an "amoe-boid" (a "constantly changing shape"). The winning medical group must be able to make any decision of any order of magnitude in less than ninety days. This will require the rapid acquisition and effective use of informa-tion and of contemporary informational systems and networks.

CHANGING ROLES, ISSUES OF REIMBURSEMENT, AND CAPITATION

If you are right but slow, you are dead[1]

In his book *Strong Medicine*,[2] George Halvorson, head of Health-Partners, advocates influencing physicians' practices by realigning pay-ments to encourage the direction toward which the payer would like to see the health care practice move. To use his example, from the perspective of a health plan, when a baby is delivered the medical providers involved should be paid for having promoted healthy mothers and healthy babies. The system providing their payment should not encourage any particular medical procedure over any other, unless that encouragement is based on clear standards for quality of care.

He further notes that fee-for-service payments do not reward quality. In many communities, physicians ignore the issue of hospital costs, since their income is based on their own fee schedules, not on the efficiency of the total care to which they contributed. This makes sense when the hospital's costs are not related to the doctors' own costs of doing business. In such a case, there is no financial incentive for the physician to use hospital care conservatively and efficiently. Once physicians become aware of the impact of their decisions upon total costs, and once they are in positions where they can keep any excess capitational payments as a reward for efficiency, but would have to pay for any excess care out of their own clinic's bank account, they will quickly become more efficient.

Halvorson contends that physicians' pay is not the financial problem; rather, the problem is physician-created expenses. Physicians make 80 percent to 90 percent of all decisions in health care, so their styles of practice drive the system. Their direct personal compensation, after overhead and expenses, probably runs only about 12 percent to 15 percent of the total bill for health care in America. That is clearly not the lion's share of costs. Their incomes are increasing more rapidly than inflation by a significant margin, but even that increase is not a truly significant problem for consumers and payers. The overwhelming problem is that the decisions they make create other substantial costs within the system. Physicians' decisions made in favor of more extensive care significantly increase the overall cost of care for each patient. Halvorson believes that no reform of the system will succeed unless it takes into consideration the leveraging impact of physicians' decisions. Once doctors become aware of the total impact of their decisions, they can quickly become more efficient.

Rewarding efficiency is the clearly heralded solution presented in the book *Strong Medicine*. Halvorson indicates that the best way to reward efficiency and not volume is to prepay teams of physicians a fixed amount of money per patient, to meet all of the medical needs of each patient. That general approach is referred to as "prepayment" and such payments are generally called "capitation," because they are paid per capita or per person rather than per service. Prepayment now has decades of experience behind it—and it works, as evidenced by the growing number of successful health plans that base their operations on this method. The science of capitation has also progressed significantly since those early days. Modern capitational approaches put the doctors at less financial risk and focus risk in issues over which the doctor has more direct control. From the perspective of a health plan, the challenge we need to face is how better to align our payments with our goals so that doctors can focus on efficiency, on quality, and most importantly on prevention and the development of healthier lifestyles in the first place.

Although efficiency has been improving, it is important to balance the health of the patients in the equation to produce a win/win outcome. Such an example of the pendulum of capitated care going too far in the efficiency direction was a recent Minnesota legislative decision (1996) to extend the amount of time health plans covered hospital stays for the mothers of newborns. Insurers had basically stated that the health plan would only cover one day of a mother's stay in the hospital after giving birth (unless there were complications). The state legislature acted to extend insurance coverage for mothers' hospital stays to two days for a normal delivery. Just because a system or plan is efficient does not mean it is effective patient care. A balance is needed and sometimes that means testing options and being willing to change when less than appropriate outcomes are documented.

PHYSICIANS AND PATIENTS FOR BETTER HEALTH

The fact remains that physicians and their patients are far better off working together to achieve healthy lifestyles. It will be most efficient, from every aspect, for health care organizations to focus on preventive educational programs rather than on programs for intervention. On behalf of their patients, physicians must be knowledgeable about available resources and services in participating health plans and hospitals.

An example follows, to show how one health care system based in Minneapolis and St. Paul addressed other improvements in health among its members and the community. The goal of the organization was to be the best model for delivering and financing health care in an integrated system that includes multiple health plans to meet any defined need; it owns or contracts hospitals in every area where members live, and includes over 3,000 physicians. The organization stated its mission to be *focused on improving the health of its members and the community.* To achieve this defined goal, specific initiatives for prevention and healthy outcomes have been implemented. Four-year goals publicly announced in 1994 include a preventive emphasis on six core areas.[3]

Four-Year Goals

1. Reduce the number of incidents related to heart disease (e.g., heart attacks) among our members by 25 percent.

Focus: Reducing deaths and hospitalizations due to myocardial infarction, angioplasty, coronary artery bypass, and congestive heart failure.

2. Increase by 75 percent to 95 percent the number of children in our system who are fully immunized for childhood diseases by age two.

Focus:	3 Polio	Adolescents:
	3 Hep B	3 Hep B
	3 HIB	4 DPT
	1 MMR	

3. Improve the early detection of breast cancer among our members, reducing by 50 percent the number of cases that reach an advanced stage before being detected.

Focus: Reducing the percentage of cases that reach Stage 3 or Stage 4 before being detected.

4. Increase the early detection of adult-onset diabetes by screening 90 percent of high-risk members. Reduce by 25 percent their progression from a high-risk state to active diabetes. Reduce by 30 percent the onset and progression of damages to their eyes, kidneys, and nerves resulting from diabetes.

Focus: Identifying persons at high risk and preventing them from advancing to the diseased state. Reducing retinopathy, neuropathy, nephropathy, and claudication among members who have diabetes.

5. Reduce by 30 percent complications in infants and their mothers among our members.

Focus: Reducing the number of preterm deliveries and repeated teen pregnancies; providing medical rather than surgical management of ectopic pregnancies.

6. Reduce dental cavities by 50 percent for all age groups among members served by our dental plan.

Focus: Reducing the number of tooth surfaces requiring restoration due to caries.

The following sections represent regional newspapers' public interpretations that described the essence of the prevention-oriented program to the Minneapolis-St. Paul and surrounding communities, and national coverage in *The Wall Street Journal* in 1994:

Minneapolis Star Tribune
Tuesday, February 22, 1994

HealthPartners to Emphasize Wellness in Goal-Setting Prevention Program

New Plan Will Focus on 6 Areas in Which Preemptive Action Can Avert Problems

HealthPartners said Monday that a new goals program would refocus its organization toward health promotion and markedly improve the health of its members.

The program, which has been under consideration for about 18 months, sets goals in six areas where the Bloomington-based health care firm said it will take steps to pursue wellness aggressively.

For instance, one goal is to reduce the number of heart attacks among its members by 25 percent over the next four years. "We are setting ourselves some specific objectives for implementing these goals," said Chief Executive George Halvorson, "rather than putting brochures in the waiting rooms and hoping people will read them."

The program will require HealthPartners to review the files of nearly all 600,000 members to identify high-risk and near-risk cases. HealthPartners includes Group Health, MedCenters, St. Paul Ramsey Medical Center, and the Ramsey Clinic. Halvorson said the program will cost $3 million to $10 million, depending on the number of potential cases it discovers. "If we show an overall 2 percent improvement in health status, we'll come out ahead," Halvorson said.

Other goals it has set include immunizing 95 percent of the children in its system by age 2, reducing advanced stage breast cancer cases by 50 percent, screening 90 percent of its members to check for diabetes, reducing infant and maternal complications by 30 percent, and reducing new cavities by 50 percent for all members in its dental network.

The company will report its progress on these goals and add new goals each year. Dr. George Isham, the company's medical officer, said the company selected goals that reflected diseases that have a high occurrence and also correspond to state public health agendas. Isham said that the company hoped to attack mental health issues in the near future, with goals such as reducing suicide and curing depression in its patients.[4]

St. Paul Pioneer Press
February 22, 1994
Largest HMO Bringing Bid for Wellness to Home Office

Ambitious Plan Urges Healthy Eating Habits

In a sharp break from its tradition of treating sick people, the state's largest health maintenance organization Monday announced a plan it hopes will keep its 600,000 members healthy.[5]

Recommendations to Promote Healthy Lifestyles

This example of preventive approach to healthy living is educationally based and aimed at patient members. To reach patient members effectively, however, and to achieve measurably improved health status, the providers (i.e., physicians, hospitals, health plans, supporting staff of each provider and any other participating providers) *must* function as teachers. It becomes necessary to teach the benefactors how to optimize the effectiveness of their services on behalf of patient members. The transfer of information from each expert source to the patient member is a main objective. In this example, the organization provided consumer education through a center on health promotions staffed with health educators, nurses, and dietitians to help members develop and maintain healthier lifestyles. By providing comprehensive educational resources and presenting consumer education programs and services, individuals were helped in making choices that promote optimal health. A brief listing of subjects addressed follows:[3]

• Stress and Relaxation • Heart Health • Smoking Cessation
• Fitness • Weight Management • Healthy Eating

Developing new skills for personal growth and enrichment:

• Parenting • Self-esteem for adults and children • Assertiveness
• Couples' Communication Workshop • Understanding Shame
• Women's Midlife Power Surge • Anger Management
• Coping with Loss

Taking an active role in managing your health conditions:

• Toward Better Blood Pressure • Fibromyalgia • Infertility
• Pulmonary Rehabilitation Program • Diabetes • Cholesterol

Give your child the best possible start in life by preparing for a healthy pregnancy, birth, and baby:

• Planning a Healthy Pregnancy • Expecting the Best: Early
Pregnancy Orientation • Breast-Feeding Your Baby
• New Baby, New Family Care Class • Childbirth Preparation Classes

Subjects of written materials available to health plan members:

Routine Physicals Get a New Twist—preventive screening, lifestyle counseling are replacing the old annual physical. Created by physicians, the guidelines specify the best way consistently and effectively to prevent a given condition in your health.

The preventive services focus calls for more than just disease testing. It also focuses on disease prevention.

FUTURE NEEDS

As the health care industry prepares for the twenty-first century, the combined targets of prevention and healthy lifestyle development will remain top priorities. The essential elements remain clear. Along with regular checkups and adherence to the fundamental preventive screening measures related to age group, the health enhancement keys include: getting physical activity; eating a healthy, low-fat diet; maintaining a healthy body weight; and not smoking.[6]

Both short and long-term return on investment are part of the payoff. In the short term, one will feel better, be more energetic, and more positive about one's own well-being. Over time, one can reduce the risk for many diseases. And, if one already has an illness, improved health habits can reduce the risk of complications. For example, by being even moderately physically active one can significantly reduce the risk for heart disease, high blood pressure, diabetes, and osteoporosis. Similar benefits exist across the board for healthy eating, an appropriate body weight, and not smoking.

Health as a commodity has considerable appeal to consumers and payers alike. In the past the measurement of satisfaction with health care was more with the process of delivery. As the product of health care, the clinical outcome is evaluated simultaneously to the way care is delivered. The physician is required to successfully orchestrate "process with outcome" to achieve excellence. Excellence is what differentiates adequate or satisfactory from superior.

If achieving excellence is not enough, the superior provider must transition the focus of practice from treating illness to preventing the disease from occurring in the first place. Although much is known about the state or nature of prevention or wellness, very little is known about the ways and means of creating or implementing an immediate prevention status among patients. The desired outcome is known as wellness, health, or an enhanced, healthy lifestyle. But each patient has his/her own health requirements and in most cases today, the provider of health care is only involved after the onset of a health condition. Intervention is the most common denominator for purposes of returning the patient's health status to balance. How can we focus on prevention when the conditions that warrant health care are predicated on and rewarded for intervention and not the promotion of health?

The challenge of shifting care away from intervention toward wellness will be a giant step for most providers today since their medical education, residencies, internships, and fellowships are focused toward "hands on" intervention methods and activities. The most highly trained specialists have had the most "hands on" intervention training in their respective specialty.

Is there a continuum between prevention and intervention toward health as a desired state or are there levels of wellness in each health state that vary from one individual to the next? The search for prevention and wellness will require an examination of both known and currently unknown factors as we move into the twenty-first century.

APPLICATIONS

Targeted Goals

Has care been delivered to each patient in a smooth and effective manner? Have all needs been met without duplication, on a low cost, high quality basis? Have patients become healthier under your medical guidance? As a group, are patients from your medical practice living longer, more disease-free lives?

Objectives

1. How do medical outcomes compare to benchmark groups' outcomes?
2. Are operating costs as low as they could be? How do they compare to similar medical groups' costs?
3. Are consumers appropriately satisfied with all aspects of care and service? Which aspects are most important to consumers?

Content

Have physicians received ongoing continuing medical education to stay a little in advance of the times? Have they been able to upgrade their patient care? Is the material on health care in curricula used in public and private schools annually updated?

Evaluation

Are consumer satisfaction scores adequate? Are they increasing in known problem areas? Is the percentage of disease-free membership/patients increasing? Where have the most significant gains been made? What is the average age of male and female patients? Are those increasing?

Continuous Quality Improvement

What refinements have been made to systems for the delivery of care and to systems for operational services? What areas need additional enhancements?

Chapter 5

Teamwork Between Physicians and Nonphysician Administrators

POINTS FOR FOCUS

The importance of building effective relationships cannot be emphasized too much. A large enough gap exists due to training alone (that in medicine as opposed to that in administration). The focus must be to reduce differences while agreeing mutually to learn more about each other's world of work. Common mission and values about management of medical practice and about desired outcomes are required.

Targeted Goal

To develop a philosophy of management that facilitates a smooth working relationship between physicians and nonphysician administrative staff.

Objectives

1. Identify clinical, organizational, and communication needs to be addressed at the administrative level.
2. Develop a plan (or plans) for communications to keep medical group staff and patients/members informed effectively.
3. Support physicians' leadership by encouraging their increased participation in the groups' planning and strategic development process, governance structure, and as public representatives of the medical practice in community activities.

Content

Physicians must be encouraged and supported as leaders of change in health care. Many physicians are not comfortable with this expectation, and need additional training in administrative leadership. The success of physicians' practices can be enhanced by understanding how to provide more services of greater quality to an increasing number of patients at lower cost. Assumptions to be considered: the pressures of costs on provision of health care will increase significantly; competitors will be in both vertically integrated systems and networks of deeply discounting providers; reform will continue to evolve locally and/or regionally through purchasers, payers, and organized groups of patient/members; and, competitors will send patients for care only to sites they own or control.

Evaluation

Develop a mutually acceptable plan based upon mission and values that shows how the partnering of roles for physicians and nonphysicians will lead to more services of high quality being delivered at lower cost and with optimal outcomes.

Continuous Quality Improvement

Be prepared to refine/enhance your plan at least annually.

THE ADMINISTRATOR'S ROLE

There is considerable variation across medical practices in methods for determining who handles what aspects of management. One way to help determine an effective working relationship is to place significant responsibility on the administrator. It is incumbent upon the administrator to ask the physician-president how he/she believes the practice should work, from its day-to-day operations to the development and management of structures for governance. There is not a right or wrong answer to how the conduct of a practice is executed. Instead it is an issue of communication and style and the development of trust. Future units will address various formal organizational structures, flow charts, and decision making apparatuses.

The essence of teamwork between administrators and physicians lies in understanding what collective outcomes are desired and in agreeing on definitions of the main targets. Once goals are set, at the level of the board and for/by the whole organization, individual style and technique will follow. The administrator is expected to design and implement various plans and strategies to attain the preset objectives of the board and the organization. Both human and financial resources will be required. It is the job of those in management to align and monitor properly the allocation of resources in order to meet the defined needs of the organization.

FIRST SEEK TO UNDERSTAND, THEN TO BE UNDERSTOOD

Stephen Covey coined this phrase, which has significant merit when applied to the development of any relationship.[1] If the administrator takes the lead to demonstrate a total and complete interest in listening to, understanding, and then acting on needs articulated by the physician-president, that physician will do everything in his/her power to see that the administrative needs are also fulfilled. The model is so simple that sometimes it is hard to understand. Proposed solutions to health care administration problems reflect ongoing changes in the health care system. Multiple challenges must be addressed and include: physician performance and behavior; financing and organization of health services; use of support services; and, physician reimbursement to mention a few. The ability to combine administrative talent and allocate responsibility and authority according to strengths and weaknesses is an essential requirement.[2] If both the physician-president and the administrator trust and understand the needs of the other and base subsequent decisions and actions on enhancing outcomes in the practice, the business relationship will be successful.

PHYSICIANS AND SOCIAL CHANGE

It is impossible to understand the problem of medical care without understanding the physician. And it is impossible to make significant changes in the medical field without changing physician behavior.[3] (p. 3)

Physicians will continue to affect substantially the patterns of medical care, of gaining appropriate standards in them, and of costs associated with delivery of high-quality care. It would be naive to assume that the enormous power of the profession that has developed during this century will, in any large part, be reversed at all quickly, despite changing conditions and the growing pool of competing physicians. Instead, it behooves administrators to take whatever time is necessary to learn how to meld and direct physicians' power toward initiatives that benefit the practice. Despite a decline in the power of the medical profession in recent years, it continues to be a significant force in the politics of health care, and what physicians think and what they do make a difference in how the systems work.[3]

It is important for administrators to understand how physicians differ among themselves and how they change in their attitudes toward broad political questions and basic issues in the organization of health care at all levels. John Colombotos and Corinne Kirchner provide significant insight into this subject, as they reflect on the reorganization of physicians' attitudes toward political issues and issues in health care.[3] Their insights are meant to help prepare nonphysician professionals in health care so that they understand physicians better during this turbulent time of change.

Attitudes Toward Political Issues and Issues in Health Care

The medical profession is often portrayed as monolithically conservative and as resistant to political change and to modifications in the organization of health care. This perception is misleading. Not only do physicians vary among themselves in their views, but they also discriminate among different features and aspects of a set of issues:

- Although they are more conservative politically than the general population, substantial numbers of physicians hold liberal political views, and slightly more than a third are "middle of the road"; one-third are Democrats.
- Considerable numbers supported a role for government in health care, the level of support varying according to specifics; indeed, a majority favored "some form" of national health insurance.
- Some favored and others opposed group practice, depending on which types of group practice; more than half considered a "small" group practice as most desirable, compared to a fourth who chose a "large" group.
- Over 80 percent favored peer reviews in hospitals, about 50 percent favoring them even in doctors' offices; three-quarters favored peer reviews under national health insurance (NHI).
- Two-thirds would have used a nurse-practitioner or physician's assistant in their practices, but they were much more willing to delegate some tasks than others.
- Fixed fees under NHI were acceptable to nearly two-thirds, capitation to a fourth, and salary to 14 percent.[3]

Physicians underestimated the support of their colleagues for some form of national health insurance—a clear instance of "pluralistic ignorance," when individuals assume that they are virtually alone in holding a certain attitude, not knowing that others privately share it. Why are physicians as a group perceived both by physicians themselves and by the general public to be more conservative than they are in fact? Colombotos and Kirchner suggest that both groups, lacking other sources of information, attributed to the profession as a whole the historically conservative policies of the AMA. The attitudes of physicians toward issues in the organization and delivery of health care, especially toward those issues that explicitly involve the participation of government, were indeed associated with their political views. Issues in health care are thus highly politicized; they are not solely professional or scientific issues, as claimed by some medical spokespersons who seek to "keep politics out of health."

Social and Professional Characteristics in Relation to Attitudes

Except for their socioeconomic origins, the characteristics of the social backgrounds of physicians, notably their religious upbringing, had strong effects on their political views and views of government in medicine. The findings were typical of those in the general population: Jews, women, those who were first-generation immigrants, easterners, and urbanites all held more liberal views than did Catholics and Protestants, men, those who were second- and third- or more generations removed from immigrant forebears, noneasterners, and nonurbanites. On all issues, physicians in an individual, fee-for-service practice were generally the most conservative, followed in declining order by those in (1) group- or hospital-based fee-for-service practices, (2) group- or hospital-based salaried practices, and (3) those whose main activity was teaching, administration, or research rather than patient care.

Considering differences by specialty, general practitioners and surgeons were the most conservative on political issues and issues of government in medicine, and psychiatrists were the most liberal. Those in the medical specialties, including pediatrics, were in between.

Does Organized Medicine Represent the Medical Profession?

The views of leaders in the AMA and in state and county medical societies were remarkably in tune with those of their membership. Who were the nonmembers? They were younger, they earned lower incomes, and they were much more likely than both leaders and members in medical societies to be in salaried positions in patient care, or in research, teaching, and/or administration. In view of the growing number of physicians in salaried settings, the leadership of organized medicine may be speaking in the future for a smaller and smaller segment of their profession.

Socialization Theory and Professional Attitudes:
A Conceptual Framework

Both diversity and change in physicians' attitudes toward political and health care issues have been analyzed in terms of lifelong socialization. Social and professional characteristics at various stages in the life cycle, have been viewed as indicators of socially patterned experiences that influence attitudes. Attitudinal differences among generations of medical trainees and physicians have pointed to the influence of broadly defined historical events, translated again as socially patterned experiences. The passage and implementation of Medicare has been viewed by those who studied its effects on physicians as an event experienced by the profession as a whole and as having a dramatic impact on its attitudes toward that relatively circumscribed issue. The extension of this general conceptual framework to research on a wider range of sources of socialization and to attitudes toward a wider range of issues (e.g., styles of practice, rates of utilization, and ethical issues), would add greatly to understanding the socialization of these professionals.

Politics and Health Care Since the Mid-1970s:
Continuity and Change

The main issues of health care leading into the 1970s—the components of the "crisis" in health care as they were perceived at the time—were cost, accessibility, and quality. The effects of these factors led to longer-term trends in organization: differentiation and specialization, the bureaucratization of medical practice, salaried reimbursement of physicians, third-party payment, reviews and controls of medical practice, and an increasing government role. It would be simplistic to view the recent changes in public and private concerns about health care in this country as having replaced the concerns of a decade ago. Rather, current issues have evolved from past issues; some are, in fact, a direct continuation of earlier ones. The adaptation of physicians to Medicare stands as a cautionary example of how they may change their minds rather dramatically within a short period as a result of specific events.

Decline of the Welfare State?

The country entered the 1970s on a wave of "agitation and reform." Conflict over national health insurance centered not on whether, but on what type of program should be enacted. Ensuring equitable access to care dominated the agenda on health policy: national health insurance appeared inevitable. Once Medicare was enacted, NHI was no longer viewed as a solution to the perceived crises of access and of cost and quality of care, and NHI became widely regarded as costly and not a practical option. The expanding regulatory structures of governmental welfare programs also came under increasingly harsh attack. Critics from the political right attacked a wide range of health and safety regulations as ineffective or inefficient. Multifaceted regulatory reforms such as utilization review by physician-services review organizations (PSROs) and limits on hospitals' capital expansion provided through the certificate of need (CON) program were evaluated on the narrow grounds of cost containment and judged a failure.

An alternative solution to the cost dilemma—the market competition approach—began to attract attention in the late 1970s. Growing out of an economic critique of regulation aimed at the providers of medical care, the market competition strategy would attempt to restore consumer sensitivity to price. Proponents argued that to the extent that comprehensive insurance benefits reduce consumers' out-of-pocket costs, consumers have little incentive to choose less costly over more costly types of care or to refrain from using services of marginal benefit. The specific steps advocated included reducing or eliminating federal tax subsidies of health insurance, and increasing consumer cost sharing through mechanisms such as increasing coinsurance.

Strategies promoting market competition also seek to promote the growth of HMOs and other alternative systems for delivery of care. As more efficient and less costly forms of care, alternative systems presumably spur price competition with other providers. According to advocates of this approach, unleashing the competitive forces of the economic market would permit elimination of much of the "burdensome" regulation now in effect. Not surprisingly, the market competition approach was embraced by political conservatives and became the centerpiece of the conservative agenda for reform of health care.

An Evolving Health Care Sector

The system for delivery and financing of health care was undergoing certain developments that had implications for the choices confronting not only physicians but society as a whole. While health economists were prescribing the enactment of procompetitive reforms as the needed antidote to burgeoning health care cost, the health care sector itself was already becoming much more competitive. The growth in comprehensive insurance benefits, including the enactment of Medicaid and Medicare, set the stage for large-scale corporate investment in health care delivery, notably in for-profit chains of hospitals. Corporate-owned hospitals, nursing homes, psychiatric hospitals, HMOs, and centers for ambulatory care and hemo-dialysis became realities. For the first time, decisions directly affecting patient care were being centralized in corporate headquarters.

The transformation of the American system for health care delivery extends beyond the increasing role of investor-owned corporations. Efforts at cost containment have reduced governmental subsidies for the capital expansion and replacement of hospitals, while traditional sources of phil-anthropic financing have also diminished. Voluntary hospitals in urban areas particularly have experienced a capital financing squeeze. In an increasingly consistent financial environment, nonprofit hospitals have turned to new types of organizational arrangements that bear a strong resemblance to those of their for-profit competitors. Nonprofit hospitals are entering into managerial contracts with corporate chains of hospitals, diversifying into new forms of service, and forming their own multi-insti-tutional hospital systems. The downward pressure on costs within an increasingly complex, competitive health care industry has related to a demand for more businesslike managerial practices: the line between the investor-owned and the nonprofit hospitals has begun to blur. Multi-insti-tutional chains of hospitals have grown significantly.

This relatively new integrated formation of hospitals has a demonstrably significant impact on physicians. It is clear that in both for-profit and nonprofit hospital settings, the need for greater efficiency has augmented the power of hospital management vis-à-vis medical staffs, and this has ramifications for physicians' clinical independence and profes-sional values. Managerial controls are further enhanced by the prospective payment system that is based on the diagnosis-related groups (DRGs) adopted for the federal Medicare program in 1983. Organization of hospitals' expenditures according to DRGs allows identification of those physicians whose case management results in nonreimbursable expenditures.

The dominance of physicians within the health care system was certain-ly affected by a second important trend: the growing numbers of physicians themselves. Job applicants began to outnumber jobs available. It is unlikely that the medical profession will declare war on new forms of organization or on their financing on ideological grounds concerning value conflicts between those in such organizations and those within the medical profes-sion. It does not appear that job openings in corporate chains or salaried practices will go short of applicants. The expanding supply of physicians is expected to continue to feed competitive pressures within our health care system.

A New Direction for Public Policy

Concerns about cost containment still dominate discussions of health care policy, and governmental cutbacks in assistance to the poor have prompted concern about access to care. Proposals to extend benefits of federally provided health insurance to the unemployed and the medically indigent have received support as pilot or demonstration endeavors. It is clear that the questions confronting national health care policy are similar to those of previous decades. Defining the appropriate role of a federal system of government in addressing key goals in health care systems is a persistent issue for analysis and debate.

Implications of Physicians' Attitudes for Policy: A Framework

What is the relevance of physicians' attitudes to the design and implementation of health care policies? The attitudes of physicians enter indirectly into the political process in two ways. First, leaders of organized medicine are influenced by, or at least take into account, what they perceive to be the views of their constituents in developing positions on policy. Second, the influence of medical leaders is enhanced to the extent that they can claim that their positions represent the views of their constituents. But that claim may be challenged when individuals or segments of the profession speak out against official organizational policies.

Physicians' Attitudes in the Mid-1980s and 1990s

What are the current views on politics and health care held by physicians—and how are they likely to change? Colombotos and Kirchner note that the medical profession will generally become more liberal, especially with respect to changes in organization. This prediction is based on (1) ongoing changes in social and professional characteristics of physicians related to their attitudes, and (2) generational differences in attitude between younger and older physicians. Major changes in the composition of the process will include:

- A sharp increase in the proportion of women in the profession, to a point where, if current enrollment practices in medical schools continue, within a few decades women will comprise a fifth of the nation's physicians
- An increase in the proportion of salaried, group-based physicians
- An increase in the proportion of physicians in primary care specialties and declines in specialties in which there are current or projected oversupplies, notably certain surgical specialties[3]

During the next decade, clinical protocols and standards, spearheaded by DRGs and by resource-based relative value scales (RBRVS) and resource-based units (RBUs), will exercise an increasing influence on the clinical decision making of physicians. In addition, the fees of physicians will be fixed, first under Medicare, and then by RBRVS/RVUs. Additional governmental and/or nongovernment-financed programs employing capitation and other such approaches will also be tested. Physicians will adapt.

Organized medicine will play a major role in the development and implementation of clinical protocols and in the negotiation of fee schedules. The clinical autonomy of physicians and their related fees are likely to fare better if clinical protocols and physicians' fees are negotiated between government and organized medicine than if they are left to the whim of market forces in a market in which the for-profit chains would have the upper hand over individual physicians competing with each other. Collective autonomy would replace individual autonomy, in both clinical decision making and physicians' reimbursement.

One unknown in this scenario is: which segments of organized medicine will gain control of these functions? Will it be (1) physicians, (2) hospitals, (3) health plans, or (4) some integrated combination of either a for-profit or not-for-profit nature? Regardless of the controlling organization of the future, it is imperative that physicians and their practice administrators function as an effective team. The goal of such teamwork is to maximize the medical practice under any scenario.

DECISION MAKING

No one would question the observation that there has been a rapid increase in the number and magnitude of financial and ethical issues affecting decisions about patient care.[2] As pressures intensify to balance social responsibility and economic reality within medical practice, the limits of ethical decision making will be tested, as was noted by Paul Hoffman in his 1991 article about collaboration between administrators and clinicians in ethical decision making.[4]

There are decreasing dollars to provide care to increasing numbers of patients at all levels. The DRG system was applied to reduce expenses in hospitals. Likewise, RBRVS and RVUs have been implemented to reduce physicians' expenses in medical practices, and HMOs and integrated health plans have been established as insuring vehicles to decrease expenses for hospitals, physicians, and insurance for growing groups of patient members. To complicate matters, in lieu of federally sponsored initiatives for the reform of health care, local/regional groups of employers are forming their own health care purchasing alliances. If your group wants to provide health care for such an alliance, it must be able to provide very accessible, high-quality care, best outcomes, low prices, geographical availability, and high rates of consumer satisfaction.

When the financial reality of staying in business demonstrates a potential to compromise patient care, it is important that administrators and physicians jointly understand those implications. There ought not to be conflict over matters of resource allocation. Hoffman's thoughts are underscored on this point. It is precisely when administrators and clinicians become adversaries that their respective constituencies are most likely to be compromised.[4] Just as there is nothing basically antiethical about a physician practicing cost-effective medicine, there is no prohibition in an administrator's job description against patient advocacy. On the contrary, the health care administrator who abdicates this fundamental responsibility is in the wrong profession.

Although it might be convenient to suggest that physicians are committed only to individual patients and that administrators are accountable either to owners and sponsors or to patient groups, this simple dichotomy is not generally the case. Given their mutual interest in allocating health resources as effectively and ethically as possible, administrators and physicians have far more to gain through collaboration than confrontation.

CONFLICTS OF VALUES IN PHYSICIANS AND HOSPITALS

Unless a physician only treats nonhospital-based patients (with no responsibilities for inpatient admissions), it is important to develop positive working arrangements with the hospital that receives the patients. The physician-hospital relationship can be mutually rewarding and strategically crucial in integration (as well as essential to strategies that plan efforts to increase market share). It is important for physicians and hospitals to know as much as possible about each other. Table 5.1 shows some values held by physicians and by hospitals, and these values may conflict.

COMMUNICATIONS

The accurate interchange of information between and among physicians, administrators, the organization, and the outside world is absolutely essential. Like any other business, the management of a medical practice requires both (1) formal and (2) informal communicative systems. In a physicians' group, communication of information may take place in the general physicians'

Table 5.1. Conflicting Values of Hospitals and Physicians

Physicians' Values	Values Held by Hospital Management
1. *Professional Autonomy*	1. *Professional Cooperation*
Physicians are trained to believe unequivocally in the necessity for their self-reliance and independent judgment. They are accountable for their actions on a highly personal level. Responsibility for patient care is directly attributed to the physician.	Management often functions through a complex process of consensus, teamwork, and structured planning. Responsibility for patient care might be delegated to the anonymous actions of a committee or a board.
Physicians:	In the hospital:
a. are antibureaucratic	a. bureaucracy can sometimes depersonalize a manager's sense of personal accountability for a decision
b. are disdainful of large institutions (often including large medical organizations)	b. managers might be individualistic in personal nature, but are trained to work within organizational hierarchies of large institutions
c. are critical of management-by-committee	c. activities are often managed by committee and by census
d. view the decision making process of most managers as "ponderous compromising"	d. there is a disdain for unilateral or arbitrary decisions
2. *Profits*	2. *Salary*
Physicians believe income should be directly related to profits generated from performance of work.	Managers are more likely to accept a salary, and expect others to do likewise (for budgetary reasons).
3. *Individualism*	3. *Team Membership*
Physicians are quick to challenge conventional wisdom.	Managers are comfortable with consensus.
4. *Ownership*	4. *Employment*
Doctors are possessive regarding their practices, patients, and professional independence.	Managers accept their status as employees with lack of ownership.
5. *Training*	5. *Education*
Medical training emphasizes decisiveness, science, exercise of judgment, and personal responsibility.	Managerial education emphasizes process, the existence of ambiguity, risk management, and business principles.

Physicians' Values	Values Held by Hospital Management
6. *Bimodal Values*	6. *Focused Values*
Business and professional values are often in conflict.	Managers have a more singular focus on priorities and decisions: there is little conflict in their values.
7. *Horizontal Control*	7. *Vertical Control*
Ownership and control are usually horizontal among physicians. Partnership votes are democratic. Authority is sparingly delegated to others. This trait is slowly changing in some groups.	The board has unrestricted authority to govern the organization. The CEO typically governs a hierarchical managerial structure.
8. *Board of Physicians*	8. *Board of Laymen*
Control lies exclusively with physicians, who are closer to issues of patient care. Group boards often micromanage their business/practice.	The board is predominantly laypersons, less directly involved in issues of patient care. Hospital boards rarely micromanage, but make policy and macrodecisions.
9. *Less Management*	9. *Middle Management*
Managerial infrastructure in a group practice is less developed than that in a hospital.	Management is often very developed, and can act condescending toward less structured medical practices.
10. *Patient Care*	10. *System Care*
Physicians believe the essence of quality care occurs in the OR, the ER, or the examination room, and that lay managers are insulated from the realities of patient care.	Managers often consider inpatient care from an impersonal, systemic point of view.
11. *Perceptions of Hospital Management*	11. *Perceptions of Physicians*
a. Managers are perceived to be preoccupied with finances, empire building, and irrelevant external activities.	a. Physicians are perceived to be organizationally undisciplined and ineffective at business; peer review and the imposition of sanctions against submarginal physicians may be necessary.

Table 5.1 *(continued)*

Physicians' Values	Values Held by Hospital Management
b. Managers are perceived to be insensitive to the needs of patients, physicians, and clinicians; they "do not recognize the customer."	b. Physicians are perceived to use issues of quality and patient care as euphemisms for personal convenience or economic benefit, or the creation of personal fiefdoms.
c. Hospital economics are perceived to be impersonal, and managers are therefore not perceived to have any real incentives to economize.	c. Physicians are perceived as wanting to maximize their take-home income and as not wanting to invest in their business.
12. *Capital Expenditures* Capital expenditures are highly personal, as they directly affect take-home income or increase debt obligation. Major expenditures often create controversy among classes of physicians (for example, by age, specialty, etc.).	13. *Capital Programs* Managers are not emotionally tied to capital expenditure programs, which are presumably made on a rational, businesslike basis and do not affect personal income.
14. *Cash Basis* Physicians account on a cash basis; financial systems are less sophisticated than those in hospitals.	14. *Accrual Basis* Hospitals account on an accrual basis; they have more complex budgeting processes.
15. *Distribute Earnings* Sensitivity to taxes precludes most physicians from significant retention of earnings. Groups are almost always undercapitalized because of this (and because of the desire to maximize current personal income).	15. *Retain Earnings* Hospitals usually retain earnings, build reserves, and are adequately capitalized.
16. *Income* Physicians have relatively simple financial structures. They rely primarily on income statements and cash flow.	16. *Assets* Hospitals tend to develop more complex financing structures and are more oriented toward balance sheets and related debt capacity ratios.

lounge, operating room lounge (and locker/dressing area), hallways, doctors' parking lot, or by telephone and e-mail and/or through other computerized networks. Information will flow through these avenues in a most free and uncontrolled manner. One way to affect this informal network positively is to make sure that all appropriate information affecting, or that has the potential to affect, the medical group is effectively being made available also through a formal system for communication.

The communication of information that is less than accurate and timely will hamper relationships among physicians and administrators. If there is a belief that administration is trying to suppress and/or color information for whatever reason, it will not work. Physicians need to receive accurate and timely information, to be most effective in teamwork with administration. Only when communication is open and direct can physicians and administrators maximize their working relationship and enhance their medical practice.

The following examples illustrate how one medical group addressed physicians' needs for communication through written surveys. Once results were analyzed, presentations were made to decision making bodies to enhance those communications that were working. Based upon the discussions, plans were made leading to implementation of summarized recommendations. In each case, follow-up planning monitored how well the changes were working. The process served to enhance ongoing communication throughout the physician group.

SURVEY OF COMMUNICATIONS
AND SUMMARY OF RESULTS

Example 1: Survey Distributed to Members of a Physicians' Clinic

TO: Members of the Clinic's Board
Members of the Council of Heads of Medical Departments
Physician Members of the Clinic

FROM: Physician President/Chief Executive Officer, _____ Clinic

DATE: April 5, 1996

RE: Effectiveness of Communication Among the Clinic's
Physician Members

Dear Colleagues,

At the July meeting of the clinic's board, issues of the effectiveness of communication within the membership of physicians were discussed. During this day and age of almost constant change, effective communication is a requirement. For purposes of improving communication, your help is needed. Please send me your comments about:

I. The effectiveness of our overall opportunities for communication. Please respond using the rating scale in the format shown, with 1 representing "very satisfied with effectiveness," 4 representing "not satisfied with effectiveness" and 5 "not aware of."

1. *Meetings of the Clinic's Board:* Meetings of the clinic's board are held in the boardroom the fourth Wednesday of each month beginning at 7:30 a.m. (Circle your response.)

Effectiveness of Communications Regarding Meetings:

1	2	3	4	5
Very Satisfied	Satisfied	Neutral	Not Satisfied	Not Aware

a. Should the time of this meeting be changed to allow for your attendance at the regular session? _____ yes _____ no. If yes, to what time should it be changed? _____

b. What changes can you suggest to improve communication about activities of the board?

_____

_____

_____

2. *Meetings of the Clinic's Physician-Membership:* Meetings of the clinic's physician membership have been scheduled on a quarterly basis.

1	2	3	4	5
Very Satisfied	Satisfied	Neutral	Not Satisfied	Not Aware

a. Should the time of this meeting be changed to make it more convenient for your attendance? _____ yes _____ no. If yes, to what time should it be changed? _____

b. What changes can you recommend to improve the meetings of our physician membership?

_____
_____
_____

3. Please indicate your opinion of communication about the clinic's board, the council of departmental heads, and other pertinent information as gathered through your departmental meetings.

1	2	3	4	5
Very Satisfied	Satisfied	Neutral	Not Satisfied	Not Aware

a. Would it be helpful if members of the clinic's board routinely attended your departmental meetings to discuss key issues? _____ yes _____ no.

b. What changes can you recommend to improve your departmental meetings?

_____
_____
_____
_____

The following section refers to various publications distributed throughout the physicians' system:

The Physicians' Clinic Presidents Report is distributed from the president of the clinic to all the clinic's physicians, board members of the hospital, and the foundation, on a monthly basis. It reports on board actions, physicians' clinical activities, and the activities of our members.

Effectiveness Scale (Circle your answer)

1	2	3	4	5
Very Satisfied	Satisfied	Neutral	Not Satisfied	Not Aware

Recommendations to improve:_____

_____

New Physicians' Announcements are distributed as new physicians begin their work at Physicians' Clinic. A current photo of the new staff member is accompanied by a biographical summary.

1	2	3	4	5
Very Satisfied	Satisfied	Neutral	Not Satisfied	Not Aware

Recommendations to improve:_____

The Physicians' Clinic Weekly Update contains weekly news-items and announcements for departmental administration, physicians, and managerial staff throughout the physicians' organizations.

1	2	3	4	5
Very Satisfied	Satisfied	Neutral	Not Satisfied	Not Aware

Recommendations to improve:_____

The Physicians' Clinic Monthly Magazine is published monthly for all staff of Physicians' Clinic, hospital, and foundation.

1	2	3	4	5
Very Satisfied	Satisfied	Neutral	Not Satisfied	Not Aware

Recommendations to improve:_____

The Physicians' Clinic Medical Journal is published four times each year and provides an overview of primary care issues; written by the clinic's physicians for referring physicians.

1	2	3	4	5
Very Satisfied	Satisfied	Neutral	Not Satisfied	Not Aware

Recommendations to improve:_____

The Physicians' Clinic Feature Bulletin in Critical Care is published four times each year and discusses a single topic in trauma, in an article written by the clinics' physicians for referring physicians.

1	2	3	4	5
Very Satisfied	Satisfied	Neutral	Not Satisfied	Not Aware

Recommendations to improve:_____

Please complete the following if you are head of a medical department:

Department Head Council Meetings: Department head council meetings are held in the board room on a monthly basis. Beginning in August 1994, the meetings will be held the second Thursday of each month beginning at 7:00 a.m., in advance of the board meeting, to allow board members to receive current department head information.

1	2	3	4	5
Very Satisfied	Satisfied	Neutral	Not Satisfied	Not Aware

Recommendations to improve:_____

_____

a. Should the time of this meeting be changed? _____ yes _____ no. If yes, to what time should it be changed? _____

b. Would it be helpful to have a few members of the board of physicians' clinic routinely attend your departmental staff meetings? _____ yes _____ no.

c. What changes can you suggest to improve the communication of activities of the council of department heads?

_____

_____

All Physicians:

II. What other suggestions should be considered for improving communications? For example, would it be helpful to distribute a specific newsletter with the latest information on activities in mergers and collaborations?

_____

_____

Your help in addressing this most important matter is sincerely appreciated. PLEASE COMPLETE AND RETURN by _____ (day) and _____ (month).

_____   _____
Name   Department

(If more space is needed to respond to any of the questions, please feel free to write on the back of this survey and/or add additional sheets.)

Example 2: Results of Survey on Communications

Board Meetings (43 respondents)

Very Satisfied	Satisfied	Neutral	Not Satisfied	Not Aware	No Rating
5 (12%)	14 (33%)	14 (33%)	9 (21%)	1 (2%)	8 (19%)

Comments

1. Minutes or a summary of actions should be distributed.

2. Meetings do not represent membership. It is only a forum for dissemination of directives created by administrators.

3. Assign a board member to each department and schedule short, informal meetings to exchange information.

4. Make sure the membership knows they may attend regular session.

5. Board members should understand their role and responsibility in helping to communicate to the rest of the membership.

Meetings of the Physician Membership (46 respondents)

Very Satisfied	Satisfied	Neutral	Not Satisfied	Not Aware	No Rating
2 (4%)	15 (33%)	15 (33%)	10 (22%)	4 (8%)	5 (12%)

Comments

1. An improved agenda (perhaps set by the membership) might improve the attendance. The department chairs need to take a more active role in encouraging attendance and to pass along communication within the department.

2. A requirement for staff privileges should be that one must attend at least one out of three or four meetings.

3. Meeting is informational only and involves no democratic actions. Perhaps the election of board members could be done at this meeting or at least the candidates could present their viewpoints.

4. Meetings should be held more frequently to enable administration to relate all significant happenings in a timely manner.

5. Two identical meetings should be held on the same day at different times to give all staff the opportunity to attend.

6. Make the membership aware of the existence of these meetings.

Communication About Board, Department Head, and Other Pertinent Information Through Department Staff Meetings (40 respondents)

Very Satisfied	Satisfied	Neutral	Not Satisfied	Not Aware	No Rating
5 (13%)	16 (40%)	5 (13%)	14 (35%)	11 (28%)	

Comments

1. It would be helpful if the physician/president or a board member would occasionally attend the department staff meetings. Provide overheads of key issues to each department chair.

2. Meetings are superficial and provide filtered information.

3. Include more clinic-wide information, not only specific department issues.

4. Information should be two directional and representative of membership.

Publications

It appears that if a respondent was satisfied with one publication he or she was satisfied with all of the publications. If dissatisfied, the same was true.

Physicians' Clinic Presidents Report (51 respondents)

Very Satisfied	Satisfied	Neutral	Not Satisfied	Not Aware	No Rating
12 (24%)	29 (57%)	5 (10%)	4 (8%)		1 (2%)

Comments

1. I like this report.

2. Report is not timely nor is pertinent information presented.

3. Too much after the fact, but does give good information.

4. Repeats information already generally available.

5. Very superficial. Report should provide more detail regarding board actions, and committee assignments, and allow for feedback.

New Physician Announcements (51 respondents)

Very Satisfied	Satisfied	Neutral	Not Satisfied	Not Aware	No Rating
21 (41%)	19 (37%)	5 (10%)	6 (12%)		

Comments

1. Very good. Helpful. Excellent.
2. Should contain more professional information and less personal.
3. These efforts are necessary and good and important on a department level.
4. Too expensive.
5. Recycle the outside packaging.
6. Announcement is immediately thrown away upon opening, sometimes before even opening.
7. Publish new physician's name in one of the other newsletters.

Physicians' Clinic Weekly Update (50 respondents)

Very Satisfied	Satisfied	Neutral	Not Satisfied	Not Aware	No Rating
14 (28%)	26 (52%)	8 (16%)	2 (4%)	1	

Comments

1. Very good.
2. Duplication of Physicians Clinic report and bulletin.
3. More in-depth information about important topics could be included.

Physicians' Clinic Monthly Magazine (50 respondents)

Very Satisfied	Satisfied	Neutral	Not Satisfied	Not Aware	No Rating
13 (26%)	27 (54%)	9 (18%)	1 (2%)	1 (2%)	

Comments

1. This publication should be distributed more frequently.
2. This is an unnecessary publication. It is a duplication of the Physicians' Clinic President's report and the update.
3. The articles are too much like pep talk. Serious statements about current issues would be more useful.
4. This is famous for its vague generality and public relations approach.

Physicians' Clinic Medical Journal (51 respondents)

Very Satisfied	Satisfied	Neutral	Not Satisfied	Not Aware	No Rating
6 (12%)	25 (49%)	12 (24%)	1 (2%)		7 (14%)

Comments

1. Publication is for outside physicians.

2. I am not sure how the topics are picked or what the purpose is.

3. Boring.

4. Serves its stated purpose.

5. More widespread topic coverage should be included, e.g., pediatrics, medicine, obstetrics, family medicine in every issue.

Physicians' Clinic Feature Bulletin on Critical Care (51 respondents)

Very Satisfied	Satisfied	Neutral	Not Satisfied	Not Aware	No Rating
8 (16%)	26 (51%)	13 (25%)	1 (2%)		3 (6%)

Comments

1. Very good.

2. Boring.

3. Serves its stated purpose.

4. Same as the monthly medical journal.

Department Head Council Meetings (14 respondents)

Very Satisfied	Satisfied	Neutral	Not Satisfied	Not Aware	No Rating
2 (14%)	3 (21%)	7 (50%)	2 (14%)	37	

Comments

1. Send minutes to the membership.

2. Develop a newsletter to the membership from the council detailing issues discussed.

3. The department head council should have a closer relationship to the Physicians' Clinic board.

4. It might help to explain department chairs' role versus board member role in decision making and how these decisions are communicated.

All physicians: What other suggestions should be considered for improving communications?

Comments

1. Information could be included in an existing newsletter.

2. Change is difficult. I think the physicians' clinic administrators are doing a good job.

3. A specific newsletter should be developed with the latest information on merger and collaboration activity.

4. Solicit information from the membership on all and any board, department head council, leadership council, etc. issues.

5. Use e-mail to distribute information quickly.

6. Quarterly (periodic) meetings with all clinic physicians should address important issues.

7. Consolidate duplicated newsletters wherever possible.

8. I think there needs to be more interaction between staff of various departments. Perhaps social gatherings of groups could be arranged to encourage face-to-face meeting and talking.

Example 3: Summary of Results and Recommendations from a Survey on Communications Completed Within a Medical Group

TO: The Clinic's Board of Directors

FROM: President/Executive Chief Officer, Physicians' Clinic

DATE: October 20, 1995

RE: Results of the Communications Survey Recently Conducted
            with the Clinic's Physician Membership

Communication in Physicians' Clinic takes many forms and ranges from informal word of mouth to formal, comprising mainly organizational meetings and the production and dissemination of newsletters. The enclosed report details results illustrating current perceptions by our membership. Two hundred fifty surveys were distributed, fifty-one completed and returned (20 percent). A summary of results follows.

Meetings

Clinic Board Meetings (43 respondents)

Forty-five percent are satisfied and 21 percent are not satisfied with the effectiveness of current board meetings. Many comments were received requesting a copy of the minutes and for board members to attend department staff meetings, to review events occurring at the board level and to answer questions.

Recommendations

1. Send minutes of previous board meeting out with agenda of upcoming meeting, which all members currently receive.

2. Divide the number of departments (eighteen) by physician members of the board (nine) and attend department staff meetings on a regular basis (i.e., each to attend staff meetings in two departments).

Physician Membership Meetings (46 respondents)

Thirty-seven percent are satisfied, 22 percent are not satisfied with the effectiveness of these meetings. Many comments requested more information and more frequent meetings.

Recommendations

1. First implement recommendations outlined above (clinic board).

   Most comments made by the membership would be addressed if they attend department meetings and read their mail (i.e., board minutes).

2. If #1 does not improve satisfaction, schedule monthly membership meetings from 12:00 to 1:00 p.m. and provide lunch.

Results of the Survey of Communications Recently Conducted with Clinic Membership

Communications Through Department Meeting (40 respondents)

Fifty-three percent are satisfied and 35 percent are not satisfied. Many comments requested board members and/or president to attend department staff meetings. Minutes and current issues could be discussed.

Recommendations

1. The noted issues should be resolved by having clinic board members regularly attend department staff meetings as outlined in the first recommendation (clinic board meeting).

Department Head Council Meetings (14 respondents/department heads)

Thirty-five percent are satisfied, 14 percent are not satisfied, with 50 percent neutral. Many comments recommended that minutes be distributed to the membership and that there should be a closer tie to the clinic board (currently an election is in process that will lead to a department head council member being elected to the board).

Recommendation

Send minutes of previous department head council meeting to the membership.

Publications

See attached specific ratings and comments for each publication. The data illustrate that if a respondent was satisfied with one publication, s/he was basically satisfied with all.

In summary, all of the publications received a majority of ratings at satisfactory or above. Currently, our public relations staff is reviewing all written communications throughout the physicians' organization for appropriateness and redundancy, with the goal of "communications enhancement." Our results will be used as a reference to help enhance system-wide communications. It is the intention of the public relations department to include board members and department heads in future communications planning as well as to provide department heads with direct information from public relations for dissemination to staff.

The last survey invited an open-ended response concerning other suggestions that should be considered for improving communications. Many comments were received about wanting to be kept informed about collaborative efforts among the clinic's physicians, and merger activities in general. For the specific purpose of keeping all interested parties updated on this activity, a newsletter has been developed for monthly distribution.

Comments and questions should always be welcome. The newsletters' acceptability and effectiveness in appropriately communicating with physician members and associated departmental staff will be monitored on a consistent basis. Enhancements will be made as needed.

RELATIONSHIPS BETWEEN PHYSICIANS AND PHYSICIAN EXECUTIVES

Physicians managed by physician executives are in fundamentally different lines of business.[5] Physicians in administrative roles are seen by their fellow physicians as administrators regardless of the amount of time physician executives care for patients. Many physician administrators believe that it is important for them to continue caring for patients for purposes of maintaining clinical capabilities and to preserve the respect of those physicians who spend a majority of time providing care.

However, once a physician begins to manage other physicians, perceptions of each other change. The various perceptual beliefs held by physician executives and physicians are important to understand, as described by Musfeldt:[5]

TABLE 5.2. Various Perceptual Beliefs Held by Physician Executives and Physicians

Issues	Perceived Differences	
	Physician Executive	Physician
Point of View	Organization wide	Patient focused
Meetings	Essential and frequent	Waste of time
Decisions	Make for good of organization	Made for good of patient and practice
Profits	Value institutional success	Value personal success
Finance	Understand and support bottom line	Want to see patients regardless of bottom line
Lawsuits	Seeks protection through maximum documentation	Documents only essential patient data (dreads depositions)
Joint commission	Supports reviews, reports, and accreditation	Couldn't care less
Ownership	Calls patient care continuum "ours"	Calls patient care continuum "mine"
Customers	Consider board chair a main customer	Considers self a main customer

Adapted from Musfeldt, CD, Ten Differences Between "Docs" and "Hocs," *Group Practice Journal,* 41-42, January/February, 1996.

APPLICATIONS

Targeted Goal

Has trust been developed between physicians and nonphysician administrative staff? How is trust measured?

Objectives

Have physicians and nonphysician staff been better informed about sensitive and strategically important clinical and organizational activities? How has an understanding of the clinical and organizational issues and concerns been measured? Is the communication network throughout the practice effective? How has effectiveness been measured? How much time and funding was spent on physicians' training for leadership, in the past year?

Content

Was the training for physicians' leadership received by medical staff evaluated to determine effectiveness? Did physicians indicate areas and topics where additional training would be helpful?

Evaluation

Can evidence be documented that shows whether high-quality services were delivered to more patients at lower costs with optimal outcomes? What additional targets should be used to show progress associated with advancements in teamwork among physicians and nonphysician administrators?

Continuous Quality Improvement

How can refinements be built into the mutual relationships of physicians to nonphysician administrators to ensure effective results of this partnering? Can effectiveness of the relationship be enhanced each year? If yes, what measurement is used to reflect the results?

Chapter 6

Physicians, Productivity, and Compensation

POINTS FOR FOCUS

As reimbursement for medical services continues to decline, physicians must understand the changes created and their impact on the management of a medical practice.

Targeted Goal

To understand the physician's role and responsibility in the production of revenue and to create ways to optimize their participation in the system for delivery of care by aligning incentives in the direction most advantageous to the practice.

Objectives

1. Assess the practice to determine changing financial needs on the basis of type and style of practice (i.e., what is the current payer mix of patients/member population, what special needs do these patients/members have, what are the overhead expenses, and so on).
2. Focus the recruitment and retention of physicians on the most effective producers.
3. Compensation must be based on fair and easy-to-understand standards for productivity. Having accurate and efficient informational systems available to provide physicians with routine data on patient care (outcomes), utilization, and related financial indicators is a basic requirement for optimizing management of the practice.

Content

Physician-directed care and supervision is the switch that turns on reimbursement. Routine analysis of standards for payment used by payer sources is required to determine how the flow of revenue is related to patterns in the practice. At least annually (usually at the time the budget is developed), next year's revenue and expenses are projected, so that these can be used as assumptions in making the budget and so that one can know when to shift the ways care must be considered.

Evaluation

Physician compensation can be compared to production and subsequently benchmarked with other physicians. Annually, similar types of physician groups from around the United States exchange information to determine what productivity-compensation ratios exist by specialty and group size.

Continuous Quality Improvement

Procedures for monitoring and enhancing revenue necessitate monthly attention, as shifts in revenue become more dramatic, with potentially devastating effects.

WHAT WILL IT TAKE TO BE SUCCESSFUL AS AN ORGANIZATION PROVIDING MEDICAL SERVICES?

- Delivery of medical services will be customer focused.
- There will be a fully linked system of medical excellence that outperforms its competition in quality, cost, accessibility, and service.
- The organization will surpass the performance of competitors on a per member, per month basis for the cost of medical services, while being able to pay physicians at premium levels for value received.
- The patient care system will serve the community.
- The system for distributing primary care will include locations convenient to the patient/members.
- The practice will include linkage with (or ownership of) capabilities for medical research with a focus on performing activities that will lead to improvements in quality and efficiency of care delivered and the creation of preventive avenues to enhance health.

KEY ASSUMPTIONS

- Reforms of health care will continue informally and/or formally.
- The competition will send their patients for care primarily to sites they own or control.
- Cost pressures on health care will increase significantly.
- The competitors will be both vertically integrated systems *and* networks of deeply discounting independent providers.
- Managed care and managed competition in the marketplace will spread. For example, in the Twin Cities marketplace in 1995, more

than 85 percent of consumers were in a managed care plan, and by 1998 that grew to 90 percent or more.

PRODUCTIVITY AND COMPENSATION BEGIN BETWEEN THE PHYSICIAN AND THE PATIENT

The physician-patient encounter has traditionally established the basis of a billable service. Depending upon the patient's payment source, some amount would be required to pay the physician. On the basis of the number and type of patients served and the type of payments received, the physician could generally regulate how busy he/she wanted to be and the amount of income needed to have a specific lifestyle. This type of practice is generally referred to as a fee-for-service approach. Physicians in many parts of the United States continue to practice some form of fee-for-service medicine, although the number of such practices is dwindling in light of sum-certain or capitated payment systems.

The intent of sum-certain or capitated payments is to increase the physician's incentive to keep the patient/member healthy at a preset, agreed-upon cost. The physician is paid the same amount per member per month (PMPM) on the basis of the number of patients (members of the plan) for which he/she has been asked to provide care. If the physician spends less than what is received in the capitated payment, the medical practice benefits (only if an appropriately capitated amount was agreed to). If the physician spends more than the capitation allows, the difference (loss) comes out of the bottom line for that physician or medical practice.

Evolving Paradox: Physicians' Compensation Based on the Amount of Service Billed, as Opposed to Sum-Certain Amounts That Do Not Regard the Amount of Service Billed.

Although the physician-patient encounter remains the focus of medical practice, the basis upon which compensation is determined changes from expenditures for services to maintaining health through education. The method of practice changes in the direction in which incentives are applied.

EVALUATION OF METHODS OF COMPENSATION

The three systems illustrated in the following section show examples of traditional, sum-certain, and transitional models for future compensation of physicians. Depending on the location, most medical practices will participate in more than one of the forms modeled.

Traditional Approach to Productivity
(Typically of Fee-for-Service Origin)

A physician's activity is compared to that of others by specialty, length of time in practice, and age, along lines of counted gross billings, outpatient visits, and hospital discharges. Charges for laboratory services and X rays are typically left out of comparisons and are pooled for overall distribution when individual comparisons have been completed.[1] Salaries are computed as follows:

Example 1: Physicians' Clinic, Salary Administration
Survey of Salary/Production

Period for Comparison _____

Clinic Location _____

Date of Hire _____

Physician _____   Age _____

I. **Survey of Salary Range*** _____   80th percentile _____

    (Includes incentive dollars if given)

Category _____

Comparative Statistics

	Gross Billings**	Outpatient Visits	Hospital Discharges

II. **Survey of Production** among all physicians in same specialty (Full Time Equivalent)

	Gross Billings**	Outpatient Visits	Hospital Discharges
1) A. Range	_____	_____	_____
2) B. Median	_____	_____	_____
3) C. Average	_____	_____	_____
4) D. 80th Percentile	_____		

III. **Intraorganizational Comparisons Across Similar Clinics**

5) A. Range	_____	_____	_____
6) B. Median	_____	_____	_____
7) C. Average	_____	_____	_____

---

*From surveys of outside practices with similar specialties and other related surveys that may be appropriate.

**Gross billings exclude charges for lab and X ray.

IV. **Personal Statistics**, Dr. _____

8) 1981 _____ _____ _____
9) 1992 _____ _____ _____
10) 1993 _____ _____ _____
Adjustments _____ _____ _____

_____ _____ _____

11) Overhead for Physicians' Clinic _____
12) Current Year Multiplied by Fee-Increase _____
13) Billings Reduced by Overhead for Physicians' Clinic _____

Formula:

14) Salary _____ Fringes _____ 20 percent***_____ Total _____
15) Formula as percentage of Production _____
16) Salary plus fringes as a percentage of net billings _____

The Sum-Certain/Quasi-Capitated System (Based on Premium Dollars)

Medical groups using a managed care basis and staff model typically employ primary care providers and the most frequently needed specialists. Table 6.1 shows physician-to-patient/member FTE ratios using various managed care examples. Other specialists, less frequently used but still essential to the overall success of the staff of physicians, are usually under contract. Often these contracted specialists are those who would be most expensive to maintain as members of the staff: neurosurgeons, neonatologists, cardiovascular surgeons. In a contracted situation, the health plan can control expenses through adherence to standards for performance which, if not met, are easier to correct than if the specialist were an employee.

Each participating physician is hired and has performance measured against services provided to an expected number of members of the health plan. Various national and regional benchmarks are used to determine the parameters for "right-sizing" this number. Premium dollars paid by the patient/members, their employers, and/or other payers are used to fund salaries for physicians on the staff and for the services of contracted physicians. Monthly allocations are budgeted by the health plan for each provider and service site. Targets for utilization and performance are established and monitored monthly (more frequently, if needed). Some guidelines for right-sizing to determine appropriate levels for numbers of physicians on the staff and targets for utilization of contracted services follow (see Table 6.1).[2]

***Unassigned overhead.

TABLE 6.1. Physician-to-Patient Ratios—1:X

	Not Aggressively Planned Metro	Managed Rural	Aggressively Managed	Medical Association	A Medical Group Model	50,000 Member Aggressively Managed HMO	Medical Economics	Groups 1990 Target Ratios	U.S. Ratios	Target Managed Care
First Contact Specialties										
General/Family Practice	2,970	3,990	1,500	2,000		2,700	2,000	4,000	4,704	2,500-3,500
General Internal Medicine	5,668	7,745	incl. above			incl. above	5,000	3,500	6,256	3,500-5,000
Obstetrics/Gynecology	9,028	10,373	41,062	9,202	9,000	7,000	11,000	10,150	12,011	8-10,000
Pediatrics	7,758	10,269	8,333			6,000	10,000	8,100	14,082	8-12,000
General Surgery	7,337	8,915	34,184	18,987	9,000	15,000	10,000	10,350	10,332	15-20,000
Consulting Specialties										
Allergy/Immunology	105,000	147,600	193,333		120,000	50,000	25,000	118,800	152,120	125,000
Cardiology	26,208	36,534	45,879	35,156	30,000	35,000	25,000	31,420	36,662	30-35,000
Dermatology	47,161	65,561	110,357		30,000	35,000	40,000	35,040	53,290	50-100,000
Emergency Medicine	33,862	46,916	144,182	20,361						
Endocrinology	135,500	190,500	103,007		120,000	100,000				>100,000
Gastrointestinal	60,103	83,222	191,692		42,000	50,000	50,000	37,460	94,850	40-50,000
Hematology/Oncology	44,623	62,125	112,091		30,000	50,000				>100,000
Infectious Disease	167,824	227,875	NA		120,000					
Neonatology										
Nephrology	110,435	154,571	88,550		84,000					>200,000

Specialty										
Neurology	46,262	63,667	67,706		42,000	55,000	60,000	44,275	78,043	>50,000
Neurosurgery	76,824	104,313	NA	150,000	84,000					
Ophthalmology	20,600	28,532	106,114		21,000	25,000	20,000	20,990	21,968	20,000
Orthopedic Surgery	18,322	25,464	20,382	20,179	15,000	20,000	25,000	16,130	21,898	15-20,000
Otolaryngology	42,000	58,381	112,947		30,000	35,000	25,000	30,440	43,297	30,000
Pathology										
Physical Med/Rehab										
Plastic Surgery	85,000	118,087	599,500		84,000		50,000	90,190	96,644	
Psychiatry	10,008	13,929	15,550	26,315	9,000	20,000	10,000	6,325	14,661	6-10,000
Pulmonary Medicine	68,875	91,167	143,611		60,000	100,000	100,000	67,640	133,274	>100,000
Rheumatology	146,850	208,500	143,238		120,000	100,000				>100,000
Thoracic Surgery	135,000	197,143	345,000	118,421	120,000		100,000	118,000	139,182	120,000
Urology	34,738	48,683	126,098	39,130	30,000	40,000	30,000	31,625	37,085	>30,000
Anesthesia			11,200	20,000		17,000				
Radiology			13,000	16,483	20,000	20,000	15,000	15,000	21,203	15-20,000
Other Specialties				5,000						

Source: Adapted from multiple national managed care benchmarks.

Future Compensation for Physicians

The Omnibus Budget Reconciliation Act of 1989 called for the establishment of a new Medicare fee schedule to be phased in from 1992 through 1996 to replace the current "customary, prevailing, and reasonable" system for payment. The health care industry, in general, tends to follow the direction of Medicare. Various models for compensation are evolving through trial and error on the basis of relative value units (RVUs) and the methodology for calculating the resource-based relative value scales (RBRVS). These RBRVS came into being under the Omnibus Budget Reconciliation Act and include relative values for the approximately 7,000 current procedural terminology (CPT-4) codes.

The method converts these relative values into dollar amounts by applying a conversion factor. Even though the scales of values were developed as a mechanism for reimbursements, the data are increasingly being used as measures of the productivity of a physician or the financial performance of a medical group. Each procedural code includes a relative weight for the work and expense of the physician, which helps to recognize the magnitude of variance in the use of resources for various procedures. Since RVUs summarize the relative weights of procedures performed by physicians for all patients, regardless of payer, they may be used as a comprehensive basis of evaluation.

The new model for compensation incorporates the aforementioned relative value scales to calculate RVUs for patient care.[3,4,5] In addition, workload resulting from teaching, research, and other activities (including departmental and organizational administration), and from outside contracts, is translated into RVUs. In other words, all recognized effort receives RVU credit based on weighting factors. The table that follows provides a summary of conversion and weight factors established by a physician-based steering committee; these are applied to internal medicine-based patient care, teaching, and research services.[6] The operating principles set forth by the committee, to govern and plan development, include:

- Provide incentives to increase departmental revenues
- Provide opportunity to increase compensation to individual members of the faculty
- Maintain budgetary discipline
- Stress individual accountability within the group
- Reward success in different services (patient care, teaching, and research)
- Maintain collegiality in the group
- Provide for administrative simplicity
- Provide flexibility to adapt to changes in the industry (e.g., managed care)

Example 2: RVU/Conversion Table:
Plan for Compensation in a Department of Internal Medicine

Activity	Production Measurements	Un-weighted RVUs	Weighted Factor	Weighted RVUs
Patient Care*	RVUs	AU1 ×	80% =	A1W
Inpatient	RVUs	AU2 ×	130% =	A2W
Outpatient	RVUs	AU3 ×	20% =	A3W
Extender	RVUs	AU4 ×	150% =	A4W
Outreach	Time/FTE	BU ×	100% =	BW
Teaching				
Funded Research**	Funding Revenue	CU ×	118% =	CW
Unfunded Research	Output (e.g., publications)	DU ×	100% =	DW
Administrative Services	Time/FTE	EU ×	100% =	EW
Outside Services	Revenue/FTE	FU ×	100% =	FW

Sw Subtotal Before Quality Adj.　Sum (Aw: Fw)
x Q (Overall Quality Adjust-　95%-105%
ment)***　Sw x Q
= Total Weighted RVUs

*Determination of weight for patient care:
- Inpatient RVUs weighted at 80% to recognize relative efficiencies in inpatient care (e.g., "captive" population/no cancellations).
- Outpatient RVUs weighted at 140% to recognize lower efficiencies in ambulatory setting (e.g., no shows, issues related to the system).
- Extender RVUs weighted at 20% to recognize ratio of MD time to that of staff nurse-practitioners, physicians' assistants, and the like.
- Outreach RVUs weighted at 150% to recognize lower efficiencies (e.g., travel time) and give incentives for gaining new business in this mode.

**Funded research weighted at 118% to recognize NIH overhead rate.

***E.g., cost effectiveness, excellence in teaching, good citizenship, or the like.

Standard

The standard used to measure productivity is the average RVU figure for departmental faculty. The standard is departmentally derived but may shift to an external benchmark as the plan evolves (and as other departments move to a productivity-based model for compensation).

Withhold

A withhold is a percentage of base salary held back until specific measures of productivity are reviewed and compared to a benchmark or standards. Interim returns on withholds will then be adjusted at the end of each quarter on the basis of the rolling average for the year to date. Final settlements on withheld amounts will occur in January of the following year, after year-end results are computed in the model for compensation.

Bonus/Incentive Awards

A bonus will be paid to physicians who exceed the standard production of RVUs. The amount of bonus paid is contingent on funds available for bonuses. The pool for bonuses is funded from the following sources:

- Departmental profits
- Withheld amounts not returned to below-standard producers (redistribution of withheld amounts)

The bonus will be paid out in a lump sum at the end of the year. The monthly reports on productivity (see next page) will include information on the overall balance in the fund for bonuses and on individual accruals toward bonuses.

Calculations for Return of Withheld Amounts and for Bonuses

If a physician exceeds the mean for production in a department, s/he will receive 100 percent of his/her amount withheld and will accrue dollars toward a bonus. If a physician meets the mean level of productivity, he will receive 100 percent of his/her amount withheld but no bonus. If a physician falls below the mean productivity for a department, s/he will lose that percentage of the amount withheld and will receive no bonus. The following provides an example of the three scenarios, given a pooled fund for the distribution of bonuses at $150,000 and given that approximately 35 percent of faculty members in the department qualify for funds from a bonus pool:

	Exceeds	Breaks Even	Falls Below
Base Salary	$90,000	$90,000	$90,000
Withhold (10%)	($9,000)	($9,000)	($9,000)
New Base	$81,000	$81,000	$81,000
Total RVUs—% of standard	124%	100%	84%
Withhold Returned	$9,000	$9,000	$7,560
Bonus	$9,000	$0	$0
Total Salary	$99,000	$90,000	$88,560

Reports of Individual Productivity and Compensation

At the end of each month, faculty will receive individual reports on production that detail where their performance stands in relation to the departmental mean. Also included in monthly reports on performance will be an estimate of the percentage of the bonus pool the individual would receive if year-end relative performance remains consistent. Starting point for collection of data for RVU production reports will be January 1.

COMPENSATION OF PHYSICIANS IN AN INTEGRATED PHYSICIAN-HOSPITAL ORGANIZATION

How can a physicians' group (Ramsey Clinic) and a hospital (St. Paul-Ramsey Medical Center) thrive on a combined rate of collection of 65 percent (physician = 58 percent, hospital = 67 percent) amidst the chaos of the Minneapolis-St. Paul health care marketplace? At Ramsey, the answer was achieved by consolidating operations to create a physician-hospital organization (PHO) for purposes of eliminating duplicated overhead expenses and combining resources to support the implementation of a jointly developed strategic plan. The study reported below, done on outcomes achieved, analyzed audited data over the course of the PHO's first five years (1987-1993).[7]

Combined net revenue was used as one of the criteria for success upon which the PHO was built, underscoring the assumption of no margin/no mission. Figure 6.1 illustrates the six-year trend (inflation adjusted to 1987 dollars). Figure 6.2 shows trends for revenue and expense in the clinic and medical center. An analysis of those factors responsible for combined net

FIGURE 6.1. St. Paul-Ramsey Medical Center and Ramsey Clinic Combined Revenues and Expenses (Inflation Adjusted to 1987 Dollars, in Millions)

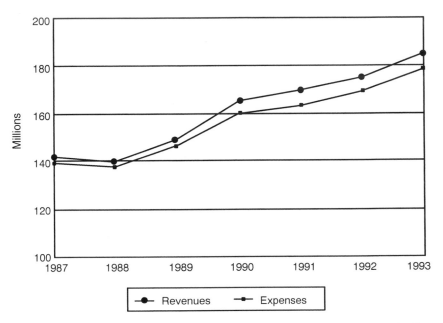

Source: Sommers, Paul A., Luxenberg, M.G., Sommers, E. P. CQI Longitudinally Applied to Integrated Service Outcomes, *Medical Group Management Journal,* 42(2): 50-54, 56-58; March/April 1995. Reprinted with permission from the Medical Group Management Association.

revenue was done by applying inferentially-based predictive methods. The findings were compared to strategies and activities preset in Ramsey's 1994 strategic plan. Adjustments were made to enhance those strategic initiatives most responsible for success while adding new initiatives. A revised 1994 plan was distributed to departments in Ramsey in June, for application where appropriate in mid-1994 and integration into departmental plans for 1995.

The managerial technology applied to guide the process from its outset is referred to as the Inferential Evaluative Model (IEM) and was originally copyrighted by Sommers in 1969.[8] The IEM is quantifiably based upon probability theory aimed at minimizing the likelihood of error related to chance that affects results unexpectedly while maximizing the occurrence of desired outcomes. Inferential statistics are characterized by *statistical*

FIGURE 6.2. Trends in Revenue and Expense at the St. Paul-Ramsey Medical Center and the Ramsey Clinic

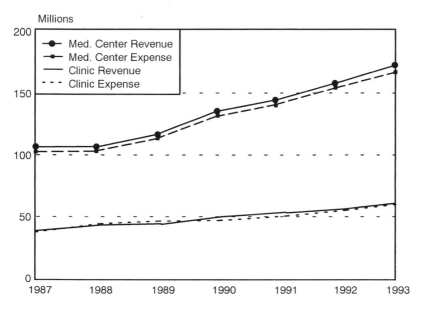

Source: Sommers, Paul A. Managing Medical Service Outcomes by Predicting and Achieving Success: An Inferential Approach, *American Medical Group Association,* 42(3): 24,26-28,30; May/June 1995. Reprinted with permission from the American Medical Group Association.

significance, which illustrates by level of probability (p-level) the degree to which chance is responsible for the results.[9] Only results with a p-level of 0.05 or less were considered to be statistically significant enough to influence additional attention and consideration at the time of resource allocation (for personnel, operating, and/or capital budgets). The IEM has helped define which factors contribute the most toward the success of the PHO annually and on a continuing basis.

Predicting Combined Net Revenues for the Medical Center and Clinic

The top five predictors of combined net revenue were compared and contrasted for 1991, 1992, and 1993 and are outlined in Table 6.2. R^2 is the amount of variance in the independent variable (combined net revenue) that can be explained by the dependent variables (year, inpatient days, referrals, outpatient clinic visits, physician salary growth as a measure of total operating expense).[10]

Interpretations

"Year" as a key factor demonstrates that the relationship between net revenues for the medical center and the clinic has grown stronger and become more predictable over the course of the six-year study. Factors found to be most predictive of combined net revenues were: increasing numbers of outpatient clinical visits and inpatient hospital days, growth in physicians' salaries as an increasing percentage of the clinic's total budget for operating expenses, and increasing numbers of admissions of patients referred by physicians in the area. Although rank ordering of these key predictors has changed slightly over the past three years, the same factors have consistently remained the top predictors of combined net revenue.

TABLE 6.2. Combined Predictors of Net Revenue (Rank Ordered from 1 to 5)

1991			1992			1993		
Predictors	**p-level**	**R^2**	**Predictors**	**p-level**	**R^2**	**Predictors**	**p-level**	**R^2**
#1 Year	.00	94%	#1 Year	.00	95%	#1 Year	.00	98%
#2 Outpatient Visits	.01	92%	#2 Inpatient Days	.00	88%	#2 Inpatient Days	.00	92%
#3 Physician Salary as % of Expense Budget	.02	92%	#3 Outpatient Visits	.01	86%	#3 Outpatient Visits	.00	86%
#4 Inpatient Days	.02	81%	#4 Inpatient Referrals	.00	85%	#4 Physician Salary as % of Expense Budget	.00	79%
#5 Inpatient Referrals	.02	79%	#5 Physician Salary as % of Expense Budget	.00	83%	#5 Inpatient Referrals	.00	79%

Implementation

How has knowledge of the top predictors been incorporated into the Ramsey system? An essential aspect of the Ramsey approach has been the interpretation and systematic application of both qualitative and quantitative information in a practical, meaningful manner. Results from these analyses have been integrated into the annually revised joint strategic plan, the budgets, and the goals and objectives for each organization. Specific implications for success focus on five main areas, of which three pertain to the medical center, one to the clinic, and one toward the combined PHO. The main component identified among factors for the physicians' group that contributes most toward combined net revenue is the increase of physicians' salary as a percentage of the budget for expenses (see Figure 6.3).

Perhaps the most controversial of these factors for success is the increase in compensation to physicians as a percentage of the total budget for operational expenses for the physicians' group. In this day of forecasting decreases in physician compensation due to shrinking reimbursements and subsequent recommendations to move payment systems toward capitation, the outcomes of this study support increasing compensation to the physicians. This is not really surprising, since the empowering of physicians has been and will remain the essential key to the delivery of effective, high-quality medical care. Physicians need to be paid for what they do.

The challenge for managers is to unburden their physician manpower while strategically creating positive, proactive roles of mutual benefit to both the physician and the organization. In his book *Strong Medicine,* George Halvorson, president and CEO of HealthPartners, addresses the need to change the incentives that have been created for both insurers and providers of care.[11] Halvorson indicates that "if we change the incentives and apply them equally to insurers and care givers, the system will restructure itself very quickly in the direction that the incentives point."

Turnover among physicians serving Ramsey Clinic (see Figure 6.4) averaged 13.5 percent per year from 1981 to 1991. When the integrated organization was established in 1987, an understanding was reached between the hospital and the clinic that the hospital would use its resources to build essential facilities and purchase necessary equipment including MRIs, CTs, lasers, and the like. The clinic agreed to focus its resources on competitive compensation for physicians, in the belief that recruitment and retention of productive physicians would contribute to instituting the programs and services called for by the clinic. Figure 6.5 shows a decrease in administrative overhead as a percentage of revenue growth. Consolidation

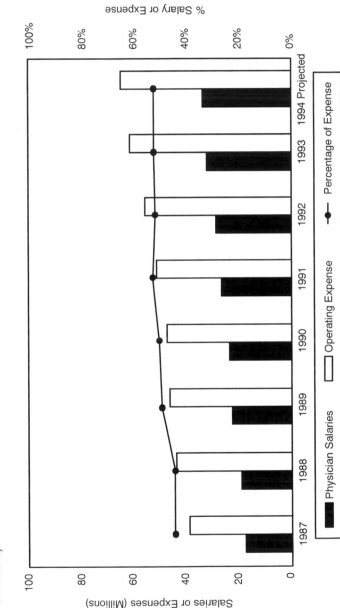

FIGURE 6.3. Growth of Physicians' Salaries as a Measure of Total Operating Expenses (Adjusted to 1987 Dollars, in Millions)

Source: Sommers, Paul A., Luxenberg, M.G., Sommers, E.P. CQI Longitudinally Applied to Integrated Service Outcomes, *Medical Group Management Journal*, 42(2): 50-54,56-58; March/April 1995. Reprinted with permission from the Medical Group Management Association.

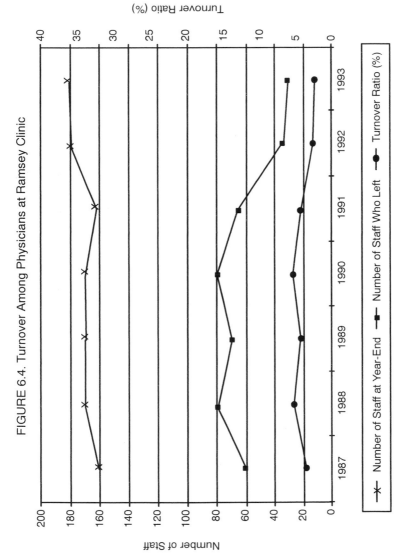

FIGURE 6.4. Turnover Among Physicians at Ramsey Clinic

✻ Number of Staff at Year-End　■ Number of Staff Who Left　● Turnover Ratio (%)

Source: Sommers, Paul A., Luxenberg, M.G., Sommers, E.P. CQI Longitudinally Applied to Integrated Service Outcomes, *Medical Group Management Journal*, 42(2): 50-54,56-58; March/April 1995. Reprinted with permission from the Medical Group Management Association.

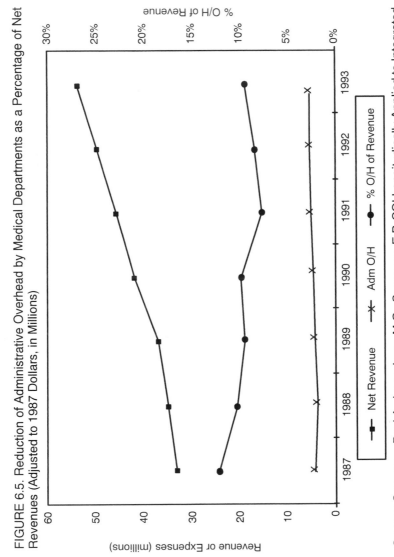

FIGURE 6.5. Reduction of Administrative Overhead by Medical Departments as a Percentage of Net Revenues (Adjusted to 1987 Dollars, in Millions)

Source: Sommers, Paul A., Luxenberg, M.G., Sommers, E.P. CQI Longitudinally Applied to Integrated Service Outcomes, *Medical Group Management Journal*, 42(2): 50-54,56-58; March/April 1995. Reprinted with permission from the Medical Group Management Association.

of duplicative administrative services contributed to favorable net revenue growth along with physician incentives for productive service. These targets for success were instituted in the strategic plan which is addressed in Chapter 9. The reader is referred to Chapter 12 for a more detailed description of inferential applications.

APPLICATIONS

Targeted Goal

How has your practice been affected by shifting revenues? What precautions are being taken to protect a stable base for net revenues? Are adequate incentives included in the system for compensation, to facilitate appropriate changes in practice?

Objectives

1. How is the practice adapting to lower reimbursements for an increasing amount of expected service? Can the payer mix be balanced by reducing operating expenses?
2. Are excellent physicians being recruited and retained? Can costs for insurance against liabilities of malpractice be lowered because of excellence in the practice?
3. Do the physicians know how to increase their compensation as the practice receives more capitated patients?

Content

What benchmarks were used to determine whether reimbursement of physicians for directed care and supervision was being optimized? Can you identify three service codes where reimbursement fluctuated the most? What did you do to offset their negative financial impact?

Evaluation

Does the practice need to consider downsizing its staff of physicians and/or nonphysicians to meet budgetary goals due to decreasing reimbursement? How many hours of continuing educational training did the staff receive that were related to enhancing coding and billing?

Continuous Quality Improvement

Were the monthly calculations of revenues and expenses on budget? What methods of operational improvement or reengineering were employed to increase efficiency and/or capacity while decreasing overhead expense?

Chapter 7

Organization and Governance

POINTS FOR FOCUS

Physicians are forming and reforming their organizations to protect and optimize market position. The manner in which organizational arrangements are constructed is in large part related to the desired outcomes.

Targeted Goal

To define desired organizational outcomes that will be required to position the practice as the provider of choice for its defined area of service.

Objectives

1. Define current leadership by physicians and potential for leadership through governance.
2. Review the organizational and decision making structure of the practice. Outline perceived strengths and weaknesses of the practice, the board, and committee structures.
3. Complete an analysis of competitors to determine current comparative organizational position. Establish desired structures in the practice with benchmarks for comparison.
4. Determine options for enhancing effectiveness of the practice through organizational and/or structural governance changes.

Content

Design structures for the organization and its governance that are supportive of each other. Outline duties, functions, and supporting services, from the consumer's perspective, with a focus on practice, mission, vision, and desired outcomes reflected in the form of goals and objectives of the practice.

Evaluation

Determine differences between what is desired and actual performance, in structures for the organization and its governance.

Continuous Quality Improvement

Reduce the difference between desired and actual results. On a monthly basis, monitor performance related to desired outcomes. Enhance performance through organizational and structural changes, as needed, to achieve or exceed desired outcomes. Conduct comprehensive evaluation at least annually.

FUNCTIONAL DEVELOPMENT

The business and organization of medical practice has initiated a period of fundamental change. Physicians are consolidating more frequently into group practices, many medical practices are affiliating with hospitals or managerial companies, and physicians in most geographic areas have started a conversion from traditional fee-for-service economics to the very different servicing and financial demands encountered with systems for prepayment. Market forces have been the primary catalyst for these changes, with anticipation of some type of reform of health care playing a subordinate role during the last year. These changes will continue, with or without reform, but their specific directions may be influenced by the final provisions of legislation mandating reforms. A continuing trend toward higher levels of prepaid enrollment, physicians' urgent need for substantial capital to reorganize and expand their practices, and the need for physicians to retain or expand their influence through organizational unity will continue to stimulate consolidation of medical practices and new affiliations with partners providing capital and service.

The supply of physicians continues to grow disproportionately to the rate of growth of the population. Increases are occurring in some subspecialty practices with the largest increases in primary care, and those physicians locate principally in metropolitan areas. Rural areas and frontiers continue to be underserved. Women are becoming an increasing percentage of all physicians, especially in the youngest age groups. Physicians and their families continue to favor urban and suburban areas as their homes.

Increasing numbers of physicians are joining group practices, or are consolidating their individual practices into groups.[1] Growth of groups as a style of practice has been increasing for many years. The size of group practices also increased significantly from 1988 to 1992, with the greatest change in the two largest classifications. The increase in the number of groups with 100 or more physicians is particularly remarkable for a recent three-year period. The average number of physicians in single-specialty groups increased from four to seven between 1965 to 1991. For the same period, the average number of physicians in multispecialty groups increased from twelve to twenty-five.

The pattern of growth in group practices and their size has changed materially during the last several years. Prior to the late 1980s, most groups grew by (1) recruiting physicians directly out of residency programs, (2) merging with other groups, or (3) acquiring small local practices. With relatively few exceptions, these transactions were entirely among physicians. An example of earlier distributions of medical group practice by size can be seen in Table 7.1.

Revolutionary changes in the organization, economics, and service characteristics of medical practice are in progress. These changes are likely to consume more than the remainder of the decade before substantial restructuring of the industry is achieved. Most physicians are uncomfortable with change, while acknowledging its inevitability. The trend in large

TABLE 7.1. Distribution of Medical Group Practices by Size (Number of Physicians)

Size of Group	1988	1991	Percentage of Change
3	4,547	3,666	-19.4
4	3,618	3,545	-2.0
5-6	3,569	3,781	5.9
7-9	1,850	2,022	9.3
10-15	1,266	1,383	9.2
16-25	672	744	10.7
26-49	403	466	15.6
50-75	147	146	-0.7
76-99	51	67	31.4
100+	118	189	60.2
Totals*	16,241	16,009	-1.4

*Totals exclude groups of unknown size.
Source: American Medical Association. *Medical Groups in the U.S.,* 1990 and 1992 Editions. Chicago, IL. Reprinted with permission.

group practices will dominate medical practice within the next ten to fifteen years, as market forces related to health care reform drive physicians into larger, more competitive, and more influential organizations as a matter of economic self-preservation. The BHCAG, composed of the twenty-four largest employers in the Minneapolis-St. Paul area, is an example of such market division reform. Many of these group practices will affiliate with health plans, hospitals, and/or other payers to form integrated health care organizations.

Large group practices will become the cornerstones of regional delivery systems, and a strong demand will continue to emerge for physicians qualified to be senior managers in those systems. These systems will require large amounts of capital and exceptional management. The risk/reward factors will be high. The trend that favored specialty practice in the second half of the twentieth century is rapidly fading. Due to measures aimed at cost containment, incentives are being shaped to encourage primary care practice as the preferred method of delivering service. It is becoming increasingly important to develop teams of physicians and non-physician administrators. Survival is the basic goal, and those groups of physicians who understand the elements of change and combine their knowledge and resource base with administrators can also learn how to thrive.

AGENTS OF CHANGE

You must think about how your competitors are positioning for the purpose of taking your business away. They want your market share and will use various tactics. Battlefield thinking and organization may be helpful. During turbulent times, *The Art of War* by Sun-tzu translated by Sawyer in 1994 offers timely considerations. This historic text emphasizes that winning any battle requires the need for rationality and self-control. It stresses the need to avoid any conflict not based upon thorough analysis, a review of all options, and one's own capabilities. Examples are described below:[2]

- Your competitors will draw your patients to them with the exciting promise of better service. They will dominate your marketplace with excellence.
- Your competitor will develop innovative products and services in your areas of strength. Move quickly to meet needs. Where you are vulnerable, your competitor will emphasize the advantages of their products.
- They will confuse you with constant innovation and superior service. Innovation is the one weapon that cannot be defended against.
- If you appear arrogant, your competitors will be humble. They will find out why you are currently favored by your constituents. Your

competitors will be patient and, with careful questions, will uncover your weaknesses.

- They will wear you out with unrelenting attention to the needs of your constituents.
- When your creativity is dulled, your commitment dampened, your enthusiasm drained, and your financing depleted, competitors will take advantage of your weakness. When that happens, no executive, however wise, can prevent the decline of his career and the loss of business.
- While we know that hastily executed competitive operations can be troublesome, we have never seen successful competitive operations that wasted time. A successful competitive operation need not be complicated. To win, do simple things well . . . and quickly!
- Strategies that waste time and exhaust resources never work.
- Physicians who cannot balance risk with opportunity cannot profit in today's business environment. Speed and innovation are the keys. Only those who are comfortable with the pitfalls and ambiguities of rapid execution can profitably manage new products and services. Only those who appreciate the knowledge gained from quick failure can achieve lasting success.
- Skillful physicians do not hesitate to utilize the resources at their command. They engage the competition immediately and gain precious information from direct contact with constituents. They do not waste time talking to corporate staff who are farther removed from the competitive situation than they are. Being one step ahead of the competition is worth more than anything else to the success of the practice. Gaining that step is the wise physician's greatest desire.
- Skillful physicians build the strongest possible team from the people in a practice. They let the competition show them how to serve better. In this way, they are always increasing their share of constituents. They build the practice through outstanding performance.
- Timely, accurate information is the lifeblood of successful competition. When obtained from outside sources, information is expensive. Expensive information wastes the company's resources.
- The most expensive information is that which is out of date. Resources spent to gather yesterday's data are wasted. Maintaining yesterday's data consumes large portions of available money and human resources.
- The wise physician harvests timely information from constituents and competitors. The accumulated data is analyzed from a product possibility perspective. One new product idea generated from discussion

with a real customer is worth any number of ideas generated by consultants.

- In order to dominate, you and your medical group—from top to bottom—must be passionate about the services you provide and the products you represent.
- To capture the spirits of your employees, you must give them clearly defined and valuable rewards. You should reward the group for gaining customer share, but people should also be able to get rewards based on individual merit.
- When someone provides outstanding service to a customer, reward that person openly. Make that service an example for others to follow by providing sure and meaningful rewards for excellence.
- Treat your employees well and train them thoroughly. The success of the organization is built on the individual success of its members.
- The important thing in competitive operations is quick results, not prolonged activity. The physician who understands how to excite the staff and dominate a marketplace will become the foundation for progress of that medical group.
- The ideal strategy is to make a competitor's products or services obsolete next to your innovation.
- The next best strategy is to create better ways of providing existing products or services.
- The next best strategy is to market yourself more effectively.
- The worst strategy is to attack a competitor's reputation or product directly. This sort of strategy is a matter of desperation. It often results in the ruin of all parties involved.
- To engage in destructive competition is ultimately self-defeating. Your aim is to provide superior service that generates high opinions among your constituents. How can you do this by ruining competitors' reputations and perhaps destroying your own in the process?
- If physicians are unable to control their impatience and seek to destroy their competitors by direct attacks, they will waste at least one-third of their resources without accomplishing much. The impact of such a strategy is disastrous.
- Skillful physicians conquer with knowledge and imagination. They create better products; they uncover unmet needs; they provide greater satisfaction. They outflank their competitors in the constituent's mind, without resorting to head-to-head battles or lengthy campaigns.
- Your aim is to take over a group of constituents intact by appearing as superior in their minds. Thus, your resources will be preserved and your profit will be greater. This is the art of effective competitive strategy.

- The philosophy of competitive strategy is this: If your customer base is already five to ten times larger than your competitors', press the competition hard through aggressive service. Dominate the situation with your presence. Spend your resources on research and innovation.
- If you have twice as many customers, make sure you understand why they are choosing your medical services and why they might choose your competitors'. Talk with your constituents. Talk with your competitors' constituents. Redefine and differentiate yourself. How are you different? How are you superior?
- Five indicators predict who will dominate:

    1. Who knows when to fight and when to retreat will win
    2. Who uses resources appropriate to the challenge at hand will win
    3. Who is enthusiastic and innovative will win
    4. Who uses accurate, timely information to make decisions will win
    5. Who is not burdened by onerous rules or troublesome staff will win

- If you know your constituents, your competitors, and yourself, your strategies will not fail, even if you are challenged a hundred times.
- If you know yourself only, but are ignorant of your constituents or your competitors, you can expect to fail as often as you succeed.
- If you are ignorant of yourself in addition to your constituents and competitors, you will fail.

GOVERNANCE AND MEDICAL GROUPS

The participation of physicians and their leadership in its governance is essential in any organization that bases its business on medical services and health care. Too often, health care organizations that have evolved outside of a medical group structure (e.g., a health plan or multihospital system) are reluctant to seek and support the best leadership and participation by physicians that is possible at the level of organizational governance. The involvement of physicians can be the factor that best differentiates your products and services from those of the competition.

Your organizational governance structure should be only as complex as is needed to conduct the medical business at hand effectively. It should be simple to understand and to explain to existing, new, and future members of your board and to policy makers. It must be comprehensive enough to involve all key participants, policy makers, and constituents. Most important, your organizational and governance structures should be designed to guide your medical organization into the future as a dominant market force and leader. Various designs are available for for-profit and nonprofit organizations. Some common structures widely used today are described in the next sections of this unit. Most groups modify conventional structures as needed to meet specific needs of their group.

Structures for Governance of Your Organization

Various structures for governance can be adapted to meet any organizational need. The following basic examples illustrate leadership by physicians and by nonphysician administrators in medical groups, hospitals, and health plans.

Example 7.1. Physicians' Group (Board Typically Ranges from Five to Fifteen Members)

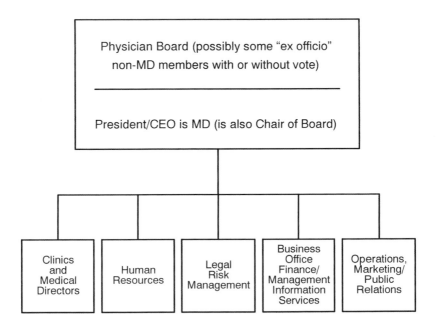

Example 7.2. Hospital Group (Board Typically Ranges from Nine to Twenty-Five Members)

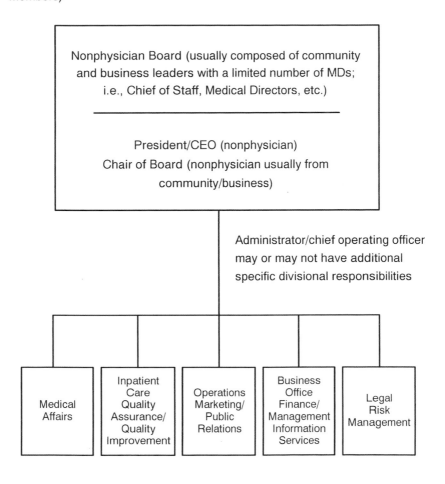

Example 7.3. Health Plan Group (Board Typically Ranges from Thirteen to Thirty-Two Members)

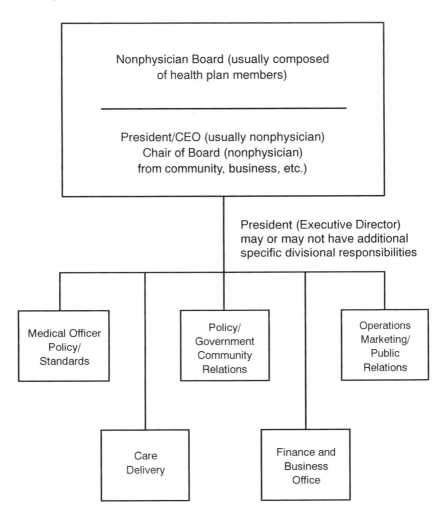

Example 7.4. Organizational Chart for Administrative Functions of a Medical Group

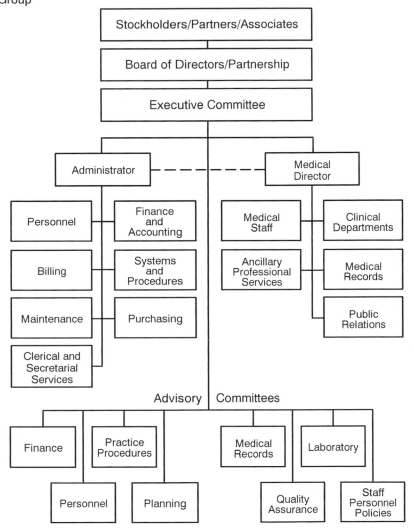

— — — Communications/recommendations

Source: Medical Group Management Association. *Considerations for Medical Group Formation.* Ballanger Publishing Co.: Cambridge, MA, 1976. Reprinted with permission.

Example 7.5a. Medical Matters

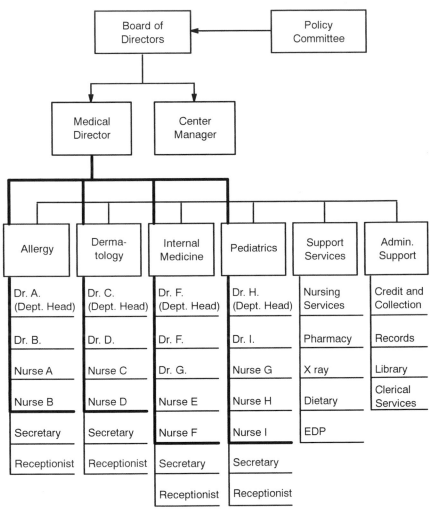

Source: Medical Group Management Association. *Considerations for Medical Group Formation.* Ballanger Publishing Co.: Cambridge, MA, 1976. Reprinted with permission.

Example 7.5b. Detailed Organization Chart for Group Practice

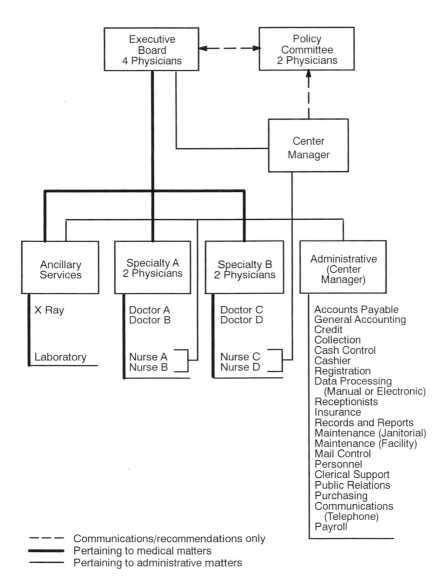

Source: Medical Group Management Association. *Considerations for Medical Group Formation.* Ballanger Publishing Co.: Cambridge, MA, 1976. Reprinted with permission.

Elements of Governance[3]

Size

Assuming that the members of a group are in general accord with respect to the intent of their role and function in a governing body, the number of members governing is secondary to their purpose of serving as policymakers. There must be leadership. Someone may formulate a proposal or motion, someone may suggest amendments, and the body of representatives must express its opinion upon those motions or suggestions, pro or con. The matter of size must be left to the discretion of the board itself or to the outside authority that determines its structure. In appraising an existing board or in making plans for a new one, it is well to begin by considering the problems that a board will face if it becomes too large or too small. At these two extremes lie the dangers of effective operation, and each board must decide what middle pathway it will take.

The ceiling on size of a board is established by the fact that it should be small enough to act as a deliberative body. A board is a collective entity, and if it grows so large that it cannot meet and make decisions, it is no longer effective. The quality of the deliberation is endangered. In a very large board, the personal involvement of each member tends to decrease. People fail to assume the responsibilities that are properly theirs. Meetings become less frequent. The quality of the membership often declines, for the satisfactions of participation are not so great; also, each member is relatively less important to the success of the board. Apathy grows. All these unhappy results, and others like them, are almost certain to result when a board grows so large that its members no longer find it possible to discuss issues easily together and to form a social unit that can effectively achieve its mission.

When a board becomes too large, it often creates an "inner" board. This entity may be given some other name, such as "executive committee," but, out of sheer necessity, it becomes the active functioning center of control. The larger group then becomes, in a sense, a kind of constituency. Sometimes the creation of an inner board is the only practical solution to immediate problems, but it is seldom a wholly desirable permanent resolution of the problem of size, since it almost inevitably gives rise to problems of strain, conflict, overlapping jurisdiction, and misunderstanding. It is far better not to let the original board grow too large.

Some large boards appear, from an outside perspective, to work quite well. Sometimes in such cases they are not true boards, though they have appropriated the name; they are groups of volunteer workers or casual sponsors, or auxiliary boards with limited responsibilities, or fictitious boards that exist to fulfill a public relations function. An individual member, an inner board, or a staff member does the real work.

The minimum size of a board is established by the fact that it should be large enough to carry the necessary responsibilities. If a board is too small, it runs into serious problems. It cannot provide adequate guidance on policy nor assistance to the agency it governs. It cannot include all the groups that should be represented for policymaking or for protection from outside attack. It becomes too closely knit and too clannish a group, or it is paralyzed by factionalism. It has difficulty getting a quorum, and therefore it is unable to operate at all or has to rely on individual decisions communicated by mail or telephone and arrived at with no opportunity for discussion or clarification of issues. Under such circumstances, an increase in size may be worth considering.

Records

Members usually have only a limited amount of time to give to the board. This time should be devoted, so far as possible, to the important rather than the trivial, to policymaking rather than to routine decisions, and to the performance of service for the program rather than to discussion of procedural details. The best way to achieve these goals is to define functions and relationships very clearly—in writing—and to keep careful records of the decisions of the board. Usually a board should have at least three kinds of written records.[3]

The first major record is its *constitution and bylaws*. Sometimes these two are separate, but often they are combined in a single document. The term *constitution* is here used in a generic sense. The actual document may be a special charter granted by a sovereign political body or an enabling law that it has enacted. It may also be a separate statement that provides the basic authorization for the institution's existence. Whatever form it takes, the constitution states the general purpose of the organization or association and defines the basic conditions of existence of the board. The bylaws are rules established to guide the procedure of the board. Generally speaking, private boards have much more control over their constitutions and bylaws than do public boards. In the latter case, there may, indeed, be an extensive body of law that defines and restricts a functional category of institutions.

The second major record of a board is its *statement of policies*. From time to time, boards make decisions about recurrent problems or issues. These decisions should be recorded and made available to all who need to know them. It often happens that a policy is not really clear unless it has been drafted, examined, and revised before being approved. In some situations, a simple list of policies is enough; in others, it is necessary to have a codification of policies, which essentially becomes a body of administrative law. Usually, the executive plays an important role in drafting, recommending, and recording policies.

The third major record of a board is made up of its *minutes*, both those of the whole board and those of the committees and other groups that carry out special responsibilities at the request of the board. Minutes are the indispensable record of the deliberations and decisions of a board. They provide the opportunity for trustees to learn about or be reminded of the board's actions. If minutes are not kept up or if they are sketchy and incomplete, confusion and conflict will almost inevitably result. Much time may be lost in disagreements among board members, the executive, and the staff about the exact nature of decisions taken and by a repetition of earlier discussions, this time with the addition of acrimony. When boards or their members come under attack by aggrieved parties or a militant press, well-kept minutes can prove to be a powerful protection for a board, both in terms of individual issues and as a demonstration of its general carefulness.

How long should a member stay on a board? This question must be of concern to every trustee. People often wonder whether they should continue to serve, sometimes being stimulated to consider the matter because a present term is nearing its end. In any such case, the member should ask him- or herself certain simple but searching questions:

1. Do I continue to be strongly interested in the mission of the institution?
2. Am I providing effective support and assistance for the program?
3. Do I have confidence in the effectiveness of the board, the executive, and the staff?
4. Am I at least as well qualified to serve as anybody who might take my place?
5. Is my continuing membership likely to strengthen the caliber and unity of the board?
6. Is the service I am performing on this board at least as significant and as personally rewarding as any other service to which I might devote the same time?

Such questions cannot produce precise answers but may help shape a decision. If the answer to all or most of them is yes, the member should plan to continue on the board if that option is open. If it is not, he/she has a clear indication that it is time to leave as soon as existing commitments or completed and he/she is able to withdraw with honor.

Length of tenure may also be decided by law, by an outside selecting authority, or by the board itself. Practices vary widely. In many cases, tradition operates; no thought-out principles govern the length of time people stay on a board. "As it was in the beginning, is now, and ever shall be" appears to be the rule. As with other aspects of the structure and operation of a board, however, it is usually wise for anyone interested in improving a board to examine present practice to see whether tradition should be continued or some better course of action might be followed.

Membership on a board is sometimes regarded as a high honor that should be widely shared. For some boards, such as those for young people's associations, part of the mission may be to involve and train as many individuals as possible. Sometimes a suspicion or fear of the board makes rapid turnover essential (Samuel Adams once observed, in another connection, that "where annual elections end, tyranny begins," and the members of some modern associations seem almost to believe him). On some boards, much work must be done, and people will not do it for very long. In some cases, it is hard to get people to serve unless they can be promised short terms. Brief tenure also helps to eliminate deadwood and to provide a constant supply of new, fresh viewpoints. Some of these values seem dubious to those who oppose short tenure for board members. A board cannot be much good, they argue, if it is so distasteful that nobody wants to serve on it for very long. Also, a short period of service does not provide enough time for the individual member to absorb what s/he needs to know, to make a substantial contribution, or to be prepared through experience for later major responsibilities.

These various arguments, taken altogether, suggest that prolonged tenure and brief tenure are both appropriate under certain circumstances, but in general, the weight of the evidence is against either extreme. In length of service, the middle way is usually best. The tenure must be long enough to provide continuity of policy and practice but short enough to secure constant freshness of viewpoint. Most boards have definite terms for their trustees, with provision for overlapping of membership.

No automatic way has been found to ensure this happy balance, but two devices are frequently suggested to help a board achieve a proper practice so far as tenure is concerned. One is the establishment of definite terms of appointment; the other is the limitation of the number of consecutive terms each member may have. These two matters are related but distinct.

Selection of the Board Chairperson

A board needs officers to carry out general coordinative functions and to undertake special assignments. Most boards have at least four such positions: the chairperson, the vice chairperson, the secretary, and the treasurer. The duties of the last three are well understood in general terms and do not need to be described here, though their specific functions should be clearly stated in the bylaws. But the chairperson is so significant as to deserve special attention.

The board's chair is the key element in the life of the board. Each new holder of that office should be chosen with great care, and the board must be constantly aware of the need to develop leaders who can eventually serve in the top post. The chairperson bears the greatest responsibility of any individual connected with the agency other than the executive; she/he must be able to rise to this responsibility and carry it out. The chairperson should be able to evoke cooperation from fellow board members and work harmoniously with the executive. She/he should be an effective representative to the constituency and the outside public. The desirable traits of an ideal board chairperson are, indeed, almost infinite, but rather than make a list of them here, it is better to let them become explicit in terms of the requirements of an effective board as they are expressed throughout this book; for, in a very real sense, the chairperson embodies and is responsible for the board.

A distinction should be made between associations and organizations, as far as board chairs are concerned. The chair of the board of an association is a member of the association, and, if it embodies a professional group, s/he is a member of the profession, e.g., a physician as president of a medical group. In such situations, there is no built-in distinction between the chair (and other board members) and the executive and staff, so far as basic expertise is concerned. In an organization, however, particularly those that provide professionalized services—in such fields as welfare, health, education, or religion—the requirements of the tripartite system suggest that the chair should ordinarily not be a member of the profession concerned. (Many authorities would apply this principle to all board members, not just the chair.) Diversity is typically lacking in board composition. There is strength and value in diversity which can be optimized as minority representatives are selected.

The chairperson of an *organization* must symbolize its community, or at least the constituency and *not the profession*. This distinction is not merely a theoretical one, as countless boards have discovered to their cost and sorrow when a chairperson assumes that the position confers on him/her a technical expertness that s/he does not in fact possess. Ideally, there should always be several people competent to take over the position as chair. One of the major tasks of an occupant of that post is to consider how s/he may develop the potential for leadership of each trustee so that, both immediately and in subsequent years, the board will always have a supply of people able to assume major responsibility. The chairperson should also be concerned with establishing a smooth transition of the office into other hands and with avoiding any of the three main problems of choosing a new chairperson with which boards are some-times confronted. All the foregoing suggests that a chair should not hold the position too long. The board itself must decide on tenure and needs to assure active and vital leadership, which, in most cases, cannot be achieved except by a periodic change of the chairperson.

Committees

Despite general criticism about the value of committees, they continue to flourish. Three different kinds of board committees exist. The most prevalent and the most criticized are *standing committees*, which may be defined as those that remain in existence indefinitely in order to consider a certain category of problems or actions. Among frequently found standing committees are those that have to do with program, personnel policies, nominations, buildings and grounds, investment, and budget. Some categories of boards have types of committees not found elsewhere: museums have collections management committees; school boards have curricular committees; and child welfare agencies have case committees. Usually, standing committees study problems in their assigned areas, provide specialized assistance and advice to the executive and staff and, most importantly, recommend policies for adoption by the board.

Special *ad hoc committees* are appointed to handle specific situations or problems; they go out of existence when those situations have been dealt with. Such a committee might be appointed to screen applicants for the post of executive, to plan a special event, to represent the board in a conference or negotiation, or to carry out any of the myriad other responsibilities that seem to arise in the day-to-day life of any board.

Coordinative committees are those that provide general direction and guidance. The executive committee is the only example of this sort on most boards. It is usually made up of the officers of the board, the chairpersons of the major standing committees, and two or three other members who can make the group more broadly representative than it would otherwise be. The immediate past president and the president elect are sometimes included. The executive committee provides a relatively small group that can meet regularly or as needed to deal with minor matters, make recommendations to the board on major issues, handle emergencies, make future plans, and appraise accomplishment. Other coordinative committees are sometimes appointed when it is thought essential to bring together subgroups concerned with several functions. A finance committee, for example, may be composed of the chairpersons of standing committees on the budget, investment, and development.

The size of the board is directly related to its need for committees. In a small board, it is wise for every member to participate in all activities so that s/he is fully involved in the total work, is well rounded in knowledge of the activities of the board, and is effective in carrying out his/her duties. Larger boards must usually set up more structured ways of achieving their purposes, and this fact almost inevitably leads to the appointment of committees. Whenever a committee is appointed, its functions should be clearly stated in writing. Standing and coordinative committees are usually provided for in the bylaws; if so, their functions should be described there and periodically reviewed. The functions of special committees should be recorded in the minutes at the time such committees are established.

A committee has only those powers delegated to it by the board and should take only those actions that it knows that the board wishes it to take. Ordinarily, the board should formally approve in advance or should ratify afterward all the actions and decisions of a committee. In emergency situations, a committee (especially an executive committee) must sometimes make a decision without consulting the whole board. In such a case, it must ask itself what it thinks the whole board would support, if possible consulting with other members to find their wishes. But emergencies should be treated as emergencies and should not give rise to new practices. Committees are usually appointed by the chair, often after consultation with the board and sometimes with ratification by it. (In some situations, there is even a formal or informal "committee on committees.") The board chair is usually an ex officio member of all committees.

If a board does not have committees, it becomes in effect a committee of the whole and in this way gains the values that good committee work provides. If there are committees, the chairperson will usually find that no other part of the job is so important as their selection and stimulation. Just as an executive must work closely with major staff members, so must the chairperson of the board with the committee chairpersons. To do so provides one of the most creative aspects of the job as s/he challenges, motivates, and blends the members of the board into a cohesive, energetic, and effective whole.

Role of the Board[4]

Governance is not management. Governance also requires recognition that it is the responsibility of members of the board to protect the long-range future of the organization and see to it that it fulfills its obligations to its constituencies, however defined. As a board member, you have to see to it that the organization is well managed, rather than managing it yourself. *The role of the board is to institutionalize the concept, the genius that created the organization.* The president/chief executive officer must make sure that the board understands what its responsibilities are. Then, however often the board meets, the CEO must make certain s/he has enabled the board to fulfill all those responsibilities.

If the board has a responsibility to review performance, then the CEO must give it a report of performance and must let it question, challenge, criticize, or praise that performance. If its responsibility is to approve a long-range strategy, the CEO has to present the plan and then let the board make it its own. Let it question, challenge, criticize, amend, and finally approve the plan. In every single case, if the board is to do its job, the CEO must enable it to do so.

Every board should annually look at its role and its relationship with management, and should discuss with managers the degree to which the board feels it has been enabled to fulfill its responsibilities. If the CEO has not done an adequate job of reviewing performance or allocating capital or whatever, then the board has an opportunity to say, "We wish you would do more of that for us." Also, when such a review occurs, the board tends to look at itself as it would not otherwise and say, "Hey, you gave us the opportunity but we really missed it." A review helps to perfect the methods and systems by which the board operates and fulfills its responsibilities.

The third thing a review triggers is a greatly improved relationship between the governors and the managers, between the board and the CEO. The most important dynamic in any organization is just such a relationship. The reviewing process gets it all on a very discussible basis focusing on "How can we do a better job together?" That is the secret of running a successful institution.

Whose Responsibility Is It to Build a Good Board?

It is clearly a shared responsibility. The chairperson of the board has a major responsibility for building a good board.[5] But any CEO who leaves the building of the board entirely to the board itself will probably find that the board becomes weakened over time. You, the CEO, have to work hard on the composition of your board, and you must help train, educate, and involve it. The only way to go about it is to build a model board, to say "What kind of a board do we really need for this organization?" If you know how you would like your board to function, then you know what kinds of directors or trustees you need to seek out. You should always be building toward the future composition of the board.

*How Are Effectiveness of Governance and Organizational
Structures Measured?*

Continuous improvement must be built into the governance and administrative/organizational structure. On an annual basis an evaluation of performance is required to determine if and/or to what extent the board members (individually and collectively) and administrative support system (individuals, functional areas, and committees) produced results toward accomplishment of the stated mission, vision, values, goals, and objectives in the organization's plan. This means that goals and objectives must be developed for board members both individually and collectively and board/organizational structures by function. If individual and/or structural functions (i.e., administrative areas and/or committees) are not performing as desired, changes must be made to enhance individual/collective board member achievement and administrative/organizational function to be useful. This usually means that board members talk to other board members about needed improvements (e.g., it is typically a responsibility of the board's executive committee to talk to underachieving board members). Functional changes to the organizational structure are usually the responsibility of the physician president and nonphysician administrator. It is their responsibility to deal with underachieving physicians and nonphysician staff. When a recommendation is prepared, it is presented to the board for approval followed by dissemination to staff physicians, management, and support personnel throughout the organization.

*Make Certain That the Board and President/CEO
Have Clearly Delineated Responsibilities*

Members of the board are ultimately responsible for the organization's welfare. The president/CEO provides the guidance and leadership. The role of the board is to institutionalize the concept of the organization and work toward the achievement of its mission.

BOARD MEETINGS THAT ARE EFFECTIVE[6]

- Have, typically, a short, well-focused agenda.
- Address a shorter, deeper list rather than an endless plethora of issues.
- Use board members' time with care; make it count.
- Do not consider meetings optional; attendance at board meetings should be high.

- Have members attend because the meetings are interesting; things are accomplished.
- Have an atmosphere of bigness and acceptance of diversity; the board is a forum for embracing diversity, not homogenizing it.
- Employ a businesslike awareness that the board is the deciding body and not a debating society. Meetings should be worth the board members' time.
- Have agendas and discussions that increasingly reflect that the organization and its mission are integral—the board gives strategic leadership.

APPLICATIONS

Targeted Goals

What are the differences between your organizational and governance structures, and what should they be to achieve appropriate participation by physicians and effectiveness at all levels? Have funds been set aside to provide essential training in leadership for those physicians expected to function and be responsible for the execution and enhancement of matters of governance?

Objectives

1. Have descriptions of roles and responsibilities been developed for each member of the board and its committees? How is performance measured? What plan is in place for phased turnover, retraining, and/or advancement into roles providing governance on the board and/or interorganizationally?
2. Since physicians' leadership and participation will distinguish the excellent health care organization of the future from others, how does your organization compare to the competition? Are physicians and nonphysician leaders partners in the process of executive management? Are compensational values shared and mutually supported by the practice? Why do you believe your governance and organizational structure and supporting outcomes are superior to (or inferior to, or about the same as) those of competitors? What can be done to maintain and enhance outcomes?
3. What options for change in governance have been implemented to enhance organizational position toward advantage in the marketplace

through physicians' leadership? List quantitative and qualitative measures.

Content

What visible and measurable evidence is documented that demonstrates congruence between the structures for governance and your organizational structures? Does your plan to accomplish desired results in the practice require modifications to organizational bylaws? Does current structure provide enough focused direction to the achieve desired position as the provider of choice in this marketplace? What can be done to enhance your positioning strategy?

Evaluation

What benchmarks have been considered that would enable quantitative and qualitative judgments to be made about the success of changes to enhance governance and organization of the practice? Is there a plan in place that is actively supported by the board of directors to accomplish the necessary changes? How much revenue is needed to support changes over the short term (three to five years) and long term (five to ten years)? How will annual and very long-term goals and objectives be set and measured?

Continuous Quality Improvement

What ongoing indicators are routinely monitored (and adjusted as needed) to measure the effectiveness of your governance, and organizational effectiveness? How does the organization embrace change to enhance the effectiveness of the practice and its market position?

Chapter 8

Operations

POINTS FOR FOCUS

Operational systems are needed to support the practice of medicine, related clinical activity, services to customers, and the functions of the business office and finances. Commonly referred to as "overhead," these are important to optimizing essential operational support for revenue-producing units of the practice.

Targeted Goals

1. To design operational support to facilitate clinical practice that is focused on customer service and satisfaction.
2. To evaluate the need to "buy or build" only essential service support.
3. To design a process for continuous quality improvement to monitor operations and provide management with information for use in achieving desired outcomes for the practice.

Objectives

1. Align supporting services to help achieve goals of the practice. Use benchmarks to guide and right-size the ratios of physicians to non-physician supporting staff.
2. Use consultants and/or managerial services for administrative needs where it is unclear whether there is need to hire full-time employees. Once the need has been established and met with supporting services, it becomes easier to evaluate whether to "buy or build" on the basis of returns on investment.
3. Continuous quality improvement is a way of doing business. Visualize ways and means to evaluate all aspects of the practice of medicine to include patient care, systems operations, and consumer satisfaction. Incorporate methods to measure, monitor, and use collected information to maintain appropriate standards for the practice and enhance those aspects documented to be in need of improvement.

Content

Operational support systems will vary by size and type of practice, by the degree to which the practice may be integrated with hospitals and/or health plans, by region of the country, by its location in an urban, suburban, or rural setting or several of these, and by any special needs and/or related interests of its physicians. Although extensive, this unit does not include all information that could address each of these sections.

Evaluation

Change is the only constant that can be counted on in health care today. From a focus on assessment of the practice, it is important to evaluate each aspect of operations, keeping in mind cost and desired effectiveness.

Continuous Quality Improvement

Viewing the administration of operational support from the perspective of CQI is a way of doing business successfully over the long term. Each aspect of operations must be viewed by comparing what exists against the expectations of the practice and regional and/or national benchmarks.

DESIGNING OPERATIONS TO MEET THE NEEDS OF MEMBER-PATIENTS

Designing optimum services with the customer in mind must be the focus for operational support in a medical group. The intent becomes one of optimizing the encounter between the physician and the patient/member while minimizing overhead and the time and effort required of nonphysician staff to run the medical practice (e.g., make appointments, schedule, keep medical records, bill, collect, cashier, and manage—administer, manage human resources, account, plan, and such).

Any activity that is not oriented to the patient members or does not add value to the consumer should be eliminated (or not considered in the first place, if it is a new service). Any activity that goes beyond adding value to medical care is not essential, does not add to the bottom line, and comes directly out of net revenue, profit, or margin. Although it is always difficult to eliminate all extraneous overhead, the practice should be able to delineate clearly how each aspect of overhead is defined and to what extent it adds value to medical care. The decision-making body can then decide matters of operational support with the interests of patient-members in mind.

What Operational Support Is Appropriate for Your Practice?

The question of whether to "buy or build" typically confronts the medical group at least annually, as the next year's budget is developed. As needs for capital equipment and/or facilities arise, other questions concerning lease/ purchase enter in as performance is developed. A rule of thumb has been to analyze such costs side by side, and to lease, rent, or contract unless (or until) the cost of buying/owning is the same or less. Special interests or conditions may change this formula; i.e., some believe that:

- Employees are more loyal than independent contractors
- Your group will have more clout as owners of buildings than as renters
- The company with whom you are negotiating for an MRI will provide better service if you lease and they maintain ownership, and so on.

Appropriately worded performance-based contracts and lease/purchase options have proven to be effective in managing decisions on whether to buy or build. But the larger an organization grows, the more prevalent this question becomes, mainly due to the principles of economy of scale, of making your own rules as your ownership base grows, and of consolidating operations to eliminate duplication.

INFORMATION SERVICES

In its 1994 annual survey of the activities and trends of medical groups, the Medical Group Management Association indicated that 17 percent of groups have computerized medical records, and 75 percent have automated scheduling of appointments.[1] Another 43 percent of groups without computerized medical records and 58 percent of groups without automated scheduling planned to begin automation in 1996. Groups were most likely (47 percent) to have real time links to commercial insurers to obtain information on insurance billings (see Table 8.1). The largest group practices were more likely than other-sized groups to use software for the automated scheduling of appointments (100 percent) and to have computerized medical records (21 percent). The largest groups were also most likely to have on-line real-time links to HMOs/PPOs and commercial insurance companies, to obtain information on insurance and billing, and medical records. Large group practices were less likely than many small and medium-sized groups to have real-time links to hospitals for medical records.

TABLE 8.1. How Group Practices Use Automated Information Systems

	Percentage of Group Practices			
	Have Computerized Medical Records	Have Automated Appointment Scheduling	Plan to Have Computerized Medical Records	Plan to Have Automated Appointment Scheduling
Size (# of FTE Physicians)				
10 or Fewer	18.5%	73.8%	40.3%	56.0%
11 - 25	13.7	71.8	45.4	58.1
26 - 50	4.0	78.4	47.8	73.3
51 - 100	12.5	87.5	47.4	100.0
101 or More	21.4	100.0	90.9	—
Specialty Composition				
Single Specialty	18.6%	73.1%	40.5%	53.6%
Multispecialty	11.5	78.4	48.6	75.6
All Groups	**16.8%**	**74.5%**	**42.8%**	**58.3%**

	Percentage of Group Practices with Real-Time Insurance/Billing Information Links To:					
	Hospitals		HMOs/PPOs		Commercial Insurance	
	Have Links	Plan to Have	Have Links	Plan to Have	Have Links	Plan to Have
Size (# of FTE Physicians)						
10 or Fewer	17.9%	42.9%	28.0%	61.1%	45.3%	66.2%
11 - 25	28.2	43.0	32.1	67.1	51.4	66.7
26 - 50	31.0	53.7	34.7	67.9	48.7	67.4
51 - 100	22.7	53.3	45.8	80.0	50.0	73.3
101 or More	25.0	90.9	66.7	88.9	69.2	70.0
All Groups	**20.7%**	**45.0%**	**30.2%**	**63.3%**	**46.9%**	**66.6%**
	Percentage of Group Practices with Real-Time Medical Records Information Links To:					
	Hospitals		HMOs/PPOs		Commercial Insurance	
	Have Links	Plan to Have	Have Links	Plan to Have	Have Links	Plan to Have
Size (# of FTE Physicians)						
10 or Fewer	25.3%	49.4%	1.3%	25.6%	0.8%	20.8%
11 - 25	25.0	48.9	1.8	27.7	2.7	18.4
26 - 50	21.3	54.6	4.0	23.9	1.4	22.7
51 - 100	16.7	61.9	12.5	42.9	4.2	35.0
101 or More	21.4	84.6	14.3	75.0	7.1	76.9
All Groups	**24.5%**	**50.8%**	**2.1%**	**26.8%**	**1.3%**	**21.9%**

TABLE 8.1 *(continued)*

	Percentage of Group Practices			
	Have Computerized Medical Records	Have Automated Appointment Scheduling	Plan to Have Computerized Medical Records	Plan to Have Automated Appointment Scheduling
Single Specialty				
Allergy/Immunology	16.7%	50.0%	—	33.3%
Anesthesiology	4.3	17.4	10.5%	33.3
General Surgery	5.3	78.9	41.2	50.0
Hematology/Oncology	25.0	81.3	72.7	100.0
Obstetrics/Gynecology	18.5	85.2	29.3	75.0
Ophthalmology	9.3	86.0	37.8	40.0
Orthopedic Surgery	20.7	89.1	47.1	60.0
Radiology/Diagnostic	40.6	50.0	21.1	37.5
All Other Single Specialty	18.6	70.9	43.3	57.6
All Groups*	**16.8%**	**74.5%**	**42.8%**	**58.3%**

	Percentage of Group Practices with Real-Time Links to Insurance/Billing or Medical Records					
	Links to Insurance/ Billing	Links to Medical Records	Links to Insurance/ Billing	Links to Medical Records	Links to Insurance/ Billing	Links to Medical Records
Single Specialty						
Allergy/Immunology	—	—	33.3%	—	50.0%	—
Anesthesiology	36.4%	52.2%	30.0	9.1%	60.9	9.1%
General Surgery	42.9	47.4	53.3	—	52.9	6.3
Hematology/Oncology	40.0	31.3	26.7	—	37.5	—
Obstetrics/Gynecology	14.3	26.4	33.3	3.9	50.9	—
Ophthalmology	—	7.1	25.0	—	54.1	—
Orthopedic Surgery	19.8	34.8	29.1	1.1	46.6	1.1
Radiology/Diagnostic	35.7	19.4	29.6	—	50.0	3.3
All Other Single Specialty	22.2	27.0	28.1	1.1	43.8	0.3
All Groups*	**20.7%**	**24.5%**	**30.2%**	**2.1%**	**46.9%**	**1.3%**

*Includes both single-specialty and multispecialty group practices.

Source: Medical Group Management Association. *MGMA Activities and Trends Survey: 1994 Report Based on 1993 Data.* Author: Englewood, CO, 1994. Reprinted with permission.

Multispecialty groups (11.5 percent) were somewhat less likely than single-specialty groups (18.6 percent) to have computerized medical records. Multispecialty groups were more likely (75.6 percent) than single-specialty groups (53.6 percent) to plan to automate the scheduling of appointments during the next two years (if they did not already have this function automated). Single-specialty groups practicing radiology, hematology/oncology, and orthopedic surgery were most likely to have computerized medical records, with 21 percent to 41 percent of groups in these specialties reporting automated systems for medical records. Automated scheduling of appointments was found in over 85 percent of single-specialty group practices in orthopedic surgery, ophthalmology, and obstetrics/gynecology.

While groups practicing anesthesiology and general surgery seldom had internally computerized medical records, they more often had established electronic links to hospital medical records and to commercial data on insurance billing. Diagnostic radiologic groups, most likely to have computerized medical records (and least likely to link to hospital records systems), were among specialties highly likely to have direct links to hospitals' and insurance companies' billing systems (not just their records). Groups practicing general surgery were most likely to have direct links to hospitals, HMOs, and PPOs to obtain data on insurance and billing. Very few single-specialty groups had real-time links to medical records systems of HMOs, PPOs, or commercial companies, but of those, groups practicing anesthesiology were most likely to have these links to outside medical records.

The MGMA, AGPA, and AMA serve as trade association contact points for any group with an interest in pursuing the names of existing representatives for computer systems for the health care industry. In addition, these associations can help put your group in contact with other members of the association who can serve as references on various systems and their costs and performance. Two needs must be addressed—daily transactions in patient care, and another that is even more important, the need for information for analysis and decision making. Overall, the median operating costs for information services per FTE physician in multispecialty groups decreased from 3.7 percent in 1993 to 3.1 percent in 1995.[2]

Physicians' Applications

According to Charles R. Meyer, MD, editor of *Minnesota Medicine* in 1994, medical education is like a shopping trip to a good hardware store.[3] In medical school, internship, and residency we acquire tools—physical, mental, and judgmental—which we apply to our trade. Every day, technology adds tools to our work belt but, until recently, one tool long adopted by most other industries had been excluded from use in clinical medicine itself—the computer. It has been in the clinic's business office, the hospital's registration and billing system, and the research lab, but it has barely nudged into view in most clinicians' daily practice. The promoters of computers in clinical medicine promise efficiency, economies, and excellence. Skeptics envision frustrated physicians, failed fail-safes, and misguided guidelines.[3]

In the same issue of *Minnesota Medicine*, a number of physicians' perspectives are presented that describe why physicians have been slow to make computers the tools of their trade. John Levitt, MD, notes that patient confidentiality and the security of any electronic records are of main concern. Levitt indicates that the primary deficiencies or dangers inherent in a comprehensive computer-based system for patients' records can be broadly grouped into the following five categories:[4]

1. Shortcomings of the physician-computer interface
2. Inadequacies of decision supporting systems
3. Defects in data coding
4. Concerns about patients' privacy
5. Distortion of patients' recorded information

Levitt further notes that proponents of computerized medical records must recognize that physicians have legitimate concerns about how records will be structured and utilized. As long as the medical record is used as a tool for providers to store data about patients, physicians are enthusiastic partners in the operation. Limited records that permit easy recall of laboratory and X-ray results and that tabulate dates of recent visits with diagnoses are already in operation and freely used by physicians in the Twin Cities and elsewhere.

But when a committee for the Institute of Medicine declares "the patient record system of the future must provide other capabilities as well. This includes links to administrative, bibliographic, clinical knowledge, and research databases," and that "computer based information management systems must be able to communicate with providers, third-party payers, and other health care entities,"[5] physicians' resistance should be considered a perfectly appropriate response to a highly controversial subject, rather than dismissed as a manifestation of computer anxiety.

Developing solutions to these issues and a host of others has been the focus of the Computer-Based Patient Record Institute (CPRI) formed in 1992 as a coalition of organizations involving health care, with the mission to initiate and coordinate needed activities to facilitate and promote the routine use of patient-based records.[4,6] The most obvious change in CPRI over its few years is growth, both in numbers and maturity. The decision to form CPRI was finalized and interim directors were seated for the first time to discuss "who we are" and "what we are up to" in January 1992, at the American Medical Association's headquarters in Chicago. Since then, the organization has increased its membership more than 500 percent. That membership comprises a variety of stakeholders in health care, so that all views and needs may be addressed. Seated at the table are physicians, nurses, hospitals, insurers, managed care organizations, vendors of hardware and software, governmental agencies, universities, patient advocacy groups, professionals in medical records, transcriptionists, pharmaceutical representatives, and many others.

Now past its adolescence, CPRI is launching itself into the adulthood of its mission and is directing its activities at the following six goals:

- Promoting the development and use of standards for structuring computer-based patient records and associated messages, communications, codes, and identifiers
- Demonstrating how computer-based systems for patient records can improve effectiveness and efficiency of patient care
- Encouraging creation of policies and mechanisms to protect patients' and providers' confidentiality and ensure security of the data
- Educating health professionals and the public about computer-based patient records
- Promoting activities that use computer-based patient records in research
- Serving as a clearinghouse for efforts to promote and develop activities related to computer-based patient records

The vision statement for the Computer-Based Patient Record Institute is as follows:

1. The health care delivery system must use a comprehensive, longitudinal patient record to provide all clinical, financial, and research data.
2. While maintaining the confidentiality of sensitive patient and provider data, the CPRI will contribute to more effective and efficient care through: universal, timely, and intuitive access to lifetime health data collected and maintained across the continuum of care; support for continuous quality improvement in health care delivery; ready access to knowledge bases to support clinical practice, administration, education, and research; and patient participation in health status documentation, wellness, and disease prevention.[7]

Dr. Meyer believes that it is just a matter of time before the computer becomes a tool used routinely by physicians. His tool-belt analogy mirrors the types of questions posed by many physicians about computers in medicine today: Will computers help clinical practice, or are they destined to go the way of "stomach freezing"? The tool analogy helps answer this question. Any computer guru worth his/her chips will tell you that, indeed, the computer is only a tool. Dr. Meyer offers his prescription for nondyspeptic assimilation of computers by medicine:[3]

1. Like any tool, the computer has to be available. If computers sit in back rooms away from the people who are supposed to use them, they will gather more dust than all the old hula hoops in basements everywhere. Computers need to be located where doctors work, if they are to use them.
2. Like tools, computers need to prove that they enhance productivity. No electric screwdrivers would sell if they did not drive screws faster and more efficiently than hand-operated screwdrivers. If computers add frustration, they are doomed to fail.
3. Users of tools and computers need to learn how to use them; for both, the quicker the learning curve, the better.
4. Both tools and computers need to operate by standards that are shared by users. Tools come in both metric and nonmetric standards, causing irritation and confusion among users. To avoid such frustration, we need concrete standardization for these computer systems.

MEDICAL INFORMATICS

The term "medical informatics" has evolved as a bridge or intersection between medical art and computer science as discussed by Clement in 1994.[8] Even the most cursory list of computer applications in clinical practice illustrates the great promise of medical informatics. But despite the vast potential for faster research, more efficient flow of information, time savings, better decisions, and improved patient care, computers have not swept over the medical world as quickly as their advocates had hoped. Clement states that David Rind, MD, Director of Harvard's Center for Clinical Computing, emphasizes that "computer phobia" is not the real reason for physicians' resistance to the clinical use of computers. "When people build bad computer systems and they're not used by doctors, they say, 'well, you know, doctors don't like computers.' And it's just not true. Doctors like things that save them time. If a computer saves them time, they use it. If it costs them time, they don't use it."[8]

Clement notes that the Beth Israel Hospital where Rind works in Boston has put in place a national example of a well-integrated system. In its hospital-based primary care practice, better than 90 percent of progress notes, lists of medications, and problem lists are now captured electronically. Virtually all lab results are available instantly to physicians via 2,000 terminals throughout the hospital and its outpatient departments. Each week, approximately 20,000 pieces of electronic mail are sent and received through the terminals, and clinicians look up approximately 50,000 items of clinical information via terminal. There are a few doctors who do not use the computer system, but it is an incredible exception.[8]

Computer education is essential. The medical school at Case Western Reserve University gives its students powerful four-pound computers that contain a 6,000-page textbook for their first two years; the computers can also tap into the university's fiber-optic network. Some Harvard Medical School professors and students are experimenting with eleven-ounce palm top computers that provide quick access to the *PDR,* the *Merck Manual,* and other reference aids. About thirty American universities offer degree programs in medical informatics, half of them sponsored by the National Library of Medicine. Medical schools in the United States offer approximately a hundred courses related to informatics, according to the American Medical Informatics Association (AMIA). The University of New Mexico's School of Medicine, for example, implemented a formal informatics curriculum two years ago. The problem in medical education has been that we have had for the past seventy years a memory-based system of education, according to Scott Obenshain, MD, Assistant Dean for Undergraduate Medical Education, who notes that all medical students at UNM now use computers in their studies. "Our projection is that . . . you're not going to be able to practice medicine without one."[9]

MANAGED CARE

From HMOs to PHOs, integrated health care systems are investing in powerful new informational technologies expressly designed for the era of managed care. Unlike most hospitals' and physicians' office computer systems, designed mainly to generate bills, informational systems for managed care help providers manage both patient care and financial risk. They perform myriad specialized functions, from verifying a patient's benefits through an HMO to calculating a physicians' group's subcapitation. What's more, these systems can automate patient records and create a knowledge base for analyzing and improving health care services and health status.

Fromberg and Bader[10] examined the development and uses of informational systems in a number of leading edge, integrated systems for the delivery of health care. While their article is neither a comprehensive survey nor an evaluation of products, we did find several important themes in it:

- *Expense reduction and enhanced service:* Computers and electronic communications will facilitate a reduction in operating expenses and improvement in consumer service.

- *Contemporary needs:* The management of care for HMO members requires information on as close to a real time basis as possible. Matching policies to member health needs and approved physicians require rapid data retrieval and analysis capabilities that can be promoted through the automated patient record.
- *Management challenges:* Knowing what information to collect, analyze, and interpret is a task every leader must be able to manage. Once the various uses for the information have been specified, it is possible to determine what type of managed care software is appropriate and whether it would be best to buy or build the information system.

Core Capabilities of an Information System for Managed Care

The information system must be able to:

- Manage member records and benefits
- Establish appointments throughout health system
- Manage referrals
- Coordinate payment plans
- Process claims while solving problems
- Case manage and review utilization and costs
- Computerize medical record

Four areas are represented by these capabilities:

1. *Operations and Administration,* such as eligibility determination and referral authorization.
2. *Financial* including payments, incentives, and balancing revenues with expenses.
3. *Utilization and decision support,* such as trend analysis and monitoring medical loss ratios to align activities with strategic targets.
4. *Care management,* such as sharing on-line information on member encounters and health status with both employed and contracted practitioners throughout the health system network.

Getting Business as Opposed to Keeping Business

Getting It: To negotiate contracts in managed care successfully, hospitals and other providers will need to capture, store, and analyze:

- Costs of care provided
- Expected reimbursement compared with actual reimbursement

- Patterns of providers' practices
- Clinical outcomes

Keeping It: To ensure a continued relationship with managed care organizations, providers will need to address:

- Real-time access to providers' data by health plans—and vice versa
- Issues of the confidentiality of clinical data
- Meeting expected levels of service to the health plan
- Issues of capitation
- Clinical and administrative information sharing[11]

HUMAN RESOURCES

Using the organization's objectives and philosophy as a guide, the human resources department develops, implements, and coordinates policies relating to all aspects of personnel administration, including recruitment, salary administration, and career development. This department oversees the provision of services such as retirement and health benefits. It reports to the organization's top administrative officer.

Operating Expenses

The largest component of operating expenses for multispecialty groups was *nonproviders' salaries*, at 43 percent of costs other than for physicians (see Table 8.2 and Figure 8.1). These included salaries for RNs, LPNs, certified nurse anesthetists, medical assistants, personnel in the administrative/business office, personnel in informational services, support personnel, secretaries, maintenance workers, security people, those in medical records and in the lab and providing radiologic services, and optical and medical ancillary servers—but no midlevel providers. *Benefits* added another 10.2 percent, in 1995, to total costs for staff in multispecialty group practices, pushing total costs for nonprovider personnel to 53 percent of all operating expenses. Costs of benefits included costs for retirement plans, profit sharing, travel, education, allowances for training, dues, entertainment, taxes, and life, health, and disability insurance.[1,2]

TABLE 8.2. Median Nonphysician Expenses per FTE Physician in a Multi-specialty Group Practice[1,2]

Category of Expense	Percentage of Total		
	1995	1992	1991
Nonproviders' salaries**	43.4%	42.4%	42.3%
Building/occupancy	11.4	11.5	12.2
Nonproviders' benefits	10.2	10.6	10.1
Medical and surgical supplies	6.9	7.0	6.2
Other nonphysician expenses	6.2	6.1	6.7
Laboratory costs	5.0	5.7	5.6
Insurance premiums	3.3	4.3	4.6
Informational services	3.1	3.6	3.5
Administrative supplies/services	3.2	3.3	3.1
Furniture/equipment	2.8	2.9	2.9
Radiology/imaging	1.9	2.6	2.8
Size of sample (# of physicians)	353	371	382

*These percentages were calculated by using a computed sum of $238,309 for 1995, $213,690 for 1992 total nonphysician expenses per FTE physician, and $213,367 for 1991.
**No midlevel nonphysician providers were included in nonproviders' salaries.

Costs for buildings or for occupancy, the second highest expenses after physicians' salaries, accounted for 11.4 percent of all nonphysician costs for multispecialty group practices in 1995, down from 12.2 percent in 1991.

Size of Group and Needs for Supporting Staff[1]

Table 8.3 demonstrates that large groups did not achieve overall economies of scale in terms of labor. The larger groups employed more staff per physician as compared to small groups. Larger groups often have larger supporting staffs than smaller medical groups because of a different mix of business. Larger groups provide more specialty care and have sicker patients. They usually provide less primary care than smaller groups.

Larger multispecialty groups employed more medical receptionists, medical records staff, and specialists in radiology and imaging, per FTE physician, than did smaller groups. The place where larger groups were more efficient and achieved some advantages of size compared with small groups was in administrative and support staff, informational services, LPNs and medical assistants, medical secretaries and transcriptionists, and laboratory technicians. Office administration—including administrative personnel, business office staff, administrative support people, receptionists and

FIGURE 8.1. 1995 Median Operating Costs per FTE Physician in a Multi-specialty Group Practice

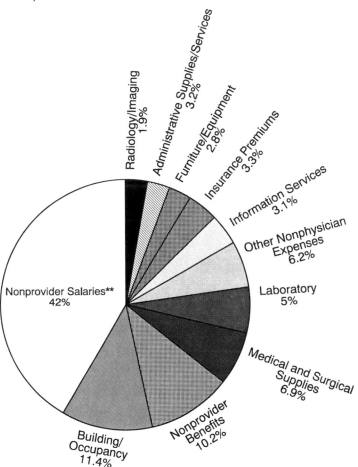

Radiology/Imaging 1.9%

Administrative Supplies/Services 3.2%

Furniture/Equipment 2.8%

Insurance Premiums 3.3%

Information Services 3.1%

Other Nonphysician Expenses 6.2%

Laboratory 5%

Medical and Surgical Supplies 6.9%

Nonprovider Benefits 10.2%

Building/Occupancy 11.4%

Nonprovider Salaries** 42%

Source: Medical Group Management Association. *MGMA Cost Survey: 1996 Report Based on 1995 Data.* Author: Englewood, CO, 1996. Reprinted with permission.

medical records staff—accounted for 47 percent of nonprovider staff per physician in small group practices, 42 percent to 44 percent of staff per physician in middle-sized groups, and 40 percent of staff per physician in large medical groups.

TABLE 8.3. Median Numbers of Nonprovider Staff per FTE Physician in Multispecialty Groups

Staff Category	10 or Fewer FTE Physicians		11.25 FTE Physicians		26–50 FTE Physicians		51 or More FTE Physicians		Weighted Average	
	1994	1996	1994	1996	1994	1996	1994	1996	1994	1996
Administrative	0.25	0.25	0.20	0.23	0.19	0.20	0.21	0.26	0.23	0.23
Business Office	0.64	0.73	0.72	0.71	0.66	0.67	0.63	0.68	0.65	0.67
Information Systems	0.22	0.14	0.17	0.16	0.18	0.10	0.16	0.14	0.21	0.14
Housekeeping/Maintenance/Security	0.15	0.20	0.12	0.15	0.13	0.10	0.15	0.16	0.14	0.14
Other Administrative Support	0.17	0.12	0.10	0.12	0.11	0.06	0.07	0.04	0.15	0.09
Registered Nurses	0.40	0.45	0.33	0.41	0.47	0.46	0.38	0.52	0.39	0.44
LPNs, Medical Assistants, etc.	0.92	0.89	0.88	1.01	0.84	0.94	0.80	0.84	0.90	0.91
Medical Receptionists	0.50	0.58	0.57	0.81	0.69	0.69	0.72	0.66	0.53	0.70
Medical Secretaries/Transcribers	0.31	0.30	0.26	0.25	0.25	0.24	0.28	0.28	0.30	0.26
Medical Records	0.33	0.33	0.35	0.35	0.39	0.39	0.34	0.47	0.34	0.37
Laboratory	0.37	0.42	0.35	0.39	0.33	0.31	0.34	0.31	0.36	0.34
Radiology/Imaging	0.22	0.20	0.18	0.23	0.22	0.20	0.28	0.28	0.22	0.23
Physical Therapy	—	—	0.09	—	0.08	—	0.06	0.08	0.02	0.08
Optical	—	—	0.06	0.09	0.07	0.05	0.05	0.05	0.02	0.05
Other Medical/Ancillary Services	0.23	0.31	0.17	0.14	0.13	0.10	0.20	0.16	0.22	0.16
Total Staff FTEs per FTE Physician	3.99	4.02	4.36	4.62	4.86	4.73	4.92	5.02	4.50	4.63

Source: Medical Group Management Association. *MGMA Cost Survey: 1994 Report Based on 1993 Data.* 1994 and 1996 Report Based on 1995 Data, 1996. 1996 Data to right of 1994. Author: Englewood, CO. Reprinted with permission.

FIGURE 8.2. Median FTE Support Staff per FTE Physician in Multispecialty Groups*

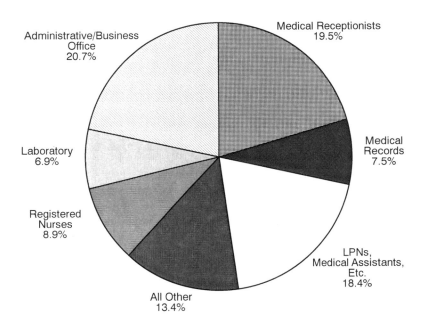

*No data on midlevel providers or physicians are included in support staff or nonprovider data.

Source: Medical Group Management Associate (MGMA). *MGMA Cost Survey: 1996 Report Based on 1995 Data.* 1996. Reprinted with Permission.

Compensation for Managers

Annually, the Medical Group Management Association conducts a survey of levels of compensation for managers; the survey is typically coordinated through human resources departments. Participation in the survey allows the medical group to compare and contrast costs for administrative staff across standard definitions for role descriptions, FTEs, compensation, and benefits.[2]

Positions in Medical Groups and Their Titles and Descriptions (1994)[1]

Administrator/Executive Director/CEO

This is the top nonmedical administrative position in many health care delivery organizations. This officer oversees, plans, guides, and evaluates all nonmedical activities of the organization and has broad responsibilities for aspects of the medical practice, including development of policy in areas such as finances and marketing. The administrator/executive director/CEO is ultimately responsible for the growth and health of the organization. In smaller organizations, this individual may also serve as the primary financial and operational officer. Reports to the organization's governing body (e.g., the board of directors).

Medical Director

This top medical administrator within a medical practice or with an HMO or PPO affiliated with a practice oversees and is responsible for all activities related to the delivery of medical programs and clinical services, such as utilization review. This officer oversees the professional physicians and in some organizations, nursing services as well. He or she must be a licensed physician. Some medical directors provide patient care. This person reports to the governing body of the organization.

Associate Administrator/Chief Operating Officer (COO)

This officer consults with, advises, and assists the top administrator in providing leadership and direction in planning, directing, and coordinating activities not associated with patient care. He or she assumes leadership of the organization in the absence of the top administrator, and reports to the top administrative officer and/or to the governing body of the organization.

Assistant Administrator

This person assists the top administrator in planning, directing, and coordinating activities not associated with patient care. Normally, an assistant administrator has a limited scope of responsibility, such as for marketing or recruiting. A medical practice may have multiple assistant administrators, who report to an associate administrator or, in some organizations, to the top administrative officer.

Chief Financial Officer (CFO)

In the organization's top financial position, the CFO develops financial policies and oversees their implementation, prepares short-range and long-term projections to ensure that the organization's financial obligations are met, and develops plans for growth of the organization. He or she reports to the top administrator and/or to the organization's governing body.

Director of Ambulatory Services

This director develops and implements policies that relate to outpatient care delivered by ambulatory service centers. S/he initiates and monitors voluntary state and federal accrediting processes, reimbursements by patients, and self-referral regulations. Usually this person reports to the organization's medical director or chief operating officer or to the top administrator.

Director of Education/Training

This person develops and delivers educational and training programs for members of the staff and for patients, evaluates programs to determine whether the goals and objectives for training have been met, and monitors the delivery of ongoing programs. Usually this director reports to the director of human resources or to the chief operating officer.

Director of Human Resources

Using the organization's objectives and philosophy as a guide, this director develops, implements, and coordinates policies relating to all aspects of personnel administration, including recruitment, training, salary administration, retention, performance evaluation, and career development, and oversees the provision of services such as retirement and health benefits. S/he reports to the organization's top administrative officer.

Director of Marketing

The organization's top marketing person develops marketing policies and programs that reflect the organization's goals and objectives, oversees or conducts research designed to evaluate the organization's market position, and performs administrative tasks such as departmental budgeting and supervision of personnel. S/he reports to the organization's top administrative officer.

Director of Planning and Development

This person oversees all activities related to the growth and expansion of the organization, manages the implementation of new products and services, and evaluates existing products and services on a regular basis. When necessary, s/he works with the organization's marketing function. S/he develops and implements the organization's budget as it relates to planning and development, and plays a major role in the organization's strategic planning process. This position reports to the organization's top administrative officer.

Director of Provider Relations

This person recruits and maintains relationships with a variety of health care providers (e.g., physicians or ambulatory care centers). Activities focus on areas such as providers' reimbursement and evaluation. This position is becoming more common in a managed care environment. Usually the person reports to the organization's medical director.

HMO/Managed Care Director

This director initiates and maintains relationships with managed care organizations and physician providers, including the negotiation of contracts with such organizations and providers. S/he may be in charge of utilization management. The position reports to the organization's top financial officer.

Director of HMO Member Services

This person develops policies and procedures that relate to the initiation and maintenance of member services, and oversees all activities of the organization related to member services, including enrollment and retention. The position reports to the organization's top administrative officer or may report to the HMO/managed care director.

Director of Management Information Services (MIS)/Information Systems Manager

This manager oversees all activities that relate to the organization's informational systems, from supervising staff members to vendor selection of both clinical and nonclinical systems, as well as resolving issues of systems implementation. S/he performs programming tasks when necessary, and reports to the chief operating officer.

Quality Improvement Director

This person develops policies and procedures that relate to the use of quantitative and qualitative information used by the organization to examine patient outcomes and utilization patterns. S/he develops programs designed to improve the quality of health care delivered. The position reports to the top administrative officer.

Facilities Director

The director develops and implements policies and procedures related to the organization's physical facilities, i.e., the buildings. S/he oversees related activities such as billing, maintenance, housekeeping, and grounds preservation, and reports to the chief officer.

Controller

The controller develops and oversees activities related to implementing and maintaining the integrity of the organization's financial reporting system, and assists with or oversees the budgeting process. The position reports to the organization's top financial officer. In smaller organizations, the controller may serve as the top financial person and would report to the top administrator and/or to the organization's governing body.

Operations Manager

This manager coordinates and directs the overall operation of specific departments, coordinating among departments to ensure that the organization meets internal and external regulatory requirements. The position reports to the top administrator or to the chief operating officer.

Business Office Manager

This manager directs and coordinates activities of the business office in an organization that has a top administrator (e.g., a CEO). Areas of responsibility include insurance processing, insurance claims processing, accounts payable, accounts receivable, credit, and collections. The position reports to the chief financial officer or the organization's top administrative officer.

Office Manager

The office manager oversees nonmedical activities of the organization, with a more limited scope of responsibility than that of an administrative director. Emphasis rests on the daily activities of the organization and not on long-term planning. Such a manager may oversee some financial activities, such as insurance processing and collections, is usually involved in the management of a smaller practice, and usually reports to managers who are practicing physicians.

Utilization Review Manager

This manager monitors activities of inpatient and outpatient care to ensure that accepted procedures for utilization management are maintained. S/he develops utilization protocols when necessary.

Compensation/Benefits Manager

This position is for developing and overseeing all aspects of the program for administering an organization's salaries/wages as well as its benefits program. This person determines eligibility for the benefits program; s/he may report to the director of human resources.

Branch/Satellite Clinic Supervisor

This person oversees the administrative and operational activities of all remote clinical sites, develops financial policy for the clinics in concert with the organization's top financial officer, supervises the clinic's managers, and indirectly supervises clinical staff. S/he usually reports to the chief operating officer.

Satellite Clinic Manager

Such a manager oversees the daily administrative and operational activities of an assigned clinic, prepares the clinic's annual budget, supervises clinical staff, and oversees financial transactions such as the purchasing of supplies. S/he reports to the supervisor of branch/satellite clinics or to the chief operating officer.

Clinical Department Manager

This person manages the operation of one or more medical/surgical departments or ancillary service departments, or an ambulatory surgical facility (usually found in larger practices). S/he assists with budgetary planning, approves departmental expenditures, and may supervise the department's non-medical staff. S/he reports to the governing body of the organization.

LEGAL SERVICES

Currently, the use of legal services among medical groups has significantly increased, in step with the acceleration of integrated organizations through mergers, affiliations, joint ventures, and consolidations. The traditional roles continue and include contract development and negotiations, antitrust considerations, prevention of fraud and abuse, monitoring of general liability, and input to provisions for management of malpractice and risk management.

Antitrust

"Ready, set . . . affiliate" sums up the atmosphere across the United States, as is indicated in an article published in the February 1995 issue of *Minnesota Physician* by Richard A. Lockridge, JD, and Henri G. Minette, JD, MPH.[12] State and federal antitrust laws essentially prohibit actions between parties that unreasonably restrain trade in the relevant market. The Sherman Act is the principal federal antitrust statute prohibiting any contract, combination, or conspiracy in restraint of trade. The Sherman Act also prohibits monopolization, attempts to monopolize, or combinations or conspiracies to monopolize. State antitrust laws generally mirror federal law.[13,14,15]

To allay providers' concerns about federal enforcement of the antitrust laws in today's rapidly evolving health care market, the Department of Justice (DOJ) and the Federal Trade Commission (FTC) issued Antitrust Guidelines for the Health Care Industry in September of 1993. The guidelines offer "safety zones" for certain activities and relationships. A relationship or activity that falls within a safety zone is unlikely to be challenged by the agencies except in extraordinary circumstances.

In 1993, the guidelines addressed: (1) mergers among hospitals; (2) hospitals' joint ventures involving high technology; (3) providers' collective provision of non-fee-related information to health care purchasers; (4) providers' participation in informational exchanges on price and cost; (5) joint purchasing arrangements among health care providers; and (6) joint ventures among physicians' networks. Because providers criticized the guidelines as being too restrictive, and because reimbursements from almost all payers continued to shrink, revised guidelines were released in 1994.[12,13] Three new areas were added and two that had previously been instituted in 1993 were enhanced.

The 1994 guidelines addressed three new areas: (1) hospitals' joint ventures involving certain specialized clinical or high-cost services; (2) providers' collective provision of fee-related information to health care purchasers; and (3) a framework for reviewing multiprovider networks, including physician/hospital organizations. The two most important enhancements over the 1993 guideline that related to physicians' affiliations addressed information sharing and physicians' networks. Lockridge and Minette note that the 1994 guidelines expanded the safety zone to include not more than 30 percent of physicians in each specialty in a relevant geographic market where the network is nonexclusive. Nonexclusive networks permit participating physicians to contract with or participate in other networks. The 20 percent safety zone for 1993 still applied to exclusive networks.[12]

In areas in which there are fewer than five physicians in a particular specialty in a relevant geographic market, as in rural Minnesota, the new guidelines provide that a joint venture by an otherwise qualifying physicians' network may include one physician from the specialty on a nonexclusive basis and still fit the safety zone. The DOJ and FTE have also committed themselves to an expedited process for review through which providers of health care can obtain rulings on the agencies' intentions concerning enforcement of antitrust laws regarding the specific proposed conduct. The agencies have indicated that they will respond to requests for business reviews or advisory opinions no later than ninety days after all necessary information is submitted regarding any matter addressed in the guidelines, except for requests related to hospitals, mergers outside the safety zone, and multiprovider networks. Nationally, numerous providers have requested expedited review of their networks' activities.

Monopoly or Not? Marshfield Clinic and Blue Cross/Blue Shield of Wisconsin

One case drawing national attention in 1994 and 1995 involved the Marshfield Clinic, Marshfield, Wisconsin, and Blue Cross and Blue Shield United of Wisconsin and its Compcare HMO. The March 17, 1995, edition of the *St. Paul Pioneer Press* noted that U.S. District Judge John Shabaz upheld a verdict that found Marshfield Clinic had illegally created a health care monopoly in northern and central Wisconsin. The article noted that the judge cut the damages from $16.1 million to $5.6 million. Because damages are tripled in antitrust cases, the amount Marshfield Clinic was required to pay Blue Cross was reduced from $48.5 million to $17 million. The jury in December 1994 found the clinic had fixed prices, driving independent physicians from the region, and had excluded competing health maintenance organizations from the market.[16]

To level the playing field, Shabaz voided agreements that Marshfield Clinic had entered into with other Wisconsin clinics and HMOs. Testimony at the trial indicated the clinic had carved up markets or engaged in other anticompetitive activity. The judge also voided noncompetition clauses in Marshfield clinic's contracts with its affiliated physicians that prevented them from practicing in the immediate area for three years after leaving the clinic. But Shabaz denied Blue Cross's request that the clinic be required to sell Lakeland Medical Center in Minocqua, which has branches in Park Falls, Phillips, and Mercer. Marshfield operates twenty-three branch clinics in central and northern Wisconsin.

Both sides declared victory, and both sides said they would review their options before deciding how to proceed. The people of northern and central Wisconsin can look forward to more competition and fairer prices for health care, according to Blue Cross spokesman Tom Luljak. The clinic has been prohibited from a wide variety of conduct with its competitors, noted James Troupis, attorney for Blue Cross. Marshfield Clinic spokeswoman Brenda Johnson Jaye said that Marshfield officials were grateful that Shabaz had refused to dismantle the clinic's satellite system of health centers dotted across northern Wisconsin. That was an affirmation of the model built over seventy-nine years, she noted. She indicated that Marshfield Clinic never intended to violate antitrust laws. The clinic appealed to the U.S. Circuit Court of Appeals for the Seventh Circuit, which yielded the following findings:

- In a strongly worded decision, the U.S. Court of Appeals for the Seventh Circuit overturned a district court verdict that Marshfield had acted as an illegal monopoly by preventing Blue Cross and Blue Shield of Wisconsin and its HMO from entering the market.
- Any monopolistic power that Marshfield holds over its rural Wisconsin markets, the appeals court found, is caused by the scarce health care resources in those areas—not a campaign by the 400-doctor clinic to block competition.
- The appellate court set aside the $17 million penalty awarded by the trial court to the Blue Cross/Blue Shield plan earlier this year as damages for Marshfield's alleged monopolistic practices. It also ordered

the insurer, which initiated the lawsuit, to pay the clinic's appeals court costs.
- The Chicago-based court affirmed only one of the lower court's findings: that Marshfield colluded with Wausau-based North Central Health Protection Plan to divide markets, in violation of the Sherman Act.[17]

In March 1996, the U.S. Supreme court denied Blue Cross's request to review the Court of Appeals decision.[18] The appellate court overturned a multimillion dollar judgment against the clinic. Although it was ruled that the clinic did not engage in price fixing, it did work with competitors to divide markets and eliminate competition. A modest financial settlement was declared by the courts. The money was directed to be used toward needy health care recipients affected by the antitrust activity.

Risk Management and Liability in Managed Care

As the practice of medicine moves further into cost-contained and managed care, the issue of increasing risk must be recognized. In an article for *Minnesota Medicine* in 1994, James Platt offered a number of steps physicians can take to reduce their risk of liability.[19] *Liability:* Physicians may increasingly be named as defendants when patients do not receive the care to which they feel entitled. As medical groups take on the dual role of provider and payer, plaintiffs may find fertile ground for alleging conflicts between patient care duties, cost containments, and economic incentives. *Considerations of risk in managed care:* Physicians entering into a managed care contract or designing a new delivery system should keep in mind their potential for liability. Physicians should always consult with legal counsel and experts in risk management ahead of time. The medical group must be aware of antitrust[19] and medicine and medical antikickback violations at all times.[20,21,22]

Some suggested precautions include the following:

1. *Provide good medical care:* Above all, physicians must continue to provide good medical care. If managed care offers an opportunity for financial gain, physicians must not allow economic factors to interfere with patient care.
2. *Inform patients of medical recommendations:* If, for example, a patient's plan will not pay for additional days in the hospital but the physician believes early discharge creates a risk, the physician should fully explain that risk to the patient.
3. *Document recommendations and decisions:* Physicians should objectively document in the patient's medical record the course of

treatment recommended and the patient's decision regarding that. In doing so, physicians should be careful about how they express frustrations with the managed care plan. In some cases, the jury reportedly would have found the physician negligent (had he been a defendant) partly because the physician noted in the medical record that the patient had to be discharged "because of pressure" from the utilization review company.[14]

4. *Avoid using terms such as "highest quality":* Physicians should question public relations releases and ad campaigns that describe their practice as "highest quality." When such terms find their way into managed care agreements, they become particularly difficult to defend.

5. *Choose the best organizational option:* The type of legal organization and how it presents itself to patients affects liability. New legal entities such as limited liability corporations and limited liability partnerships may afford networks an ability to protect members from negligence committed by other members in the network.

6. *Design cost-containment incentives so they don't influence patient care:* Managed care organizations that work with capitated or risk-bearing medical groups are being advised to reduce their risk by disclosing that the gatekeeper or capitated physician is financially at risk for decisions in health care. This strategy may focus attention on the primary care group and how it makes decisions. Physicians must avoid making decisions concerning patient care for financial gain.

7. *Challenge decisions by the utilization reviewer:* Was the decision of the reviewer made by qualified medical professionals? Was a denial of surgery or extended hospitalization reviewed by a licensed physician? Was a specialist involved? Be satisfied that qualified staff reviewed each step of the process.

8. *Help patients take advantage of their right to appeal:* Physicians must become advocates for the rights of patient members. Be available as a resource to help patients understand the system and the care received for which they are fiscally responsible.

9. *Be certain the practice can meet the patient's needs:* Medical groups that have signed capitated contracts or serve as gatekeepers should be careful that the practice can appropriately address the needs of potential patient members. Physicians must be careful, if they are responsible for determining which specialists to refer to and when a referral is appropriate, particularly if the decision has a financial impact on the practice.

10. *Maintain adequate malpractice insurance and be aware of policy exclusions:* Policies typically do not cover nonmedical claims such

as for defamation, breach of contract, and antitrust violations, which may be involved when providers do their own credentialing and utilization review.

11. *Handle credentialing carefully:* Medical groups that handle their own credentialing should carefully analyze how physicians are credentialed. In several cases, hospitals and HMOs have been found to be responsible for inappropriate credentialing.

12. *Have legal counsel review contracts for managed care and new arrangements for delivery of care:* Overly broad indemnification clauses appear in many managed care contracts. These clauses can obligate the medical group to reimburse the managed care organization or network for legal fees and court costs if a claim results from the medical group's actions.

Pitfalls in Computerized Patient Records

The transition from the traditional paper medical record to a computerized patient record (CPR) continues to present risks of liability. The following summarizes a few of the more common areas:[21]

1. *Invasion of Privacy:* When a wrongful disclosure of medical records is made by a health care provider, invasion of privacy has often been the basis of an action. Four causes of this action include: (a) disclosure of private or embarrassing facts; (b) the appropriation of a person's likeness (as in a medical publication); (c) invasion of a person's solitude; and (d) the placing of a person in a false light to the public.

2. *Defamation:* An inadvertent disclosure of a false statement about a patient could also lead to a defamation suit. Generally, elements of defamation are: (a) defamatory language (i.e., language that tends to affect another's reputation adversely); (b) the defamatory language must be of or concerning the plaintiff (i.e., it must reasonably identify the defamed person); (c) publication of the defamatory language (i.e., communication to a third person who understood it); and (d) damage to the defamed party's reputation.

3. *Negligence:* If a medical record is disclosed to someone who is not authorized to see that record, there may also be a viable claim for negligence, depending upon the circumstances. To prove negligence, the plaintiff must show: (a) a duty to use reasonable care existed; (b) there was failure to conform to this required duty; (c) there was a reasonably close causal connection between the conduct and the resulting injury; and (d) there was actual loss or damage.

4. *Malpractice:* If the patient's condition is adversely affected by the disclosure of sensitive information, or if the treatment is based upon inaccurate information, there may also be a basis for a malpractice claim.

Pechette's recommendations to minimize the risks of unauthorized disclosure include the following:[21]

1. *Restrict Access:* Create a security system that allows access to patient records only to those who have a legitimate need to know the particular information sought. Ways to accomplish this include allowing extremely sensitive information to be accessed only from designated CPUs; using methods for encryption, where appropriate; limiting access to portions of patient's records solely related to the user's responsibilities; tracking and coding highly sensitive information stored in the system (for example, the results of tests for HIV antibody, records of celebrities or public figures, psychiatric records, records of abortions, and records of patients treated for alcohol and drug abuse); using a coded identifier instead of patients' names; requiring the use of passwords or other security clearances to access the system; using locks and fire walls to prevent unauthorized access; and enforcing systems that would prevent access to a terminated employee.

2. *Audit Regularly:* Audits should be conducted periodically. Although a formal audit might be an administrative burden for a small group practice, some form of monitoring should be done on a regular basis.

3. *Plan for Disaster:* Though its computer-based patient record system may be on a smaller scale than a hospital's, a group practice nevertheless relies heavily on its records. Thus, it is critical to plan for a potential disaster before it hits. Consider the following safeguards: have in place and advise all key employees of a contingency plan that can be deployed immediately in the event of a disaster; have ready a disaster recovery "hot site"; store valuable data and information off-site on a regular basis; provide an uninterrupted power supply for the informational system; install fire prevention equipment in the data center; and make sure that the insurance policy includes comprehensive coverage such as for interruption of business, errors and omissions, defamation, and invasion of privacy.

4. *Raise Consciousness:* Sensitize all individuals who may acquire access to patients' records about the importance of maintaining confidentiality and the potential liability for failing to do so.

5. *Confidentiality:* As a policy, every individual who may gain access to patients' records should sign a confidentiality agreement acknowledging that a computerized patient record is confidential and privileged

and that the individual is obligated to maintain its confidentiality, and that passwords, key cards, and access codes are for personal use only, with appropriate sanctions for violation of the policy.

6. *Indemnification:* Seek indemnification from the vendor for inaccuracies in medical records, or for system errors that allow for unauthorized access to the records, when those are attributable to the vendor. Seek indemnification from high-level employees whose job it is to monitor and enforce the security controls, for violations that they could reasonably have prevented. Also consider obtaining indemnification from third party laboratories that provide test results to the group practice, for negligence in following procedures to ensure confidentiality. Should litigation ensue, a right to sue for indemnification could prove very valuable.

Malpractice and Risk Management

Expenses incurred by physicians to protect themselves from inappropriate claims of negligence have been increasing, which in turn has caused an increase in overall costs of health care. These costs are generally passed on to physicians in the form of increased premiums for insurance against malpractice and/or liability.[22] Sizable indirect costs, such as physicians giving up their practices or declining to perform certain procedures, have yet to be defined. Various attempts are being made to cap or limit the amount of malpractice awards, in the belief that overall costs of health care will diminish or at least stabilize if awards are made to meet the needs of the affected individual but are not excessive. An emphasis is being placed on reasonableness, as the sizes of awards are determined.

Attempts to prevent or at least minimize liability are referred to as "risk management." Risk management embodies various functions that identify, manage, and prevent risks of liability and devise means to fund those risks. Physicians and health services managers are becoming increasingly aware that effective risk management can improve the quality of care and protect providers' assets. Therefore, whether your practice is primarily office- or hospital-based, you need to understand and become active in risk management.[23]

Risk management was originally developed to promote safety and control costs of liability in industry. It was first applied in health care in the early 1970s, spurred on by increases in awards by juries for remedial malpractice and by out-of-court settlements against hospitals and physicians, which in turn were caused by a national trend of increased consumer activism and the proliferation of high-technology medicine, with its attendant benefits and risks.

In the malpractice insurance crisis of the mid-1970s, many companies began charging sharply higher rates. Some refused to renew long-standing accounts, or they withdrew entirely from the medical malpractice market, leaving their customers at risk. This spurred hospitals and physicians to organize innovative insurance arrangements. It also stimulated them to implement risk management programs, in the belief that they could help control liability risks and financial losses. The concept of risk management also appealed to patients' groups and the general public because it was equated with improved patient safety and hence better health care. The concept and practice of risk management gained widespread acceptance as a means to protect both hospitals and physicians from costly malpractice claims and to improve the quality of medical care.

Increasingly, the diagnosis and treatment of serious ailments occurs not only in hospitals but also in clinics and doctors' offices where a variety of high-risk medical technology is being utilized. As an office-based physician, you also probably maintain hospital privileges and perform a portion of your work in a hospital setting. Risk management and quality assurance are in place in one form or another in almost all hospitals in the United States, and their activities will affect your practice in that setting and will warrant your attention and active involvement.

Risk management has a number of functions. It is concerned with the orderly and cost-effective transfer of risk through various insurance arrangements. It is concerned with the reduction of risk through the identification of sources of liability, particularly those stemming from personal injury to patients. It facilitates and carries out actions to reduce the extent of injury after it has occurred to an individual patient. It also provides information about prior risks, so that changes in the system may be implemented to prevent future risks of injury and consequent liability. Risk management is concerned with effective communication and documentation among providers and patients. It seeks to help providers optimize their handling of problem situations and problem patients. Risk management, in order to be successful, requires physicians' active participation.[22]

Protection of assets, a basic element of risk management, is accomplished primarily through professional liability insurance, in which the risk of loss of assets is transferred to a third party. Malpractice litigation is so ubiquitous these days that practicing physicians must have a plan in place for protection of their assets. A few have concluded, for personal reasons, that they will not or cannot purchase professional liability insurance, and they thereby expose their personal assets to potential loss. The means by which these assets may be protected from loss in litigation varies from state to state. Those who intend to practice with or without professional liability insurance protection should consult experts in their communities to determine what collateral protection they need and what may be available. Mills, Lindgren, and Brown describe various aspects of this concern, in the sections to follow.[22]

Different types of professional liability insurance are available to physicians through insurance companies and various self-insuring organizations. The oldest and safest form is the "occurrence" type of coverage, which protects the policyholder for the particular patient's injury regardless of the date when that injury precipitated a lawsuit. Claims-made policies are the type presently available to most physicians in North America. Physician-controlled insuring organizations, for example, provide claims-made policies at beginning rates that are substantially less than those required for occurrence policies. However, the premiums increase until about the fifth year, when the premium for the claims-made policy is approximately the same as that required for the occurrence policy. So, although claims-made coverage is more affordable for the beginning practitioner, ultimately it will cost the same as occurrence policies.

In effect, a claims-made insurance policy weds the policyholder to the insurer. The only way to break that relationship and maintain subsequent protection is to buy what is called "tail coverage" from the insurer. This policy is sold to you for a specific price to cover you for subsequent claims arising from events in the years for which you purchased claims-made coverage from that company, even after you have terminated that policy. Because not all potential claims are clearly identifiable at the time of occurrence, it is generally advisable to purchase tail coverage, but, depending upon the vagaries of the insurance market at any particular point in time, tail coverage can be expensive and difficult to obtain.

Risk-retention groups, cooperatives, and self-insuring programs of larger group practices are other means by which to protect your assets, including "offshore" captive insurance companies in Bermuda, the Cayman Islands, and such, which are exempt from U.S. federal taxes. These may provide you with coverage at a premium substantially below that quoted by regular insurance companies and may offer other advantages and disadvantages. In most states, insuring organizations are subject to review by state insurance agencies and are backed up by that state's guarantee law requiring that claims against a bankrupt insurance agency be paid by other insurance companies doing business in that state.

These alternative forms of coverage may also be completely accessible—that is, you may be responsible for ultimate losses that exceed the company's premium structure. If the premium quoted to you seems unusually low, you need to determine the question of accessibility and the extent to which the company comes under the jurisdiction of the state's guarantee laws. You should also inquire into the financial strength of the company and the extent to which you would receive any protection through reinsurance or excess insurance coverage that they purchase.

The attraction of risk retention groups is that they often write coverage for a number of states in a region. This means that if you move from one state to another, you may not need to seek new means of professional liability coverage. This is a definite advantage over doctor-controlled companies that are restricted to one state and write only claims-made policies.

Record Keeping and Communication

For medicolegal purposes it is imperative that you create records that will allow a recreation of the findings, decisions, and medical management you provided. These records are mandatory for your own credibility in the event your patient disagrees with your findings, recommendations, or treatments. Another reason to create and maintain a complete patient record is reimbursement. Increasingly, both government and private payers are basing payment on the level of care and intensity of service reflected in the office chart.[23]

Original records in your office should be retained as long as practicable. For patients under current management, old records must be retained indefinitely. For patients who have left your practice, records should be retained at least ten years; in some highly litigious regions of the country they should be retained indefinitely. If space is limited or too costly, records may be placed in lower cost, long-term physical storage or captured on microfilm or electronically. Your state's medical society is usually a reliable source of guidelines for the retention of records. A telephone conversation between you and a patient may be just as critical as a face-to-face communication in your office. In both instances, the essence of the information conveyed should be documented. Lab and radiology reports need to be reviewed before they become part of the patient's record.

Care must be taken to modify existing medical records appropriately. You may cross through what was written incorrectly and write the correction immediately thereafter. Do not erase or obliterate incorrect words or phrases—this creates the impression of a cover-up. Once your original page has been created and a day or two passes, do not go back and correct the original page. Leave the original page in place and create a new page, noting alterations and augmentations.[22]

No patient should leave the doctor's office with instructions for care at home that are not in writing.[24] Patients are invariably anxious when being seen by the physician and more likely than not will forget your recommendations for care at home. Providing these instructions in written form, therefore, will improve outpatient management and compliance. Hospitals already do this, and you should too, in your office practice. With the increasing emphasis on ambulatory care and outpatient, rather than inpatient, treatment this is especially important. There are times when you will be required to warn patients, to avoid possible future harm. For instance, you have a duty to warn your patients about the sedative effects of prescription drugs. Failure to give such a warning may leave you vulnerable to lawsuits by the patients or by people you have never seen before.

Patient Relations

Claims for malpractice result from both real and perceived negligence. Three areas account for claims: (1) the standard of care within a specialty, (2) legal obligations, and (3) your relationships with patients.

MARKETING AND PUBLIC RELATIONS

Marketing was once seen by physicians as inappropriate, unethical, and not something done by the medical profession. Even today, some physicians would prefer not to engage in such a process, which has been associated with the buying and selling of used cars, houses, and (to some extent) "snake oil," that is, products or services that are not what they are advertised to be. The truth of the matter is that marketing and public relations constantly take place in each of our lives, whether or not we care to recognize it.

Every interaction we have with another human being reflects a level of communication. The type of interaction can be visual, auditory, or tactile. It can be verbal or nonverbal. In each instance, some aspects of our belief system have been inspired to communicate voluntarily and involuntarily. In most cases, we decide the nature and form of our communication, i.e., whether it will be pleasant, informative, sell an idea, make a request, inform, or whatever. The effect of communication in its simplest form is no more than marketing and public relations. We do it constantly, whether or not we care to admit it. Henceforth, since we do it anyway, why don't we do it in the most effective and optimal way possible?

Developing Effective Communications

Formalized marketing and public relations imply structure and purpose. Public relations aims at informing the public about your activities, policies, and *image* in a way that creates favorable opinions about your medical practice in general. The essence of marketing is to present your product and its place, price, and promotion. Keeping in step with the need for operational support in general, the purpose of marketing should be to identify patients' needs and to design and implement services and programs to meet the defined needs. Activities for continuous quality improvement are incorporated to ensure that the services and programs are doing what they are designed to do and that consumers (e.g., patients, payers, referring professionals) are sufficiently satisfied, to the extent that they will return for services when needed in the future and will refer others for care from the same providers (you).

By placing yourself in the patient's shoes, it is possible to understand better what is expected of the medical staff. Too often patients are expected to follow rigorous directions and procedures; written orders and guidelines may be handed to them that, in many cases, are too complex and detailed. Patients may be given pills for very good reasons yet often fail to understand why it is important to comply with the frequency or number to be taken, as recommended. Multiple procedures for registration, and requirements to complete seemingly endless and often redundant forms and applications are forced upon them but rarely understood by most patients.

The total process associated with delivery of medical care can benefit from a timely examination and reasonable modification to improve its less-than-favorable services. Evaluative review of procedures conducted at the nurses' station, at the appointment desk, and in the physician's exam room, as well as in the administrative processes of any organization, is appropriate. Is medical service being provided with an eye on consumers' needs? Such a question must be asked about all phases of the system. Many executive meetings in health care service organizations find discussions aimed at one subject: the need to see a certain number of patients on a daily, weekly, monthly, or yearly basis. Office budgets, practitioners' profits, and the financial strength of a progressive group all necessarily depend upon consumer satisfaction—yet, few health care providers appropriately design services for the consumer. The organization that can effectively establish a consumer-oriented program will progressively grow to become a service truly interested in its patients—and all the other concerns will fall in line.

The age-old question "Will the patient have a real voice in determining the nature of their continuing health care?" continues to be addressed in many texts and journals on health care. Answers vary, in as wide a distributive pattern as there are providers of health care asking the question. Similarly, when the administrator of a health care organization is asked "How satisfied are your patients with services provided them?" a typical response would probably indicate "Patients are generally satisfied—we still have patients, don't we?" Yes, but that does not say much about anything. Systematic participation by patients is needed to help your staff assess patient satisfaction after medical intervention. Care provided to both individuals and groups of patients getting similar services needs to be evaluated. Less-than-favorable ratings of satisfaction must be eliminated.[24,25]

Evaluators of health care often recognize the need to include consumer information in an assessment of how well their services are being provided, yet they may fail to conduct systematic evaluations that adequately reflect consumer satisfaction. Many doctors neglect to assess objectively any aspect of their patients' satisfaction. Others collect information that is so general it is impossible to compare or relate it to anything but the most generalized goals and objectives, far removed from the actual day-to-day practice of medicine. Still others ask the wrong questions, leading to the collection of useless information.

If there is an interest in assessing patient satisfaction and using the information obtained to improve less-than-favorable services, further definition of "satisfaction" is necessary. Cast aside what is thought to be the patient's need and ask the patient what his/her expectations are—then fulfill them. By examining those activities which patients say are important to them, a patient-oriented system can be built to meet both patient and organizational needs.[24]

Marketing and Development of a Business Plan

Planning for marketing begins by establishing clear objectives for the practice, ones that can be quantified. To achieve each objective, there needs to be a specific action or set of actions that a physician intends to implement.

For example: To increase by 20 percent the volume of new patients seen in a practice, one might:

- Increase the number of patients from a desirable geographic area by 10 percent
- Increase the number of contracts for managed care by ten
- Increase the number of patients who return for follow-up appointments by 30 percent
- Establish a new office practice with a patient base of 200 within the first six months

Factors to Consider

1. *Demographics:* Who are the people in the community?
2. *Targeted markets:* Who are the people in the community whom the physician would most like to reach?
3. *Competition:* Who are the other providers of health care in the area? What are their strengths and weaknesses?
4. *Unique features:* What is special about your practice that would be perceived as important by members of the community?

5. *Trends in the practice:* What is happening in the practice? Is your practice strong in terms of reimbursement mix and balance of patients?
6. *Physical environment:* Do any changes need to be made in your office space?
7. *Actions:* What specific actions is the physician planning to take in the above areas, to achieve the objectives?

Image and Recognition of Brand Name

1. *Image:* Who are the people with whom the physician interacts? How do they perceive the physician?
2. *Bedside manner:* How does the physician respond to patients and families?
3. *Patients' perceptions:* How effective is the physician's combination of styles with patients?
4. *Appearance:* What message is the physician's personal image and style communicating to people with whom he works?
5. *Actions:* What specific actions is the physician planning to take to improve his or her personal image?

Patient Relations

1. *Telephone:* How are telephone calls to the practice being handled?
2. *Scheduling:* Are patients' waiting times acceptable?
3. *Billing:* Is the office responsive to patients' financial issues?
4. *Education:* Does the practice have sufficient educational materials available?
5. *Environment:* How does the physical environment appear to patients?
6. *Actions:* What changes is the physician planning to make to improve the patient's experience in the office?

Doctor-to-Doctor Relations

1. *Referrals:* Is the physician responsive to his or her sources of referred patients?
2. *Contacts:* Is the physician developing professional contacts in the community?
3. *Actions:* What actions can the physician make to improve his or her relations with other professionals?

Participation in Hospital Programs

1. *Hospital marketing:* Is the hospital's marketing program supporting the physician's activities?
2. *Hospital programs:* Does the hospital sponsor particular programs that can benefit physicians?
3. *Managed care:* What are the opportunities in managed care to develop the practice?
4. *Medical staff:* Does the physician know how the medical staff operates within the hospital?
5. *Physicians' services:* Does the hospital have a department specifically designed to assist physicians?
6. *Hospital's community relations:* Does the hospital sponsor programs in the community in which a physician can become involved?
7. *Actions:* In what programs or services is the physician planning to become involved?

Managed Care

1. *Information:* Does the physician have a clear understanding of the volume and trends in managed care in the area?
2. *Participation:* Is the physician participating in the right managed care plans? Are there organized groups of physicians in the community to deal with contracts in managed care?
3. *Actions:* In which managed care plans or physicians' groups is the physician going to participate?

How to Use Your Community

1. *Community groups:* Are there important groups that the physician should join?
2. *Professional visibility:* Are there opportunities for the community to hear the physician's message?
3. *Participation in the community:* Is there an opportunity to participate in community events?

Processes of Communication

1. *Options:* What pieces of communication might the physician might want to use?
2. *Production:* How does the physician arrange to have these pieces created?

3. *Identifying system:* What is the image and continuity of image that should exist?
4. *Distribution:* How well will people receive the proposed communication?
5. *Actions:* What system of communication is the physician going to create?

DEVELOPMENT OF A BUSINESS PLAN

Criteria for Initial Evaluation of New Business Ideas

A. Description

   1. Briefly describe who will benefit from the idea and how it will work:

   _____

   _____

   2. Must we pioneer this idea? _____ yes _____ no

   3. What other successful models can we look at?

   _____

   _____

B. Mission

   1. Is this idea compatible with and supportive of defined organizational missions, goals, and strategic plans? _____ yes _____ no

   2. Briefly explain:

   _____

C. Competition

   1. What competing ideas currently exist?

   _____

   _____

   2. How might competing organizations respond to our initiative?

   _____

   _____

D. Assessment of the Market

   1. Does the potential market demand for this idea exceed the capacity of existing providers? _____ yes _____ no

2. If yes, on what information do you base your answer?

_____

_____

3. How did input from end users (patients, referring professionals, business and industry, paramedical personnel) play a role in developing this idea?

_____

_____

4. What research has been done to support this idea?

_____

_____

E. Experience

1. Does your physicians' group currently have the experience and talent to develop and manage this idea successfully? _____ yes _____ no

2. If no, how will these be provided?

_____

_____

F. Space Requirements

1. Do you currently have access to space in which to implement this idea effectively? _____ yes _____ no

2. If yes, is this space easily accessible by users of the idea? _____ yes _____ no

3. If no, what is the plan for meeting spatial needs?

_____

_____

G. Staffing

Primarily, how many and what types of people will be required to implement this idea?

Number of FTEs: *New*   *Existing*   *Job Class*

_____   _____   _____

H. Capital

1. What is the preliminary estimate of the initial cost of equipment $_____ and facilities $_____ required to implement this idea?

I. Financial Results

    1. Is this idea believed likely to meet the financial evaluation criteria for the approval of new business proposals? _____ yes _____ no

    2. If yes, on what information do you base your answer?

    _____

    _____

J. Timing

    1. How long will it take to develop the idea?_____

    2. Is the timing of introduction or development of the idea a factor critical to its success? _____ yes _____ no

K. Organizational Conflicts

    1. Does this idea present any potential conflict with the interests of other physicians, departments, clinics, or services? _____ yes _____ no

    2. If yes, briefly describe:

    _____

    _____

L. Departmental Approval

_____   _____
Signature of medical department head   Date

_____   _____
Signature of administrative officer   Date

If the plan received approval at the screening/review level, it would proceed to the development of a business plan.

Criteria for Approval of New Business Proposals

A. Business Plan

    1. Plans must address the first three years of operation.

    2. Plans must satisfactorily respond to all criteria for initial evaluation.

    3. Plans must state timetables and responsibilities for implementation.

4. Promotional requirements must be outlined.

5. Evaluative criteria to be used to measure success of the project must be explicitly stated.

6. A contingency plan must address what will be done with staff, space, equipment, cash, receivables, and liabilities, if operations of the project do not meet expectations.

B. Financial Evaluation

1. A pro forma statement of revenues and expenses must be provided for the first three years of operation.

   a. Projects undertaken with an expectation of financial gain:

   Physicians' Group—The proposal must show a positive margin of net revenue over expenses, including the costs of promotion, by the second year of operation. The proposal must also recover any losses from the first year of operation by the end of the third year.

   Hospital (if involved)—The proposal must have a positive net present value of cash flows at an 8 percent discount factor.

   b. Projects not undertaken for economic reasons must generate sufficient net revenue to at least meet the expenses of operation, including the costs of promotion, by the third year of operation.

2. All assumptions regarding major business risks associated with the proposal—about volume, market conditions, charges, sources of payment, operational expenses, promotional costs, bad debts, discounts, and capital costs—must be explicitly stated and shown to be reasonable and consistent with community norms.

3. Total requirements for capital, recovery periods, rates of return, and the like must be shown to be reasonable and in accordance with organizational requirements.

4. If more than the physicians' group is participating, the physicians' group and each of the other participants must be detailed.

C. Other Considerations

1. Any regulatory, legal, or accrediting requirements must be anticipated and addressed.

2. Administrative responsibilities must be resolved. (For example, who will manage the idea? To whom will managers report?)

3. The availability of developmental funds or funds from foundations or grants to supplement startup operations must have been considered.

Annual Review of Developments of New Business

Program Name: _____

Date Approved: _____

Anniversary Date: _____

Date Operational: _____

A. Objective

   1. Has the primary goal or objective been achieved to date? (explain)

   _____

   _____

   2. Is this program still compatible with the physicians' defined missions, goals, and strategic plans? (if not, explain)

   _____

   _____

B. Results

How do the actual volumes of service and financial results compare to the original pro forma projections? (Please attach an updated pro forma showing projected and actual results.)

_____

_____

C. Financial Viability

   1. Is the program now self-supporting? (If not, explain how and when that will be accomplished.)

   _____

   _____

   2. Will the program require additional operating or capital funds to continue? (If yes, explain why additional funds will be necessary.)

   _____

   _____

   _____

D. Changes

Does the program need to change from what was originally proposed? (explain)

_____

_____

E. Approvals

_____   _____

Signature of medical department head   Date

_____   _____

Signature of administrative officer   Date

RELATIONS WITH REFERRERS

If the medical practice is dependent upon (or could benefit from) referrals from other physicians and/or health care-related professionals, effective communications with referrers are essential. The essence of such communication is rapid notification of the referred patient's condition to the primary care physician (or the related health care professional) who referred the patient. Once a treatment plan has been developed, it is crucial to return the patient, along with the plan, to the primary care physician. If the referred patient required hospitalization or other immediate intervention, the physician to whom the patient was referred should notify the primary care physician of this status and any other significant change.

The importance of referrals to organizations who count on them, is significant. For example, a longitudinal analysis of results associated with the integration of Ramsey physicians and Ramsey Hospital in St. Paul, Minnesota found that referred hospital admissions constituted one of the five most important predictors of growth in combined net revenues for the integrated organization. Ramsey Clinic and St. Paul-Ramsey Medical Center consolidated into an integrated organization in 1987.[25,26] Figure 8.3 shows the volume of referrals of inpatients (hospitalized) as a ratio of admissions through 1994. Figure 8.4 illustrates the trends in average length of stay and inpatient referrals.

Table 8.4 shows the role of inpatient referrals as a predictor of combined net revenue. "Year" as a key predictor demonstrates that relationships among sources of net revenue in the combined medical center and clinic have grown stronger and become more predictable over the course of the six-year study. Factors found to be most predictive of combined net revenues were: An increasing number of outpatient clinical visits and inpatient hospital days; growth of physicians' compensation as a percentage of the clinic's total budget for operating expenses; and increasing numbers of patients referred for admission to the hospital from area physicians. Although rank order had changed slightly, the same factors consistently remained the top predictors.[25]

FIGURE 8.3. Volume of Inpatients Referred, as a Ratio of Admissions

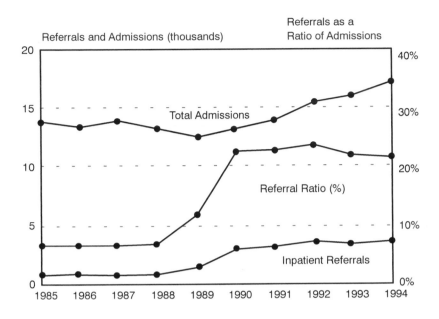

Source: Sommers, P. Managing Medical Service Outcomes by Predicting and Achieving Success: An Inferential Approach. *American Medical Group Association,* 42(3): 24,26-28,30; May/June 1995.

System Referral Network

An example of a medical group and hospital referral system follows to serve as a guide for communicating with primary care physicians.

Availability of Staff to Take Telephone Consults/Transfers

Physicians on the staff of Physicians' Clinic personally respond to the referral's beeper code (2000) within five minutes, or will ask another member of the staff to accept the call. Pages for referrals will use the standard beeper codes: 1 = stat, 2 = ASAP, 3 = routine, 4 = outside call. Outside calls are considered to have priority.

Prompt Communication with Referring Professional

Contact by telephone with the referring professional occurs within twenty-four hours after admission of the patient and at any time when a

FIGURE 8.4. St. Paul-Ramsey Medical Center—Average Length of Stay (Days) and Referred Inpatients (in Thousands)

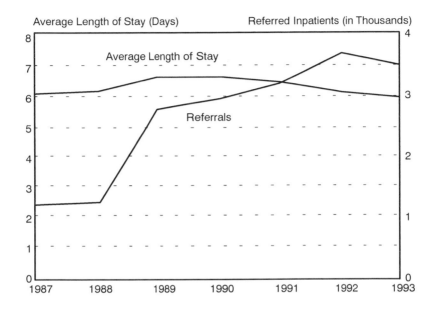

Source: Sommers, P. Managing Medical Service Outcomes by Predicting and Achieving Success: An Inferential Approach. *American Medical Group Association,* 42(3): 24,26–28,30; May/June 1995.

significant development occurs. If the patient is transferred to another service, the attending physician must again contact the referring physician by phone within twenty-four hours. Periodic surveys of satisfaction among referring professionals will be conducted, and reports will be sent to departmental chairs.

Discharging Summaries Processed Promptly

Discharging summaries are completed and mailed to the referring professional within ten days after discharge. Departmental chairs are notified as needed of discharging summaries dictated late or not at all within the ten-day grace period.

TABLE 8.4. St. Paul-Ramsey Clinic and Hospital Predictors of Combined Net Revenues (Rank Ordered from 1 to 5)

1991			1992			1993		
Ranked Predictors	p=	R^{2*}	Ranked Predictors	p=	R^2	Ranked Predictors	p=	R^2
1. Year	.01	94%	1. Year	.01	96%	1. Year	.01	98%
2. Outpatient Visits	.01	92%	2. Inpatient Days	.01	88%	2. Inpatient Days	.01	92%
3. Physician Salary Percentage of Expense Budget	.02	92%	3. Outpatient Visits	.01	86%	3. Outpatient Visits	.01	86%
4. Inpatient Days	.02	81%	4. Inpatient Referrals	.01	85%	4. Physician Salary Percentage of Expense Budget	.01	79%

*The R^2 coefficients were derived from simple pairwise regression analysis with combined net revenue.

Source: Sommers, P. Managing Medical Service Outcomes by Predicting and Achieving Success: An Inferential Approach. *American Medical Group Association,* 42(3): 24,26-28,30; May/June 1995.

Patients Returned to Primary Physicians

Every effort will be made to return the referred patient to the primary care provider or the referring professional. Satisfaction of referring professionals will be measured through periodic surveys. Reports are made to departmental chairs on a quarterly basis.

Departmental Chairs Responsible for Compliance

Departmental chairs have the authority and responsibility to monitor physicians' compliance with this policy. The network maintains monitoring systems and reports to departmental chairs on a regular basis.

Service Offered for Referring MDs

Hotline

Toll-free twenty-four hour access to physicians on Physician's Clinic staff for consultation or assistance in transport or transfer.

Referral Representative

This liaison to referring professionals (MDs, nurses, hospital staff, clinic managers, and others who influence referrals) will provide information, meet needs, and promote use of the referred system, acting as a troubleshooter and ombudsman.

Admit/Discharge Report

Referral system staff review all admissions to identify referred patients and their primary physicians. Staff then send written notice of the condition of a referred patient, at admission and again at discharge, for the referring professional's medical records. A backup system is in place providing for regular calls by physicians to referrers.

Patient/Family Support

Offer discounted hotel reservations, maps, and support to patients' families.

Services for Physician's Clinic Medical Staff and Administrator

Database and Reporting on Referrals

Tracks referral history of every referring professional in the region: type of patients sent, current attitude, last visit by system referral representative, payer mix, and resulting revenue to hospital and clinic. Maintains up-to-date address and profile for physicians and other referring professionals in the region. Posts notices of referrals on clinic and hospital information systems, patient's chart, and attending doctor's office.

Promotions

Administration identifies outreach opportunities where staff physicians can provide continuing medical education or consultation in outlying practices. Referral system provides receptions and other opportunities for its physicians to meet and establish relationships with primary care physicians. Announcements of new staff are mailed to clinics and hospitals in the area.

Research

Referral system staff measure awareness by and preferences of referring physicians, at regular intervals, through surveys, focus groups, and other research.

Functions Related to Communications

Inbound Calls from Referring Physicians—Requests for:

1. Instant consultations
2. Scheduling for patients
3. Updates of information
4. Information on referred patients
5. Assistance to families of patients

Information Center for Medical Referrals

1. Collects and tracks admissions of inpatients
2. Obtains name/address/telephone of referring/primary physician for inpatients by:

- Checking history and physical in medical chart
- Visiting in their rooms patients who did not provide "source of referral" during admission
- Checking with emergency transport personnel

3. Notifies primary physicians whose patients have been admitted
4. Asks referring physicians how frequently (and in what form) they would like to be updated

Outbound Calls to Referring Physicians

- The referral center will place calls to referring MDs at the attending physician's request

Mailed and Faxed Communications to Referring Physicians

1. Referral center staff sends out summarizing letters at admission and discharge
2. The preliminary discharging report is sent within twenty-four hours of the patient's discharge

Communications with Referring Physicians

There are three rules for attending physicians who receive referrals from the hotline:

1. The attending physician is to call the referring physician upon completion of a major procedure or test or within twenty-four hours of admission

2. The attending physician will contact the referring physician with information related to any significant change in the patient's condition

3. The attending physician is to send a report within three days of discharge

The importance of an efficient and effective referral physician communications system cannot be overestimated. Without referrals, any multispecialty group or service will fail. An example of how one physician group and hospital evaluated and enhanced its referral communication system is described in the following case study.

EXAMPLE OF A CASE STUDY: HOW CONTINUOUS QUALITY IMPROVEMENT IS APPLIED TO COMMUNICATIONS BETWEEN REFERRING PROVIDERS AND PHYSICIAN AND HOSPITAL SERVICES IN A TRAUMA CENTER

Purpose

The overall objective of this quality improvement case study conducted by Paulus[27] was to first determine current status and then improve the communication of patient-related information between physician and hospital (medical center staff) and health professionals who either refer trauma patients to the medical center or provide primary medical care to those patients. This objective was intended to be accomplished through collaboration between medical center departments who had some defined role in the communication of this information.

Definitions

Physicians who initially treat the trauma patient and then refer the patient to the medical center will be referred to as "referring medical doctor" (RMD). These physicians reside throughout and are often not permanently based in the local emergency department (ED). The ED is the site from which patients are most frequently referred. Together with the RMDs, nurses in the local ED are part of the group who will be referred to as "referring providers." Any emergency medical service (EMS) agency that transports a trauma patient will be referred to as an "EMS agency." This group includes agencies in the outstate region as well as metro agencies. Lastly, physicians who provide the primary source of medical care for the patient admitted at the medical center for an injury will be referred to as "private medical doctor" (PMD). These PMDs may be outstate or metropolitan physicians including those in the physician group at the medical center. Most frequently, with trauma patients, the RMD and PMD are two different physicians; obviously not every trauma patient has an RMD.

Background

The activities in place to accomplish the project's objective followed an accepted seven-step problem-solving process used in continuous quality improvement. Departments that were to collaborate on this project included trauma center administration (TCA), the department of surgery, referral network (RN), and emergency medical services.

Activities

The activities completed during each of the seven steps of the project are summarized as follows.

Steps of Process

1. Identify the problem
2. Observe the problem
3. Analyze its causes
4. Act on the results
5. Check the results
6. Standardize the changes

- Two information gathering meetings were held with the RN staff, staff of TCA, and two members of the department of surgery
- Market research conducted by medical center marketing was reviewed

Discussion

During these activities, the referral network and trauma center administration became familiar with specific tasks in the role each plays in communicating information between the medical center and outside providers. The communication involved that initiated by outside providers to staff at the medical center, and that initiated by staff at the medical center to the outside provider. Major content of these communications includes:

- Requests by outside providers for medical information to manage a patient

- Requests to transfer a patient to the medical center
- Oral reports on condition of the patient and feedback on medical center patients to the referrer (RMD)
- Oral reports on condition and feedback on medical center patients to that patient's PMD
- Written reports on condition of the patient, to the RMD or PMD
- Acknowledgment of the arrival of a patient
- Instructions on patient's discharge, per hospital information system
- Physician's dictated summary for patient's discharge

Both staffs were trained with the forms and processes currently being used to accomplish communication of the above information. From these discussions, a flow chart was constructed that illustrated all the steps to be taken in transferring information from outside of the medical center to inside, and vice versa. Activities also done by the TACS physicians (Trauma and Critical Services), the physician in the EMD, and the nursing staff were included at this point so that the medical center ED staff could become familiar with them.

Data were gathered from numerous researches that had been done by the medical center marketing department on the needs and wants of the community and of outstate physicians and EMS agencies. Major interests of the group included:

- EMTs want to know what happens to a patient they have brought to the emergency room.
- RMDs want a call from a medical center physician on the day of admission that provides information relative to diagnosis and feedback on premedical center care that patient had received.
- PMDs want to know that their patient has been hospitalized at the medical center. They also want to know the patient's injuries and progress. Information was requested either by phone or letter.
- PMDs want the patient to come back to their local clinic for follow-up care.
- PMDs want timely and applicable information about their patients upon discharge from the medical center so that the PMDs can provide quality care in clinical follow-up.

During the above data gathering, problems in the current process were identified, along with possible causes. The most significant problems with identified causes were:

Problem	Cause
Approximately 20 percent compliance with recommendation that medical center ED staff call RMDs	Lack of time Not seen as priority No consequence for not doing Not enough information on patient's ultimate diagnosis at the time when phone call should be made
Poor compliance of TACS physicians with recommendations to make phone calls to RMDs and PMDs	Lack of time Not seen as priority No consequence for not doing RMDs and PMDs unable to be reached by phone, resulting in much communication with support staff Names, phone numbers of RMDs, PMDs inaccurate Patients have little relationship with the PMDs identified in records of previous medical center encounters Data collection by RN does not occur over the weekend. This may result in a PMD not being identified until day of discharge
Incomplete compliance data on medical center MDs providing RMDs and PMDs with feedback on patients	Data for evaluation of process compliance requires filling out an additional form
Delay in PMDs receiving dictated summary of discharge	Residents'/MDs' delay in dictating summary
Patients not referred back to local PMD after care at medical center	Residents/MDs make discharge plans (unaware of local PMDs or importance of this referral back to community) (Easier for resident to arrange a medical center physician follow-up appointment than to arrange a follow-up by the patient's PMD)

Act on the Results

New procedures and standards for communication of information were developed.

Discussion

The focus of the project at this point became limited to communication initiated by medical center staff and given to outside providers. These new procedures and standards were developed by staff from the TCA and the RN, and by the trauma director. The procedures and standards were divided into three phases of patient care. These were: admission (front end), hospital stay (interim), and discharge (back end). The procedures affected four groups of outside providers (customers of the medical center's communication): EMS agencies, referring ED nursing staff, RMDs, and PMDs. The new procedures were applied just to those trauma patients who were admitted to the TACS service.

Major changes in the new process involved:

- Assigning responsibility for initial verbal contacts with the RMD and PMD to the trauma nurse clinician, as opposed to medical center physicians. Calls initiated by medical center MDs would only be made upon request of the RMD or PMD.
- Strengthening the identification of the PMD by incorporating this responsibility into assessment by the trauma nurse clinician.
- Developing hospital information system screens (changing current screen) that provide a working tool for staff at the medical center involved in the processes, as well as providing a source of data for later measurement of compliance and utilization.
- Verbally communicating patient outcomes back to EMS agencies for those patients who required activation of the trauma team. This was a totally new process, and the assistance of the medical center's department of EMS was enlisted.
- Strengthening the efforts to refer medical center patients back to a local PMD for follow-up after injury, when appropriate.
- Including operative reports in the packet of information sent to the PMD upon the patient's discharge.
- These changes were initiated in response to specific causes of problems, those identified on the previous pages.

a. Check the results
b. Standardize the changes

- Evaluation of specific aspects of the new process and standards was carried out in the subsequent two-month period.
- One evaluative meeting was held after the evaluation period.

DISCUSSION

Data were collected to evaluate the new process and determine compliance with standards. Sources of data to evaluate the new processes included clinical case management cards filled out by the trauma nurse clinician, and the information systems worksheets that contained information on RMDs and PMDs. The documents contained information about the actual activities specific to each patient such as phone calls and letters written by both trauma nurse clinicians and TACS physicians. Other sources of data included summaries of their activities done by the staff of the EMS department, and a listing of discharging summaries sent by the RN. In a very limited number of situations, TACS physicians were asked actually to recall their communication with a PMD.

Several major changes and future activities were planned as a result of the evaluative meeting with the RN and TCA. Other activities that were noted to be very successful in completing the objectives of the project were standardized.

In this project, it was noted that data on the RMD and PMD were being collected by both the RN and the TCA. The two databases, however, had different uses and varying abilities to retrieve the data for analysis. A strength of the system in the RN was the accuracy of names and addresses. A strength of the database in the TCA was that data on RMDs and PMDs were specifically linked to the patient, and this was computerized. At the beginning of the project, one-third of the fields in the TCA's database on RMDs and PMDs were incomplete. As a result of this project, concurrent data on RMDs and PMDs collected by the RN is shared with the TCA for inclusion in their database.

Following a joint meeting to discuss the study results a standard form for communicating with EMS agencies was developed. Implementation will occur as soon as approval is received from legal counsel concerning data privacy appropriateness. A standard form letter to RMDs and PMDs has been drafted. The process has been reviewed with legal counsel. Implementation of the form letters has been set for distribution.

Future Plans

Future plans for continued improvement in this area of communications with referrers has been prioritized as follows:

1. Implement a streamlined method to document the multiple activities associated with these processes. See the following section, Project Limitations and Pitfalls.
2. For patients who will not be required to follow up with the TACS clinic, achieve greater compliance in having medical center MDs communicate with the PMD prior to the patient's discharge.
3. For patients who are initially admitted to TACS but then transfer to a different service, improve the communication with PMDs.
4. In the remonitoring of timing of discharge letters, ensure that the PMD who receives discharge summaries is the correct PMD.
5. Extend the communication with EMS agencies not only to the transporting agency but to the first responders as well.
6. Examine the quality of information on discharge summaries that are for use by PMDs.

Project Limitations and Pitfalls

1. Clearly, the greatest weakness of this project was that the recording of activities was not computerized. The medical center information system was chosen as the most appropriate system, as data on RMDs and PMDs is already available. Also, both trauma nurse clinicians and TACS physicians have access to the system. A request for enhancements in the information system associated with this project was made as a result of the project and is pending final approval.
2. A second limitation of the project was the variability in patterns of practice of TACS physicians. Attending physicians see trauma patients in various locations for follow-up: in the TACS clinic, or at offices as PMDs. This makes it difficult for the trauma nurse clinician to predict how s/he should address the PMD initially.

Summary of Major Quality Improvements from This Project

1. Prior to the project, no formal information on patients was being sent to EMS agencies. During the study, this improved, to a current occurrence at 62 percent. With recent changes implemented, this rate will increase to 100 percent for EMS agencies that transport seriously injured trauma patients.
2. Prior to the project, calls to referring MDs were being made by one trauma nurse clinician. Compliance with this activity was never measured, and the timing of the call was variable. In some cases, there had been duplication of calls to the RMD because some TACS physicians also made a call. The improvement noted in this project was that no

duplication occurred, the calls were done in a timely way, and compliance was measured at 85 percent. It is important to note, however, that due to the limitations of phoning mentioned earlier, this should not be interpreted as actually reaching 85 percent of RMDs.

3. Prior to the project, there was limited consistency in the communication given PMDs. Regarding the role of a PMD after the patient's discharge, little formal discussion occurred up front from the medical center team on where the patient would be followed up. When discharge was soon to occur, due to lack of preplanning it was easier to have the patient followed up in the TACS clinic rather than with the PMD.

   In this project, compliance with attempting to reach the PMD was measured at 73 percent. It was also determined in the period studied that 16 trauma patients were returned directly to their PMD for follow-up care, and that in 75 percent of these cases, there was actually communication between the MD at the medical center and the PMD. It is assumed that this is a marked improvement, as review of many records by the trauma registry staff over the past three years revealed that follow-up appointments with PMDs were rare. The quality of follow-up care is markedly improved when an MD-to-MD report occurs rather than only communication by written summaries.

4. The information that PMDs received has improved with the addition of operative reports in the pack sent to PMDs upon the patient's discharge. It should be noted, however, that this was not measured in the period studied.

5. Utilization of data collected by the RN has improved, and accuracy of information in the trauma registry regarding RMDs and PMDs has also improved.

PUBLIC RELATIONS: PLANNING COMMUNICATION

The role of public relations is to inform the public and consumer groups about your medical activities, policies, and image in a way that creates favorable opinions. Development of the communications process amounts to a successful positive image. Once in place, the image is to be carefully built upon toward establishment of the reputation your practice has agreed to strive to attain. A positive image does not occur by chance. Instead, a communications plan is developed upon defined needs of the physicians.

Example 1: Plan for Communications in the Consolidation of Physicians' Group and Hospital Services in a Rural Community, for Purposes of Strategic Planning

Introduction

At present, strategic planning is ongoing between Physicians' Clinic and Hometown Medical Center, as options are explored and implemented for more consumer-oriented and efficient health care operations in Hometown. As decisions are made and plans develop, providing information to the appropriate audiences will be important to ensure a clear understanding and goodwill throughout. The following communications plan is intended as a guideline for timely and consistent release of information regarding the strategic plans of Physicians' Clinic and Hometown Medical Center.

Goals

To promote internal understanding, because external public relations are so dependent on it, and promote external understanding and goodwill among all audiences.

Targets

Internal:

- All employees
- Staff and courtesy physicians
- Board of directors
- Volunteers/auxiliaries

External:

- Patients
- Residents in the community
- Local media
- Village board

Communication

Internal communication:

1. Develop a communicative piece with its purpose to keep internal audiences updated. Secondary purposes of the piece: Minimize anxiety and panic among employees, discourage the spread of inaccurate rumors, link employees together by promoting a sense of "we" rather than "we vs. they," contribute to a more consumer-oriented attitude among staff, and send an unstated message that employees are valued and important enough to be kept updated.

   Frequency: Written information will be provided to internal audiences as often as necessary.
   Writing: The communicative piece will be written by marketing/public relations as information is received from administration. Facts will be presented in straightforward statements and will address particular questions in a question/answer format.
   Distribution: Employees (via departmental supervisors), physicians, members of the board, volunteers.

2. Host meetings of the staff as necessary, to present dated information and respond to rumors, questions, and concerns. Staff meetings will be videotaped for employees unable to attend.
3. Remind staff of administration's open door policy as an option for employees with specific individual concerns or questions.

External communication:

1. Keep residents of the community updated with the timely release of significant information to local media. News releases will be prepared by marketing/PR as information is provided, and to the media on Tuesdays.
2. Updated information will be included in mailings to all stakeholders.
3. Inserts for envelopes will update current patients on issues that could potentially affect them.
4. Administration will update the village boards via written correspondence.

Example 2: Postmerger Assessment of Internal Communications Survey with Employees and Physicians

Cover Letter to New Corporate Officers

Today's Date

To: Newly Merged Organization

From: Communications Director

Re: Internal Communications Survey

Late last year, we began a process to assess communications with employees and physicians. We completed an overview of our current internal communications vehicles, conducted interviews with selected managers and supervisors, and conducted six focus group sessions that included staff from the merged organizations.

Now we are looking more closely at employee communications, with the attached survey that is being mailed this week to all merged staff. Persons receiving this survey have been randomly selected, as were the participants in the focus groups. We plan to use this insight as a basis for redesigning the "mix" of our communications vehicles for the new organization.

Members of your staff might receive this survey. We hope you will encourage them to respond. Thanks for your support, and we will report the results of our research efforts and recommendations following completion of the survey.

Letter to Staff (on letterhead)

Today's Date

Dear New Organization's Staff:

We need a few minutes of your time to help us serve our communications needs better. Part of the job of the corporate communications staff is to create newsletters, presentations, and other ways of sharing important information with you.

Our organization has experienced significant changes during the past several years, and we want to ask you how well our communications efforts are working. Having current information about our organization helps us all do a better job—now here's your chance to tell us what's working, and what needs to be changed or updated.

Please take a few minutes to respond to the enclosed survey and return it through interoffice mail, by a specific date. (Instructions on returning the survey are enclosed.) The survey's results will be tabulated by an independent, outside research firm—your responses will be totally confidential. Once the surveys have been reviewed and your recommendations have been studied, we'll be implementing ways to improve our publications and other communications efforts.

Thank you for participating. Please return your survey by specific date.

Sincerely,

(Name and Title)

Corporate Communications

New Organization's Communications Survey

Confidential

Please participate in this survey about communications at the New Organization. Your responses, along with those of other employees throughout New Organization, will be used to evaluate and improve communications. The survey is completely confidential, so please answer each question as candidly as possible.

Communications Climate

Check the box that most accurately describes your opinion about each of the following statements.

	Strongly Disagree	Disagree	Neither	Agree	Strongly Agree
1. The organization tries to keep me well informed.	☐	☐	☐	☐	☐
2. Senior management gets high marks for listening to employee ideas.	☐	☐	☐	☐	☐

3. Communications have improved in the last two years. ❏ ❏ ❏ ❏ ❏

4. I can trust communication to be candid. ❏ ❏ ❏ ❏ ❏

5. Employees don't see enough of top executives or senior managers. ❏ ❏ ❏ ❏ ❏

6. Informal communication channels are more reliable than formal ones. ❏ ❏ ❏ ❏ ❏

7. This organization communicates a balance of good and bad news. ❏ ❏ ❏ ❏ ❏

8. I have a clear understanding of the organization's goals and priorities. ❏ ❏ ❏ ❏ ❏

9. Communication has suffered, with recent mergers and affiliations. ❏ ❏ ❏ ❏ ❏

10. The organization is doing a good job of communicating our cultural diversity efforts. ❏ ❏ ❏ ❏ ❏

11. I have a clear understanding of prevention and wellness, and why they are important to the organization. ❏ ❏ ❏ ❏ ❏

12. CQI is making a positive difference in the way we do business. ❏ ❏ ❏ ❏ ❏

13. The organization is doing a good job of communicating its plans for integrating each of the subsidiary organizations into the new organization. ❏ ❏ ❏ ❏ ❏

14. Managers and supervisors share important news with employees in a timely manner. ❏ ❏ ❏ ❏ ❏

15. How does the organization NOT meet your needs for information?

_____

_____

_____

Publications

Following are questions about specific publications. Please choose the response that most accurately describes your opinion. If you are unfamiliar with the publications, please continue with the next section.

	Clinical Newsletter			Management Brief		
	Seldom	Some-times	Often	Seldom	Some-times	Often
16-17. Is valuable and worth my time.	❑	❑	❑	❑	❑	❑
18-19. Covers the right topics.	❑	❑	❑	❑	❑	❑
20-21. Is a publication I read.	❑	❑	❑	❑	❑	❑
22-23. Is timely and current.	❑	❑	❑	❑	❑	❑
24-25. Is candid and straight-forward.	❑	❑	❑	❑	❑	❑
26-27. Is essential to my under-standing of the company.	❑	❑	❑	❑	❑	❑

28. What do you like best about *Clinical Newsletter?*

_____

_____

29. What do you like least about *Clinical Newsletter?*

_____

_____

30. What do you like best about *Management Brief?*

_____

_____

31. What do you like least about *Management Brief?*

_____

_____

Other Sources of Information

For each of the following communications vehicles, rate its value to you by checking the appropriate box.

	Waste of Time	Marginal Value	Good Value	Essential
32. Employee/staff meetings.	☐	☐	☐	☐
33. Voice (phone) mail.	☐	☐	☐	☐
34. Electronic mail.	☐	☐	☐	☐
35. Electronic bulletin board.	☐	☐	☐	☐
36. Memos from the president.	☐	☐	☐	☐
37. Grapevine.	☐	☐	☐	☐
38. Memos from other officers/managers.	☐	☐	☐	☐

Messages and Distribution

39. From the following list, choose three topics that are most important *to you.* (Identify the top three by writing the corresponding letter in the blank next to "1" for the topic most important to you, "2" for the second most, and "3" for the third most important.)

40. Then, from the same list, choose the three topics you think are most important *to the organization.* (Again, choose the top three by placing the corresponding letters next to numbers "1," "2," and "3.")

A. Business strategy
B. CQI initiatives and progress
C. Employee benefits and policies
D. Mergers
E. Financial performance
F. New products, services, and contracts
G. Personnel moves/appointments
H. Marketplace changes/competition/ legislation on reform of health care
I. Operational procedures and improvements
J. Employee recognition/achievement
K. Member/patient satisfaction
L. Departmental activities
M. Cultural diversity

39. Important to me.
1. _____
2. _____
3. _____

40. Important to the company.
1. _____
2. _____
3. _____

Demographics

41. Your age: a. 18-25 b. 26-35 c. 36-45 d. 46-55 e. over 55
42. Your gender: a. male b. female
43. Your years of service: a. less than 1 year b. 1-5 years c. 6-10 years
    d. 11-20 years e. more than 20 years
44. Job category:

Direct patient care	Nonpatient care
a. Nurse	a. Manager/Supervisor
b. Ancillary	b. Clerical
c. Other health care professional	c. Other nonpatient position

45. Location: a. Main office b. Clinic c. Other

BUSINESS SERVICES

Operational requirements for financing and functions in the business office typically support accounting, financial services, patient accounts, and business services. For example:

Accounting	Financial Services	Patient Accounts	Business Services
Financial Accounting	Reimbursement	Credit and Collections	Fee Management
Budgeting	Managed Care Contracting	Billing	Customer Representatives
Financial Reports	Internal Auditing	Accounts Receivable	Referral Relations
Accounts Payable	Cost Accounting		
	Payroll		
	Cash Management and Treasury Functions		

In larger multispecialty physicians' groups, multihospital systems, and health plans, there is usually a chief financial officer (CFO) who has responsibility and authority for functions of the business office. The CFO may report to the CEO, president, or chief administrative officer (CAO). The CFO, CAO, and president will function as the senior administrative team, which requires close cooperation and alignment of goals toward the mission of the organization.

Benchmarking Operational Standards

The type and amount of operational support needed by a medical group will relate to the size and nature of the practice.[28,29] The American Medical Association (AMA)[30,31] and Medical Group Management Association (MGMA) publish comparative rate bases.[32,33] On an annual basis the MGMA publishes a cost survey. Data for the survey are used as a benchmark against which medical practices throughout the United States can compare themselves. For example, *MGMA Cost Survey: 1994 Report Based on 1993 Data* presents confidential data on charges, revenue, expenses, earnings, and staffing in medical practices for calendar year 1993 or for the respondent's most recent twelve-month fiscal period as of the February 1994 date of distribution of this survey.[1] The following example shows how data is annually collected.

Hoechst Marion Roussel produces an annual report that combines data supplied by the MGMA and the American Medical Group Association (AMGA), Alexandria, VA. The MGMA is the national professional and trade association and in 1997 represented 6,753 medical group practices that included 169,049 physicians. The MGMA and its Center for Research in Ambulatory Health Care Administration (CRAHCA) maintain the nation's largest collection of medical group practice management materials and databases about medical groups. The 1997 report contains data on AMGA members that included 236 medical group practices representing a reported 46,778 physicians.[2] Surveying questionnaires and booklets of definitions were mailed to 6,565 MGMA member practices in February 1994. There were 1,349 questionnaires returned, representing a rate of response of 20.5 percent. Not all responses were used to prepare the tables in this report. Questionnaires were deleted from the database if not all the mandatory questions were answered, if the respondent was a practice plan for faculty in a medical school and/or clinical science department, if the respondent was a hospital, if the respondent was a practice owned by a hospital, if not twelve months of data were reported, or if the medical practice did not consist of at least three full-time equivalent physicians. The net result was that 1,166 questionnaires were admitted to the final database, for a net response rate of 17.8 percent.

The information is updated annually and presented to assist leaders in medical practice in measuring the performance of their organizations vis-à-vis the performance of a self-selected population responding to this survey. It must be stressed that this survey is not based upon a stratified random sample of practices of members of the MGMA nor of all medical practices in the United States.

Since the surveying questionnaire was only distributed to practices who are members of MGMA, and since all responses were purely voluntary, multiple elements of bias may apply to these respondents. Any comparisons of data on individual practices to the values reported in these tables should be made cautiously, with the realization that values for the respondent population are not necessarily representative of all medical practices in the United States nor even of medical practices in the MGMA. Although this disclaimer is true, there is not currently a better set of benchmarks against which to compare operational costs in a medical practice.

In examining data presented in this report, the leadership in a medical practice might want to consider the following:

1. What is the difference between the data reported by the practice and overall medians presented in this report, in dollars per FTE physician, in dollars in FTE provider, and in percent of total net medical revenue?
2. Do these differences indicate that the practice's performance is significantly out of line with the statistics on costs surveyed? Such differences may help identify some areas of the practice's business that require closer scrutiny.
3. Are the differences explainable either through the practice's method for collecting data, reporting data, and/or defining data, or because of special goals in the practice?
4. By what methods can these financial indicators be changed or controlled within the medical practice?

The reader should also be aware that MGMA has other sources of information on revenues and costs in a medical practice besides data presented in this report. *The Academic Practice Management Survey: 1994 Report Based on 1993 Data* presents similar types of data for academic practices.[34] The *Performance Efficiency Evaluation Report*[29] provides participating medical practices with a customized report comparing a practice's performance to that of similar types of practices, on a quarterly and/or annual basis. Examples from MGMA groups that participate in the survey appear in the following tables and figures. Current year information is available by contacting MGMA offices in Englewood, Colorado (Telephone: (303) 799–1111).

TABLE 8.5. Frequencies

1. State

MGMA Membership Frequencies			Survey Respondent Frequencies		
State	Count	Percent	State	Count	Percent
Alaska	15	.23%	Alaska	7	.60%
Alabama	128	1.95%	Alabama	12	1.03%
Arkansas	95	1.45%	Arkansas	20	1.72%
Arizona	130	1.98%	Arizona	28	2.40%
California	535	8.15%	California	70	6.00%
Colorado	161	2.45%	Colorado	36	3.09%
Connecticut	74	1.13%	Connecticut	10	.86%
District of Columbia	22	.34%	District of Columbia	1	.09%
Delaware	24	3.67%	Delaware	3	.26%
Florida	340	5.18%	Florida	39	3.34%
Georgia	198	3.02%	Georgia	21	1.80%
Hawaii	14	.21%	Hawaii	2	.17%
Iowa	92	1.40%	Iowa	26	2.23%
Idaho	41	.62%	Idaho	10	.86%
Illinois	252	3.84%	Illinois	50	4.29%
Indiana	190	2.89%	Indiana	39	3.34%
Kansas	93	1.42%	Kansas	16	1.37%
Kentucky	81	1.23%	Kentucky	12	1.03%
Louisiana	111	1.69%	Louisiana	16	1.37%
Massachusetts	110	1.68%	Massachusetts	15	1.29%
Maryland	122	1.86%	Maryland	15	1.29%
Maine	51	.78%	Maine	8	.69%
Michigan	213	3.24%	Michigan	38	3.26%
Minnesota	200	3.05%	Minnesota	56	4.80%
Missouri	224	3.41%	Missouri	35	3.00%
Mississippi	68	1.04%	Mississippi	6	.51%
Montana	26	.40%	Montana	13	1.11%
North Carolina	263	4.01%	North Carolina	45	3.86%
North Dakota	31	.47%	North Dakota	8	.69%
Nebraska	74	1.13%	Nebraska	16	1.37%
New Hampshire	49	.75%	New Hampshire	11	.94%
New Jersey	98	1.49%	New Jersey	8	.69%
New Mexico	41	.62%	New Mexico	8	.69%
Nevada	50	.76%	Nevada	5	.43%

TABLE 8.5 *(continued)*

State	Count	Percent	State	Count	Percent
New York	191	2.91%	New York	28	2.40%
Ohio	257	3.91%	Ohio	43	3.69%
Oklahoma	76	1.16%	Oklahoma	15	1.29%
Oregon	119	1.81%	Oregon	38	3.26%
Pennsylvania	316	4.81%	Pennsylvania	51	4.37%
Rhode Island	23	.35%	Rhode Island	3	.26%
South Carolina	81	1.23%	South Carolina	10	.86%
South Dakota	47	.72%	South Dakota	6	.51%
Tennessee	234	3.56%	Tennessee	48	4.12%
Texas	378	5.76%	Texas	48	4.12%
Utah	23	.35%	Utah	10	.86%
Virginia	179	2.73%	Virginia	34	2.92%
Vermont	10	.15%	Vermont	2	.17%
Washington	224	3.41%	Washington	68	5.83%
Wisconsin	140	2.13%	Wisconsin	45	3.86%
West Virginia	33	.50%	West Virginia	6	.51%
Wyoming	18	.27%	Wyoming	6	.51%
TOTAL	6,565	100.00%	TOTAL	1,166	100.00%

2. Geographic Section

MGMA Membership Frequencies

Geographic Section	Count	Percent
Eastern Section	1,565	23.84%
Midwest Section	1,496	22.79%
Southern Section	2,107	32.09%
Western Section	1,397	21.28%
TOTAL	6,565	100.00%

Survey Respondent Frequencies

Geographic Section	Count	Percent
Eastern Section	240	20.58%
Midwest Section	327	28.04%
Southern Section	298	25.56%
Western Section	301	25.81%
TOTAL	1,166	100.00%

3. Single Specialty Practice Type

MGMA Membership Frequencies

Single Specialty Practice Type	Count	Percent
Allergy/Immunology	27	.67%
Anesthesiology	203	5.02%
Cardiology	272	6.73%
Dermatology	25	.62%
Emergency Medicine	37	.92%

MGMA Membership Frequencies

Single Specialty Practice Type	Count	Percent
Allergy/Immunology	7	.87%
Anesthesiology	41	5.11%
Cardiology	71	8.84%
Dermatology	6	.75%
Emergency Medicine	7	.87%

TABLE 8.5 *(continued)*

Endocrinology/ Metabolism	10	.25%	Endocrinology/ Metabolism	1	.12%
Family Practice	463	11.46%	Family Practice	100	12.45%
Gastroenterology	70	1.73%	Gastroenterology	13	1.62%
Geriatrics	5	.12%			
Gynecology (only)	9	.22%			
Hematology/Oncology	74	1.83%	Hematology/Oncology	18	2.24%
Infectious Disease	8	.20%	Infectious Disease	2	.25%
Internal Medicine	225	5.57%	Internal Medicine	53	6.60%
Neonatal Medicine	14	.35%	Neonatal Medicine	4	.50%
Nephrology	31	.77%	Nephrology	8	1.00%
Neurology	60	1.48%	Neurology	23	2.86%
Nuclear Medicine	1	.02%			
Obstetrics/Gynecology	360	8.91%	Obstetrics/Gynecology	51	6.35%
Occupational Medicine	18	.45%	Occupational Medicine	1	.12%
Ophthalmology	247	6.11%	Ophthalmology	38	4.73%
Otorhinolaryngology	91	2.25%	Otorhinolaryngology	18	2.24%
Pathology	60	1.48%	Pathology	7	.87%
Pediatric Cardiology	4	.10%			
Pediatrics	114	2.82%	Pediatrics	29	3.61%
Physical Medicine	32	.79%	Physical Medicine	5	.62%
Psychiatry	28	.69%	Psychiatry	4	.50%
Pulmonary Disease	38	.94%	Pulmonary Disease	10	1.25%
Radiation Oncology	20	.49%			
Radiology: Diag.	250	6.19%	Radiology: Diag.	35	4.36%
Rheumatology	9	.22%	Rheumatology	1	.12%
Surgery			Surgery		
Cardiovascular	52	1.29%	Cardiovascular	11	1.37%
Colon and Rectal	8	.20%			
General	89	2.20%	General	21	2.62%
Hand	14	.35%	Hand	4	.50%
Neuro	58	1.44%	Neuro	19	2.37%
Orthopedic	565	13.98%	Orthopedic	149	18.56%
Pediatric	3	.07%			
Plastic	32	.79%	Plastic	4	50%
Vascular/Thoracic	24	.59%	Vascular/Thoracic	12	1.49%
Urology	118	2.92%	Urology	28	3.49%
Other Single Specialties	273	6.76%	Other Single Specialties	2	.25%
TOTAL	4,041	100.00%	TOTAL	803	100.00%

TABLE 8.5 *(continued)*

4. Practice Type

MGMA Membership Frequencies

Practice Type	Count	Percent
Single Specialty	4,041	74.63%
Multispecialty	1,374	25.37%
TOTAL	5,415	100.00%

Survey Respondent Frequencies

Practice Type	Count	Percent
Single Specialty	803	68.87%
Multispecialty	363	31.13%
TOTAL	1,166	100.00%

5. Legal Organization

MGMA Membership Frequencies

Legal Organization	Count	Percent
Business Corp.	389	7.12%
Nonprofit Corp.	435	7.96%
Partnership	565	10.34%
Professional Corp.	3,939	72.10%
Sole Proprietorship	84	1.54%
Other	51	.93%
TOTAL	5,463	100.00%

Survey Respondent Frequencies

Legal Organization	Count	Percent
Business Corp.	203	18.22%
Nonprofit Corp.	43	3.86%
Partnership	86	7.72%
Professional Corp.	765	68.67%
Sole Proprietorship	1	.09%
Other	16	1.44%
TOTAL	1,114	100.00%

6. Total At-Risk Managed Care Revenue Percentage

MGMA Membership Frequencies

Total At-Risk Managed Care Revenue %	Count	Percent
No Managed Care	3,389	51.62%
10% or Less	1,252	19.07%
11% to 50%	1,636	24.92%
51% to 100%	288	4.39%
TOTAL	6,565	100.00%

Survey Respondent Frequencies

Total At-Risk Managed Care Revenue %	Count	Percent
No Managed Care	481	46.97%
10% or Less	196	19.14%
11% to 50%	272	26.56%
51% to 100%	75	7.32%
TOTAL	1,024	100.00%

7. Number of Satellite Facilities

MGMA Membership Frequencies

Number of Satellite Facilities	Count	Percent
1 to 2	1,730	58.84%
3 to 4	626	21.29%
5 to 6	262	8.91%
7 or more	322	10.95%
TOTAL	2,940	100.00%

Survey Respondent Frequencies

Number of Satellite Facilities	Count	Percent
1 to 2	400	59.35%
3 to 4	135	20.03%
5 to 6	68	10.09%
7 or more	71	10.53%
TOTAL	674	100.00%

Source: Medical Group Management Association. *MGMA Cost Survey: 1994 Report Based on 1993 Data.* Author: Englewood, CO, 1994. Reprinted with permission.

FIGURE 8.5. Mean Gross and Adjusted Collection Percentages for Multi-specialty Practices for Fee-for-Service Activity Only—1980 through 1993

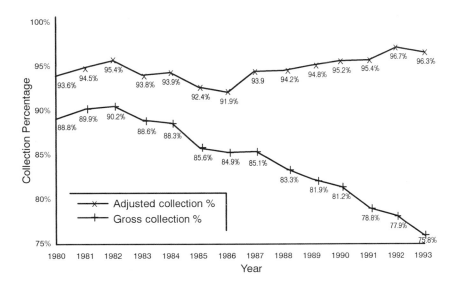

Note: The increasing gap between the adjusted collection percentage and the gross collection percentage can be interpreted as an increase in adjustments over time. Adjustments include charge restrictions imposed by Medicare and contractual adjustments required by third party payers such as commercial insurance carriers, managed care organizations, etc.

Source: Medical Group Management Association. *MGMA Cost Survey: 1994 Report Based on 1993 Data.* Author: Englewood, CO, 1994. Reprinted with permission.

The AMA is a resource for benchmarking operational development, for physicians and medical groups. Although members of the AMA are found across medical groups of various types and sizes, they have been more frequently found in the smaller groups and solo practices that have composed the influential base of the association's organizational structure. Excellent guides available through the AMA are particularly helpful in establishing and running a practice[30] and in buying and selling medical practices.[31]

FIGURE 8.6. Median Nonprovider Expense Categories as a Percentage of Total Nonprovider Expenses for Multispecialty Practices—1993

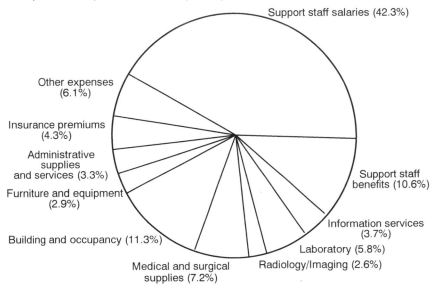

Note: These percentages are calculated by using a computed sum of $225,446 for "Total nonprovider expenses per FTE physician" as opposed to the published median of $235,786. This computation forces the pie chart slices to equal 100 percent. "Other expenses" include the expense categories of Physical therapy; Optical; Outside professional fees; Promotion and marketing; Interest; Health, business, and property taxes; and Other nonprovider expenses.

Source: Medical Group Management Association. *MGMA Cost Survey: 1994 Report Based on 1993 Data.* Author: Englewood, CO,1994. Reprinted with permission.

MANAGED CARE OPERATIONS

The American Group Practice Association (AGPA) and the Unified Medical Group Association (UMGA) participated in the development of the *Managed Care Digest, 1994: Medical Group Practice Edition, Hoechst Marion Roussel Managed Care Digest, Medical Group Practice Digest, 1994.* Data were supplied by Medical Group Management Association (MGMA), Englewood, Colorado, and American Medical Group Association (AMGA), Alexandria, Virginia, under the sponsorship of MGMA.[32] The *Managed Care Digest* focuses on medical group practice activities by illustrating cross-sectional presentations of benchmarks in managed care

Nonprovider Expenses	Practice Type							
	Multispecialty							
	Count	Mean	Std. Dev.	10th percentile	25th percentile	Median	75th percentile	90th percentile
Total Support staff salaries	362	$101,947	$33,800	$67,764	$80,687	$95,316	$117,333	$142,852
General administrative	302	$10,994	$7,793	$5,303	$6,882	$9,116	$12,520	$18,606
Business office	299	$14,199	$7,783	$7,476	$9,375	$12,700	$16,785	$21,566
Managed care administrative	77	$4,788	$4,600	$664	$1,314	$3,182	$6,570	$11,584
Information services	207	$3,732	$2,167	$1,263	$2,164	$3,280	$5,139	$7,068
Housekeeping/maintenance/security	211	$2,668	$1,680	$765	$1,484	$2,436	$3,526	$4,773
Other administrative support	138	$3,156	$4,290	$357	$856	$1,974	$3,733	$7,204
Registered nurses	251	$15,099	$10,503	$3,165	$7,399	$12,744	$21,206	$28,675
LPNs, medical assistants, etc.	265	$18,226	$10,148	$7,496	$11,337	$17,226	$22,265	$30,257
Medical receptionists	269	$11,692	$7,649	$4,555	$7,235	$9,961	$14,153	$19,841
Medical secretaries/transcribers	264	$5,605	$3,123	$2,045	$3,499	$5,114	$6,909	$9,572
Medical records	261	$5,897	$3,371	$2,460	$3,765	$5,663	$7,241	$9,223
Laboratory	268	$9,076	$4,582	$4,462	$6,215	$8,535	$11,085	$14,636
Radiology/imaging	265	$6,317	$3,912	$2,432	$3,614	$5,545	$8,185	$10,313
Physical therapy	77	$3,700	$6,558	$251	$744	$2,272	$4,052	$6,968
Optical	78	$2,111	$3,539	$399	$799	$1,286	$1,955	$3,900
Other medical/ancillary services	168	$7,713	$10,390	$894	$2,216	$4,276	$8,758	$17,305
Total support staff benefit expenses	360	$25,659	$11,015	$14,762	$18,859	$23,933	$30,503	$39,982
Taxes: FICA, payroll, etc.	316	$9,204	$4,497	$5,650	$6,921	$8,307	$10,639	$13,193
Insurance: health, life, etc.	314	$9,380	$5,293	$3,834	$5,742	$8,132	$12,099	$15,970
Retirement and profit sharing	294	$6,394	$4,005	$1,935	$3,779	$5,634	$8,063	$11,410
Other benefits	253	$1,677	$1,871	$356	$684	$1,123	$1,972	$3,677
Total information services expenses	331	$9,319	$5,437	$4,161	$5,728	$8,436	$11,387	$15,164
Telephone/telecommunications	321	$4,105	$2,036	$2,150	$2,885	$3,682	$4,983	$6,225
Equipment/rent/depreciation/maintenance	276	$3,770	$3,357	$711	$1,542	$2,735	$4,856	$7,852
Service bureau fees	139	$2,602	$2,617	$239	$726	$1,731	$3,962	$5,977
Supplies and miscellaneous	206	$1,509	$2,549	$186	$380	$838	$1,630	$3,205

TABLE 8.6 (continued)

Total laboratory expenses	319	$13,527	$6,679	$5,579	$9,468	$13,064	$17,049	$21,812
Outside services fees	282	$5,981	$5,309	$727	$2,640	$4,807	$7,544	$12,678
Equipment rental/depreciation/maintenance	240	$1,596	$1,576	$196	$649	$1,248	$2,106	$3,127
Supplies and miscellaneous	285	$7,299	$4,058	$2,247	$4,623	$6,960	$9,311	$12,743
Total radiology/imaging expenses	307	$7,750	$6,756	$1,450	$2,795	$5,767	$10,894	$16,576
Outside services fees	165	$3,395	$4,624	$53	$257	$1,369	$4,374	$9,440
Equipment rental/depreciation/maintenance	233	$3,186	$4,148	$207	$544	$1,568	$3,900	$8,076
Supplies and miscellaneous	286	$3,562	$2,677	$1,086	$1,825	$2,683	$4,614	$6,967
Total physical therapy expenses	91	$2,203	$3,585	$89	$291	$723	$2,403	$6,471
Total optical expenses	84	$1,648	$1,806	$35	$210	$1,082	$2,659	$3,874
Total medical/surgical supply expenses	333	$18,125	$10,143	$7,614	$10,903	$16,155	$23,387	$31,127
Drugs and medications	297	$10,524	$8,037	$2,331	$5,013	$8,939	$13,362	$21,065
General medical supplies/instruments	308	$8,250	$5,163	$3,234	$4,718	$7,196	$10,315	$14,405
Laundry and linens	279	$624	$528	$105	$231	$514	$837	$1,282
Total building/occupancy expenses	333	$27,236	$12,665	$13,346	$18,184	$25,510	$34,589	$42,341
Rental/depreciation/occupancy	322	$21,695	$11,552	$8,220	$13,474	$20,234	$27,813	$36,238
Utilities	295	$3,123	$1,986	$974	$1,929	$2,933	$3,871	$5,270
Housekeeping/maintenance supplies	292	$1,558	$1,642	$260	$537	$1,008	$2,002	$3,397
Other	230	$2,563	$2,533	$248	$757	$2,014	$3,711	$5,571
Total furniture/equipment expenses	307	$7,352	$5,610	$922	$3,208	$6,446	$9,834	$14,716
Rental/depreciation	288	$6,249	$5,138	$851	$2,673	$5,187	$8,092	$13,355
Other	221	$1,831	$1,747	$375	$833	$1,487	$2,206	$3,703
Total administrative supplies/service/expenses	325	$9,257	$8,762	$3,072	$5,155	$7,453	$11,008	$15,213
Total insurance premiums	331	$10,527	$5,562	$4,618	$6,417	$9,603	$13,787	$17,647
Professional liability	321	$9,629	$5,425	$3,784	$5,585	$8,834	$13,026	$16,576
Other	284	$1,135	$1,731	$258	$418	$729	$1,268	$2,275

Source: Medical Group Management Association. *MGMA Cost Survey: 1994 Report Based on 1993 Data.* Author: Englewood, CO, 1994. Reprinted with permission.

TABLE 8.7. MGMA Survey Ranking Report

Cost Survey: 1995 Report Based on 1994 Data Report Based on Multispecialty Practices

Group Practice: MGMA Sample Group Practice

Department Performance Indicators	Reported	Percentile	Median	Count
Total net revenues (per FTE physician):				
Net fee-for-service revenue	$342,228	53	$320,771	36
Net prepaid revenue	$170,938	61	$155,436	26
Net other medical revenue	$3,083	35	$5,254	24
Total net medical revenue	$516,249	64	$461,954	36
Months adjusted FFS charges in Accounts Receivable				
Formula: Total AR / [(1/12) Adjusted FFS charges]	3.02	47	3.54	30
Gross collection percentage				
Formula: (Net FFS revenue x 100 / Gross FFS charges)	45.23%	31	76.65%	31
Adjusted collection percentage				
Formula: (Net FFS revenue x 100 / Adjusted FFS charges)	79.99%	38	95.68%	30
Gross patient charges by payer type:				
Medicare: capitated	*	*	*	0
fee-for-service	3.10%	25	17.75%	30
Medicaid: capitated	*	*	*	0
fee-for-service	2.80%	32	6.00%	27
Managed care: capitated	48.00%	67	32.60%	18
at-risk discount FFS	27.10%	*	*	0
not at-risk discount FFS	*	*	16.74%	16
Commercial, private, etc.	19.00%	37	39.64%	30

271

TABLE 8.7 *(continued)*

Department Performance Indicators	Reported	Percentile	Median	Count
Total FTE midlevel providers	.23	57	.19	33
Total FTE support staff	6.01	61	5.20	34
General administrative	.17	49	.18	32
Business office	.59	50	.59	32
Managed care administrative	.16	52	.14	16
Information services	.20	53	.17	29
Housekeeping/maintenance/security	.09	15	.90	31
Other administrative support	.06	43	.08	21
Registered nurses	.39	47	.41	30

*Cannot report: value not reported, value cannot be calculated, or insufficient sample size (count under 10).

Source: Medical Group Management Association. *MGMA Cost Survey: 1994 Report Based on 1993 Data.* Author: Englewood, CO, 1994. Reprinted with permission.

across small, medium-sized, and very large medical practices. The 1993 group practice database included 6,107 members in medical group practice in the MGMA. This number was up 8.8 percent, from 5,612 group practices in the MGMA database in 1992. These groups were made up in 1993 of 3,838, or 70 percent, single-specialty practices and 1,641, or 30 percent, multispecialty practices (excluding 628 with unknown specialty).

Some data in this digest are from an exclusive survey, the *MGMA Activities and Trends Survey,* conducted in April and May, 1994. This digest also contains information from other reports of surveys by MGMA and CRAHCA. In 1994, the following reports were included. As an annual report, the *Managed Care Digest* compares the most current information available:

- *MGMA Cost Survey: 1993 Report Based on 1992 Data* and *1994 Report Based on 1991 Data*
- *MGMA Physician Compensation and Production Survey: 1993 Report Based on 1992 Data* and *1992 Report Based on 1991 Data*
- *CRAHCA Performance Efficiency Evaluation Report (PEER):* 1993, 1992 and 1992 Annual Reports
- *CRAHCA Physician Services Practice Analysis (PSPA) Comparison: 1993 Medians*

This digest also contains data from the exclusive survey by AGPA, their *1994 Group Practice Activities and Trends Survey* conducted in April and May, 1994.[34] Example of types of available information on an annual basis:

1994 Summary

- Four percent of all medical group practices and 24 percent of groups with over fifty FTE physicians had ownership interests in HMOs in 1993. Multispeciality groups were twice as likely as single-specialty medical groups to have equity interests in HMOs.
- Nearly nine of every ten medical groups (89 percent) had managed care contracts with HMOs or PPOs in 1993, up from only 56 percent in 1992; 95 percent of groups with managed care contracts had one or more PPO contracts.
- Revenues from contracts for managed care accounted for 20 percent of total revenues of medical group practices in 1993, up from 17 percent in 1992.
- Fifty-five percent of medical group practices derived revenue from at-risk managed care contracts in 1993, up from 50 percent in 1992.

- Though integrated systems are under development nationwide, relatively few group practices (3.9 percent) were actually owned by hospitals in 1993, and just 2.5 percent participated in a "clinic without walls" arrangement (see Table 8.8).
- Groups relying heavily on managed care employed 5.34 staff per FTE physician in 1992, compared with only 4.37 in groups with no revenues from managed care.
- Fifty-eight percent of group practices had branches or satellite clinics in 1992; groups with satellites averaged 3.5 satellites per medical group (Table 8.9).
- Physicians in group practices typically performed three procedures per patient for the first six months of 1993, resulting in median relative value units (RVU) of 3.67 per patient. Each physician in a group practice typically worked with 1,301 patients in the six-month period.
- Group practices owning pharmacies experienced a 9 percent increase in average revenue per prescription, in 1992, to $27.57, up from $25.29 in 1991.
- Directors of medical group practices believe guidelines for practices and standards of care will be a high priority in the next five years; 31 percent of groups had formal treatment protocols, in 1993.

Multispecialty groups with a majority of revenues from contracts for at-risk managed care used many more midlevel providers per FTE physician, reflected in high costs for compensation for allied health professionals. These groups also had much lower annual fees per FTE physician to outside medical consultants (referral fees) as illustrated in Figure 8.7.

Eighty-three percent of medical groups were free-standing practices in both 1992 and 1993. In 1993, the remaining 17 percent were affiliated with hospitals (12 percent), universities (3 percent), had other affiliations (2 percent), or were government- or industry-affiliated (less than 1 percent). The affiliations of another 869 medical group practices were unknown.

Three-fourths of group practices in both 1992 and 1993 included ten or fewer FTE physicians. Another 16 percent had between eleven and twenty-five physicians. Two percent of groups reported fifty-one to ninety-nine physicians, while 3 percent had 100 or more physicians. Groups in orthopedic surgery (10 percent) and family practice (7 percent) accounted for the largest percentages of single-specialty groups in 1993 (see Figure 8.8).

Medical groups most often reported having diagnostic X-ray facilities (56 percent) and clinical laboratory facilities (41 percent) as part of their operations, followed by diagnostic imaging facilities (24 percent). But the percentage of groups whose operations included diagnostic X-ray and clinical laboratory facilities actually declined by several percentage points between

TABLE 8.8. Medical Group Practices

	Number of Medical Group Practices		Percentage Change	Percentage of All Groups**	
	1993	1992	1992-1993*	1993*	1992*
Affiliation					
None (Freestanding Practices)	4,489	4,341	3.4%	82.5%	82.8%
University	166	158	5.1	3.1	3.0
Industry/HMO	19	64	-70.3	0.4	1.2
Government	10	12	-16.7	0.2	0.2
Hospital	644	539	19.5	11.8	10.3
Other	110	127	-13.4	2.0	2.4
Unknown/Na*	669	371	—	—	—
Total	**6,107**	**5,612**	**8.8%**	**100.0%**	**100.0%**
Size (# of FTE Physicians)					
10 or Fewer	4,484	4,130	8.6%	73.4%	73.6%
11 - 25	949	870	9.1	15.5	15.5
26 - 50	344	314	9.6	5.6	5.6
51 - 99	149	127	17.3	2.4	2.3
100 or more	181	171	5.8	3.0	3.0
Total	**6,107**	**5,612**	**8.8%**	**100.0%**	**100.0%**
Single Specialty					
Allergy/Immunology	17	16	6.3%	0.3%	0.3%
Anesthesiology	200	189	5.8	3.7	3.6
Endocrinology	7	6	16.7	0.1	0.1
Family Practice	399	389	2.6	7.3	7.4
General Surgery	87	84	3.6	1.6	1.6
Hematology/Oncology	71	64	10.9	1.3	1.2
Obstetrics/Gynecology	344	334	3.0	6.3	6.3
Ophthalmology	231	222	4.1	4.2	4.2
Orthopedic Surgery	547	506	8.1	10.0	9.6
Pediatrics***	110	99	11.1	2.0	1.9
Radiology/Diagnostic	36	34	5.9	0.7	0.6
All Other Single Specialty	1,789	1,725	3.7	32.7	32.7
Total Single Specialty	**3,838**	**3,668**	**4.6**	**70.0**	**69.6**
Total Multispecialty	**1,641**	**1,605**	**2.2**	**30.0**	**30.4**
Unknown/NA	628	339	—	—	—
Total	**6,107**	**5,612**	**8.8%**	**100.0%**	**100.0%**

*Excluded from this data are groups whose specialty composition or affiliation are unknown. The 1993 affiliation percentages are calculated on a base of 5,438 groups, without 669 groups of unknown affiliation or composition. The 1992 affiliation percentages are calculated on a base of 5,241 groups, excluding 371 groups whose affiliations or composition were not identified.

**Includes 38 medical/faculty foundation members. Column totals have been rounded.

***Excludes pediatric subspecialties such as peds pulmonology, peds neurology, peds gastroenterology, and peds endocrinology.

Source: Medical Group Management Association. *MGMA Activities and Trends Survey: 1994 Report Based on 1993 Data.* Author: Englewood, CO, 1994. Reprinted with Permission.

TABLE 8.9. Medical Group Practices with Satellite Clinics or Branch Offices

	Number of Branch/Satellite Offices Owned*		
	1-2	3-4	5 or More
Size (# of FTE Physicians)			
10 or Fewer	71.3%	18.1%	10.6%
11 - 25	41.6	32.5	26.0
26 - 50	35.0	21.7	43.3
51 - 100	4.4	21.7	73.9
101 or More	7.1	7.1	85.7
Specialty Composition			
Single Specialty	64.4%	21.5%	14.1%
Multispecialty	42.3	18.7	38.7
Overall Average	57.8%	20.6%	21.6%
Sample Size: 876			

*Base is the 510 group practices (58%) with at least one satellite or branch office.

Source: Medical Group Management Association. *MGMA Member Database: 1991-1993.* Author: Englewood, CO, 1994. Reprinted with permission.

FIGURE 8.7. Expenses per FTE Physician

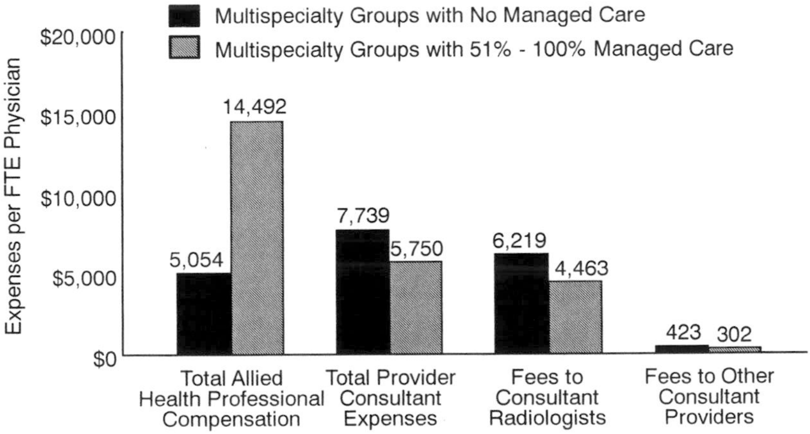

Source: Medical Group Management Association. *MGMA Cost Survey: 1994 Report Based on 1993 Data.* Author: Englewood, CO, 1994. Reprinted with permission.

FIGURE 8.8. 1993 Number of Single-Specialty Medical Group Practices

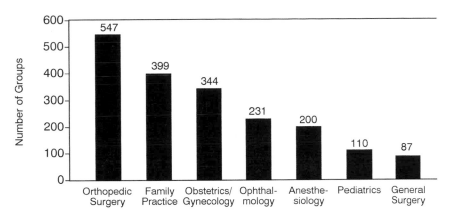

Source: Medical Group Management Association. *MGMA Cost Survey: 1994 Report Based on 1993 Data.* Author: Englewood, CO, 1994. Reprinted with permission.

1991 and 1993. Medical group practices were most likely to offer patients extended hours (37 percent), formal programs in patient education (29 percent), and cardiologic stress testing (29 percent), in 1993. Fewer than 10 percent of groups offered dialysis (5 percent), home health care (7 percent), multiphasic screening (7 percent), or MRIs (9 percent). The percentage of group practices that offered extended hours for patient care increased several percentage points to 37.3 percent in 1993, from 35.4 percent in 1991. A lower proportion of groups offered stress tests in 1993 (29.2 percent) than in 1991 (31.4 percent).

USING RELATIVE VALUE UNITS
TO STANDARDIZE MEASUREMENTS[33]

Data on medical groups can be used successfully to measure and compare their productivity. Data on their RVUs can also provide a baseline for calculating capitated rates. Relative value units can only be determined by establishing frequencies of use for each procedure. An RVU is the measure used by the federal government as the basis for calculating physicians' payments for services. Other payers also use the RVU method of determining such payments. Other than office visits by patients, the most frequently performed procedures typically involve drawing blood, performing hemograms, analyzing urine and tissue, and handling specimens, according to data from medical group practices (see Table 8.10). Together, these activities account for very high frequencies of tasks performed.

TABLE 8.10. The Most Common Procedures of Medical Group Practices

Procedure	Relative Frequency per 10,000 Procedures	CPT-4 Code*
Office/Outpatient Visit, Est., Level 2	1,352.5	99212
Office/Outpatient Visit, Est., Level 3	1,126.9	99213
Drawing Blood	507.3	36415
Automated Hemogram	454.1	85025
Post-op Follow-up Visit	414.1	99024
19 or More Blood/Urine Tests	386.2	80019
Automated Hemogram	327.6	85024
Urinalysis with Microscopy	300.2	81000
Tissue Exam by Pathologist	249.3	88305
Tissue Exam by Pathologist	249.3	8830526
Tissue Exam by Pathologist	249.3	88305TC
Mammogram, Screening	248.2	76092
Automated Hemogram	223.4	85022
Urinalysis Nonautomatic w/o Scope	211.4	81002
Prothrombin Time	204.2	85610
Specimen Handling	198.1	99000
Office/Outpatient Visit, Est., Level 1	197.2	99211
Office/Outpatient Visit, Est., Level 4	193.2	99214
Automated Hemogram	189.7	85027
Assay Thyroid Hormone	166.8	84443

*CPT-4 codes over five digits designate a professional or technical component of the CPT-4 code.

Source: Medical Group Management Association. CRAHCA Physical Services Practice Analysis Comparison: 1993 Medians. Copyright, 1994. Reprinted with permission.

Example of RVU information applied:

Activity Summary
(Medians for Six Months of Procedures)

FTE Physicians/Group Practice	28.76
Patients/Group Practice	45,488
Procedures (six months)	96,099
RVU Count	115,779.30
Procedures/Patient	3.04
Procedures/FTE Physician	3,530
Patients/FTE Physician	1,301
RVUs/Procedure	1.10
RVUs/FTE Physician	4,310.60
RVUs/Patient	2.67

Comparisons of Productivity

Study of the office visit profiles of RVUs performed by medical specialty enables group practices to compare their activities and productivity to those of a national sample of medical groups, using the resource-based relative value scale developed by the Health Care Financing Administration. The RBRVS was developed to establish a new relationship between cognitive and procedural services for purposes of reimbursement.

Rates of Reimbursement per RVU

The following standard conversion factors are not geographically adjusted:[2]

$35.42: primary care services
$40.80: surgical services
$34.63: other nonsurgical services[35]

Group practices may develop an individualized RVU comparison using activity reports generated internally by their own practices and coupling those with software developed to calculate RVUs per physician per month, by specialty. Two examples of RVU calculations are provided to allow comparisons within similar specialties and to familiarize readers with methodology in using RVUs. See Table 8.11 and Figure 8.9.

Relative value units provide a unique view into a medical specialty by focusing on procedures consuming the most resources, either by the frequency with which they occur or by the complexity of the procedures. For

TABLE 8.11. Procedure Code Profile by Specialty

CPT-4 CODE	Allergy/Immunology (17.55 FTEs) Description	RVUs*
95117	Immunotherapy Injections	62.08
95115	Immunotherapy, One Injection	49.18
99213	Office/Outpatient Visit, Est.	43.46
99214	Office/Outpatient Visit, Est.	24.33
99244	Office Consultation	22.82

CPT-4 CODE	Noninvasive Cardiology (29.83 FTEs) Description	RVUs*
93307	Echo Exam of Heart	129.03
93015	Cardiovascular Stress Test	56.26
99213	Office/Outpatient Visit, Est.	54.51
9330726	Echo Exam of Heart	47.16
99254	Initial Inpatient Consult	26.83

CPT-4 CODE	Family Practice (115.113 FTEs) Description	RVUs*
99213	Office/Outpatient Visit, Est.	139.64
99212	Office/Outpatient Visit, Est.	67.58
99214	Office/Outpatient Visit, Est.	34.06
59410	Obstetrical Care	23.01
99215	Office/Outpatient Visit, Est.	22.92

CPT-4 CODE	Invasive Cardiology (30.17 FTEs) Description	RVUs*
92982	Coronary Dilation	118.49
93307	Echo Exam of Heart	68.65
93325	Doppler Color Flow	61.14
99213	Office/Outpatient Visit, Est.	38.14
99231	Subsequent Hospital Care	23.72

CPT-4 CODE	Diagnostic Radiology (37.85 FTEs) Description	RVUs*
71020	Chest X Ray	94.53
76700	Echo Exam of Abdomen	29.25
76090	Mammogram, Both Breasts	17.84
76805	Echo Exam of Pregnant Uterus	17.38
76091	Mammogram, Both Breasts	5.14

CPT-4 CODE	General Surgery (49.170 FTEs) Description	RVUs*
19120	Removal of Breast Lesion	22.97
49505	Repair Inguinal Hernia	22.42
99212	Office/Outpatient Visit, Est.	18.11
44140	Partial Removal of Colon	14.47
19240	Removal of Breast	13.82

Hematology/Oncology (41.1 FTEs)

CPT-4 CODE	Description	RVUs*
99214	Office/Outpatient Visit, Est.	61.89
99213	Office/Outpatient Visit, Est.	51.35
96410	Chemotherapy, Infusion Method	30.33
99215	Office/Outpatient Visit, Est.	18.79
99231	Subsequent Hospital Care	13.86

OB/Gyn (62 FTEs)

CPT-4 CODE	Description	RVUs*
59400	Obstetrical Care	313.54
59510	Cesarean Delivery	101.57
59410	Obstetrical Care	90.63
99213	Office/Outpatient Visit, Est.	71.66
59515	Cesarean Delivery	53.83

Orthopedic Surgery (89.397 FTEs)

CPT-4 CODE	Description	RVUs*
27447	Total Knee Replacement	76.05
29881	Knee Arthroscopy/Surgery	65.16
27130	Total Hip Replacement	46.61
29877	Knee Arthroscopy Surgery	26.68
63047	Removal of Spinal Lamina	17.13

Internal Medicine (203.5 FTEs)

CPT-4 CODE	Description	RVUs*
99214	Office/Outpatient Visit, Est.	83.41
99213	Office/Outpatient Visit, Est.	29.06
99212	Office/Outpatient Visit, Est.	28.68
99232	Subsequent Hospital Care	12.29
71020	Chest X Ray	7.93

Ophthalmology (28.8 FTEs)

CPT-4 CODE	Description	RVUs*
66984	Remove Cataract, Insert Lens	235.78
92014	Eye Exam and Treatment	88.75
99213	Office/Outpatient Visit, Est.	51.76
67210	Treatment of Retinal Lesion	39.15
99202	Office/Outpatient Visit, New	4.18

Pediatrics (80.44 FTEs)**

CPT-4 CODE	Description	RVUs*
99213	Office/Outpatient Visit, Est.	97.31
99212	Office/Outpatient Visit, Est.	63.97
99214	Office/Outpatient Visit, Est.	7.95
99203	Office/Outpatient Visit, New	4.42
99202	Office/Outpatient Visit, New	3.53

*Represents mean RVU per FTE physician per month.
**Pediatrics excludes subspecialty pediatrics such as pulmonology, neurology, gastroenterology, and endocrinology.

Source: Reprinted with permission from the Medical Group Management Association. CRAHCA Physician Services Practice Analysis Comparison: 1993 Medians, Englewood, CO, 1994.

FIGURE 8.9. Procedure Code Profile—Internal Medicine

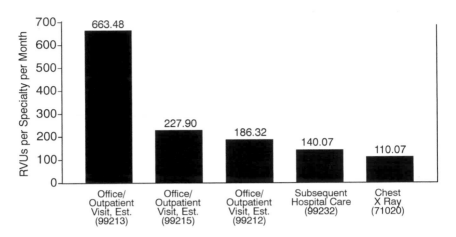

Source: Reprinted with permission from Medical Group Management Association. *CRAHA Physician Services Practice Analysis Comparison: 1993 Medians.* Author: Englewood, CO, 1994.

example, a total knee replacement in an orthopedic practice has an average RVU per month of 76.05, with an RVU per occurrence of 53.35, as is seen in studying the value schedule published by the government. This equates to an average of 1.43 procedures of this type per orthopedic surgeon per month (76.05 divided by 53.35, or 53.35 multiplied by 1.43). The conclusion to be drawn is that knee replacements consume large amounts of resources in orthopedic physicians' work and overhead. For pediatricians, the top procedure by RVU in that specialty is an outpatient office visit with an established patient, consuming 97.31 RVUs per physician per month—just under one hundred occurrences of this procedure. Each office visit has a low relative value, as published in the federal schedule, but their high frequency indicates that these procedures consume a large amount of resources for this specialty.

Production Trends Used to Calculate RVUs per FTE Physician

The frequencies and total numbers of procedures/encounters performed in group practices are used to determine the total RVUs, RVUs per specialist, and RVUs per procedure. Table 8.12 shows, for each specialty, the

TABLE 8.12. Procedure Frequency per Specialist per Month*

CPT-4 CODE	Invasive Cardiology (30.17 FTEs)			Noninvasive Cardiology (29.83 FTEs)			Family Practice (115.113 FTEs)		
	Freq/Mo/FTE	% of Total	% Freq.	Freq/Mo/FTE	% of Total	% Freq.	Freq/Mo/FTE	% of Total	% Freq.
99201	0.17	—	0.2	0.53	0.033	0.5	2.99	0.338	1.0
99202	0.44	—	0.5	0.53	0.100	0.5	8.74	1.477	2.9
99203	1.41	0.184	1.7	0.73	0.133	0.7	4.50	0.963	1.5
99204	1.97	0.287	2.4	1.30	0.077	1.2	1.70	0.318	0.6
99205	2.43	0.436	3.1	2.21	0.398	2.1	.74	0.139	0.2
99211	1.32	0.218	1.6	4.64	0.387	4.4	5.51	0.791	1.8
99212	14.76	1.298	18.1	8.24	1.051	7.7	100.11	22.391	33.7
99213	39.92	8.648	48.3	56.17	6.193	52.7	140.09	29.364	47.2
99214	17.77	2.458	21.8	25.64	2.356	24.0	22.87	3.676	7.7
99215	1.79	0.149	2.3	6.56	0.310	6.2	9.74	2.233	3.3

CPT-4 CODE	General Surgery (49.17 FTEs)			Hematology & Oncology (41.1 FTEs)			DEFINITIONS OF CPT-4 CODES
	Freq/Mo/FTE	% of Total	% Freq.	Freq/Mo/FTE	% of Total	% Freq.	
99201	3.02	0.716	3.4	0.12	0.048	0.1	99201: Office/outpatient visit, new, Level 1
99202	3.50	0.822	3.9	0.63	0.038	0.5	99202: Office/outpatient visit, new, Level 2
99203	1.29	0.464	1.5	1.73	0.143	1.2	99203: Office/outpatient visit, new, Level 3
99204	0.27	0.063	0.3	1.18	0.248	0.9	99204: Office/outpatient visit, new, Level 4
99205	0.29	0.084	0.3	1.04	0.153	0.7	99205: Office/outpatient visit, new, Level 5
99211	24.25	3.708	27.5	18.63	2.177	13.4	99211: Office/outpatient visit, established patient, Level 1
99212	30.89	9.671	34.9	13.97	0.831	10.0	99212: Office/outpatient visit, established patient, Level 2
99213	22.30	5.394	25.2	52.94	6.532	38.0	99213: Office/outpatient visit, established patient, Level 3
99214	2.19	0.211	2.5	41.26	8.146	29.6	99214: Office/outpatient visit, established patient, Level 4
99215	0.41	0.042	0.5	7.93	1.776	5.6	99215: Office/outpatient visit, established patient, Level 5

TABLE 8.12 (continued)

CPT-4 CODE	Internal Medicine (203.5 FTEs)			Ophthalmology (28.8 FTEs)		
	Freq/Mo/FTE	% of Total	% Freq.	Freq/Mo/FTE	% of Total	% Freq.
99201	1.25	0.221	0.7	0.89	0.250	0.9
99202	3.43	0.636	1.9	2.79	0.985	2.9
99203	2.95	0.869	1.7	5.20	1.085	5.5
99204	2.23	0.408	1.2	3.90	0.284	4.2
99205	2.68	0.279	1.5	0.07	0.033	0.1
99211	3.62	0.595	2.0	6.45	0.000	6.9
99212	42.18	6.837	23.6	22.51	9.229	23.6
99213	88.74	17.067	49.7	42.24	11.916	44.1
99214	19.13	18.26	10.7	10.19	3.755	10.7
99215	12.26	2.400	6.9	0.92	0.050	1.1

CPT-4 CODE	Orthopedic Surgery (89.397 FTEs)			OB/Gyn (62 FTEs)			Pediatrics (80.44 FTEs)**		
	Freq/Mo/FTE	% of Total	% Freq.	Freq/Mo/FTE	% of Total	% Freq.	Freq/Mo/FTE	% of Total	% Freq.
99201	10.19	0.534	6.0	1.72	0.164	1.1	1.65	0.658	0.7
99202	16.88	4.879	10.2	4.44	0.434	2.8	2.78	0.974	1.2
99203	12.70	1.349	7.7	3.60	0.590	2.3	2.54	0.665	1.6
99204	1.85	0.341	1.2	2.30	0.213	1.5	1.73	0.181	0.8
99205	1.04	0.252	0.7	.55	0.049	0.4	.36	0.087	0.1
99211	10.39	2.890	6.3	6.99	0.812	4.5	5.93	1.579	2.7
99212	70.45	12.835	42.6	51.45	8.436	32.8	94.08	23.205	43.1
99213	32.04	5.217	19.4	73.87	8.403	47.2	100.32	29.264	46.0
99214	7.59	1.467	4.6	8.49	1.303	5.4	5.30	1.747	2.3
99215	2.19	0.430	1.3	3.22	0.377	2.0	3.32	0.423	1.5

WHAT THIS DATA MEANS

Freq./Mo.: The median number of procedures per physician per month. **Example:** For orthopedic surgery, Procedure 99201 occurred 10.19 times per month per physician.

% of Total: The percentage of all procedures per month. **Example:** For orthopedists, Procedure 99201 occurred 10.19 times and was 0.534% of all procedures for that specialty. This field will not add up to 100%; only the top 10 codes are shown.

% Freq.: The percentage each procedure represents of the 10 procedures shown. **Example:** For orthopedists, of the 10 procedures, 6.0% were office outpatient visits (99201). The percentages add up to 100% for this column.

TABLE 8.12 *(continued)*

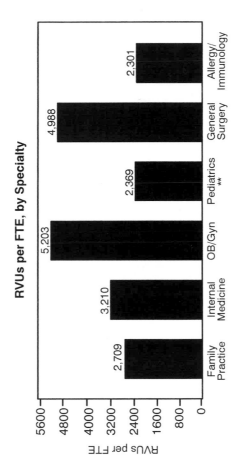

RVUs per FTE, by Specialty

285

TABLE 8.12 (continued)

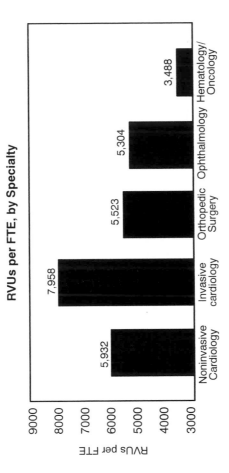

RVUs per FTE, by Specialty

*All numbers are medians for all groups for six months, January through June 1993.
**Excludes pediatric subspecialties such as pulmonology, neurology, gastroenterology, and endocrinology.

Source: Medical Group Management Association. *CRAHCA Physician Services Practice Analysis Comparison: 1993 Medians.* Author: Englewood, CO, 1994. Reprinted with permission.

percentages of total encounters or procedures for the ten most common types of office visits. Sixty-two percent of total encounters and procedures for family group practices were reported among these ten office outpatient procedures. Conversely, 38 percent of total encounters for family group practices were not codes for office visits. Pediatric group practices experienced a pattern of very high volumes of office visits (59 percent of total procedures). Total RVUs for family practice groups were 26,611.97 for office visits, resulting in 2,709.41 RVUs per FTE physician. (Some data are not shown.)

Groups Can Use RVUs per FTE to Compare Their Productivity

Total RVUs for each specialty comprise the frequency per month for each procedure or office visit and the total FTEs in each specialty. The total RVUs for a group practice are indicators of the complexity of procedures and of case intensities. Case intensity is a measure of the difficulty of a patient's case and of multiple problems. This explains why the RVUs per FTE physician of 7,958 RVUs for invasive cardiologists are so much higher than the 2,709 RVUs per FTE for family practitioners. The conclusion to be drawn is that cardiologic procedures are roughly three times as complex as procedures in family practice.

OPERATIONAL IMPROVEMENTS

Various terms are used to describe operational improvements including reengineering, value improvement, cost quality adjustment, and others. The underlying intent is to determine ways and means to increase efficiency, enhance quality, and produce more for less cost. Competitive marketplaces in health care are experiencing price wars resulting in shifts of members under managed care among competing plans, due to significant underbidding to buy the business at cost, or more frequently below cost. Buying business at cost or at loss is the only way for some groups to increase their market share in competitive environments.

Operational improvement is being used to supplement efforts to grow. Coupled with shrinking reimbursement from virtually all sources of payment, organizations are becoming more proactive in seeking new ways to enhance operations and reduce expenses. An example of how a physician group and hospital organization was guided through operational improvement follows.

Goal

To strengthen physician and hospital services by improving operational efficiency and reducing costs, without compromising the quality of care or service provided.

Planned Outcome

The physicians and hospital will be able to compete successfully in a very competitive marketplace.

A four-phased approach was recommended; it provides the structure to achieve continuous operational improvement. A steering committee of key staff are selected to guide the process. If current administrative staff are not familiar with the process, outside consultants will be required. This approach also helps to focus on those areas that present the greatest opportunity to reduce costs and improve quality of service. An overview of each phase follows:

Phase I: Establishing the Imperative to Change

The goal of this phase is to define the magnitude of the project and to select areas for further review. In this phase, a "helicopter view" of the organization is taken. Various techniques are used to make comparisons between this physicians' practice and its competitors, and national benchmarks. Interviews are conducted with all key staff. Tours of the practice and hospital sites are done. Several analyses are performed, including a review of skill mix, productivity, nonsalary costs, organizational structure, span of control, and utilization management. With the findings from Phase I, the steering committee is able to prioritize and select areas that offer the greatest opportunity for enhancing quality and service and reducing costs.

Phase II: Creating Shared Vision

Within this phase, administrative staff serving as the project's directors and/or the consultants spend significant time in each area selected in Phase I to gain a thorough understanding of operations. Interviews are conducted with managers, staff, physicians, and patients involved in the examined area of operations. Extensive observations of work flow are made. Various area-specific analyses of productivity and cost are performed. With this information, opportunities to improve the operation and reduce costs are quantified and documented. Opportunities are not limited to the selected areas; consideration is also given to improvement of interdepartmental relationships.

The Phase II Review takes approximately four to six weeks per area examined. An executive sponsor from the steering committee is assigned to each area. The executive sponsor provides managerial oversight and is accountable for the project's success. The administrative director and/or consultants work closely with the executive sponsor and managers in the area examined, to develop a report for formal presentation to the steering committee.

Phase III: Redesigning

This phase begins with the development of an overall plan for implementation to address the findings outlined in Phase II. In most cases this requires establishing teams for redesign, typically three to four for each area needing work. Goals for quality, service, and financial concerns from Phase II are further refined for the area as a whole and for the individual teams, as applicable. Oversight is provided by the executive sponsor. Members of the team include individuals not only from the specific area, but also physicians and other representatives from outside the area as necessary. Teams working on redesign use an approach based on continuous quality improvement. They develop detailed plans for implementation, outlining specific resources, timing, work steps, and responsibilities for the various tasks. Full-scale implementation begins in this phase.

Phase IV: Maintaining Change

In the final phase, the objective is to achieve and sustain measurable operational improvement. Implementation continues, as well as monitoring of performance against established standards defined in Phases II and III. During this phase, the mechanism for meeting targets and for continuous improvement that has been put in place continues.

Example of This Process Applied to a Physicians' Group and Hospital

Phase I

Phase I of operational improvement officially kicked off and completed within two to three months. Several conclusions were identified during Phase I. They include:

- Historically, increases in revenue have mirrored trends in cost increases
- Overall direction in this practice is similar to that of other providers in our marketplace
- The patient population in this practice is not as critical as many perceive
- This practice must align its resources with actual patient acuity
- Overall gains have been made in productivity, with increased volume of business
- Interdepartmental barriers seem to impede operational efficiencies and dilute our focus on patients
- Reductions in staff are inevitable
- Everything is on the table for review

On the basis of findings in Phase I, there were sufficient opportunities for enhancements of quality and service and for cost savings to proceed with the project. Those areas where the opportunities were the greatest were selected for further review. Criteria for selection included the extent of interdependence with or influence on other departments, degree to which the area does not meet expectations for providing service or quality, and areas where comparisons with competitors and with benchmarks indicated there were opportunities for cost reduction. The areas identified for further review in Phase II included:

- Medical surgical nursing
- Intensive care nursing
- Pharmacy
- Bedside delivery of ancillary services
- Pathology
- Surgical services
- Business office
- Business/customer services
- Management of human resources
- Utilization management
- Physicians' practice operations
- Radiology
- Information systems

Phase II

The goal of Phase II was to find opportunities for cost reduction or improvements in service or quality. Initiatives identified from the work in Phase II are highlighted below:

Nursing

- Achieve improved morale and job satisfaction among employees
- Demonstrate enhanced patient satisfaction
- Demonstrate improvement in physicians' satisfaction with the delivery of patient care
- Incorporate strategies that result in increased collaboration between physicians and nurses
- Achieve cost reductions and increased productivity associated with restructured staffing and changes in skill mix

Pharmacy

- Redesign to combine roles of pharmacists
- Improve functions in nonclinical support, such as in the distribution and billing of stocked medications
- Redesign processing for outpatient prescriptions, with an increased focus on customers and an improved policy on prescriptions at the patient's discharge
- Restructure management and organization functions
- Initiate a cost-benefit analysis of the programs in teaching and research
- Achieve cost reductions and increased productivity associated with the above and with changes in skill mix

Bedside Ancillary

- Consider delivery of bedside ancillary care utilizing a unit-based multiskilled caregiver
- Improve quality and consistency of caregiver/patient communication
- Eliminate interruptions in patient care due to uncoordinated scheduling
- Achieve cost reductions associated with the above

Pathology

- Reduce labor costs via an alternative managerial structure, increased cross training, and changes in skill mix
- Further evaluate costs/benefits of educational programs for medical technicians (MT) and medical lab technicians (MLT)
- Implement strategies to evaluate the limiting of standing orders and to reduce utilization of stat orders
- Achieve cost reductions associated with the above

Surgical Services

- Improve case scheduling and increase utilization of the operating room
- Reengineer the overall organization of anesthetic services
- Reduce costs of supplies via expanded use of expertise in materials management
- Redesign the teaching model by further evaluating the teaching programs
- Achieve cost reductions associated with the above

Business Office Functions and Business/Customer Services

- Develop improved customer service initiative
- Increase number of claims billed electronically
- Target reduction of gross days of revenue outstanding in accounts receivable
- Reduce late charges
- Redesign cashier's office
- Implement collection of copayments, "up front"
- Continue to expand registration and scheduling done in centralized areas
- Develop guidelines for financial counseling for the underinsured
- Achieve cost reductions associated with the above

Phase III

Those areas that moved into the activities of Phase III began the task of further defining their goals for quality, service, and financial concerns identified in Phase II. In most areas, it was anticipated that three or four redesigning teams would be established to develop specific plans for implementation to meet the goals. Recruitment for the teams was initiated, using an interdepartmental approach followed by the development of specific plans for activities of each team, and a schedule including an estimated date for completion. As in the other phases, the executive sponsor provided leadership for activities of the teams. The administrative project director and/or consultants were involved either in assisting to develop teams or in providing oversight. Updates and progress were to be reported to the steering committee.

Communications

Consistent with the plan for communications, key findings of the project are formally presented to management and to the physicians' group. Operation Improvement Update is a standing item on agendas for regularly scheduled administrative and physicians' meetings. As key points are achieved along the way, updates are presented at physicians' board meetings.

Summary of Key Activities, Expected Outcomes, and Potential Cost Savings

Determining the Need to Change

- Select members of steering committee
- Select project manager and members of project team
- Hold kick-off meeting for project, to communicate:

> Mission and strategy
> Organization and work plan
> Timetable

- Conduct preliminary analysis and benchmarking in:

> Productivity
> Layers of management/span of control
> Nonsalary cost analysis
> Analysis of competitors
> Analysis of internal trends
> Business (line profitability)
> Analysis of skill mixes
> Analysis of core processes

- Conduct interviews with executives and physicians to identify issues of quality and service

Expected Outcomes: Criteria and format for selection of areas on which to focus for redesign; an imperative for a commitment to change

Specification of Objectives for Evaluation

Select areas of focus for redesign on the basis of criteria of cost, service, and quality

- Conduct in-depth reviews by department/clinic and/or focus area using:

> Interviews with managers
> Interviews with customers and focus groups
> Observation of key processes and work flows

- Analyze supportive data
- Identify cross-functional drivers of costs
- Refine opportunities using:

    Strategy sessions for members of teams to define objectives for evaluation
    Selection of opportunities, quantification, and prioritization

- Identify opportunities in:

    Presentations to the steering committee
    Agreements on priorities

- Develop preliminary strategies for implementation

Expected Outcomes: Opportunities for redesign will be identified and quantified; objectives will be defined and expectations for performance delineated.

Development of the Work Plan

- Develop strategies for organizational implementation
- Involve physicians and other internal and external customers in planning implementation
- Prioritize departments/clinical areas to be implemented
- Define requirements for tracking performance
- Develop detailed plans for implementation:

    Time frames
    Work steps
    Benchmarks for performance
    Tracking systems

- Initiate implementation:

    Conduct required training
    Pilot and refine as necessary
    Track performance

Expected Outcomes: A plan for organizational implementation; detailed plans for implementation with defined criteria for performance; tools for managers to track performance; redesigned processes that can become operational.

Continuous Quality Improvement

- Internalize continuous process of improvement by:

    Ongoing training of the staff
    Development of leadership and training of managers
    Strategies for improving transitional operations to redesign under framework of total quality management improvement

- Assess readiness of informational systems to implement new reporting for management
- Evaluate outcomes:

    Evaluate/monitor results against established targets
    Evaluate targets on an ongoing basis

Expected Outcomes: Ability to maintain change and adapt to new environment; documentation of actual results as compared to expected results; elimination of gaps yielding improved performance; reevaluation of performance thresholds following achievement of initial objectives.

Potential Enhanced Efficiencies in the Operating System and Related Cost Savings

Example: Ambulatory Care Practice

To summarize, opportunities in ambulatory care, by major area, generally focus on the development of clinical modules of "clusters," and break down as described in Table 8.13.

Example: Integrated Physician-Hospital Organization

Summary of Goals for Quality/Service:

- Improve patient satisfaction
- Improve physician satisfaction
- Improve employee morale and job satisfaction
- Improve quality and consistency of communications with caregivers
- Eliminate interruptions in patient care due to uncoordinated scheduling in delivery of care and/or in personnel
- Improve interdisciplinary coordination/collaboration

TABLE 8.13. Breakdown of Opportunities in Ambulatory Care, by Major Area

System	Current System	Prospective System	1996 Annual Operating Dollar Impact*#
First Appointments/Registration	Individual Clinics	Automated and Clusters	$226.800
Reception/Waiting	Individual Clinics	Clusters	120,000
Medical Records	Manual Unitized	Chart Tracking Optical Disk	341,200
Clinic Support Personnel	Individual Clinics	Clusters	670,800
Exam Rooms/Schedule Flow	Individual Clinics	Clusters and Smothered	169,400
Procedure Rooms	Individual Clinics	Clusters	8,000
Transcription	Departments	Central Support	151,200
Repeat/Cross-Clinic Appts/Testing	Individual Clinics	Automated Scheduling	167,200
Cashiering for Outpatient	—	Clusters	0
Blood Draw Stations	Central Support and Satellite	Central Support & Ambulatory	0
Charge Entry	Central Support and Individual Clinics	Clusters	396,000
Billing Production/Accts Receivable	Central Support and Departments	Central Support	0
Information/Customer Service	—	Central Support	(93,000)
Support Services	Central Support	Central Support	0
Clinic Administration	Departments	Departments	0
			$2,157,600

*Inflation assumed at 6% per year, $1 in 1996 = $0.75 in 1991.
#Preliminary and subject to change.

Source: Sommers, PA, Luxenberg, MG, Sommers, EP. Continuous quality improvement longitudinally applied to integrated service outcomes. Internal work papers used to show integrated approach. *Medical Group Management Journal*, 42(2): March/April, 1995.

- Develop strategies to eliminate provision of unnecessary tests/procedures/supplies/drugs
- Design processes that support continuity of caregivers
- Streamline processes used for documenting care provided
- Redesign processes for creation and delivery of reports that facilitate smooth delivery of care
- Increase caregivers' time at the bedside
- Incorporate a teaching model that provides a reasonable teaching experience, quality patient care, and efficiency
- Simplify patients' requirements to do paperwork to eliminate unnecessary delays and redundant processes

Potential Savings Targeted

Phase I: $15.7-$29.5 million

Phase II: Initial target—$12.8-$22.1 million; opportunities not yet pursued in initial Phase II—$2.9-$7.4 million; final confirmed—$11.9-$16.7 million

Phase III:	*In Progress*	*Planned*	*Combined*
Teams with consultant	$4.7 - $6.3 million	$5.7 - $7.9 million	$10.4 - $14.2 million
All teams	$6.2 - $8.8 million	$5.7 - $7.9 million	$11.9 - $16.7 million

APPLICATIONS

Targeted Goal

1. What differences were found to exist between desired clinical practice focused on customer service/customer satisfaction and those focused on operational support?
2. Which services should the practice buy and which build? Why? At what point (if ever) should you build/hire your own?
3. Define practical applications of CQI. Analyze return on investment gained by activities in CQI. What will be done differently on the basis of results from CQI?

Objectives

1. What overhead expense can be compared to accomplishment of each goal for your practice?

2. Was an outside consultant or managerial service worth the expense? Could the activity be enhanced?
3. Is CQI a way to conduct a practice? How has its impact been measured? Could the process be improved? How?

Content

Since every practice is different, how can your organization benefit from additional content (either through adding more or different subject matter to each area or adding new sections of different operational content)? What specific changes should be made? Why? What unique characteristics of your market warrant the enhancements?

Evaluations

Define elements of change in your practice. How will your practice embrace change as a way of doing business?

Continuous Quality Improvement

What observable differences exist between current outcomes in your practice and those that are desired? Where does performance in your practice stand, from the perspectives of regional and national performance? What will be changed as a result of your assessments in CQI?

Chapter 9

Mission-Based Planning

POINTS FOR FOCUS

Where do you want your practice to be when it gets to where you are going? Whether your practice succeeds or fails should not come as a surprise. Optimize success through planning.

Targeted Goals

1. To establish a vision and mission focused on meeting the health care needs of defined groups of consumers.
2. To define core values upon which to base the delivery of medical services.
3. To appraise the environment in your marketplace by defining strengths, weaknesses, opportunities, and threats (SWOTs).

Objectives

1. Specify key strategies for positioning.
2. Outline goals, strategies for implementation, objectives, and programs.
3. Apply the processes for CQI to monitor performance and manage necessary enhancements to optimize desired outcomes.

Content

A physicians' practice based upon clear vision and mission establishes the context for planning. Specification of desired quantifiable goals and objectives is described. Budgets are developed to support achievement of measurable goals and objectives.

Evaluation

Measure performance-based goals/objectives. Determine the differences between desired and actual outcomes on at least an annual basis.

Continuous Quality Improvement

Monitor progress toward defined targets. Maintain appropriate activity and enhance performance determined to be less than adequate.

STRATEGIC PLANNING

Planning is the process used to guide the physicians' practice from where it is today to where it should be in the next one, five, ten, and fifteen years. In order to provide a complete picture of the organization's future direction, and given the competitive nature of health care, strategic thinking (positioning the medical practice to take advantage of competing health plans) becomes a principle upon which plans are developed. The plan is based on direction from the board and the partners and should include similar thoughts from others who are seen as valued and vested partners, to attain mutual gain from such joint efforts: other physicians and hospitals where the group's physicians practice. The value of joint planning with others who have mutual interests includes additional resources to focus on specific activities; potential cost savings through consolidation of duplicated activities and systems, and overall greater market leverage associated with more points of influence on key indicators of success of the system.

The strategic planning process identifies a mission that is a view of the future and defines goals as targets to be achieved to move the practice forward (see Figure 9.1). Strategies are maneuvers selected to guide planned activities toward achievement of desired outcomes. Since plans will be affected by market conditions and the environment in general, they will need to change and evolve. And regardless of the size of an organization, there are basic concepts that must meld if the plan is to develop.

Continuous quality improvement is applied to measure system-wide performance against targeted goals and objectives. At least annual evaluation of progress is required, while quarterly updates can serve as markers of outcome in the intervals. The ability to capitalize on change is a significant strategic advantage. As your data from CQI show new or changing strengths among key factors, it is important to make the necessary adjustments in the plan, that is, to identify resources to support an initiative if warranted.

FIGURE 9.1. Model for Mission-Based Planning

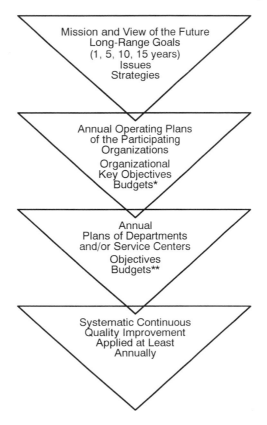

*Incentive dollars available for achieving organization-wide goals/objectives
**Incentive dollars available for achieving individual merit and department-wide goals/objectives

The concept of a dynamic or "rolling" plan optimizes this. Simply put, the basic plan, predicated on the mission and vision of your medical practice, that represents the main product lines of its physicians, moves (rolls) from year to year without a great deal of variation. The successful practice establishes its reputation by being excellent in specific areas that allow for the concentrated focus of resources. Over time and through repeated focus and superior performance, its main product lines acquire a reputation for excellence. A dynamic plan invites changes organized for inclusion into the main product lines and, if warranted, past activities are dropped when their factors no longer significantly contribute to the attainment of your defined goals. Consider the following example.

CASE EXAMPLE: STRATEGIC PLAN DEVELOPMENT FOR METROPOLITAN-BASED MULTISPECIALTY PHYSICIAN GROUP AND REGIONAL TERTIARY CARE HOSPITAL

Development of Mission and Vision

A *mission statement* summarizes what we are expected to do over the long term, while a *vision statement* outlines our hopes and dreams for the future of the medical practice. For example, the medical practice will:

- Continue to be the innovator in services for critical care through leadership in research and education
- Develop efficient and convenient outpatient services through dedication to the needs and preferences of patients
- Remain true to its tradition of community service through commitment to conservative financial management
- Become the obvious choice for healthcare in the area, through rigorously high standards of patient care
- Continue to develop networks with providers who share its mission

Core Values

Core values outline the medical group's expectations for each individual within the organization. Six individual commitments are key to achieving its mission and vision of the future:

1. *A commitment to integrity.* The physicians are a multitude of individuals, all of whom will act ethically, with personal honesty and mutual respect. Many come from professional disciplines that each have a code of conduct. While the group's success depends on effective working relationships among all individuals, it is equally important that individuals rigorously adhere to their own ethical and professional standards.
2. *A commitment to merits.* Our decisions are based on facts and substance, not form and procedure. Concordance with the group's mission, vision, goals, and strategies will take precedence over the desires and opportunities of individuals.

3. *A commitment to openness.* We plan and act with the greatest possible openness and participation. Individuals are encouraged to speak their minds and adopt a positive, questioning attitude, both of their own thinking and that of colleagues.

4. *A commitment to equal opportunity.* We are committed to equal opportunity for all, regardless of race, color, creed, religion, national origin, sex, sexual or affectional orientation, marital status, status with regard to public assistance, membership or activity in a local commission, disability, age, political affiliation, or place of residence.

5. *A commitment to using resources responsibly.* We are committed to conservative and economical use of human, financial, and other resources, because any waste of resources impairs our ability to perform our mission.

6. *A commitment to learning.* To succeed, we must be willing to learn. We must continuously learn in order to achieve our vision, care for our patients, manage effectively, and teach others.

Summary of Strategic Plan

The strategic plan states our commitment to achieving our mission and vision of the future. The plan is not rewritten every year, but is reviewed regularly and changed when appropriate. The strategic plan consists of:

- *Goals:* Broad actions that define how we will achieve our mission and fulfill our vision. The physicians' group has seven goals:

  1. Provide unified medical leadership and strategic direction
  2. Provide care and service of high quality
  3. Improve internal corporate culture and external image
  4. Increase the patient base by improving services, facilities, and technology
  5. Strengthen the financial position and improve net income
  6. Recruit qualified staff to support this vision and mission
  7. Enhance activities of continuing medical education, to be seen as excellent in the practice of family medicine and critical care

- *Strengths, weaknesses, opportunities, and threats (SWOTs):* These are issues we face that must be managed, that is, either exploited or overcome.
- *Strategies:* These are approaches the physicians take to address issues. Strategies provide direction for services and/or departments.

For example, "here is a specific opportunity; here is how we will use it." For purposes of emphasizing current-year opportunities of group-wide importance, the strategies within this plan are listed in prioritized order. Subsequent years' emphases may or may not remain the same, but will be based on analyses done for CQI.

- *Objectives and programs:* These are specific ways to deal with SWOTs and to implement strategies. Generally, they are quantifiable in terms of dates, actions, and the like, and are incorporated into capital and operating budgets. Objectives should fit stated strategies; otherwise, why expend the resources? These objectives, seen as key indicators of specific strengths in our service, were extracted from more detailed lists.

Key Strategies for Positioning

The medical group has six overarching or "positioning" strategies. They are selected from the plan and are emphasized here to indicate our strategic intent, and the reputation, image, and points of difference from our competitors that we wish to place in the minds of our customers:

- Succeed as part of an integrated system of care that seeks to improve health
- Combine academic physicians' group practice and a teaching hospital
- Use continuing medical education to create superior health care capabilities
- Maintain a leadership role and a dominant market share with our ER and trauma care
- Continue to develop the ER, clinics on the main campus, and branch clinics to provide an outpatient base for the majority of hospitalizations and specialty referrals
- Strengthen service commitment to, and relationships with, referring MDs

Goal #1: Provide Unified Medical Leadership and Strategic Direction in Concert with Hospital and Health Plan

SWOTs

S: Physician-hospital partnership.

S: Reputation as a teaching facility has a positive effect (e.g., cutting edge, high-tech).

S: Expanded vertical integration with health plans as integrated service network.

Strategies

Combine academically inclined physicians group and teaching hospital.

Use continuing medical education to create superior health care capabilities.

Place physicians in lead role in marketing and planning.

Adopt managed care as a way of doing business enroute to successfully integrating Ramsey into the HealthPartners organization.

Objectives/Programs

Clearly define mission, vision, core values, goals, and strategies.

Effectively communicate corporate message to nonphysician personnel and seek their commitment.

Determine expected utilization target and activity patterns by physician and hospital inpatient and outpatient departments.

Develop MIS capability to provide department with the managed care technology to analyze and interpret information.

Goal #2: Provide Quality Care and Service

SWOTs	Strategies	Objectives/Programs
W: Long waits for appointments and long waiting times in clinics. W. Communication with referring MDs inconsistent. O: New, powerful customer groups have emerged (e.g., payers and purchasers of care, referring professionals, prehospital providers) with explicit expectations for information outcomes and service. T: Payers and purchasers imposing stricter utilization controls. T: Patients have many choices, therefore, technical excellence is not enough. T: Government and purchasers rapidly moving to service contracts based on cost, outcomes. T: Important payers will tend to use their own care systems. W: Continuing medical education model may influence certain aspects of care.	Meet or exceed expectations of customers for service quality and value. Restructure referral services as an operations activity under business office/customer services and include outpatient referrals in addition to inpatients. Become an active participant in health care guideline utilization. Demonstrate top management commitment to Continuous Quality Improvement.	Seek to design new clinic space to make it more "patient friendly." Seek to improve systematic, timely feedback to referral sources for outpatients and inpatients. Develop outcomes measurement and reporting methods. Develop internal capability to respond to multiple data needs of providers, patients, payers, and purchasers. Establish and formalize practice guidelines. Monitor patient surveys to improve responsiveness to patient demands. Implement demonstration projects at department level showing use of consumer satisfaction information to improve operation, e.g., pediatrics, surgery.
T: External demand for outcome measures. T: Cost reimbursement rates are declining. T: State legislation calls for control of high technology equipment. S: Physicians commitment to continuous quality improvement (CQI).	Standard patient–care quality improvement model. Utilize care delivery models that maintain quality while taking into account reimbursement rates. Coordinate CQI planning and activities.	Maintain quality improvement model through continuing education, database analysis, and process enhancement. Develop plan to provide customized services that maintain quality of care. Develop plan to ensure access to necessary new technology and equipment. Incorporate appropriate CQI training and coordinate among all providers. Compare and contrast quarterly performance and focus continuing education on eliminating the difference between expected and actual performance.

Goal #3: Improve Internal Physician Group Culture and External Image

SWOTs	Strategies	Objectives/Programs
W: Many nonphysician employees do not understand the strategies and direction.	Make understanding of strategic plans an important priority.	Communicate key strategies to the appropriate audiences.
W: Intradepartmental and external referral patient flows are relatively low in comparison to other settings.	See internal and external MDs and residents as customers.	
O: MDs control patient hospital volume.	Involve physicians early in decision making.	
S: The external public has a relatively strong understanding of the integrated physician groups' role and identity.	Retain present positioning as an excellent critical care provider.	Develop a communications plan to support an integrated organizational identity program and positioning and to enhance external image.
S: A member of an integrated physician-hospital health plan organization.	Participate in helping establish the value of an integrated organization to individual patients and each group of consumers.	Develop a communications plan to optimize physicians as members of the integrated group.

Goal #4: Increase Patient Base by Improving Services, Facilities, and Technology

SWOTs	Strategies	Objectives/Programs
T: Aggressive competition critical care services are moving into marketplace.	Maintain emergency and trauma care leadership role and dominant market share.	Achieve Level 1 Trauma and critical care service.
O: Inpatient services provide financial base but require even larger outpatient base.	Integrated organization to become provider of choice for specialty referrals, trauma, critical care, and emergency/urgent care services.	Design and implement new ambulatory care building, remodeled ER, and walk-in clinic.
S: MD and EMS transport patterns show increased use of physician and good understanding of service specialists.	Strengthen service commitment to and relationships with referring MDs.	Develop plan to bid on competitor contracts with primary care physicians for their specialty care needs. Monitor sources of referring revenue.
O: Substantial portion of existing business comes from referring MDs.	Seek competitive advantage over closest competitor.	Strengthen MD support of Physician Referral Network.
T: Current market share is increasing, but competitors directly compete with group.	Increase continuing medical education skills and latest outpatient techniques.	Transition the management of referral physician services from marketing into operations, e.g., business/customer services. Strengthen and emphasize cardiology and orthopedics.
O: Total orthopedic and trauma volumes have grown modestly over the past four years.	Reposition Physicians' Clinic within the network to counteract new primary care competitor.	Consider the integration of select services as valued added options for community. Consider relation of Physicians' Clinic.
T: A new competitive threat has moved into your primary catchment area.	Have superior ability to interface with county and state government.	Strengthen OB and Urology coverage to enhance primary care. Coverage and value-added specialty urological services.
O: Government support is critical to facilities, numerous contracts, and reimbursement arrangements.	Strengthen OB to contain competitive threats from the new primary care competitors.	Strengthen our relationship with community service. Review psychiatry to increase services without expanding campus facilities.
S: Pediatric Service has expanded.	Meet the pediatric care needs of the community through collaboration with other providers. Seek opportunities to extend mental health and chemical dependency services "reach" off campus.	Meet with select health plans interested in capitated mental health and chemical dependency programs. Develop community provider relationships to be attractive as a referral service resource.

Goal #4 *(continued)*

SWOTs	Strategies	Objectives/Programs
T/O: Demand for psychiatry services has been steadily growing with relatively weak competition, but managed care cost controls are strictly limiting benefits and eroding with inpatient market.	Optimize the integrated organization options (i.e., health plan options, prevention versus intervention leading toward healthier patients/members, use of practice guidelines).	Expand inpatient service capabilities with private and semi-private rooms.
S: Full-service, integrated, tertiary care provider with expertise in critical care.		Determine physician service needs by specialty and regulate FTEs accordingly.
S: MD-hospital—partnership.	Develop and market managed care arrangements to increase market share and diversify customer mix (as an integrated origination there is strength in producing and marketing various health plan options which are based on consumer need/preference).	Provide technology needed to establish Physicians' Clinic as the specialty care center of choice.
W: Lower preference for, and use of Physicians' Clinic suburban areas.		Capture and track patient data on cost, utilization, and outcome with linkage of the inpatient, outpatient, and branch systems.
W: Physicians' Clinic has perceived lower proficiency/quality in some services (e.g., cardiovascular).		Provide incentives for cost-effective medical management.
		Expand network for distribution of services to competitor patients and employer purchases.
O: Growing market interest in "wholesale" and "sole-source" purchasing of health care services.	Position Physicians' Clinic to retain current Medicare volume in a capitated/managed care environment.	Develop globally priced packages within selected specialties for direct contract sales.
O: State law requires small employer health plans.	Meet community needs of branch market areas with on-site specialty coverage.	Enhance the "preferred" health benefit product for employees, and develop it further for external sales.
T: Increasingly more people are enrolled in managed care plans and this will include Medicare.	Increase market share of specialty referrals from neighboring state.	Work with health plan to identify and/or establish managed care programs.
T: Managed care contracts restrict choice of provider, use of specialists/services, length of stay, charges.		Medicare patients can be enrolled as members.
		Increase specialty coverage in gynecology, ENT, orthopedics, and cardiology.
		Develop a marketing strategy for neighboring state.
O: State law calls for programs to support rural health care.	Actively nurture relationships with communities of color and new Americans.	Meet key opinion leaders. Sensitivity training for staff. Participate in community events designed for minorities.

Goal #4 *(continued)*

SWOTs	Strategies	Objectives/Programs

O: Influx of younger professionals into branch market areas.

O: Populations of neighboring state counties in service area are growing.

T: Increasing competition for primary and specialty services in neighboring state.

O: Minority populations in main catchment area are growing and the Physicians' Clinic has unique strength in helping these groups.

Goal #5: Strengthen Financial Position and Improve Net Income

SWOTs

T: Health care reimbursement is increasingly uncertain and most likely will decrease.

S: HealthPartners can provide a steady flow of patients.

O: State will have capitated service networks and an all-payer system, parallel to federal program. Regulations are not published and there is opportunity for input.

Strategies

To ensure continued financial strength, increase efficiencies, and control operating costs and capital spending.

Seek revenue enhancements from current business.

Maintain a conservative financial position.

Use physician and hospital(s) strength to maintain each other's financial position.

Support integrated organization in health policy development at the county, state, and federal levels.

Objectives/Programs

Operation Improvement Program. Reengineer current physician group, hospital, and health plan operations to increase customer service, improve quality, and reduce costs.

Seek mutual cost-saving opportunities within the integrated organization.

Goal #6: Recruit Qualified Staff to Support Physicians' Group and Mission

SWOTs

T: Shortages in some classes of health care workers.

W: Physicians' Clinic MDs are relatively unrecognized.

W: MD turnover is somewhat higher than peer group average.

Strategies

Offer higher quality services through physicians and other staff members who receive compensation that meets or exceeds competitive levels.

Seek to enhance teamwork between physicians, nurses.

Seek public recognition and prestige for MDs as key sources for increased patient volumes. Continuing medical education opportunities present visibility through networking interactions.

Enhance perception of clinic within medical community to attract and retain quality staff.

Objectives/Programs

With MD input, consider the cost-effectiveness and impact on quality of using more physician extenders.

Continue MD recognition program for contributions in patient care, teaching, research, and community service.

Goal #7: Enhance Activities in Continuing Medical Education, Research, and Undergraduate/Graduate Education

SWOTs	Strategies	Objectives/Programs
W: Academic and continuing medical education role is not well known by our public.	Have superior environment for residents and students.	Identify/implement enhancements that would make Physicians' Clinic resident programs unique and desirable.
T: Potential decrease in residents in area University medical training programs.	Strengthen affiliation with area medical schools through collaborative efforts for services not provided by the Physicians' Clinic.	Develop an alumni relations program.
W: Research is costly and reduces MD patient care income.	Stress external research grants.	Increase the number of residents trained through Physicians' Clinic family medicine program.
T: Increased pressure for cost containment may include reduction of public funding for medical research and education.	Actively promote and participate in a process to revise funding system for medical education and research.	Reconstituting the Physicians' Clinic medical education committee to address ways/means of transitioning managed care into the training curriculum.
S: Incorporating managed care into the Physicians' Clinic medical education program.	Organization to become a demonstration center to teach managed care techniques and management principles to medical students.	Develop collaborative educational programs between integrated organization's providers (physician and hospital) and health plan. Seek outside funding for demonstration medical education program teaching medical students how to be effective managed care providers.

CQI TO ACHIEVE AND ENHANCE EXCELLENCE AND SUCCESS

Systematic evaluation of integrated programs including physicians, hospitals, and/or health plans is essential to determine whether the "new" business is doing what the plan for integration initially intended. Today's health care environment finds most provider organizations considering some form of integration as a means to strengthen and enhance their capabilities in an increasingly competitive marketplace.[1] At the Eastern Symposium on Integrated Healthcare—A Summit Meeting for Innovators, held on November 7 and 8, 1994, on Amelia Island, Florida, David Ottensmeyer, MD, president and CEO of Lovelace Institutes, a long-term "mature" integrated organization in Albuquerque, New Mexico, defined integrated health care as "a process in which the elements needed to provide all aspects of health care services to a population of people are brought together in a coordinated and accountable fashion."[2]

His message underscores the importance of coordination of health care and the need for accountability. Coordination is a process necessary to melding programs and activities into integrated networks, while accountability requires consideration of a system, science, or art of keeping, analyzing, and explaining the resulting outcomes. Although many providers' organizations with an interest in integration have addressed consolidation, as is evidenced by the growing number of formally integrated organizations, few of the emerging hybrids have quantifiably documented the results.[3]

Development of a Database

Knowledge of the relationships between and among the key factors comprising the physicians' health care practice is a key element needed for application of CQI to a system. It is necessary to develop reliable and valid sources of information (a database) that can be tracked over time. For example, the factors in Tables 9.1 and 9.2 represent one group practice, followed by data on the group's primary hospital activity. Most of the information presented has data from both physicians and the hospital. This report is typical of what would be presented at monthly or quarterly meetings of a board of directors.

As important as the physicians' information is the hospital's database associated with the physicians' practice. Physicians who are already part of an integrated organization have the advantage of combining resources (human, capital, and financial) to achieve excellence and success. From the perspective of a system for CQI, it is important to evaluate results for physicians, the hospital health plan, and the overall organization (combined). The hospital's financial information and the combined volume/activity factors for the physicians and hospital together are shown in Table 9.3.

SELECTING TARGETS

Is the business doing what was originally intended? It is essential to have a process to use in determining which factors are most important for achieving the plan's mission and vision. Questions about quantitative outcomes and the ability of results to stand the rigor of scientific inquiry and the test of time must be addressed. Because multiple factors may have a bearing on preferred outcomes, a process of evaluation capable of analyzing such situations is necessary.

A multidimensional approach involving inferential statistics is well suited for use in the evaluation and management of systems for the integrated

TABLE 9.1. Physicians' Clinic Actual and Budgeted Administrative Expenditures—1987 Through 1995
Dollars in Thousands

ADMINISTRATIVE COSTS	Actual 1987	Actual 1988	Actual 1989	Actual 1990	Actual 1991	Actual 1992	Budget 1992	Actual 1993	Budget 1993	Actual 1994	Budget 1994	Actual 1995
Executive Office	891	771	842	685	531	535	538	502	519	552	550	619
Legal	N/A	N/A	N/A	N/A	N/A	86	101	164	173	119	171	113
Marketing and PR	624	287	353	50	50	71	71	114	114	117	117	94
Operations	78	104	73	76	0	0	40	0	0	0	0	0
Medical Director's Office	N/A	N/A	(30)	51	43	43	40	37	41	68	54	58
Risk Management	70	70	58	80	82	103	112	103	116	106	132	105
Human Resources	156	219	284	305	352	304	346	338	362	336	371	382
Professional Services	N/A	N/A	N/A	N/A	N/A	82	99	142	140	149	162	169
Managed Care/Quality Control	N/A	15	24	31	64	73	72	78	78	90	90	74
Accounting			347	398	429	495	489	509	509	504	504	702
Financial Services			0	0	(94)	69	69	35	121	52	(56)	251
Credit and Collections			993	1042	983	1127	1108	1273	1226	1290	1291	1230
Management Information Services			704	703	730	767	807	886	934	970	970	1068
Investment Income Fee Management			240	208	40	0	0	0	0	0	0	0
Central Registration			40	40	0	0	0	0	0	0	0	0
TOTAL BUSINESS OFFICE	1964	2179	2264	2391	2088	2458	2473	2703	2790	2816	2709	2896
Business Services Reps	N/A	N/A	N/A	N/A	N/A	N/A	N/A	186	150	246	269	437
Surgical Coding Department	N/A	N/A	N/A	N/A	0	8	0	(14)	0	11	22	27
Zoned Registration	N/A	N/A	N/A	N/A	N/A	N/A	N/A	56	56	95	95	0
Parent Company	N/A	N/A	N/A	N/A	69	157	153	337	198	233	218	218
Ambulatory Care	N/A	N/A	N/A	N/A	N/A	N/A	N/A	99	101	103	104	114
General Fund and Other	248	(105)	(482)	346	173	128	166	204	173	202	221	197
TOTAL ADMINISTRATIVE OVERHEAD	4031	3540	3386	4060	3452	4048	4171	5049	5011	5243	5291	5503
Medical Department Net Revenue	33503	35073	36666	41693	45622	49546	50686	53798	53969	57594	57133	60019
Medical Department Direct Expense	25382	28000	31466	34922	39446	42558	44326	46426	46843	50064	49351	52104
Medical Department Net Income Available to Cover Corporate and Indirect Expenses	8121	7073	5200	6771	6176	6988	6360	7372	7126	7530	7782	7915
Administrative/Overhead as a percentage of Medical Department Net Revenue	12.03%	10.09%	9.23%	9.74%	7.57%	8.17%	8.23%	9.39%	9.28%	9.10%	9.26%	9.17%

315

TABLE 9.2. Physicians' Clinic Actual and Budgeted Administrative Expenditures—1987 Through 1995

Dollars in Thousands

CORPORATE COSTS	Actual 1987	Actual 1988	Actual 1989	Actual 1990	Actual 1991	Actual 1992	Budget 1992	Actual 1993	Budget 1993	Actual 1994	Budget 1994	Actual 1995
Branch Administration	229	322	282	205	193	184	193	315	261	169	146	277
Branch Clinics	795	944	1003	1116	574	650	351	930	304	743	671	733
Ambulatory Care	N/A	118	95	88	51	107	89	N/A	N/A	N/A	N/A	N/A
Campus Clinic	185	451	346	516	409	479	523	353	532	387	501	454
Neonatology	N/A	N/A	159	157	200	212	188	322	204	277	285	317
Neurosurgery	N/A	N/A	N/A	262	158	151	61	103	83	79	40	13
Walk-in Clinic	109	N/A	N/A	N/A	N/A	27	0	116	100	128	46	163
Specialties	N/A	27	10	19	0	10	0	0	0	0	0	0
Emergency Medical Services	291	107	132	30	115	259	258	262	262	271	271	244
Contribution to Foundation	332	168	0	307	67	0	0	0	0	150	150	150
Venture Funds	N/A	22	137	132	2	173	267	204	329	(14)	108	99
Workers Compensation Program	N/A	N/A	N/A	N/A	N/A	N/A	N/A	0	0	46	70	55
Incentive Plan	500	0	0	0	0	0	0	0	0	0	0	0
Insurance Contingency	600	1031	927	(913)	(674)	(54)	0	(114)	0	(18)	0	0
Corporate Profit (Loss)	787	193	(1260)	2994	2781	1144	410	255	483	587	500	602
Other Corporate Costs	273	18	0	4	0	(108)	66	154	59	63	68	0
Total Corporate Costs	4101	3401	1831	4917	3876	3223	2406	2900	2617	2868	2856	3106
Total Corporate and Administrative	8132	6941	5217	8977	7328	7271	6577	7949	7628	8111	8146	8609
Net Clinic Revenues	39105	43234	44356	49779	53220	55863	57595	60883	60843	64140	64865	67792
Clinic Expenses	38318	43041	45616	46785	50439	54719	57185	60628	60360	64553	64365	67109
Corporate Profit or (Loss)	787	193	1260	2994	2781	1144	410	255	483	587	500	602
Physician Salaries	17115	18918	22040	23322	26093	27831	27848	31284	30035	34883	32625	35129
Physician Salaries as a Percentage of Operating Expenses	44.67%	43.95%	48.32%	49.85%	51.73%	50.86%	48.70%	51.60%	49.76%	54.04%	50.69%	52.20%
Affiliation $ as a Percentage of Net Revenue	12.68%	13.22%	14.36%	13.85%	14.06%	14.17%	13.84%	13.47%	13.48%	13.88%	13.69%	14.68%
Affiliation $ as a Percentage of Medical Center Total Expenses	4.88%	5.54%	5.58%	5.28%	5.87%	5.23%	5.28%	5.05%	5.03%	4.99%	5.20%	5.21%

TABLE 9.3. Hospital Financial and Physician/Hospital Volume/Activity—Historical Financial Data 1985-1994
(Dollars in Thousands)

	1985	1986	1987	1988	1989	1990	1991	1992	1993	1994
Licensed Beds	427	427	427	427	427	427	427	427	427	427
Beds in Service	292	292	292	292	292	292	292	292	292	292
Average Daily Census	231.3	219.3	228.6	220.8	226.8	234.2	244.1	257.1	260.1	268.7
Percent Occupancy	79.2	75.0	78.4	75.3	77.2	79.4	83.6	82.4	83.1	85.8
Patient Days*	84,441	80,038	83,437	80,830	82,776	85,491	89,088	94,118	94,924	98,078
Admission*	13,607	13,276	13,725	13,211	12,495	13,001	13,921	15,401	16,005	17,164
Average Length of Stay*	6.21	6.03	6.08	6.10	6.60	6.60	6.40	6.10	5.90	5.70
Observation Status Patients				305	1,778	1,827	1,275	405	511	1,055
Outpatient Clinic Visits**	219,471	230,971	241,270	242,477	253,836	269,324	268,345	265,635	278,859	283,671
Emergency Room Visits**	53,830	54,067	55,795	57,421	54,779	57,090	55,745	59,437	56,626	56,584
Deliveries	1,257	1,217	1,118	1,086	1,171	1,396	1,658	1,649	1,601	1,674
Operating Room Cases			7,029	6,515	6,015	6,297	6,396	6,124	6,093	7,115
Radiology Procedures			106,900	105,126	110,189	113,028	111,542	113,252	113,456	
Lab Procedures			586,686	611,492	692,340	718,283	718,751	723,382	724,267	757,551
Full Time Equivalents			2017.8	1949.3	1956.2	2051.2	2149.8	2151.3	2180.7	2281.9
Inpatient Referrals										
Net Patient Revenue	98,022	84,695	96,697	99,816	110,240	124,811	133,868	146,507	157,279	173,864
Other Operating Revenue	7,238	8,792	9,631	6,136	6,618	9,749	10,045	11,803	13,444	13,479
Operating Expenses	88,913	92,919	104,630	102,633	113,366	131,536	140,088	154,121	165,806	181,631
Income from Operations	16,347	568	1,698	3,319	3,492	3,024	3,825	4,189	4,917	5,901
Prior Year Adjustments	0	0	0	3,598	(504)	(3,323)	(881)	0	(19,869)	0
Nonoperating Revenue	1,048	867	685	577	985	597	361	363	(2,346)	(42)
Excess of Revenue Over Expenses	17,395	1,435	2,383	7,484	3,973	298	3,305	4,552	(17,298)	(5,859)
Operating Fund Cash	6,639	3,068	6,247	8,480	5,187	509	3,660	9,769	17,433	20,552
Depreciation Fund Cash	9,056	8,858	7,318	9,060	9,894	9,774	9,010	9,428	9,764	9,893
Patient Accounts Receivable	13,423	12,555	14,706	18,152	20,477	24,953	26,832	25,406	27,667	31,858
Net Land, Buildings, & Equipment	34,391	37,573	38,263	39,516	43,206	48,744	50,306	52,581	55,189	70,951
Additions to Land, Buildings, & Equipment	7,560	8,061	5,924	6,431	8,863	11,100	7,385	8,732	9,696	24,050
Total Assets	73,665	76,926	80,704	90,950	97,993	104,605	113,236	199,883	167,257	178,997
Fund Balance	47,542	49,958	53,474	61,992	67,056	68,501	73,037	78,661	62,364	67,686

*Statistics from 1985 to 1991 have been adjusted to remove data related to neonatal and convalescent nurseries.
**Walk-in Clinic visits in all years are included in outpatient clinic visits.

organization, since a successful organization is based upon the appropriate mix of elements of service and needs for health care in the market to which services are provided. It is necessary to determine both the influence of market conditions on the provision of medical services, and the influence upon each other of interactive services and needs. Basic statistical longitudinal analysis using simple regression methods has been applied to the data shown on physicians and hospitals in Table 9.3. For example, using combined net revenues for the physicians and the hospital as an indicator of success, it is important to know which factors among all the possibilities are most important in predicting growth in combined net revenues. Once the top factors have been identified, resources (human, capital, and financial) should be disproportionately directed toward those factors and underlying services most related to the top predictors, to gain further increases in combined net revenue. Chapter 12 discusses the inferential approach in greater detail.

ANALYSIS OF THE RAMSEY DATA

Linear regression analyses were applied to data collected from 1987 to 1991 for Ramsey Clinic and St. Paul-Ramsey Medical Center data to examine predictive relationships between the factors accounting for the positive results in revenue for the combined medical center/clinic. Several key factors were identified by level of importance (rank order); they were (1) year R^2 = 97 percent; (2) clinic visits R^2 = 92 percent; (3) growth in physicians' salaries as a measure of total operating expense R^2 = 90 percent; (4) referrals R^2 = 88 percent and inpatient days R^2 = 66 percent. Table 9.4 displays the results associated with the analysis.

The reader is referred to Chapter 6 for details of this analysis in its original discussion. These key factors receive significant consideration in budgets, to maximize their contributions to the medical center and clinic. Annual follow-up evaluation monitors outcomes, providing a quantitative basis for changes in programs and the delivery of services, and refinements in the allocation of resources. Each year the jointly developed strategic plan is enhanced to reflect the changes supported in the operational budgets.

INTERPRETATION OF ONE YEAR'S RESULTS FOR CONSIDERATION IN NEXT YEAR'S STRATEGIC PLAN

Results from these analyses have been integrated into the annually revised joint strategic plan, the budgets, and the current year's goals and objectives for each organization. Specific inclusions from the current study

TABLE 9.4. Prediction of Combined Medical Center and Clinical Revenues—1987-1991

Variable	B Slope	t	P	R²
Year	13621.0	10.56	.002	97%
Patient Days	6.074	2.43	.093	66%
Referrals	20.911	4.64	.091	88%
Admissions	1.820	0.09	.935	2%
Clinic Visits	1.467	5.97	.009	92%
Physician Salary Growth as a Measure of Total Operating Expense	6884.8	5.07	.015	90%
Administrative Overhead as percentage of Medical Department Net Revenue	-11586	-2.84	.066	73%

Correlations

	Year	Patient days	Referral	Admits	Total Visits	Physicians' Salary as a % of Expense Budget	Administrative Overhead
Combined Revenue							
Year	.987	.815	.937	.015	.960	.946	-.853
Patient days		.730	.925	-0.17	.942	.921	-.913
Referrals			.670	.538	.718	.831	-.556
Admits				-.245	.919	.941	-.811
Total Visits					-.080	.049	.059
Admin Overhead						.846	-.729

Source: Sommers, P. Longitudinal Analysis of a Physician-Hospital Collaboration That Works: The Ramsey Model. *Group Practice Journal,* 43(3): 14, 16-18, 20, 22-23, 26, 55, 1994. Reprinted with permission.

focus on four main areas, of which two pertain to the hospital, one to the clinic, and one to the combined system of hospital and physicians' clinic. A delineation of the applications follows.

Hospital Factors

Continued positive outcomes require increased admissions of patients with appropriate reimbursement. This outcome relates to two main factors in the study: referrals and outpatient/ambulatory clinical visits.

Referrals

Actions taken: Strong emphasis is being given to enhancing the existing program in referral relations; refining and expanding the network of branch clinics giving primary care; adding courses in continuing medical education that appeal to referring physicians; making enhancements to the software used by the inpatient referral communications service; and construction of a new burn center to expand further the capabilities of this specialty service for patients with burns and trauma. The following changes were implemented in the program in 1993-1994: (1) a new program for communications of outpatient referrals; (2) a broader network of affiliations with primary care providers for purposes of becoming their hospital providing specialty services in critical care; and (3) communicating to primary care providers the significance of and capabilities associated with recent recognition from the American College of Surgeons of our center as a Level I Trauma Center.

Outpatient/Ambulatory Care Clinical Visits

Actions taken: Additional primary care providers are being added to the network/system of physicians' clinics, both on and off our central clinical location; construction has begun on a new ambulatory care center; and an enhanced and expanded emergency medicine center on the hospital campus began to be implemented in early 1993-1994.

Physicians' Clinic

The recruitment and retention of physicians at the central location and within the neighboring state's network of branch clinics are required outcomes.

Physicians' Compensation

Actions taken: Strong emphasis has been placed on the development of competitive packages for compensation, with the opportunity for physicians to do research and participate in the medical education program as desired. Incentive programs driven by medical-department-based productivity have been established to extend further opportunities for compensation to interested physicians.

Hospital and Physicians' Clinic Combined

Continued combined success will require ongoing trust and joint support of an excellent working relationship, now and in the future.

Analysis of Trends

Annual analysis is conducted to determine whether the desired targets for success are being met, and which factors deserve more, less, or maintenance levels of allocated resources. New opportunities that relate to mission and vision can be funded from new ventures or from development funds throughout the budgetary year. Requests for new business proposals must address organizational mission and must include a two-year business plan. (See Chapter 8 for process of application for new business.) The new business activity will subsequently be evaluated on its merits for its contribution to achieving one or more of the organization's targets for success such as growth in combined net revenues. Table 8.4 in Chapter 8 shows an analysis of the trends in top predictors of combined net revenue from 1991, 1992, and 1993.

CURRENT APPLICATION AND RESULTS: A CASE STUDY

Outcomes derived from the 1991 analysis were integrated into the joint strategic plan for 1992. The 1992 analysis developed recommendations that were included in the joint strategic plan for 1993. The 1993 results, along with recommendations to consider in developing the joint 1994 strategic plan, are presented here as a case study. The project was published in the May/June 1995 issue of *Group Practice Journal* and is titled "An Outcome Study of the Ramsey Physician and Medical Center Service Delivery System, 1987-1995."[4]

Applications

How has knowledge of the top predictors been incorporated into the Ramsey system? An essential aspect of the Ramsey approach has been the interpretation and systematic application of both qualitative and quantitative information in a practical, meaningful manner. Results from these analyses have been integrated into the annually revised joint strategic plan, the budgets, and the goals and objectives for each organization. Specific implications for success focus on five main areas, of which three pertain to the medical center, one to the clinic, and one toward the combined PHO. A delineation of the outcomes follows.

Saint Paul-Ramsey Medical Center

Factors in success for the hospital relate to inpatient days, referral of inpatients, and outpatient/ambulatory care visits.

Patient Days

Although the average length of stay has been decreasing over the course of the study, the number of days related to inpatient admissions has been increasing. Figure 9.2 shows the trends.

Considerations

- Until the number of noncapitated patients significantly declines, it is to the hospital's advantage to market all services that lead to admissions (primary, secondary, and/or tertiary care).
- In preparation for an increasing volume of capitated/managed care patients, it is essential for the hospital to (1) strengthen and improve operations while reducing costs, and (2) shift delivery of care for primary and secondary cases to an outpatient setting.

FIGURE 9.2. St. Paul-Ramsey Medical Center—Average Length of Stay and Inpatient Days

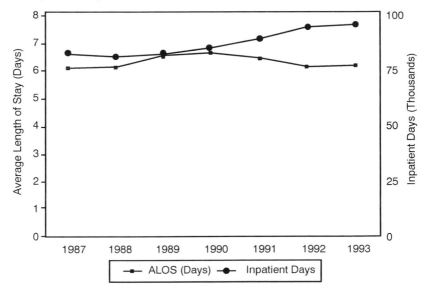

Source: Sommers, P. Managing Medical Service Outcomes by Predicting and Achieving Success: An Inferential Approach. *American Medical Group Association,* 44(3): 24,26-28,30, May/June, 1995. Reprinted with permission.

Inpatient Referrals

Ramsey's emphasis on critical care services has provided a consistent contribution to increasing referrals of inpatients, which have tripled over the course of the study—accounting for more than 20 percent of the total admissions for the past six years. Figure 9.3 illustrates the trend in referrals of inpatients, length of stay, and number of admissions.

Considerations

- The existing network for communications regarding referral of inpatients, which has been serving as an informational bridge to referring physicians, has been restructured from a supportive feature of marketing to a fundamental way of doing business in the customer service unit of the business office. This transition has also eliminated extra steps, forms, and FTE employees.
- A new burn center has been constructed and is open for business, while construction of an enhanced emergency center is well underway.
- Formal efforts at marketing have been implemented and need to continue, in the critical care areas of burns, trauma care, and emergency medical services.
- Courses in continuing medical education, of specific interest to physicians in the area, are being continued, while at the same time we continue to highlight Ramsey's staff and capabilities in critical care.
- Research activity continues to increase and expand Ramsey's skill and reputation as the experts who teach primary care physicians about state-of-the-art medical care and technology.

The following changes in program were implemented in 1994-1995:

1. Combining a network for referral of outpatients with the existing program for inpatients to allow for appropriate communication with referring physicians about *all* referred patients
2. Establishing a broader network of communications with primary care providers for purposes of becoming their center for specialty services in critical care
3. Communicating to primary care providers the significance of and related capabilities associated with the recognition from the American College of Surgeons received by Ramsey as a Level I Trauma Center

Outpatient/Ambulatory Care Clinical Visits

An increasing population base from which outpatients are drawn is needed to maintain and/or increase admissions to the hospital and patient

FIGURE 9.3. St. Paul-Ramsey Medical Center—Inpatient Referrals and Admissions

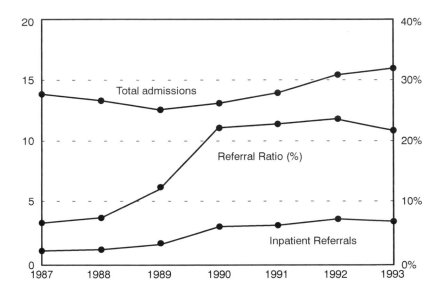

Source: Sommers, P. Managing Medical Service Outcomes by Predicting and Achieving Success: An Inferential Approach. *American Medical Group Association*, 44(3): 24, 26-28, 30, May/June, 1995. Reprinted with permission.

days, as length of stay decreases and the shift occurs from inpatient to outpatient care. Figure 9.4 shows the trends.

Considerations

The design of a new ambulatory care center on the St. Paul campus is in process, to serve as the east metropolitan location of choice for outpatient specialty care, surgery, and services in critical care. At the same time, services in primary care are being reorganized on a more effective, customer-oriented basis. Table 9.4 illustrates needed action at the level of programs/services.

A change in strategic direction has been implemented, following the merger with HealthPartners. Instead of the premerger strategy of diversifying services in primary care geographically to expand the patient base from which to draw outpatients, Ramsey has made preparations to serve an increasing number of capitated/managed care patients from the primary care physicians at HealthPartners:

FIGURE 9.4. St. Paul-Ramsey Medical Center—Outpatient Visits and Inpatient Admissions

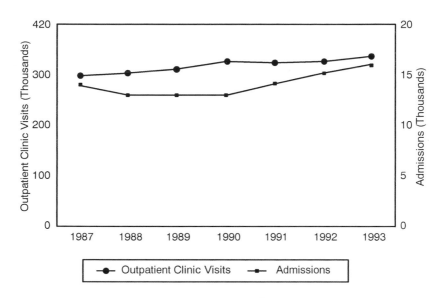

Source: Sommers, P. Managing Medical Service Outcomes by Predicting and Achieving Success: An Inferential Approach. *American Medical Group Association*, 44(3): 24, 26-28, 30, May/June, 1995. Reprinted with permission.

- In anticipation of accelerated price wars in the Twin Cities, Ramsey recognized that its cost structure was too high to compete effectively. For the past year, Ramsey has been working with a nationally recognized consulting firm to reengineer the systems for delivery of both inpatient and outpatient care, to reduce operating and overhead costs while increasing service effectiveness.
- The recruitment and retention of physicians of high quality throughout Ramsey Clinic continues to be a model. It is predicated upon physician leadership, followed by an organization-wide commitment to instituting the programs and services called for by the physicians. The targets for success are instituted in the jointly developed strategic plan. When the PHO was formed in 1987, an understanding was reached between the hospital and the clinic that the hospital would use its resources to build essential facilities and to purchase the necessary equipment such as for MRI, CT, lasers, and the like. The clinic agreed to focus its resources on competitive plans for compensation of physicians.

TABLE 9.4. Predicting Combined Net Revenue—1991-1994

Results	Factor	Implications
Five key factors accounted for the prediction of combined net revenue in 1991-1992-1993. Although the factors rotated their order slightly over the years, the *same* five remained the top predictors.	*Year:* The longer the partnership lasted, the more combined net revenue growth.	*Needed Action:* Continue integrated physician-hospital partnership.
	Patient Days: Inpatient hospital days	*Needed Action:* 14. Encourage referral of increased fee-for-service business through excellent care, low costs, and high consumer satisfaction. 15. Operations improvement. Reduce costs/improve operations. 16. Anticipating increased capitation shift care delivery from "in" to "outpatient," i.e., same-day surgery, home care, promotion of healthier lifestyles, etc.
	Referred Inpatients: Patients referred for inpatient hospital care by area primary care physicians.	*Needed Action:* 1. Make rapid and accurate communication back to referral source through referral communication network a way of doing business. 2. Target marketing dollars on specialty service utilization versus primary care. 3. Opened new burn center and new ER. 4. Expand CME offerings about critical care skill enhancements to primary care physicians. 5. Market research findings about referral center capabilities to underscore state-of-the-art, leading-edge medical care services.
	Outpatient/Ambulatory Care: Patients seen by physicians in an outpatient/ambulatory care setting.	*Needed Action:* 1. Expand referral communication network to respond to outpatients referred for specialty service needs. 2. Operations improvement (improve customer services while decreasing costs). 3. Prepare space and facilities to serve patients in a seamless, customer-oriented manner.
	Physician Compensation: Total compensation with incentive dollars included.	*Needed Action:* 1. Increase incentive opportunities for physicians in the direction you would like to see their practices move. 2. Reduce administrative and non-revenue producing overhead. Begin zero-based budgeting.

Physicians' Compensation

Strong emphasis has been placed on the development of competitive packages of compensation, with the opportunity for physicians to do research and participate in the medical education program as desired. Incentive programs driven by medical department-based productivity have been established, to extend opportunities for compensation beyond base salary to interested physicians.

Considerations

Since its formation as a group of physicians, 1991, 1992, and 1993 marked the most successful years, financially, for Ramsey clinic. This coincides with implementation of departmentally based incentive plans to extend physicians' compensation beyond annually budgeted salaries.

Because some departments have not been able to generate incentive dollars because of low rates of collection, a pilot program was implemented in 1994 whereby all departments would be eligible to receive incentive dollars if targets for production were met. The rate of turnover of physicians at Ramsey has decreased from a ten-year average of 13.4 percent to 6.1 percent at the end of 1993. Figure 9.5 shows the results, and Table 9.5 illustrates needed action at the level of programs/services.

Reduction of administrative overhead as a percentage of net revenues of medical departments (Figure 9.6), net revenues for clinics (same figure), and the growth of physicians' salaries as a measure of the total operating budget for the clinic (Figure 9.7) were the top three predictors accounting for decreasing turnover of physicians.

The continued success of Saint Paul-Ramsey Medical Center and Ramsey Clinic combined will require ongoing trust and joint support of the annually enhanced strategic plan. On an annual basis, Ramsey will reexamine the status of key factors for success and adjust its focus and operations for purposes of maximizing predetermined outcomes.

MARKET RESEARCH

Many sources of information are needed to gather accurate and timely information about the markets and populations your group is interested in doing business with. A significant amount of information is available by request through local, regional, and state departments of public health, health and social services, office of the insurance commissioner, bureau of labor and workforce statistics, bureau of census and population characteristics, and various public and private planning agencies. Contact should be made and continued with each of these and other planning/resource-based organizations throughout your defined business services areas.

FIGURE 9.5. Turnover Among Physicians

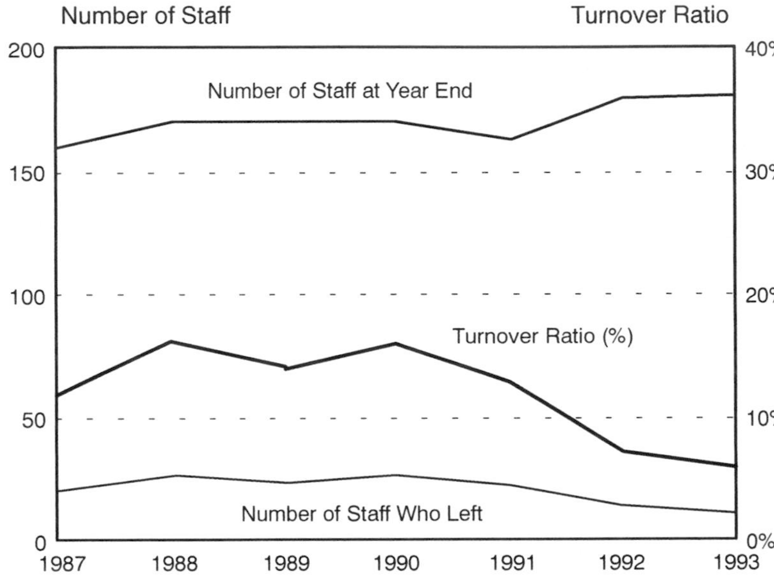

Source: Sommers, P., Luxenberg, M., and Sommers, E. CQI Longitudinally Applied to Integrated Service Outcomes. *Medical Group Management Journal*, 42(2): 50-54, 56-58; March/April, 1995. Reprinted with permission.

An example of a feasibility study used to (1) determine a community's need for a primary care clinic; and, (2) an example to develop a community-based strategic plan follows.

CASE EXAMPLE: CONDUCTING A FEASIBILITY STUDY TO DETERMINE HEALTH CARE NEEDS AND ESTABLISHMENT OF A PRIMARY CARE CLINIC

A community clinic market research study was conducted to assess the level of demand for a proposed clinic.

Methods

Six hundred households from communities within a ten-mile radius of the proposed site were selected by random digit dialing and contacted

TABLE 9.5. Predicting a Decrease in Physician Turnover

Results	Factor	Implications
Three key factors accounted for the prediction of decreasing physician turnover and are presented in rank order	*Factor 1:* Administrative overhead reduction as a percent of medical department net revenue.	*Needed Action:* 1. Reduce expenses supporting non-revenue producing services. Use zero-based budgeting process. 2. Ask departments to consider LPNs for RNs and PAs instead of additional physicians. Cross-train support staff wherever possible. 3. Consolidate duplicated services.
	Factor 2: Net clinic revenue.	*Needed Action:* Complete each recommendation outlined in Table 9.4.
	Factor 3: Physician salary growth as a measure of the clinic's operating expense budget.	*Needed Action:* 1. Implement department-based, productivity-driven incentive plans. 2. Supplement department incentives with clinic-wide incentive opportunities. 3. Instead of hiring new physicians, ask existing staff to see one new patient per day and/or add more capitated members to their practice.

between May 8, 1995 and May 15, 1995. The head of household was asked to respond to a four-page survey, developed to assess interest and determine need. The six hundred households, with an average of 2.77 persons per household, represent 1,664 persons or 5.2 percent of the total service area population (32,324).

Findings

Favorable Demographic Characteristics

The current county population in which the clinic would be located is 34,000. There is projected steady growth over the next twenty-five years, reaching 42,000 by 2020. Much of this growth is occurring in the thirty- to fifty-year-old age group, meaning many families with young children. Only 15 percent of area residents commute to the Twin Cities for work, which is positive as distance from home is a more important indicator of clinic usage than distance from work.

The county economic base is stable given the diversity of manufacturers and the percentage of the population employed by the county government

FIGURE 9.6. Reduction of Administrative Overhead as a Percentage of Net Revenues

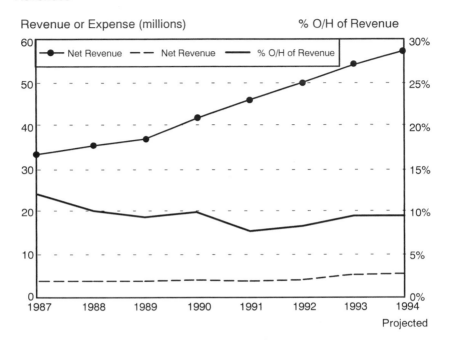

Source: Sommers, P., Luxenberg, M., and Sommers, E. CQI Longitudinally Applied to Integrated Service Outcomes. *Medical Group Management Journal,* 42(2): 50-54, 56-58; March/April, 1995. Reprinted with permission.

or by the local school district. In 1993, the county unemployment rate was 5.9 percent, below the national average of 6.4 percent. The county per capita income is higher than national average.

Findings in Favor of the Clinic

- Of the six hundred households surveyed, 1.5 percent indicated they were very likely to use the clinic. Extrapolating to the actual service area population (32,324), the anticipated number of visits to the clinic, multiplying the households very likely to use the clinic (1,342) by the average number of visits, is between 5,500 and 6,500. The market research indicates there is enough to support one full-time provider.

FIGURE 9.7. Growth of Physicians' Salaries as a Measure of Total Operating Budget

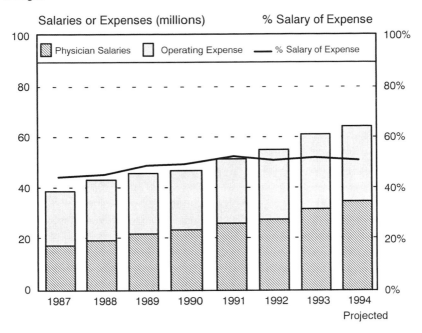

Source: Sommers, P., Luxenberg, M., and Sommers, E. CQI Longitudinally Applied to Integrated Service Outcomes. *Medical Group Management Journal*, 42(2): 50-54,56-58; March/April, 1995. Reprinted with permission.

- One of the clinic development sponsors has been a health care provider in the vicinity of the proposed site for approximately eight years and has established name recognition for primary and tertiary care.
- Sixty percent of the very likely to use are currently going to a main competitor whose location is also in the vicinity of the proposed site.
- Twenty-seven percent of the population surveyed had one or more members of the household over 65. The older population often have more visits to a medical provider, and many appreciate shorter travel distances.
- Steady population growth in the area, particularly among the thirty- to fifty-year-old age group who often have young children, will potentially increase the patient volume at the clinic.

Barriers to Establishing the Clinic

- Many surveyed residents have long-established relationships (average 10.6 years) which may be an initial barrier to building the patient base, although those who were very likely to use the clinic also had lengthy relationships with their provider (10.5 years).
- Of those very likely to use the clinic, 84.1 percent are insured. There is the potential that a higher uninsured rate could negatively impact the financial operations of the clinic, although this potential effect could be minimized with a sliding fee schedule, if the clinic does well, with reduced charges. Additionally, if grants are awarded to this project, there may be a stipulation to provide care to all, regardless of ability to pay.

Tables 9.6 to 9.10 illustrate the summarized results of the survey findings.

TABLE 9.6. Likelihood of Clinic Use

Response	Frequency of Response	
Very Likely	11.5%	(69)
Somewhat Likely	21.5%	(129)
Not Likely At All	63.2%	(379)
Do Not Know	3.8%	(23)
Total	100%	(600)

TABLE 9.7. Provider of Choice

Response	Frequency of Response	
Family Practitioner	88.2%	(529)
Specialist	4.7%	(28)
Physician Assistant	4.0%	(24)
OB/GYN	1.8%	(11)
Other	1.3%	(8)
Total	100%	(600)

TABLE 9.8. Reasons for Choosing a Facility

Response	Frequency of Response	
Distance from Home	49.1%	(287)
Previous Personal Experience	14%	(82)
Quality of Staff	6.3%	(37)
Quality of Care	6.0%	(35)
Previous Experience of Friends/Family	5.8%	(34)
Insurance Requirements	4.5%	(26)
Distance from Work	3.6%	(21)

TABLE 9.9. Medical Facility of Choice

Response	Frequency of Response	
Clinic 1	41.2%	(246)
Clinic 2	19.6%	(117)
Hospital 1	8.0%	(48)
Hospital 2	3.9%	(23)
Hospital 3	3.5%	(21)
Hospital 4	3.5%	(21)
Clinic 3	3.0%	(18)
Clinic 4	2.8%	(17)
Clinic 5	1.2%	(7)
Clinic 6	1.2%	(7)

TABLE 9.10. Likelihood of Use by Current Facility

Facility	Very Likely	Somewhat Likely	Not Likely At All	Do Not Know	Total
Clinic 1	8.7%	17.1%	23.5%	0.0%	19.8%
Clinic 2	60.9%	43.4%	35.6%	56.5%	41.2%
Hospital 1	5.8%	9.3%	7.1%	21.7%	8.0%
Clinic 3	2.9%	2.3%	3.1%	4.3%	3.0%
Other	21.7%	27.9%	30.6%	17.4%	28.2%
Total	100.0%	100.0%	100.0%	100.0%	100.0%

Community Clinic Stakeholder Benefits

- Delivery of primary care medical services with a clinic location at the unified school site offers a great convenience for residents of the area communities.
- Community control regarding the services and operations of the clinic (e.g., provider selection, hours of operation).
- Improved services through communication lines developed during the clinic planning and organizational development (governance) process as well as through the patient advisory committee.
- Opportunity to access an integrated service network, offering a comprehensive range of health care services.
- Build on existing positive patient-provider relationships.
- Participate in the development of innovative health care systems for rural communities.

Sponsor Hospital Benefits

- Helping to meet a need within the community, within sponsor service area (20 percent of area residents currently use the sponsor hospital).

- Potential of increasing presence in the communities.
- Increased referrals, both inpatient and outpatient.

Sponsor Clinic's Benefits

- Strengthen community relationships through the community involvement model for organizing and financing primary care, with potential applicability for other communities in which the sponsor clinic is currently involved or may be in the future.
- Increased market share and referrals to the sponsor's local main clinic and its companion tertiary care referral center.
- Share the risk for delivering rural primary care.
- Open consumer input channels in order to get in better touch with what services the clinic consumers' value.
- Create a culture or stimulate a process for exploring alternative models of health care delivery in rural communities.

CASE EXAMPLE: DEVELOPING
A COMMUNITY-BASED STRATEGIC PLAN

The following example is used to demonstrate a community-based approach to be used by an integrated physician-hospital-health plan organization to build its primary care network.

Introduction

Primary care clinic development is crucial to long-term success. To be most effective, primary care service must be founded on the principle of local solutions to local problems. The focus of efforts is on ways and means to build networks from the individual communities up rather than from the top down. Building effective networks requires education of the participants and identification of benefits to provide the will, a carefully defined networking process to provide the way, sufficient financial and technical resources to provide the means, adequate time to build trust among the participants and participant commitment and follow-through to ensure the attainment of mutual goals.

The organization can inspire needed change by supporting the development of community-based planning processes to enhance local health systems. Accompanying this effort should be strategies to:

- Enhance local leadership skills
- Educate and involve local citizens
- Support the integration of existing health resources between and among communities
- Develop a vision of services that clearly identifies the continuum of care citizens can expect

Mission and Vision

A mission statement summarizes what we are expected to do over the long-term future, whereas vision relates to organizational expectation.

Regional Development

Mission and Vision

The mission of regional development is to support the mission of the parent organization for our members and our community by supporting planning processes to enhance local health systems. Visionary expectations are founded upon an organizational reputation as the care delivery system of choice.

Core Values

Core values outline expectations for each individual within regional development:

- *A commitment to local leadership.* Our efforts must focus on ways and means to build networks from the individual community up rather than from the top down.
- *A commitment to the education and involvement of local citizens.* Building of effective networks requires education of the community-based constituents.
- *A commitment to self-examination and change beginning from within each individual leading to supporting the integration of existing health resources between and among communities.* Through education, community residents will be taught how to optimize and consolidate scarce human, fiscal, and capital resources because any waste of resources impairs our ability to perform our missions.
- *A commitment to a vision of services that clearly identifies the continuum of care citizens can expect.* In order to succeed, we must be willing

to learn. We must continuously search among care alternatives for ways and means to optimize the health and wellness of each citizen.

Strategic Plan Summary

The strategic plan states our commitment to achieving the mission and vision of the future. The plan is not rewritten every year, but is reviewed regularly and changed when appropriate. The strategic plan consists of goals—board actions that define how we will achieve our mission and fulfill our vision.

Within the context of our parent organizational mission, regional development has five goals:

1. Provide unified development and management services for internal and external consumers. Desired outcome: *Provide leadership to guide caregivers toward achievement of effective services delivered at the community level throughout the network.*
2. Provide high-quality, low-cost program consultation to contracted primary, specialty, and hospital caregivers. Desired outcome: *Achieve consumer satisfaction and enhance consultation on a continuing basis.*
3. Improve the management and effectiveness of administrative linkages between the parent organization-owned clinics and contracted caregivers. Desired outcome: *Enhance/expand services.*
4. Enhance supportive and integrating care delivery processes. Desired outcome: *Improve/extend caregiving capabilities.*
5. Optimize the delivery and transformation of information communication capabilities with a consumer-oriented focus toward state-of-the-art performance. Desired outcome: *Enhanced communications measured by internal and external consumer satisfaction which is refined on a continuing basis.*
6. Recruit qualified staff to support physicians' group and mission.
7. Enhance activities in continuing medical education, research, and undergraduate and graduate education.

Strengths, Weaknesses, Opportunities, and Threats—Issues We Face That Must Be Managed, i.e., Either Exploited or Overcome

Strategies—The approach the organization takes to address issues. Strategies provide direction for departments. For example, "here is a specific opportunity; here is how we will use it."

Objectives and programs—Specific ways to deal with SWOTs and implement with adequate strategies. Generally, they are quantifiable in terms of dates, actions, etc., and are identified in the capital and operating budgets. Objectives should fit the strategies—otherwise, why expend the resources?

Key Positioning Strategies

1. Establish reputation and skill as the management services organization of choice among contracted groups. *Save money while increasing effectiveness and achieving both internal and external consumer satisfaction.*
2. Strengthen service commitment (caregiver/provider and management) and improve relationships with contracted groups. *Benchmark care outcomes, utilization targets, and service standards—develop/ implement network-wide plan to measure and achieve through continuous quality improvement.*
3. Create state-of-the-art expertise and methods for practice guidelines development and practical approaches toward the evaluation of healthier populations (i.e., members and patients), expand/extend capability through electronic information exchange including telemedicine and teleconferencing, and enhance and extend medical and continuing education programs to both internal and external consumers. *Use medical and continuing education and research to create superior health care, administrative, management, and service capabilities.*
4. Enhance communication capabilities to meet caregiver/provider and management needs to deliver superior internal and external consumer service. *Create/enhance comprehensive service networks to meet caregiver and management needs.*

Goal #1: Provide Unified Medical Development and Management Services for Internal and External Organizational Consumers

SWOTs	Strategies	Objectives/Programs
S: Physician-hospital-health plan partnership.	Combine network-wide resources toward collective priorities.	Clearly define mission, vision, core values, goals, and strategies.
S: Reputation as a community-oriented, full-service, vertically integrated health care organization.	Focus services on internal and external consumer needs.	Reorient the delivery of services in the owned and contracted clinics and hospitals to enhance customer satisfaction and follow-up at all levels, e.g., offer needs assessment/consumer satisfaction evaluation to determine baseline.
S: Owned clinics will be marketed under one coordinated marketing plan.	Use existing owned clinics and hospital to demonstrate integrated approach to meet health needs of constituents.	Promote the value of the family medical clinics and local community hospitals. Educate the community on the broad scope of primary caregiver capabilities from delivering babies to performing colposcopies to counseling adolescents, e.g., marketing plans of owned and contracted primary care groups must reflect unique attributes and produce the necessary outcomes to become network of choice.
S: Owned and contracted groups create an extensive medical service distribution system across the seven-county metro area, eastern Minnesota and western Wisconsin. The network represents virtually unlimited health care service capabilities to a potential market of more than one million patients/members.	Place physicians in lead role to market and deliver products.	Promote the "hometown clinic" you've grown up with on a personal basis.
		Encourage the physicians to participate in community events, the local schools, and athletic endeavors. The organization should offer resources as needed, e.g., a tailor-made health plan for the industrial park/Small Business Purchasing Alliance.
		Develop a permanent presence in western Wisconsin by establishing an organizational office. Regional office established in 1998.

Goal #2: Provide High-Quality, Low-Cost Program Consultation to Contracted Primary, Specialty, and Hospital Caregivers

SWOTs	Strategies	Objectives/Programs
T: Hospitals may close, be purchased by another organization, or consolidate.	Provide management and consulting services to help communities and hospitals through the transition to help them prepare to meet community health care needs of the future.	Seek to be the organization most helpful to local communities in implementing educationally based wellness and healthy lifestyle programs.
		Offer resources to local physician groups and hospitals to facilitate health care planning, e.g., conduct community education needs assessments and offer follow-up plans to help communities meet defined needs.
O: Competitors interested in western Wisconsin are not currently organized to systematically begin to take control of shaping the health care system of the culture.	Serve local hospital and physician constituencies by helping them identify needs and options to meet current and future health care needs.	Create the provider network needed to compete more effectively with other integrated systems. May require consolidation of duplicative services among caregivers, e.g., area physicians and hospitals for primary and secondary care; the hospitals of surrounding counties for home care; the physicians and hospitals of an adjacent county for emergency room service, etc.
		Appoint a medical director to help marshall resources necessary to train local physicians and hospitals about managed care, e.g., connect clinics to organization electronically. Offer management information and claims processing systems. Interface with network practice guidelines.
		Prepare and implement a strategic development plan for enrollment growth and for commercial risk contracting, medicare risk contracting, and other managed care opportunities, e.g., small employer purchasing alliances.

Goal #2 *(continued)*

SWOTs	Strategies	Objectives/Programs
		Oversee utilization management and quality assurance functions, including clinical outcome documentation and other support services which can help local physicians and hospitals.
		Coordinate and manage specialists' panels across the network.
		Prepare and implement a strategic development plan for enrollment growth and for commercial risk contracting, medicare risk contracting, and other managed care opportunities, e.g., small employer purchasing alliance.
		Help to administer/allocate risk pools pursuant to risk-sharing arrangements between hospitals and physicians. Become a licensed HMO in Wisconsin. May need to develop PPOs and other companion managed care products to market through the network, e.g., industrial park model.
W: Currently no marketing plan has been developed to focus efforts on western Wisconsin.	Market the network to employers and consumers.	Begin to strategically develop organizational connections throughout St. Croix, Polk, Pierce, and Dunn counties initially, e.g., implement enhancements derived from the emergency room demonstration project between the four hospitals and physician groups of St. Croix County. Maintain oversight role while providing ongoing medical and continuing education to hospital and physician staff. Complete home care business plan for the three hospitals of Polk County and remain active in an oversight/source role.

Goal #3: Improve Management and Effectiveness of Administrative Linkages Between Owned and Contract Caregivers

SWOTs

S: The comprehensive physician-hospital-health plan network.

Strategies

Become the network support system of choice for primary care providers.

Objectives/Programs

Provide consultation on practice management and enhancement.

Assist in physician development, recruitment, and retention for network growth.

Provide CME Category I credit for physicians and appropriate continuing education for other staff.

Provide administrative services on an "as-needed" basis to participating physicians and hospitals as requested.

Manage selected practices (solo and/or group) as requested, e.g., north suburban clinics.

Seek new/expand existing relationships in collaboration with local communities, e.g., Random Lake, etc.

Goal #4: Enhance Supportive and Integrating Care Delivery Processes

SWOTs	Strategies	Objectives/Programs
O: No organized management service organization is effectively serving physicians and hospitals in western Wisconsin.	Develop an organized management/services approach toward helping primary and specialty caregivers and hospitals optimize their service in the communities of western Wisconsin.	Provide administrative assistance to physicians and hospitals. Conduct hospital/practice needs assessment to determine the best way to help each group (physician and hospital).
		Present proposal to each provider/hospital group on the following basis: flexible structure; no minimum physician or hospital requirement; can serve multiple physician groups and hospitals as well as solo practitioners; equal opportunity can be offered to both physicians and hospitals.
		Provide selective administrative services to physicians, individuals, and groups. Less "radical" may be most acceptable model to some physicians; medical group retains control over practice including "ownership" of patients and medical records (can build as much independence into each community as they desire).
		From hospital's perspective— no pressure to buy good will from physicians.
		Minimum regulatory requirements.
		Begin by approaching all area primary care groups to discuss ways and means of promoting community understanding of health care needs and fostering leadership toward healthier lifestyles.

Goal #5: Optimize the Delivery and Transformation of Information Communication Capabilities with a Consumer-Oriented Focus Toward State-of-the-Art Performance

SWOTs	Strategies	Objectives/Programs
W: Long waits for appointments and long waiting times in clinic.	Meet or exceed expectations of customers (members, patients, other payers, purchasers, and other referral sources).	Develop outcomes measurement and reporting methods to monitor key consumer satisfaction performance.
T: Payers and purchasers imposing stricter utilization controls.	Encourage active participation in the developing practice guidelines network.	Promote practice guidelines among owned and contracted groups. Provide electronically managed outcome and utilization reporting systems.
W: Expensive and time-consuming methods of providing specialty services to distant primary caregivers.	Use telemedicine capability to reach out and provide specialty care throughout western Wisconsin initially and subsequently throughout the organizational network.	Establish connectivity between the organization's specialty service center and distant primary care groups. Connect physically via electronics, cable, TV, and/or other yet-to-be-defined forms to promote ready access and immediate feedback of information about clinical care, outcomes, information updating, satisfaction, patient/member choices, ongoing education, and promotion of healthy lifestyles.
T: Important payers will tend to use their own care systems and support services.	Network services must become exemplary from cost, quality, effectiveness, and consumer satisfaction perspectives.	Become the network of choice based upon ability to deliver most effective service at lowest cost to totally satisfied consumers. Network effectiveness to be demonstrated by meeting defined needs one customer at a time.
T/O: There will be several competing major players in western Wisconsin.	Use existing owned and contracted network to "seal out" competitor movement on market share of defined product lines.	Sponsor and help develop and implement jointly developed strategic plans in collaboration with physicians and hospitals of western Wisconsin.

Goal #6: Recruit Qualified Staff to Support Physician's Group and Mission

SWOTs	Strategies	Objectives/Programs
T: Shortages in some classes of health care workers.	Offer higher quality services through physicians and other staff members who receive compensation that meets or exceeds competitive levels	With MD input, consider the cost effectiveness and impact on quality of using more physician extenders.
	Seek to enhance teamwork between physicians, nurses	
W: Physicians' Clinic MDs are relatively unrecognized.	Seek public recognition and prestige for MDs as key sources for increased patient volumes. Continuing medical education opportunities present visibility through networking interactions.	Continue MD recognition program for contributions in patient care, teaching, research, and community service.
W: MD turnover is somewhat higher than peer group average.	Enhance perception of Ramsey within medical community to attract and retain quality staff.	

Goal #7: Enhance Activities in Continuing Medical Education, Research, and Undergraduate/Graduate Education

SWOTs	Strategies	Objectives/Programs
W: Academic and continuing medical education role is not well known by our public.	Have superior environment for residents and students.	Identify/implement enhancements that would make Physician's Clinic resident programs unique and desirable.
T: Potential decrease in residents in area university medical training programs.	Strengthen affiliation with area medical schools through collaborative efforts for services not provided by Physicians' Clinic.	Develop an alumni relations program.
W: Research is costly and reduces MD patient care income.	Stress external research grants.	Increase the number of residents trained through Physicians' Clinic family medicine program.
T: Increased pressure for cost containment may include reduction of public funding for medical research and education.	Actively promote and participate in a process to revise funding system for medical education and research.	Reconstituting the Physicians' Clinic medical education committee to address ways/means of bringing managed care into the training curriculum.
S: Incorporating managed care into the Physicians' Clinic medical education program.	Organization to become a demonstration center to teach managed care techniques and management principles to medical students.	Develop collaborative educational programs between integrated organization's providers (physician and hospital) and health plan. Seek outside funding for demonstration medical education program teaching medical students how to be effective managed care providers.

Goal Summary:
Program/Budget/Activity Responsibilities

Program Activity	Projected Budget Needed	Assigned Responsibilities
Goal #1:		
• Offer consultative assistance to the owned and contracted clinics for needs assessment/consumer satisfaction evaluation and follow-up services.	$ In Kind Support	Managing Director Physician Liaison
• Offer consultative services to help owned and contracted services to develop effective marketing plans to promote local market share growth in each community.	$25,000	Managing Director Marketing Department
• Complete design and actuarial work related to Industrial Park Small Business Purchasing Alliance PPO model.	$ In Kind Services	Insurance Account Rep.
• Develop a permanent presence in western Wisconsin by establishing an agency office. Initial steps in 1996.	$15,000	Managing Director VP Network Services
Goal #2:		
• Conduct community education needs assessment and work with each community to develop a plan to meet defined needs.	$10,000	Managing Director Marketing Department
• Approach communities with offer to help coordinate consolidation of duplicated services between hospital and physicians for purposes of eliminating duplication and excess expenses while demonstrating how working together provides mutual benefit.		Managing Director
• Establish connectivity between organization and owned/contracted clinics, i.e., electronic communications and/or telemedicine	$ In Kind Support	Director, Network Management VP, MIS
• Assign account representatives to oversee utilization review, quality assurance, and clinical outcomes documentation.	$ In Kind Services	VP, Network Management

Goal Summary *(continued)*

Goal #2 *(continued)*

• Secure an HMO license to sell products in western Wisconsin.	To be determined by insurance department.	
• Implement coordinated emergency medical service program between physicians and hospitals in the county.	$ In Kind Service	Managing Partner
• Complete home care business plan for the three hospitals of the county.	$25,000	Managing Partner Director, Home Care

Goal #3:

• Offer consultative services to owned and contracted primary care clinics to increase management efficiency.	$ In Kind Services	VP, Network Management Managing Director
• Complete feasibility plans concerning Random Lake and Indo Scandian.	$25,000	Medical Director Regional Services Administrator, Regional Services

Goal #4:

• Provide consultation on practice management and educational development in communities as basis for management services organization. Interface CME/EMS training, education, and consultation services.	$25,000	Managing Director Physician Liaison
• Approach hospitals and physicians throughout the regional counties with proposal to help examine ways and means of enhancing community understanding of health care needs while fostering leadership toward healthier lifestyles.	$ In Kind Services	VP, Network Management
• Develop a systems approach to monitor outcomes/reporting measures.	$ In Kind Services	VP, MIS Director, Network Management
• Sign clinics up/help prepare for participation in practice guideline collaboration.	$ In Kind Services	Medical Director Practice Guidelines
• Establish connectivity (See Goal #2 which covers same activity)	$ See Goal #2	
• Offer to develop joint strategic plans with interested physicians and hospitals of western Wisconsin.	$ In Kind Services	Managing Director

1996 Total $125,000

APPLICATIONS

Targeted Goals

1. Does the practice publish a defined vision and mission statement? Where are they posted?
2. List core values for your practice. Do they reflect the commitment and strength underlying your vision and mission?
3. Rank order your strengths, weaknesses, opportunities, and threats. How do they compare to those of your competition? What is the plan to correct weaknesses and optimize strengths?

Objectives

1. Can you measure the effectiveness of key strategies for positioning your practice?
2. Quantify progress toward outcomes related to your goals, strategies for implementation, objectives, and programs.
3. Enhancements of CQI must be measurable. What analysis can help identify elements to be enhanced?

Content

Outline the vision, mission, core values, goals, and objectives of the practice. List new elements added to enhance last year's plan. What activity was dropped because it is no longer relevant?

Evaluation

Define differences between desired and actual outcomes for each goal/objective. How will enhancements be considered for next year's plan?

Continuous Quality Improvement

Do measures of CQI reflect increasing positive refinements? What measures of progress are reported on a monthly basis?

Chapter 10

Financial Management

POINTS FOR FOCUS

The development of budgets follows establishment of the annual plan that outlines desired performance in the practice through defined programmed activities. The philosophy of constructing a "zero-based budget" is recommended. A zero-based budget implies that each item of expense requires annual review/justification and approval before reinclusion (i.e., just because an expense was in last year's budget does not mean it should automatically be included in next year's budget). Zero-based budgeting is a defense against creep up in numbers of FTE employees and in support for nonproductive activities.

Targeted Goals

1. To define budgetary needs based upon desired achievement of outcomes in the practice/program.
2. To plan budgets to balance decreasing reimbursement from third-party payers with needs for medical care of good quality.
3. To establish a monitoring system that routinely (at least monthly) reports the status of each budgeted activity producing revenues and expenses.
4. To enhance financial management of the practice by systematically predicting and achieving desired successes.

Objectives

1. Implement a zero-based budgeting process that requires annual review/ justification and approval of each item of expense. If the expense is not directly related to productive activity, it should not be included.
2. Define each source of reimbursement and verify its status for the next years. Each payer should be asked to indicate planned changes in

amounts they will be reimbursing your services for each of the next three years. Your plan must reflect changes to decreasing reimbursement from virtually all sources of payment.

3. Monthly (or more frequent if needed) reports on "key indicators" must be made to executive staff/board of directors on the status of revenues and related items of expense. Without close attention to key indicators, the practice will spend unnecessary time worrying about finances when the focus should be on medical practice and achievement of desired outcomes in customer service.

4. It is important to identify those factors/activities most responsible for the achievement of a desired outcome in the practice. Once identified, the most important factors must receive appropriate support/enhancement if expected success is to be attained.

Content

Successful financial management of medical practice has become (or is becoming) more difficult, due to decreasing reimbursements from third-party payers, increased competition from providers and health plans, and regional/local initiatives toward reforms of health care sponsored by various business- and employer-sponsored alliances and groups. Physicians can prepare to succeed through effective financial management founded on sound practices. Current issues, reporting systems, and methods are described in this chapter.

Evaluation

Meeting or exceeding budgetary expectations on a regular basis is the ultimate test of financial management. Assessing how well revenues, expenses, and estimates of volume and activity were achieved is an essential analysis.

Continuous Quality Improvement

Ongoing refinements must be sought by systematically comparing actual results to budget. Key indicators are helpful to follow, since targets for success are generally predictable on the basis of knowledge of the top four or five key predictors.

THE BUSINESS OF MEDICINE

Knowing what business the medical practice must focus on to be successful has been an oxymoron until recent reforms of health care became a national and statewide issue. The business of medicine, although not new from the point of view of the Internal Revenue Service nor of commerce, has never before had to consider tactics and strategies usually reserved for those companies found among the Fortune 500, on the New York Stock Exchange, or on Wall Street. Make no mistake about it, medicine has become a most competitive business. Each existing medical practice, regardless of size, must recognize and address its competitive needs.

Finances support the medical practice—if there is no margin, there is no mission. Although most physicians do not enter medicine for the money, there is an expectation of a comfortable living. The challenges of competition in contemporary health care are such that the finest physicians' minds can be the contributing factors that swing advantage in the direction of those groups with the most significant leadership by physicians and participation by them in business planning and financial matters. Physicians need to know how each action creates positive, negative, and neutral reactions. Those in private practice know this lesson well, but the number of physicians in private practice and in small medical groups is rapidly diminishing, due to an inability to compete. Tactics and strategies that are needed to provide physicians with a competitive edge to enhance their practices proactively and to provide their businesses with opportunities for growth include:

- Reimbursement will shrink, from virtually all payers, who will follow trends in Medicare and Medicaid.
- Costs must be reduced, to remain competitive in a rapidly changing marketplace.
- Opportunities for improvements in the practice that complement and build on previous operations and efforts at cost containment must be identified.
- Complete in-depth reviews must be done of focus areas, examining the operations of the practice as well as major business processes that cross boundaries among primary care and various specialties.
- Practices must build consensus among management, staff, and physicians on key strategies, through a participative approach toward common needs.
- Operations must be reengineered, using principles of CQI to integrate the components of the physicians' delivery system and to improve customer service.
- Operations of the practice must be strengthened to meet the demands associated with the continuous shift toward ambulatory care and away from inpatient admissions to the hospital.

- Plans must be developed for implementation of all opportunities, assessing their priority, benefit, level of risk, level of effort, and time frame.
- Managers must assist with the implementation of cost reductions and strategies for enhancement of service/quality to off set static and shrinking reimbursements.

UNDERSTANDING THE ISSUES

Changing characteristics reflecting medical group behaviors are routinely reviewed and described by MGMA. The following summaries appeared in the *MGMA Physician Compensation and Production Survey: 1993 and 1992 Reports Based on 1992 and 1991 Data:*[1]

Activity in Managed Care Increases Administrative Efforts

Medical groups who had a majority of revenues from contracts for at-risk managed care in 1992 employed more staff than groups without managed care, in certain key areas including administrative and supporting staff, staff in informational services, registered nurses, medical receptionists, medical records specialists, radiologic and imaging technicians, and staff for other medical ancillary services. But groups with more than half of revenues from managed care employed only 55 percent as many medical secretaries and transcriptionists per physician as groups with no revenues from managed care. Groups with more than 10 percent of revenues from managed care had significantly more supporting staff than groups with no contracts for at-risk managed care or with only minimal revenues from managed care. Groups relying most heavily on managed care employed 5.34 FTE staff per FTE physician in 1992, compared with only 4.37 staff per physician in groups without managed care.

Ownership by Physicians

A small minority of group practices (just over 4 percent) had equity in health maintenance organizations (HMOs) in 1993, while about the same percentage (just under 4 percent) had ownership interests in preferred provider organizations (PPOs). Group practices with more than fifty FTE physicians and multispecialty group practices were much more likely to have equity interests in HMOs. Twenty-nine percent of all groups with fifty-one to one hundred FTE-physicians had ownership interests in HMO plans in 1993, followed by 14 percent of groups with more than 100 physicians. In contrast, only 3 to 5 percent of smaller medical groups had such ownership in HMO plans in 1993. About 6 percent of multispecialty groups had ownership interests in HMOs, compared with 3 percent of single-specialty groups. Slightly more than 4 percent of multispecialty groups had ownership interests in PPOs, compared with just under 4 percent of single-specialty group practices.

Revenues from Managed Care

Medical group practices derived a median of 20 percent of total revenues for medical care from contracts for at-risk managed care in 1993, up from 17 percent in 1992. Revenues from capitated contracts as a percentage of total medical revenues decreased to 13 percent in 1993, from 15 percent in 1992. At-risk, discounted, and fee-for-service revenues were 11 percent of total medical revenues in 1993, up from 10 percent in 1992. Fifty-seven percent of multispecialty group practices derived some revenue from contracts for at-risk managed care in 1993, up from 53 percent in 1992. Multispecialty group practices (57 percent in 1993) were somewhat more likely than single-specialty groups (54 percent in 1993) to receive revenue from HMO/PPO contracts, in both 1992 and 1993.

Fifty-five percent of groups derived revenue from contracts for at-risk managed care in 1993, up from 50 percent in 1993. Groups of more than 100 FTE physicians were most likely (69 percent in 1993) to have revenue from contracts for at-risk managed care in both years. More than half of all small groups derived revenue from contracts for at-risk managed care in 1993, though they were the least likely of all groups to do so.

Issues of Productivity

Basing physicians' compensation solely on productivity (measured as total gross charges) was most common in 1992. Some 26 percent of physicians' groups were compensated solely on the basis of productivity; 29 percent of physicians received 50 to 99 percent of their compensation on the basis of their productivity, while other factors were taken into account, and 25 percent of physicians were paid salaries plus incentives of various kinds (see Tables 10.1 and 10.2).

Family practices (13 percent) and internists (12 percent) had the highest percentages of revenues from capitated managed care of the five single-specialty groups shown. Too few single-specialty groups in obstetrics/gynecology, orthopedic surgery, and cardiology reported revenues from capitated contracts for reliable conclusions to be drawn. Cardiology and internal medicine received the highest shares of revenues from Medicare fee for service.

TABLE 10.1. Physician Compensation for Established Providers

	Percentage of Physicians Compensated by:						
	Productivity			Salary Plus Incentives	Straight Salary	100% Equal Shares	Other
	100%	75% - 99%	50% - 74%				
Size (# of FTE Physicians)							
10 or Fewer	26.1%	10.2%	9.9%	28.0%	9.8%	12.6%	3.4%
11 - 25	30.4	16.4	6.9	26.1	10.3	7.2	2.8
26 - 50	36.6	22.2	8.8	20.0	6.7	2.9	2.8
51 - 99	39.6	30.7	12.8	11.9	2.9	0	2.0
100 or More	7.3	17.5	14.7	31.7	28.8	0	0
Specialty Composition							
Multispecialty w/PC	27.5%	22.4%	12.0%	21.8%	15.3%	0.2%	0.8%
Multispecialty w/o PC	23.1	17.2	10.0	26.1	4.3	15.5	3.8
Average Multispecialty	27.3%	22.2%	11.9%	22.0%	14.8%	0.9%	0.9%
Single Specialty							
Allergy/Immunology	24.2%	4.5%	0%	47.0%	13.6%	10.6%	0%
Anesthesiology	14.4	3.7	0	33.9	8.4	25.7	13.9
Cardiology	5.3	2.5	10.2	43.5	9.4	25.7	3.3
Family Practice	20.4	9.6	9.8	45.4	11.3	1.9	1.6
General Surgery	12.9	22.6	12.9	9.7	17.2	17.2	7.5
Hematology/Oncology	12.3	3.8	19.8	15.1	19.8	29.2	0
Internal Medicine	48.3	8.3	2.8	34.3	0.8	2.4	3.0
Obstetrics/Gynecology	32.1	6.8	6.8	32.4	12.3	9.7	0
Ophthalmology	20.4	20.9	19.4	32.7	0	1.5	5.1
Orthopedic Surgery	35.1	13.0	15.4	15.6	7.0	12.5	1.2
Pediatrics	3.9	26.4	3.9	27.9	32.6	5.4	0
Radiology/Diagnostic	5.8	5.8	0	40.4	13.6	29.5	4.8
All Other Single Specialty	19.3	10.3	8.2	28.0	11.6	13.7	8.9
Average Single Specialty	22.0%	9.2%	8.1%	31.9%	9.9%	14.0%	4.9%
Average All Specialties	25.8%	18.5%	10.9%	24.8%	13.4%	4.6%	2.0%
Sample Size: 20,367 providers/1,306 groups							

Source: Medical Group Management Association. *Physician Compensation and Production Survey: 1993 and 1992 reports based on 1992 and 1991 data.* Englewood, CO, 1994. Reprinted with permission.

As the groups illustrate, 2.8 percent of medical groups that differentiated how physicians were compensated for services to managed care patients in 1992 used capitation as the basis for compensating physicians, up from 19.7 percent in 1992. In 1992, another 19.5 percent of groups that differentiated how physicians were compensated for services to managed care patients paid physicians by using a combination of capitation and discounts/reductions, up from 9.1 percent in 1992.

TABLE 10.2. Sources of Revenue

Single-Specialty Groups*

	Medicare		Medicaid		Managed Care			Com-mercial, Private, Etc.
	Capi-tated	Fee For Service	Capi-tated	Fee For Service	Capi-tated	At Risk Disc. FFS	Not At Risk Disc. FFS	
Single Specialty Family Practice	—	16.1%	—	8.4%	13.0%	20.0%	18.0%	50.0%
Internal Medicine	—	41.0	—	3.0	11.7	15.5	18.2	34.2
Obstetrics/Gynecology	—	2.0	—	4.0	—	23.5	30.0	56.0
Orthopedic Surgery	—	19.8	—	4.0	—	10.0	15.2	60.3
Cardiology	—	46.0	—	3.4	—	6.0	10.0	34.5

Multispecialty Groups*

	Medicare		Medicaid		Managed Care			Com-mercial, Private, Etc.
	Capi-tated	Fee For Service	Capi-tated	Fee For Service	Capi-tated	At Risk Disc. FFS	Not At Risk Disc. FFS	
Size (# of FTE Phys.) 10 or Fewer	—	27.8%	—	8.0%	9.5%	13.1%	11.0%	44.2%
11 - 25	—	25.0	—	7.1	16.0	10.0	10.4	48.0
26 - 50	—	27.1	—	7.1	18.0	8.7	13.7	48.0
51 or More	8.9%	22.4	1.4%	6.7	22.0	6.9	13.9	43.8

*Percentages are medians and do not total 100%.

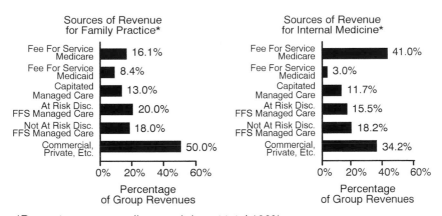

Sources of Revenue for Family Practice*

Sources of Revenue for Internal Medicine*

*Percentages are medians and do not total 100%.

Source: Medical Group Management Association. *MGMA Cost Survey: 1993 Report Based on 1992 Data.* Author: Englewood, CO, 1994. Reprinted with permission.

Definition of Methods of Compensation

- *100 percent productivity:* All of the physician's compensation is based on his or her individual productivity.
- *75 to 99 percent productivity:* 75 to 99 percent of a physician's compensation is based on productivity, and the remainder is based on other factors.
- *50 to 74 percent productivity:* As above.
- *Salary plus incentives:* The physician is paid a salary and an incentive based on productivity, overall performance of the group, or other factors determined by the medical group. Salary may encompass an equal-shares situation.
- *Straight salary:* 100 percent of the physician's compensation comes from a fixed salary.
- *100 percent of equal shares:* All physicians in the medical group are paid equal amounts based on overall performance of the group.

DEFINING AND SYSTEMATICALLY USING INFORMATION FROM KEY INDICATORS

Effective financial management requires a working knowledge of those factors most important to the growth and development of your business. One model is not appropriate for all physicians' practices, and a "best fit" of useful information will require your group's active participation. The remainder of this chapter will address the application of financial information and information on volume and utilization in the managerial process.

Financial Reporting

To be useful, information on key indicators must be tracked, processed, and reported, on at least a monthly basis. Most physicians' practices hold monthly meetings of the board of directors, and it is appropriate that this information should become a part of each such meeting. An example of a fairly standard consolidated statement of income for a physicians' group appears in Example 10.1. It includes data related to the hospitals that are part of each physician's practice.

For purposes of aligning other factors important to the practice with financial information, customized formats for reporting are helpful. For example, selected financial indicators and indicators of volume can be pulled out of the consolidated statement of income and included with a

EXAMPLE 10.1. Physicians' Clinic, Consolidated Statement of Income, Shown with Key Indicators of Volume and Utilization—1995 Year-to-Date (Through April 30) (Dollars in Thousands)

Current Month's Budget				Budget Year-to-Date		
Actual	Budget	Variance	Income Statement	Actual	Budget	Variance
			(Physicians' Group Only)			
$3,518	$3,891	($373)	Net Revenues from Patients	$15,566	$15,609	($43)
$1,729	$1,737	($8)	Other Operating Revenues	$6,766	$6,948	($182)
$5,247	$5,628	($381)	Total Operating Revenue Expenses	$22,332	$22,557	($225)
$2,998	$2,974	$24	Physicians' Salaries and Benefits	$12,160	$11,814	$346
$1,139	$1,290	($151)	Non-Physicians' Salaries and Benefits	$5,219	$5,490	($271)
$475	$512	($37)	Purchased Services	$2,100	$2,045	$55
$189	$205	($16)	Professional Liability	$783	$819	($36)
$455	$514	($59)	Supplies and Other	$1,852	$2,058	($206)
$77	$79	($2)	Provision for Bad Debts	$334	$320	$14
$5,333	$5,574	($241)	Total Expenses	$22,448	$22,546	($98)
($86)	$54	($140)	Operating Income	($116)	$11	($127)
$26	$18	$8	Non-Operating Income	$105	$73	$32
($60)	($72)	($132)	Net Income	($11)	($84)	($95)
		Selected Statistics on Volume (Data from Hospital and Physicians' Practice)				
7,315	7,446	(131)	Adult and Peds Patient-Days*	29,994	29,492	502
574	633	(59)	Patient-Days, Intensive Care	2,292	2,500	(208)
352	527	(175)	Patient-Days, Nursery	1,341	1,571	(230)
1,420	1,401	19	Admits, Adults and Peds	5,960	5,525	435
14	10	4	Admits, Intensive Care	56	41	15
126	146	(20)	Deliveries, Newborn	491	547	(56)
4,482	4,430	52	Visits to ER	18,121	17,615	506
19,715	20,190	(475)	Clinical Visits	82,997	84,798	(1,801)
			Cases in the Operating Room			
547	589	(2)	Main Campus	2,302	2,233	69
298	380	(82)	Same-Day Surgery	997	1,460	(463)
548	566	(18)	FTEs	559	566	(7)

*Indicates data associated with hospital's physicians' practice.
**Indicates data for physicians' practice only

Source: Paul Sommers.

major category of expenses in overhead, human resources, indicators of service/quality, and comparisons of hospital occupancy (see Examples 10.2 and 10.3 and Figures 10.1 through 10.4 in this chapter). Customization is governed by the needs of the physicians' group practice concerning how best to track and utilize information. The information and/or reporting format should be routinely reviewed to determine its effectiveness. Enhancements should be made as needed as long as the information is adequately protected to insure accurate ongoing interpretations.

EXAMPLE 10.2. Key Indicators to Review Monthly/Annually (Includes Financial Indicators and Statistics on Utilization and Volume)*

- Financial
    Operating Income
    Days' Cash on Hand
    Days' Net Revenue in Net Accounts Receivable

- Volume
    Patient Days in Hospital
    Hospital Admissions
    Visits to Emergency Center (specify admitted or nonadmitted patients)
    Cases in Operating Room
    Ambulatory/Outpatient Visits

- Indicators from Human Resources
    Total FTEs
    Rate of Turnover for Physicians
    Rate of Turnover for Employees
    Number of Staff Physicians by Year
    Percentage of Minorities

- Indicators in Service and Quality
    Complaints from Inpatients
    Complaints from Outpatients
    Complaints from Patients in ER
    Rates of C-Sections Done
    Mortality Rates

*To give as complete a picture as possible, data on physicians' practice should include related information on hospital practice.

EXAMPLE 10.3. Summary of Occupancy in Hospitals in the Catchment Area for This Physicians' Group Monthly Report

Hospital	Reported Beds	Average Daily Census	Occupancy %
East Catchment Area			
1.	230	126	55
2.	116	84	72
3.	60	12	20
4.	205	94	46
5.	140	123	88
6.	375	175	47
7.	313	276	88
8.	358	284	79
Combined East Catchment Area	1,797	1,174	65
West Catchment Area			
1.	625	461	74
2.	208	130	63
3.	185	113	61
4.	10	1	10
5.	149	132	89
6.	121	64	53
7.	331	222	67
8.	562	401	71
9.	341	231	68
10.	373	275	74
Combined West Catchment Area	2,905	2,030	70
Combined Catchment Area	4,702	3,204	68

GUIDELINES FOR HEALTH CARE: FINANCIAL IMPLICATIONS

The development of guidelines will have a direct impact on measurable results in the quality of patient care and physicians' expenses. Physicians have been in the lead and continue to play a major role in assessing technology and developing evidence-based outcomes.[2] The Institute for Clinical Systems Integration (ICSI) was created by Group Health, Mayo Clinic, Park Nicollet Medical Center, and HealthPartners in response to consumers' and employers' demands for greater access to reasonably priced quality care with greater accountability from providers.[3] The primary tools used by ICSI are measurements of medical outcomes, continuous quality improvement, and guidelines for health care. Dr. David Eddy's

FIGURE 10.1. Displaying Physicians' Practice and Related Hospital Indicators—Volume Indicators

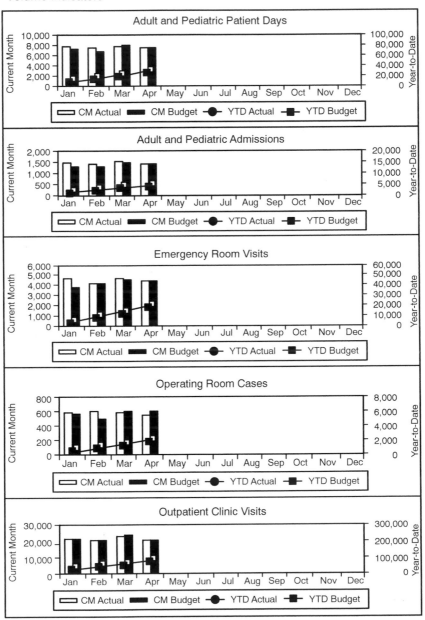

FIGURE 10.2. Displaying Physicians' Practice and Related Hospital Indicators—
Financial Indicators (Dollars in Thousands)

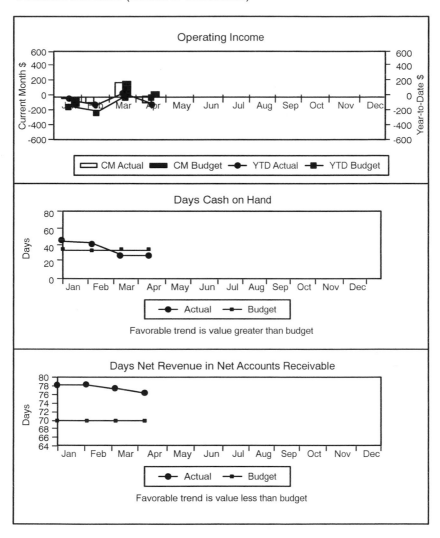

FIGURE 10.3. Displaying Physicians' Practice and Related Hospital Indicators—
Human Resource Indicators

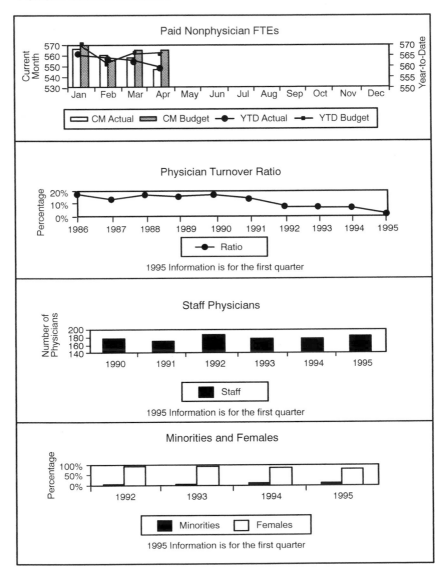

FIGURE 10.4. Displaying Physicians' Practice and Related Hospital Indicators—Quality Indicators

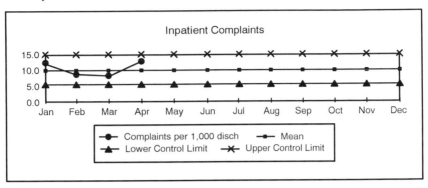

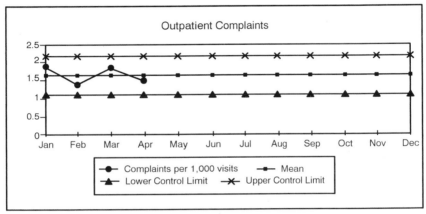

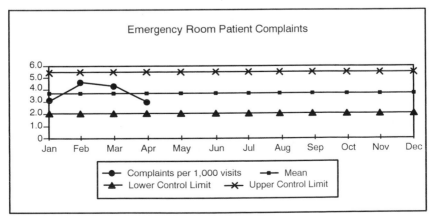

FIGURE 10.4 *(continued)*

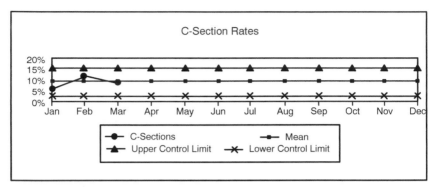

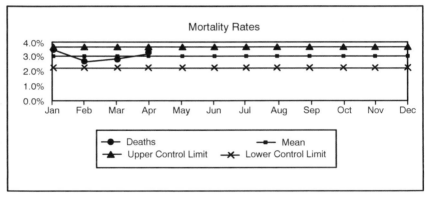

article on guideline development published by the AMA in 1990 substantiate the use of scientific evidence rather than consensus-based decisions.[2]

As guidelines are implemented in clinical practice, anticipated results should include (1) more efficient, more effective, and less costly care to patients, resulting in better outcomes, less cost, and healthier lifestyles; (2) physicians who adhere to guidelines will experience less risk and lower costs of liability for malpractice.

Measurement is a fundamental part of the ICSI program. Data from claims records, medical charts, and other sources are considered in all phases of the process of continuous quality improvement. Each guideline includes a plan for measuring concordance (the match between the recommended and the actual practice) and/or short-term effects. Reports of measurements of guidelines are used by participating medical groups to target areas for continuous quality improvement as well as by ICSI to determine the need for changes in guidelines. In 1996, ICSI expanded its collaboration with more than twenty medical groups in Minnesota that focuses on the development and implementation of clinical guidelines.

Although it takes time to determine if the use of clinical guidelines actually improves care, some evidence has been received that supports the efforts. Noteworthy results were reported by a University of California San Francisco/Mount Zion Medical Center research team to the scientific sessions of the American Heart Association held in Orlando, Florida, in November 1997. The research team used the congestive heart failure treatment guidelines developed by the Agency for Health Care Policy and Research. The results were encouraging:

- fewer readmissions
- decreased cost
- decreased length of stay

Specifically, the use of guidelines helped boost use of recommended post-hospital medications from 59 percent of patients to 76 percent.

Computers provided an added benefit to guideline use for the UCLA Emergency Department. The research published in the November 19, 1997 *Journal of the American Medical Association,* tested a computer charting system with treatment guidelines for handling health care workers who get stuck with a needle or otherwise expose themselves to body fluids. Researchers found that the physicians were much more likely to document seven essential items regarding patient history in the medical record. But the improvement disappeared as soon as the computerized chart was taken out of service. Results indicated that compliance with five treatment guidelines increased from 83 percent to 96 percent with the computerized chart use.

SELECTING KEY FACTORS TO ENHANCE FINANCIAL PERFORMANCE

Although routine reports from the financial and business office include more than adequate amounts of information, a process is needed to focus on key factors that account for specific goals and objectives in the physicians' practice. For example: How can a physicians' group (Ramsey Clinic) and a hospital (St. Paul-Ramsey Medical Center) thrive on a combined collection rate of 65 percent (physicians = 58 percent, hospital = 67 percent) amidst the chaos of the Minneapolis-St. Paul health care marketplace? At Ramsey the answer, in part, was achieved by consolidating operations to create a physician-hospital organization (PHO) for purposes of eliminating duplicated overhead expenses and combining resources to support the implementation of a joint strategic plan. This study reports on outcomes achieved by analyzing audited data from the PHO (1987-1993).[4,5,6] Chapter 6 discusses how key factors can be identified and applied to predict desired outcomes; e.g., revenue growth, a decrease in physician staff turnover, and so on.

DEVELOPMENT OF BUDGETS

The development of a program or organizational plan outlining proposed services or activities for a given period of time requires consideration of related expenses. Many organizations plan revenues to offset expenses through a fairly formal budgeting process. Following is an example of what can be included in the budget development process.

Overview for Next Year's Budget for Physicians' Clinic (includes outpatient and inpatient hospital consultations)

- Next year's budget will be prepared in a way consistent with the strategies and objectives of Physicians' Clinic.
- An average daily census of 244 patients is budgeted for acute patients, twenty-one for those in extended care for mental health/chemical dependency, and twelve for those in the hospital's nursery.
- Our acute admissions are budgeted on 16,800 patients for the year and reflect declines in specific areas from certain third-party payers.
- The average length of stay for acute patients is budgeted at 5.3 days.
- Outpatient activity reflects increases in psychiatry and in family practice, with all others remaining consistent with last year's activity.
- Visits to the ER are budgeted at last year's projected levels.
- Net income is budgeted at $400,000 or .6 percent, compared to $370,000 or .6 percent projected for last year.
- $1,268,000 of departmental net income is budgeted by the medical departments in the new year. Consistent with prior years, this amount is assumed to be distributed under the Physicians' Clinic incentive plan as compensation to physicians.
- Gross revenues include an increase in rates of 4 percent, effective January 1 of the new year.
- It is assumed that sources of revenues (i.e., the payer mix) will be consistent with last year, with the exception of a further shift toward the managed care option for recipients of Medicaid.

- Reimbursement was calculated using the most up-to-date information available. The average collection percentage is projected to be 55.4 percent next year, 1.8 percent less than projected collections for the current year.
- Net revenue from patient services (after write-offs and contractual deductions) is budgeted at $48,515,000, an increase of 5.2 percent from projected totals for the current year.
- Other operating revenue is budgeted at $20,615,000 for next year, an increase of 3.1 percent from projected results for the current year.
- Operating expenses are budgeted at $68,730,000, an increase of $2,999,000 or 4.6 percent from projected results for the current year.
- The budget includes an overall increase in rates in physicians' and nonphysicians' salaries and wages of 4.0 percent.
- The expense of physicians' salaries and benefits is budgeted to increase approximately $1,598,000, or 4.7 percent from projected levels for the current year.
- The budget allows payment for 562.9 FTE employees; this represents a decrease of approximately 2.6, or 0.5 percent, from projected levels for the current year.
- Total indirect expenses in departments are budgeted to increase 3.9 percent for the new year.
- The total amount allocated for the corporation (expenses for programs recognized to benefit Physicians' Clinic generally) is budgeted at the current year's level of $2,986,000, for next year. Distribution of the corporate allocation to the medical departments was made in accordance with the methodology approved by the Physicians' Clinic board of directors when the current formula was established.
- Total venture project funding for next year is $598,000. Of this, $48,000 is funding for expansion in psychiatry, and $550,000 is for unspecified projects.
- Cash is budgeted to decrease $1,396,000. Days cash on hand is expected to decrease to thirty-four days from forty-four during the past year.

Typically, each service unit is required to project or forecast its future operations on predetermined assumptions. For the physicians' practice, the following budgetary assumptions could be considered.

Assumptions

Volume

No overall increase in volume is contemplated by the Physicians' Clinic in 1995. Medical departments will budget for changes in volume depending on their individual circumstances. Changes in volume will be coordinated between primary care and physicians in specialties (and hospitals where appropriate).

Fee Increase

An overall fee increase of 4 percent is anticipated for Physicians' Clinic, to be effective January 1 of the new year.

Payer Mix

The budget assumes the clinic's payer mix will be comparable to data for the actual current year.

Payer	Percentage of Total
Medicare	19
Medicaid	29
HealthPartners	6
Blue Cross	8
All Other HMOs	6
Commercial	11
Self-Pay	12
Other	9
	100

Reimbursement

Increases in annual net revenues were projected by payers using existing regulations and contracts where applicable. Rate increases included in the budget are:

Payer	Percentage Increase
Medicare	1.5
Medicaid	0.0
Blue Cross	2.5
HMOs	2.0
Commercial	4.0
Self-Pay	2.5
Other	2.5

Specific rates of recovery for each department and/or service will be budgeted by financial planning based on the information presented above and the historical payer mix for each specific department/service.

Other Operating Revenue

The amounts from physicians' affiliation agreements will be budgeted at last year's levels, with adjustments made after determination of the actual amounts for next year's budget.

Salaries and Benefits

Physicians' Clinic will budget for a 5 percent increase in salaries for the new year, for both physicians and nonphysicians. Health and dental insurance has been budgeted for the new year at the current rates, due to favorable experience during the current year.

Professional Liability

Financial Planning will provide each department and each single-specialty physician with the amount of expense for professional liability that should be included in the new budget.

Indirect Expenses

Total indirect expenses are expected to be held to a 4 percent increase.

Corporate Allocation

The corporate allocation for next year is being held at the level for the current year.

Expense Inflation

Next year's operating expenses have been increased by anticipated inflation. Inflating factors included in the budget are:

- Salaries   4%
- Other   3-6%

Format for Statement of Income

EXAMPLE 10.4. Statement of Income for Physicians' Clinic—Next Year's Budget (Dollars in Thousands)

	Next Year's Budget	Current Year's Budget	Increase/ Decrease Amount	Percent
Operating Revenue				
Net Patient-Service Revenue	$48,515	$46,099	$2,416	5.2
Other Operating Revenue	20,615	20,002	613	3.1
Total Operating Revenue	$69,130	$66,101	$3,209	4.6
Operating Expenses				
Physicians' Salaries and Benefits	$35,639	$34,041	$1,598	4.7
Nonphysicians' Salaries and Benefits	$16,827	15,868	959	6.0
Purchased Medical Services	5,642	5,949	(307)	-5.2
Professional Liability	2,388	2,417	(29)	-1.2
Supplies	1,411	1,361	50	3.7
Occupancy	2,039	2,137	(98)	-4.6
Purchased Services	540	494	46	9.3
General and Administration*	2,454	1,787	667	37.3
Provision for Bad Debt	$68,730	$65,731	$2,999	4.6
Net Income	$400	$370	$30	8.1
Total Margin	0.6%	0.6%		

*Increase is primarily due to venture project funds of $498,000 budgeted to be expended next year with no expense for this item projected in current year.

Format for Balance Sheet

EXAMPLE 10.5. Balance Sheet for Physicians' Clinic—Next Year's Budget (Dollars in Thousands)

	Next Year's Budget	Current Year's Projected Balance
Assets		
Cash and Cash Equivalents	$2,521	$3,917
Net Receivables from Patients	10,774	10,004
Other	505	505
Current Assets	$13,800	$14,426

Investments Including Board Designated	3,919	3,919
Net Cash, and Investments Designated for Professional Liability Claims	3,253	3,102
Investment in Professional Liability Company	250	250
Net Land, Buildings, and Equipment	1,283	1,283
Deferred Compensation Investment Fund	878	554
Total Assets	$23,383	$23,534
Liabilities and Fund Balance		
Accounts Payable	$1,886	$1,886
Accrued Salaries and Benefits	3,361	4,236
Other Accrued Expenses	1,970	1,970
Current Liabilities	$7,217	$8,092
Accrued Professional Liability Claims	2,031	2,031
Deferred Compensation Payable	878	554
Total Liabilities	$10,126	$10,677
Fund Balance	13,257	12,857
Total Liabilities and Fund Balance	$23,383	$23,534

Projection of Net Income by Department/Service

EXAMPLE 10.6. Physicians' Clinic: Net Income by Department/Service—Next Year's Budget (Dollars in Thousands)

	Net Operating Revenue	Net Operating Expense	Net Income
Ophthalmology	$1,690	$1,570	$120
Otolaryngology	931	905	26
Family Practice	2,390	2,354	36
Internal Medicine	10,585	10,581	4
Psychiatry	11,982	11,981	1
Neurology	1,271	1,107	164
OB/GYN	4,507	4,496	11
Physical Medicine	756	756	0
Orthopedics	2,543	2,490	53
Pediatrics	1,919	1,913	6
Surgery	5,349	5,206	143
Urology	818	799	19
Emergency Medicine	4,758	4,745	13
Anesthesiology	3,092	3,011	81
Pathology	1,892	1,704	188
Medical Imaging	3,748	3,345	403
Departments Before Accrual	$58,231	$56,963	$1,268

372 MEDICAL GROUP MANAGEMENT IN TURBULENT TIMES

Departments' Net Income Accrual	($1,268)
Corporate Net Income Included in Net Operating Expense	400
Net Income	$400

EXAMPLE 10.7. Physicians' Clinic, Corporate Allocation—Detail Next Year's Budget (Dollars in Thousands)

Corporate Costs Before Net Income

Branch Clinics	$964
Venture Projects	550
Psychiatry Initiative—East Suburb	48
Neonatology	322
Emergency Medical Services	244
Contributions to Foundation	150
Neurosurgery	101
Workers Comp Managed Care Program	55
Dermatology	(11)
Total Corporate Costs Before Net Income	$2,586
Net Income	400
Total Corporate Allocation—Next Year	$2,986
Corporate Allocation—Last Year	2,986
Percentage of Change	0.0%

EXAMPLE 10.8. Physicians' Clinic, Other Operating Revenue, and FTEs Detail—Next Year's Budget (Dollars in Thousands)

Other Operating Revenue

	Next Year's Budget	Current Projected	Increase/ Decrease Amount	Per- cent
Physicians' Affiliations	$9,449	$8,692	$757	8.7
Reimbursements for Indigent Care	824	824	0	0.0
Capitation in Psychiatry	3,331	4,246	(915)	-21.4
Other	$20,615	$20,002	$613	3.1
Full Time Equivalents (FTEs)				
Medical Departments	332.2	331.1	1.1	0.3
Indirect Departments	102.7	102.5	0.2	0.2
Corporate Departments	128.0	131.9	(3.9)	−3.0
Total	562.9	565.5	(2.6)	−0.5

EXAMPLE 10.9. Physicians' Clinic, Assumptions on Census/Volume—Next Year's Budget

	Next Year's Budget	Current Year's Projected	Past Year's Actual
Admissions			
Acute	16,800	16,679	15,870
Extended Care	130	133	144
Deliveries	1,600	1,600	1,601
Patient Days			
Acute	89,000	89,292	87,394
Extended Care	7,700	7,717	7,368
Newborn	4,470	4,470	5,121
Average Length of Stay			
Acute	5.3	5.4	5.5
Extended Care	59.2	58.0	51.2
Outpatient Visits			
Emergency Room	54,600	54,600	56,626
Outpatient Clinics	255,400	247,656	247,464
Surgical Cases			
Inpatient	4,175	4,080	3,781
Outpatient	7,775	3,220	2,186
	11,950	7,300	5,967

REIMBURSEMENT TRENDS

The health care market in Minnesota continues to be referred to as a barometer for trends in the reimbursement and delivery of services. The Twin City area, in particular, continues to serve as a national laboratory demonstrating self-improving reforms. In the May 1995 issue of the *Managed Care Industry Overview*,[7] Brown described systems for delivery and payment in the Minneapolis-St. Paul area as among the most organized in the United States. The Twin Cities area is being shaped by a strict regulatory environment and an exceedingly liberal local government. Business coalitions and purchasing alliances have become strong negotiators, extracting extremely favorable health care packages for participating employees.

Milliman and Robertson, a national actuarial firm in health care, surveyed Minnesota's health care costs in early 1995 and found that mean rates for premiums in the Minneapolis area were about 85 percent of the nationwide mean rates.[8] From the perspective of cost, medical care here ranges 15 percent to 20 percent below the national average. Costs have been steadily declining for the past ten years. With a nationwide factor of 1.0, the area factor for Minneapolis-St. Paul was .98 in 1985 and decreased to .82 in 1994.

Brown noted that the Department of Health and Social Services recorded over $1 trillion for health care costs in 1994 in the United States. This $1.06 trillion was a 12.5 percent increase over 1993 expenditures. Approximately 85 percent of the U.S. population (about 215 million people) are insured by a carrier, by the federal government, or by self-insuring programs. Government programs, which cover about 30 percent of the insured population, accounted for 53 percent of such expenditures. Private expenditures amounted to 47 percent of spending and covered about 70 percent of the insured population.[7]

Sources of Funds for Health Care

Private Sources

Health Insurance	39%
Out-of-Pocket Payments	18%
Total Private Funds	47%

Government Sources

Medicare	22%
Medicaid	18%
Other Programs	13%
Total Public Funds	53%

Uses of Funds in Health Care

Hospital Care	37%
Personal Care (dental, home health, vision, durable medical equipment)	24%
Physicians' Services	19%
Administration, Research, and Construction	12%
Care in Nursing Homes	8%
Total	100%

Source: Brown, A. *Managed Care Overview.* Alex Brown and Sons, Inc. Baltimore, MD, May 5, 1995. Reprinted with permission.

PAYERS

Payers for health care include governmental agencies, employers who shift risk to managed care and indemnity carriers, and employers who self-insure (see Figure 10.5). Federal and state governments account for more than half of spending in health care. Of the population served by the health care industry 60 percent paid privately for services, 26 percent used governmental sources, and 14 percent were uninsured. The distribution of payers for services was divided: 47 percent private and 53 percent governmental sources.

Medicare

The Medicare model has encouraged other payers (e.g., private insurers, HMOs, employers' business coalitions, and the like) to become aggressive in decision making about health care, to force lesser demand for services. This movement implies lower income for MDs, and less need for their services.

FIGURE 10.5. Payer Shift to Public Sector (Share of Expenditures for Health Services and Supplies)

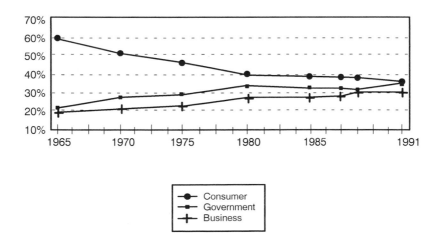

Source: Health Care Financing Administration, *Health Care Financing Review*, Spring, Washington, DC, 1993.

Factors associated with the way financing is changing the practice of medicine are reflected as follows:

- Physicians in solo practice will be forced into groups to combat competition and share in the costs of liability for malpractice.
- There will be incentives against hospitalizations, creating a need for fewer beds and encouraging programs in cost containment and a move toward outpatient surgery and as much general ambulatory care as possible. For example, there will be consolidations and mergers between physicians and hospitals.
- Rates will be cut in Medicare/Medicaid.
- Use of DRGs will mean fewer hospitalizations and more ambulatory care.
- Rates for ambulatory care will be controlled by resource-based relative value scales (RBRVS) that consider physicians' time spent as compared to spending on procedures.
- The initial reactions of health care providers to the preceding factors resulted in cost shifting to other payers, e.g., to private insurers, HMOs, employers, patients, and other government payers—a virtual reform.

Medicare is the fastest growing portion of the federal budget, consuming an ever-increasing share. Lawmakers face two conflicting tasks: (1) reduce the federal deficit; and (2) keep Medicare benefits relatively intact. Taxpayers are demanding decreased spending but, generally, not at the expense of the elderly and others with special needs. In 1994, Medicare provided benefits to approximately thirty-six million Americans at a federal expenditure of $158 billion. The total spent on Medicare was projected to increase from its 1980 rate at 6 to 12 percent, $177 billion, in 1995, and increase at a rate greater than 10 percent a year through 1999, according to the Congressional Budget Office. In an era of public scrutiny of governmental spending, Medicare is accounting for an increasing percentage of the federal budget.

Eligibility for Medicare extends to three groups: (1) those over age sixty-five who are eligible for Social Security; (2) those under age sixty-five who are disabled and have received Social Security benefits for two years; and (3) those who have had a kidney transplant or are on kidney dialysis.

Indemnity Coverage

Medicare is not a comprehensive health care program. Coverage is provided in two parts: Part A is hospital insurance; Part B is medical insurance for physician services. Part A is provided at no cost. Part B is optional; if a recipient chooses coverage under Part B, he/she must pay a premium of about $40 per month, which is deducted from his/her Social Security check. Blue Cross Systems are the predominant fiscal intermediary for recipients of Medicare, handling approximately 33 million (greater than 90 percent) of the beneficiaries.

Medigap Insurance

Most seniors purchase "Medigap" policies to fill in the gaps, or to supplement coverage under Medicare. Medigap policies were standardized by federal law in 1992, to make comparison among policies easier. There are currently ten standardized supplemental plans. Supplemental policies range from coinsuring the beneficiary for the 20 percent of charges not covered by Medicare to a high-end policy that adds a limited benefit covering prescription drugs. Prices for policies range from $30 to $150 per member per month.

Medicare Risk in Coverage by an HMO

When a recipient of Medicare joins an HMO program, all benefits are administered through the HMO. Except for emergency care, no care outside the HMO system is covered by either the HMO or the federal government. The HMOs provide all coverage that is standard under Medicare. In addition, they usually cover annual physical exams and other preventive care. There are generally no deductibles, coinsurances, or claims forms. The HMOs must accept any applicant covered by Medicare except those being treated for kidney disease at the time of application or those already enrolled in a hospice program under Medicare (see Figure 10.6). An HMO can charge a recipient a premium for coverage; nearly half of all HMOs do not charge recipients of Medicare a premium, at present.

Brown issued the following forecast:[7]

> We believe that the federal government will continue to encourage recipients to join HMO risk programs, because it shifts the risk of utilization to the HMO (which has more sophisticated systems to manage the risks). In addition, we believe that HCFA will remain motivated to encourage HMOs to serve the Medicare population. We do not anticipate a dramatic change in reimbursement for at least the next five years.

Medicaid

Medicaid is a state-run program that provides health care benefits to the poor and disabled. Approximately one-half of its funding comes from the

FIGURE 10.6. Medicare Risk Contracts—per Member per Month Premiums Charged to Seniors

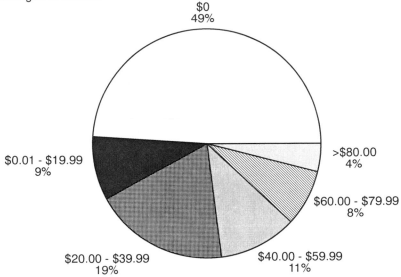

Source: Health Care Financing Authority, U.S. Government Finance Office, Washington, DC, June 1994.

federal government. About one-third of the expenditures are spent on two-thirds of the beneficiaries: families with a single woman as head of household (mothers on AFDC). Expenditures under Medicaid have been growing at an alarming rate and are projected to increase more than 10 percent annually until the year 2000. Approximately thirty-four million people are covered by Medicaid.

Distribution of Population Receiving Medicaid

	Distribution	1993
Mothers with Children	68%	33%
Disabled	15%	39%
Elderly	13%	28%
Other	4%	—
	100%	100%

Source: Health Care Financing Authority. U.S. Government Finance Office, Washington, DC, June 1994.

Distribution of 1993 Spending, by Service

Acute Care	45%
Institutional Care	30%
Home Health	6%
Other	19%
	100%

Source: Health Care Financing Authority. U.S. Government Finance Office, Washington, DC, June 1994.

Distribution of Medicaid Recipients by Coverage

	Total in Millions	Percent of Total	# of Plans
HMO	3.9	12	210
Primary Case Management (PCP)	2.4	7	80
Prepaid Health Plans (PHP)	1.4	4	50
Other (not Managed Care)	26.2	78	
Total	33.9	100	340

Source: Health Care Financing Authority. U.S. Government Finance Office, Washington, DC, June 1994.

MANAGED CARE AS A WAY OF DOING BUSINESS

Physicians need to make preparations for changes in reimbursement that will negatively impact partners in practice and their bottom lines. Medicare/Medicaid is but one example necessitating a deliberate change in the way medical care is delivered. Along with significantly reduced reimbursement from governmental payers, a major (and growing) source of reform is private and public groups who believe that they are paying too much for health care. In many areas various businesses and organizations are getting together for the sole purpose of reducing health care costs. The end product is an "alliance" or agreement to pool employees, members, and other necessary resources to create leverage for buying health care.

Rules and operating principles are internally agreed on by participants in such an alliance. Any expenses are typically shared on a *pro rata* basis. As a providers' organization, you must be ready, willing, and able to compete for the right to serve the members of such an alliance. Usually your group must respond favorably to fairly specific and defined needs to be considered as a potential provider. The following request for proposal (RFP) outlines the requirements of a consumer-oriented partnership of locally based providers of primary health care dedicated to controlling the cost of care by improving the health of their community. The group outlined what they were seeking in a relationship with tertiary/specialty physicians. Respondents interested in providing health care services to the group had to respond financially and progammatically to successfully become providers.

Example of Questions to Be Answered by Potential Tertiary/Specialty Physicians Which Must Be Considered in the Budget

Please address each one of the following areas in your response to this request for proposal. Your responses should be specific and with as much detail as needed for clarity. To simplify your response, we would be willing to review materials developed for other reporting purposes, if they address these issues (the alliance noted its current regional service capabilities below).

1. Identify all providers involved in the proposal. Describe locations of inpatient and ambulatory care services.
2. Provide information on inpatient and ambulatory practice protocols/guidelines and care pathways that are in use in your facilities or with your specialists. Compare these to the targeted DRGs outlined in this request for proposal.
3. Provide information on your standards for measuring quality and patient outcomes.
4. Describe your case management process and coordination of care for patients referred to your tertiary hospital. Also describe how the care of the patient will be transferred back to the primary care physician in the alliance's region.
5. Describe how you will effectively control the utilization of health care resources in the care of patients. We are particularly interested in how you will reduce the duplication of diagnostic tests and other services that have been previously performed by a physician or hospital for the alliance prior to transfer to your facility.
6. Describe methods you will use to communicate with the alliance's providers regarding the status of patients who are referred either to your hospital or your physician specialist (e-mail, fax, phone, paper).
7. Describe any telemedicine or on-line clinical data-sharing capabilities (lab, X ray) you currently use in working with out-state providers. How might these be used with providers from the alliance?
8. Identify how data on patient care episodes can be provided to the alliance.
9. Describe your capabilities for providing specialist physician outreach to clinics and hospitals in the alliance's service area.
10. Describe your proposed reimbursement for the target DRGs. Indicate whether these reimbursement levels reflect a bundling of ser-

vices provided to the patient including physician services, diagnostic testing, and inpatient services during the patient's inpatient stay in related ambulatory care (see Table 10.3).

11. For inpatient or ambulatory specialty physician services not included in the above DRG rates, we are seeking a reimbursement proposal based upon the CPT coding, which would be a multiple of the Medicare allowable charge.
12. Provide information about any transplant services available through your care delivery system.
13. Describe your credentialing process for medical staff and for any physician specialists without hospital privileges.
14. Document what types of tertiary/specialty services are unavailable in your network of providers. Examples may be transplant care, burn units, etc.

Regional Services Capabilities

- Adult and pediatric medical and surgical
- High-risk pregnancy management (transfer deliveries < 30 weeks)
- Level II nursing (transfer ventilatory dependent cases)
- Neurosurgery (transfer cerebral aneurysms)
- Thoracic surgery (transfer mediastinal aneurysms)
- Trauma and limb reattachment (transfer multiple trauma)
- Acute MI thrombolytic therapy
- Cardiac catheterization and angiograms (transfer invasive cardiac surgery)
- Acute detoxification

Potential Services Bundling

HOSPITAL FEES

- Hospital stay
- Radiology
- Preadmission testing
- Organ procurement/marrow harvesting
- Outpatient procedures
- Medication laboratory work
- Supplies

TABLE 10.3. Target DRGs

MDC	DRG	Description	MDC	DRG	Description
1	1	Craniotomy age >17 except for trauma	7	193	Biliary tract proc w cc exec only
1	2	Craniotomy for trauma age >17	7	201	Other hepatobil. or pancr. OR
1	3	Craniotomy ages 0-17	5	110	Major cardiovascular procedures w/cc
2	36	Retinal procedures	5	111	Major cardiovascular procedures w/o
4	75	Major chest procedures	5	112	Percutaneous cardio-vascular proc.
4	475	Respiratory system diag. w/ve	5	113	Amputation for circ system disorders
5	104	Cardiac valve proc./ pump & wc	5	114	Upper limb & toe amputation for circ.
5	105	Cardiac valve proc./ pump & w/o	5	115	Perm cardiac pace-maker implant/AMI
5	106	Coronary bypass w cardiac cath	5	116	Other permanent cardiac pacemaker
5	107	Cor. bypass w/o cardiac cath	5	117	Cardiac pacemaker revision exc. de
5	108	Other cardiothoracic procedures	5	118	Card. pacemkr dev replacement
8	217	Wound debrid & skin graft exc hand	5	121	Cir. disorders/AMI & C.V.
8	471	Bilat. or mult. major joint proc.	5	122	Circ. disorders/AMI w/o C.V.
8	471	Bilateral or multiple major joint proc.	5	123	Circ. disorders w AMI, expired
7	191	Pancreas, liver & shunt proc.	22	458	Non-exten. burns w skin graft
5	124	Circ. disorders except AMI, w	24	484	Craniotomy for mult. signif.
5	125	Circ. disorders except AMI, w/o	24	486	OR proc. for mult. signif.
5	126	Acute & subacute endocarditis	ALL	468	Exten. OR proc. unrelated
6	148	Major small & large bowel proc.	15	387	Prematurity w major problems
6	154	Stom., esophag. & duodenal proc.	15	388	Prematurity w/o major problems
11	302	Kidney transplant	15	389	Full-term neonate w major problems
14	373	Vaginal delivery w/o complic. dia	16	392	Splenectomy age >17
15	385	Neonates, died or transf. to anoth.	17	410	Chemotherapy w/o acute leukemia as
15	386	Extr. immaturity or resp. distress	17	492	Chemotherapy w/acute leukemia as
8	209	Major jt & limb reattchmt proc.	19	430	Mental health
8	214	Back & neck procedures w cc	23	462	Rehabilitation
8	215	Back & neck procedures w/o cc			

MDC	DRG	Description	MDC	DRG	Description
15	390	Neonate w other signif probs	24	485	Limb reattchmt, hip & femur pro
15	391	Normal Newborn	25	488	HIV w extensive OR procedure
17	473	Acu. leukemia w/o maj OR proc	ALL	482	Tracheostomy w mouth, larynx
18	415	OR proc. for infectious & para			

PROFESSIONAL FEES

- All physicians' fees
- Surgeons' fees only
- All professional fees
- Anesthesiologists' fees
- Other specialists' fees
- Psychologists' fees
- One-year follow-up exam

Possible Transplant Services

- Kidney
- Heart
- Liver
- Pancreas
- Bone Marrow
- Pancreas/kidney
- Heart/lung

Projected Enrollment (Alliance Service Area)

Product/Market	1996	1997
Self-insured	3,700	6,600
Sm. business/indiv.	5,000	11,000
Medicaid/MN Care	6,000	14,000
Medicare Suppl.	1,680	3,900
	16,380	35,500

PURCHASERS DIRECTED SERVICE

Purchasers of health care services have set reform in motion. The RFP illustrated above and actions such as those instituted by the Buyers Health Care Action Group in Minneapolis/St. Paul will help create the momentum needed to ignite the same type of purchaser directed health care services across the United States. Preparation for change is imminent.

Requirements for Change

Providers of care will be practices or groups that can bear financial risk and are dominated by primary care physicians. Financial strategy and accuracy must be weighed with the type and amount of service to be provided.

Operating Principles

Primary care	Specialty care
Through interdisciplinary teams that efficiently match the skill required for the care with the training of the professional doing the care.	Through colleagues within the group or through contracted colleagues outside the group who bear financial risk.

Standards of Care

- Internally Derived—Disease Management
- Externally Derived—Regulations

Figure 10.7 shows an array of available care options on the community/home-based care level, with the elimination and narrowing of specialized inpatient high-tech options.

Development and Use of Technology

- Restrictions due to its cost
- Practical applications are required before technology becomes standard practice
- Research confined to fewer institutions
- Purhcasers will continue to place a premium on doctors/health providers who listen to them
- Will retain entitlement philosophy
- Will become responsible for larger percentage of their medical bills
- Will reflect demographic changes

FIGURE 10.7. Levels of Care

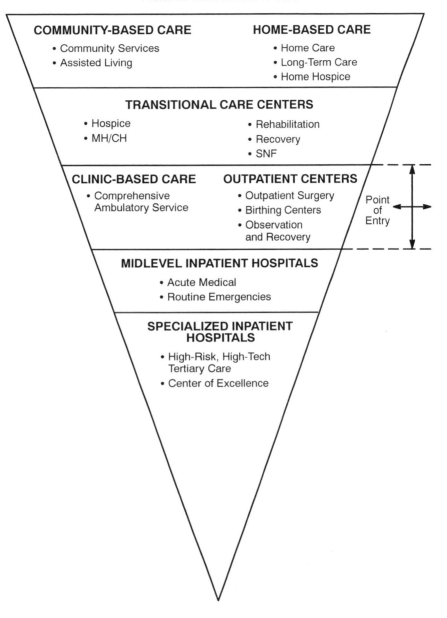

Change and Required Action

1.	Change the way we think.	• develop comfort with uncertainty
		• examine the common practices of our time and conclude that much is based on habit, not science
2.	Change the basis on which we make our decisions	• demand greater practical application in clinical research
		• be mindful that we are continually at risk of drawing conclusions on the basis of our recent experience
		• request and utilize data relevant to our clinical practices
3.	Change the emphasis of our clinical practices	• think and practice prevention rather than intervention
4.	Change the way we relate to patients	• think about caring for "populations"
		• enhance our skills in gaining trust
		• develop extreme comfort/skill with death and dying
		• understand that "medical care" and "medical treatment" are not synonymous
5.	Change the way we relate to other health professionals	• recognize training and expertise
		• focus on joint problem resolution
		• work in teams

Redefinition of Role as Physician

Primary Care

- Visibly lead the team
- Orchestrate members of the team to meet patients' needs
- Delegate clinical responsibility and authority
- Define specific parameters for consultation
- Develop precise expectations for patients

Specialty

- Practice in a more precisely defined role based on customers' need
- Recognize the primary care physician as the customer alongside the patient
- Support role of primary care physician as team leader

FUNDAMENTAL CHANGES OCCURRING IN HEALTH CARE

Specialized -------- ➤ Primary Care
Cost Unaware ------ ➤ Cost Accountable
Technology Driven -- ➤Humanely Balanced
Institution Based---- ➤Community Focused
Professional ------- ➤Managerial
Individual --------- ➤Population
Acute ------------ ➤Chronic
Treatment --------- ➤Management/Prevention
Individual Providers - ➤Team
Competition ------- ➤Collaboration

Figure 10.7 illustrates levels of care. Future requirements will focus moving the delivery point away from hospital toward home care.

According to Group Health of Puget Sound, the six elements of managed care include:

1. Vertical integration and teamwork
2. Effective management of capitation; willingness and ability to optimize risk
3. Sound science
4. Effective prevention
5. Excellent information
6. Superb customer service

DETERMINING CONSUMER SATISFACTION

Consumer satisfaction involves determining what the consumer wants, providing the service, and subsequently measuring the product; i.e., did your service meet the consumers' need? The only way to tell is to ask the consumer/purchaser to help you complete a report card that reflects whether or not the efforts of the practice met the needs. Although a standard approach to satisfaction for each practice setting does not exist, there are various measures of customers' perceptions that are helpful when assessing their satisfaction with the delivery in a system of managed care. The attributes of satisfaction for services in managed care include:

General Attributes

- Quality of medical care
- Outcomes of medical care, how much patient was helped

- Thoroughness and completeness of care
- Medical knowledge, skills, experience, and training of clinic's doctors
- Thoroughness of examination and accuracy of diagnosis by clinic's doctors
- Attention to what patient has to say
- Personal interest in patients and their medical problems
- Reassurance and support offered by clinic's doctors and staff
- Amount of time spent with doctor during visit
- Access to medical care whenever needed
- Overall satisfaction with the primary care clinic

Waiting Time Indicators

- Level of acceptance with appointment-to-visit waiting time for routine appointment
- Level of acceptance with waiting room waiting time

Indicators for Prevention of Disease

- Had a general checkup in past five years
- Had a tetanus booster in past ten years
- Received advice on cholesterol
- Uses tobacco products on a daily basis (tobacco users given advice to quit smoking, by clinic staff)
- (Females) Had PAP smear in past two years
- (50+ Females) Had mammogram in past two years
- (Seniors) Given advice last fall to have a flu shot
- (Seniors) Had a flu shot last fall

PROFILES AND TRENDS

In the *Hoechst Marion Roussel Managed Care Digest, 1994: Medical Group Practice Edition,*[9] noteworthy financial profiles substantiated the growing importance of readiness to provide managed care. Multispecialty groups with more than half their revenues from managed care spent proportionately less for insurance premiums and for laboratory and radiologic expenses per FTE physician than did groups without managed care. The percentage of revenues generated by contracts for at-risk managed care that called for discounted fees-for-service ranged from a low of 6 percent for a single-specialty group in cardiology to a high of 24 percent of groups in obstetrics/gynecology.

The largest multispecialty group practices (those with more than fifty physicians) were the only subgroup reporting in sufficient numbers to determine revenues from capitated Medicare (9.9 percent of total revenues) and capitated Medicaid contracts (1.4 percent of revenues).[10] The smallest multispecialty groups received a median of about 10 percent of revenues from contracts for capitated managed care, while the largest multispecialty groups received 22 percent of revenues from contracts for capitated managed care.

THE POWER OF QUALITY IN MEDICAL CARE

Perhaps the most significant yet elusive factor to measure in medical care, "quality," is sought after by all, but often left up to individual interpretation from the perspective of attainment of outcomes. Expectations of quality are linked to virtually all aspects of medicine, ranging from the care delivered and received to how well the operating systems worked to support the delivery of medical care. The problem with quality has to do with the fact that every physician and medical practice believes that they provide the quality that their customers/patients and other consumers (e.g., third-party payers, referring professionals) are looking for; but if the consumers' definitions (expectations) are different from the doctors', what evidence can be associated with quality?

Excellence Is Everything

In the pursuit of excellence one must:

- Care beyond what others think is wise,
- Envision more than most feel is practical,
- Chance beyond what others see as safe, and
- Anticipate more than others think is possible.

—adaptive verse by M. R. Mittelstadt, 1990

Quality is the target of both clinical and service excellence in health care today. Although providers and related caregiving facilities, services, and programs have established standards of practice, the ultimate determiner of quality is a total voluntary commitment by providers to embrace patient-focused care. Combine this fact with the reality that it is the consumer's perception which totally determines the degree of excellence or quality.

Quality assurance organizations help to formalize policies and procedures for providers and health care systems. Accreditation requirements have added safeguards that ensure and preserve the highest level of care and treatment in each patient. In this regard, a shift is occurring toward patient-focused systems founded on continuous quality improvement. Accreditation by the Joint Commission (formally the Joint Commission on Accreditation of Healthcare Organizations or JCAHO) gradually is moving its focus from assurance of service of good quality to improvement of its quality. [11] Improvement of outcomes for the patient, the enhancement of organizational responsibility, and the implementation of principles for continuous improvement in quality of service are moving to the forefront of JCAHO activity. The Joint Commission is a not-for-profit organization that performs accreditation reviews primarily on hospitals, other institutional facilities, and outpatient facilities. Most managed-care plans require any hospital under contract to be accredited by the Joint Commission. [12]

The National Committee for Quality Assurance (NCQA) is a private not-for-profit organization that assesses and reports on managed care plans on several levels. The information on accreditation that the NCQA provides is intended to enable purchasers and consumers of managed care to distinguish among plans based on quality. The NCQA is the leading accrediting body for managed care plans, as well as for some of the performance measures used today. [13] It evaluates how well health plans manage all parts of its delivery system—physicians, hospitals, other providers, and administrative services in order to continuously improve health care for its members.

The Accreditation Association for Ambulatory Health Care (AAAHC) primarily accredits ambulatory surgery centers, although it has accredited several managed care plans using two groups of standard that are applied as appropriate. Core standards apply to and include rights of patients, governance structure, administration, quality of care provided, quality management and improvement (which includes peer review, quality improvement, and risk management), clinical records, professional improvement, and facilities and environment. [14]

Quality, Consumer Satisfaction, and the Practice of Medicine

Cast aside what is thought to be the patient's need and instead ask the patient about his or her expectations. Once the expectations have been defined, it is up to the physician and supporting staff to fulfill them. [15] Best defined as perception, consumer satisfaction is a style, a total quality experience, a voluntary commitment by providers to deliver health care and achieve excellence. Health care is primarily a physician-driven service. Without the commitment, leadership, and follow-through of physicians in the area of consumer satisfaction, little (if any) progress can be sustained. It is essential, therefore, that physicians take a leading and active role in identifying and implementing the changes that need to occur to make consumer satisfaction a way of doing business in hospitals and medical practices. By caring enough about their patients to make these changes, physicians will find that their patients will remain loyal to them and will return to them whenever they have a problem in health care.

The practice of medicine has been a confidential and privileged relationship between physician and patient. The nature of the physician-patient interaction is embodied in the Hippocratic Oath, which outlines the duties and obligations of physicians. When a physician enters the business of medical practice, therefore, he or she must run that business in association with high-quality medical care. Yet even high-quality care can be delivered without consumer satisfaction, as indeed it often has been in the past. More and more frequently, however, medical professionals are recognizing the importance of providing high-quality service as well as high-quality care to their patients. They have found that such a consumer-oriented approach makes good business sense. It also goes a long way toward assuring that the patient receives the very best care possible.

Incorporating consumer satisfaction into a medical practice does not cost the typical physician any more than does the old, not-so-service-oriented approach. Cost is a nonissue, because it does not cost any more to treat the consumer right the first time he or she comes into the hospital or clinic. In fact, not treating the consumer right can be very costly. First, all such complaints from patients must be documented and dealt with, which costs time and effort; and second, some of those complaints may develop into expensive lawsuits for malpractice. In addition, the dissatisfied consumer may go elsewhere for care, another costly problem. Studies have found that it takes five times as much money to attract a new customer as it does to retain an existing one. By multiplying by five the annual value associated with *one* patient's outpatient and inpatient charges (including laboratory and X ray charges), it is easy to see the loss of revenue from one unhappy consumer of health care.

Many providers of health care are unaware that their patients are dissatisfied with the care they are receiving, because patients seldom complain directly to providers. In fact, research has shown that 96 percent of unhappy customers never complain to the people providing them with a service. But they do tell their families and friends. Research has also shown that each dissatisfied customer tells nine other people about concerns, and 13 percent tell as many as twenty other people. Word gets around.

Patients Differentiate Quality by the Nature of Care and Treatment Received

For physicians to thrive instead of just survive in the contemporary marketplace for health care, traditional approaches to achieve excellence in medical practice will have to change. Quality assurance through adherence to accreditation standards is part of the success formula and a basic requirement for every health care system. However, excellence can only be attained on a patient-by-patient level. Every consumer must believe that he or she is receiving personalized care that is totally focused on meeting or exceeding defined needs.

The attitude one takes to address excellence in patient care and treatment is often just as important as the technical skill used to treat the specific health care conditions. Without clear and distinct leadership and proactive participation by physicians at each level within the universe of health care as it is defined today, there will be less effective health care, health products-related services, and less than excellence in both the clinical and service quality of the care provided.

APPLICATIONS

Targeted Goals

1. Were outcomes for your programs achieved within budget?
2. Were payer sources accurately estimated?
3. Were financial reports and reports of activity accurately presented on a monthly basis?
4. What are key predictors of net revenues in the practice?

Objectives

1. What items of expense were eliminated during development of the zero-based budget? What expenses were added?
2. What net revenue replaced the diminishing reimbursement from third-party payers? Was it dollar-for-dollar replacement?
3. What key indicators are regularly (e.g., at least monthly) reported to the governing body of the practice and/or the board of directors?
4. What methods are used to differentiate financial support for various levels of productivity in the practice? Demonstrate accuracy of the methodology.

Content

Anticipated revenues, expenses, and activity in patient care are covered in this unit. Since revenue has become a most variable factor, careful study of potential fluctuations is at least an annual requirement. Are all essential financial considerations present in the system? Is progress of each element monitored?

Evaluation

Were budgetary targets achieved? What indicators of revenue, expenses, or activity failed to achieve projected results?

Continuous Quality Improvement

How were discrepancies in revenues and expenses identified and corrected? Describe the process used to incorporate refinements on an ongoing basis.

Chapter 11

Positioning the Medical Group

POINTS FOR FOCUS

Adopting change as a way of managing a practice will give your business a significant lead on the competition. Agents of change affecting your practice must be identified before the medical group can be positioned. Once a clear understanding of that has been established, it is possible to position the practice and achieve desired results.

Targeted Goals

1. To develop a strategy for the practice to enhance your medical group's market position through integration. Integration of physicians, hospitals, and health plans has been increasing, with significant frequency.
2. To establish your system for delivering medical service as the "provider of choice" for your service area.
3. To focus specific services toward customers' needs. To achieve the highest levels of consumer satisfaction with each of the major health care organizations in your catchment area.

Objectives

1. Examine the potential for integration of your groups.
2. Describe what it will take to become the provider of choice for your specialty.
3. Develop each service to meet customers' needs. Include measurable activities to assess consumer satisfaction appropriately.

Content

Change in health care today presents opportunity to the medical group that is prepared to:

1. Provide more high-quality service for less cost.
2. Sacrifice a quick buck for a mutually beneficial long-term relationship.
3. Design and deliver customized member/patient-centered service.
4. Expand member/patient-centered service.

Evaluation

Is the group better off now than before, as a desired outcome? The move from survival to thriving status, over the long term (seven to ten years), will be hallmarked by groups who are willing to change and become proactive. Integration has offered opportunity to consolidate resources toward achievement of common vision, mission, and goals while combining services to produce a highly effective and comprehensive unified customer-service system.

Continuous Quality Improvement

The achievement and ongoing refinement of desired outcomes is exemplified by unified team/partnership combinations that magnify effects beyond those that could be achieved independently.

THE NEED TO POSITION MEDICAL GROUPS

Contemporary medical practice warrants contemporary leadership by physicians and positioning of the medical group. Practices are rapidly changing, for reasons not unlike the game of musical chairs where once the music has stopped, someone is left without a chair. Although specialists are more affected than primary care providers, it is clear that for much of the United States, there is an excess of physicians. Competition among providers continues to increase, along with consumer expectations of easily accessible satisfactory care of the highest quality, priced right, that produces excellent outcomes. There has never been a time of greater opportunity for the field of medicine.

Physicians can position their practices to optimize growth and development during these turbulent times, mainly due to opportunities created by the shift of patient services to outpatient/ambulatory care and the requirements of managed care in a practice. Those physicians' groups who understand that the growth of managed care is shifting financial risk from payer to provider, and who prepare to enhance their skills as prudent providers of managed care, can increase their market share. As hospitals receive less reimbursement and have to determine how to reduce costs due to an over-abundance of beds, effective and well-positioned physicians' groups can be a significant asset by reducing inpatients' length of stay, ordering fewer tests, enhancing clinical and systems outcomes, helping establish outpatient centers for surgery and other procedures, combining duplicative administrative services and sharing expenses, and either developing capabilities for a system to serve managed care, buying the services from a third-party administrator (TPA) or service bureau, or forming/joining a health plan.

The strength of physicians' leadership will be required to move the current focus of medical care from intervention toward prevention and the overall development of longer lives and healthier lifestyles. Although hospitals and health plans can play active roles in establishing the imperative to change, to move from intervention to prevention, these can play no more than a supporting role. Only physicians are licensed to admit and discharge patients at the hospital, prescribe medicine or other therapy, and authorize medically necessary procedures. Without active, positive leadership by physicians, hospitals and health plans have less than adequate effectiveness. In a mutually beneficial integrated partnership among physicians, hospitals, and health plans, however, routine achievement of jointly developed goals and objectives becomes a way of doing business.

INTEGRATION AND RELATIONSHIP BUILDING

Integrated networks for delivery of health care, developed to provide comprehensive, seamless, consumer-oriented care and service, have rapidly become the standard. Optimal integration of physicians, hospitals, and health plans requires community stakeholder involvement and consensus on mission, vision, goals, and objectives. Integrated delivery systems can be defined as partnerships among essential providers who assume shared risk through common ownership, governance, financing, planning, and/or management (see Figure 11.1). Figure 11.2 shows basic organizational structures from which numerous variations are possible.

Strategy for Vertical Integration from the Perspective of the Health Plan

1. Capture premium
2. Control doctors
3. Cut costs
4. Keep the difference

FIGURE 11.1. Fully Integrated Model

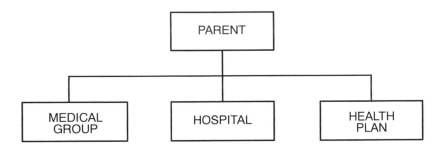

FIGURE 11.2. Health System Organization Models

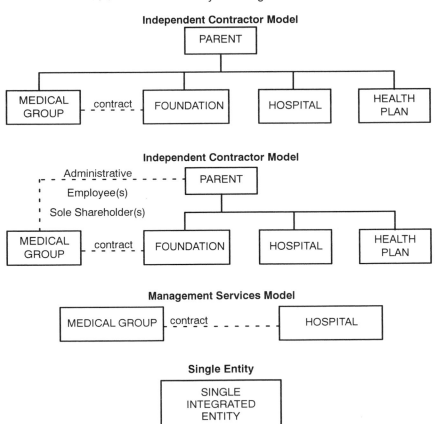

Provider Strategy

- Health care is a buyers' market
- Payers (employers, government, and patients) control the money and try to control the risk
- He who keeps the risk, keeps the reward—the goal of the providers' group must be to accept the risk and manage the care
- Pete Drucker: "know your customer"
- W. Edwards Deming: "meet our customer's needs"

Market-driven health care reform offers medical groups very specific outcome, price, utilization, and access "targets" to consider as physicians and hospitals position themselves to compete for business from purchasing groups composed of large companies, coalitions of large businesses, and health alliances established on behalf of Medicaid populations, small businesses, and others. Figure 11.3 illustrates sources of revenue and the flow of activity and dollars in the market-driven reform.

FIGURE 11.3. Sources of Revenue

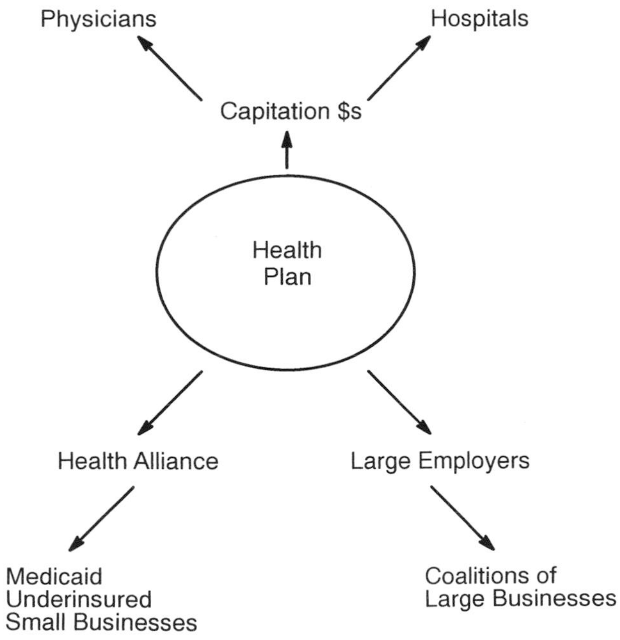

Family practices (13 percent) and internists (12 percent) had the highest percentages of revenues from capitated managed care of the five single-specialty groups shown. Too few single-specialty groups in obstetrics/gynecology, orthopedic surgery, and cardiology reported revenues from capitated contracts for reliable conclusions to be drawn. Cardiology and internal medicine received the highest shares of revenues from Medicare FFS.

Figure 11.4 shows a continuum of practice systems available as physicians, hospitals, and health plans position themselves in the marketplace.

Most major health care systems are developing integrated networks for the delivery of care, designated to compete effectively. Physician-led practices in primary care provide the essential focus on medical care. As physicians plan for enhanced participation through integration of systems, the following issues (identified by Ross Stromberg in his models for development of success for integrated health systems) are shown.[1]

PRINCIPLES OF UNDERSTANDING[2]

Effective physicians position themselves and their services in situations where they will survive. Then they wait for an opportunity to act. Survival depends on one's own actions; the opportunity to gain market share depends on the actions of others. Therefore, while effective physicians can always manage to survive, they may not necessarily be able to gain market share.

Survival depends on a careful defense; enhancement of market share results from taking the initiative and acting at the right moment. If your physicians' group is in the midst of intense competition, do not institute large-scale organizational change yourself. Stick with acceptable, easily understood methods and procedures. Maintain stable organizational patterns. Keep administrative matters simple and clear. Do not waste time with unnecessary paperwork.

You can manage competition more easily when your emotions, your organization, and your constituency are stable. Different competitive situations may require different tactics for success but, as far as possible, try to maintain stability during conflict situations. Do things the easy, well understood way. Operate from positions that can be defended.

Most physicians' groups like stability. People work better with methods, procedures, and equipment they understand. They are more comfortable if they know what is going on. They dislike being in the dark. People who are comfortable and stable have healthier emotions and sharper minds. Healthy emotions and sharp minds are necessary for competitive success.

When you face a challenge or obstacle, focus on the benefits of success. Create motivation through enthusiasm. In this way, your group draws

FIGURE 11.4. Continuum of Practice Systems

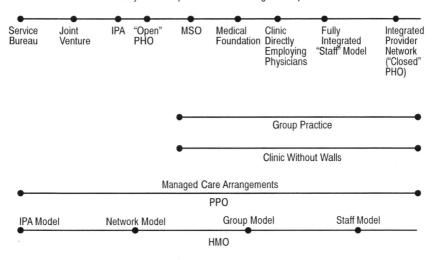

Physician-Hospital-Health Plan Integration Options

| Service Bureau | Joint Venture | IPA | "Open" PHO | MSO | Medical Foundation | Clinic Directly Employing Physicians | Fully Integrated "Staff" Model | Integrated Provider Network ("Closed" PHO) |

Group Practice

Clinic Without Walls

Managed Care Arrangements

PPO

| IPA Model | Network Model | Group Model | Staff Model |

HMO

Issues

Physicians	Health Plan/Network	Hospital Ownership
Ownership	Marketability to:	
	-payers	
	-patients	
	-physicians	
	-hospitals	
Governance/control	Capital funding	Geographic boundaries
Autonomy	Managing risk across the network	Hospital relationships
Structure	Role vis-à-vis local MSOs (management service organizations) and foundations	Physician relations
Compensation	N/A	Control
Pension plans		Multiple tertiary programs
Specialists relationships	N/A	How to assure referrals
Hospital relationships	N/A	N/A

Adapted from Stromberg, R.E. *Success Models for Integrated Health Systems Development.* Presented at Eastern Symposium on Integrated Health Care, Amelia Island, Florida, November 7-8, 1994.

strength from each others' examples. When there is excessive change or uncertainty in a situation, it will affect your ability to compete. If you must work within a rapidly changing environment such as a merger, wait until the change is manageable.

There are also dangers inherent in every competitive situation because of rumors. Stay away from spreading rumors. If your competitor bases his movements on such things, push him as far as possible in the direction he is going. Most rumors do not prove true, and competitors who perpetuate them will self-destruct. If your competitor exaggerates, in advertising or public statements, it is a sign of weakness. This should be documented in your planning process as an opportunity to be exploited, as an indication of turmoil. Resources are too scarce to be used as scare tactics or to embarrass the competition through public opinion. During these situations, effective physicians remain focused on their mission and continue to enhance customer-oriented services to their patients.

When your competitor deeply discounts his prices too often or hands out too many rewards, he has lost the ability to motivate his group. When your competitor publicly criticizes fellow staff or affiliated colleagues, mutual trust is not possible, and this weakness should be documented and exploited in the planning process. When you have penetrated deeply into another's territory and have expended large amounts of resources, a critical situation has been entered. Desperate groups are more apt to engage in risky business and to use valuable resources to buy market share, which in many cases makes it impossible to achieve a return on investment.

In managing competitive actions, effective physicians make it difficult for competitors to defend all aspects of their positions. They make it difficult for competitors to coordinate use of resources. They make it difficult for competitors to support weaker organizational elements. Effective physicians advance their position when it is advantageous and stop when it is not. Speed is the major factor in successful competitive action. You must take advantage of the situation before your competitor arrives.

The business of medical leadership brings all the forces together and puts them into an effective pattern. Lead physicians by actions, not by words. The staff of those skilled in leadership are responsive to well thought-out and deliberate plans of action. It is the goal of leadership to unify the various parts into a unified whole with focused direction. Cooperation among members of the group is essential for success. Cohesion through group commitment to a common mission and purpose is the ingredient to build upon to sustain long-term success. The requirement for successful medical leadership is to bring human, financial, and capital resources together to achieve predetermined group goals.

PROACTIVE CONSIDERATIONS

- Teamwork through physician/hospital/health plan integration: equal partnership to maximize resources and unify direction. Execute through joint strategic plan.
- Quality must pervade as the one overriding principle cornerstone.
- Focus on customer service and consumer satisfaction. Must adopt consumer satisfaction as a way of doing business.
- Accessible and affordable service is a must! Do not price service too high—although customers will pay for quality care, do not make price an issue.
- Continuously refine outcome analysis and improvements in your capabilities for service. Systematically focus on clinical outcomes to demonstrate technical competence and consumer satisfaction—the results of which may very well determine whether the patient returns for care needed tomorrow.
- Managing care requires the group's and the individual's consideration. For example, physicians can directly influence cost savings by reducing lengths of stay in the hospital, being aware of at-risk populations, competing against indemnity insurers, supporting aggressive cuts in premiums, and seeking improved relationships through discounted care.
- Become committed to participating actively in community initiatives that focus on wellness, health education, and prevention of disease. The mission of leading healthy, longer, and enriched lives is embraced by all and can be influenced significantly by physicians' commitment and active participation. It is a "win-win" situation. The patient becomes healthier and lives a longer enriched life under the watchful eye of the physician, who cultivates a larger, healthier practice that flourishes under capitated reimbursements for managed care.

WHAT PHYSICIANS NEED TO KNOW ABOUT MARKET CONDITIONS

Market conditions affecting medical practice:

- Shortage of primary care physicians
- Surplus of specialists and declining volumes but continuing needs of patients for chronic care
- Declining net incomes from solo practice
- Increasing administrative complexity

- Competition from group practices
- Declining value of practice "equity"
- Behavioral transition to managed care
- Need for capital, management, and access to contracts for managed care
- Increased trend toward electronic transmittal of patient information will permit more accurate basis for decision making.

The value of mission and vision in integration:

- The ultimate goal is to create a comprehensive system of physicians, an acute hospital, outpatient services, home care, and preventive and wellness services that are geographically dispersed yet efficient and fully coordinated—a system that can assume and effectively manage the full risk for delivering services for a fixed payment.
- Once full integration is achieved, an individual using the services can move from the physician's office to a hospital service to a home care service, with ease of admission and coordinated records, and can expect to receive the same quality of care throughout the system.

What insurers want from physicians:

- A long-term relationship
- To align insurer and provider functions and incentives
- To increase accountability for costs and quality through sharing risks and rewards
- Greater efficiency in delivering a comprehensive continuum of services
- Increased communication of utilization and outcome data for report card development and purchaser review
- Secure, loyal base of primary care physicians

What to look for from an integrated organization:

- A comprehensive continuum of services
- Geographically dispersed, yet coordinated
- Physicia, hospital, and insurance incentives aligned
- One managerial and administrative supporting structure
- An informational system that connects all parts of the system
- Costs and values that are continuously measured
- Highly competitive on cost, quality, and access

The market pressure on hospitals:

- Recessionary economy and employer activism
- Increase in managed care

- Threat of reforms in health care
- Declining use of hospitals
- Eroding base of primary care
- Aggressive competitors
- Operating losses
- Threat of exclusion

Defining quality knowing that cost is part of the problem:

- Quality is either acceptable or indistinguishable to most consumers
- The market will stabilize price through capitation
- Cost is the problem, and quantity is the villain
- Continuous quality improvement reduces cost, and:

> Is driven by data and facts
> Has statistical quality control
> Reduces waste and rework
> Increases productivity
> Builds in quality
> Abandons inspection
> Utilizes training, education, and feedback
> Drives out fear and blame
> Applies single-source contracts with suppliers

Focusing on consumer needs:

- Embrace the philosophy of continuous quality improvement
- Document and differentiate high-quality care and customer satisfaction
- Be cost effective by reducing waste, duplication, and reworking
- Operate a medical practice driven by primary care, prevention, and outcomes
- Provide consumers with necessary data and information to profile your performance
- Be a "one-stop shop" for the "best of the best" practice with providers who deliver the highest quality at the least cost
- Accept the risk and share the reward

USING HEALTH PLAN EMPLOYER DATA AND INFORMATION SET (HEDIS) INFORMATION AS A POSITIONING STRATEGY[3]

As previously noted in Chapter 1, the major areas of performance addressed by HEDIS include quality, member access and satisfaction, membership and utilization, finance, and descriptive information on management and activities in the health plan. The cornerstone of HEDIS is comparable measurement. Data in HEDIS provide tools and building blocks upon which to improve quality of care and reduce cost. By evaluating performance against defined measures in HEDIS, a health care organization can demonstrate its value and be held accountable for its performance as it positions itself with business and industry as an efficient and effective provider.

The HEDIS provides information:

- For individuals to make comparable, informed choices about health care. This information makes quality a factor in choice of health plan and allows individuals to select a plan that best meets their needs.
- For purchasers of health benefits to do their jobs better on behalf of their employees. Standard measures of a plan's performance demonstrate a plan's value.
- For providers of health care to improve continuously the care they deliver. Comparable information allows providers to gauge their performance and focus efforts at quality improvement on specific areas of their delivery of care.
- For policymakers, to guide their efforts to find solutions to improve the health care system.

Data Integrity

The HEDIS represents the state of the art in comparable reporting and is a major step forward in the health care industry. As the industry better understands what measures to report and how to report them, HEDIS will go through many generations. The next generation of HEDIS is likely to address issues that affect comparability, such as health status and other risk factors like the social and economic background of members of a health plan.

In July, 1994, the NCQA named MedStat as the group responsible for auditing its national report of the pilot project on care. The MedStat Group specializes in the strategic application of health care information and offers knowledge-based systems, consultation, and research for improving the quality and total value of health care. The company, with over 1,000 clients in both the private and public sectors, is headquartered in Ann Arbor, Michigan, with offices in Boston, Nashville, Sacramento, San Francisco, Santa Barbara, and Washington, DC. Having the audit performed by a team of MedStat professionals provides assurance that data are being consistently defined to meet requirements for each measure of performance in

HEDIS included in the collecting and reporting processes, general policies and procedures for informational management, internal auditing, and quality control. The company conducted site visits with each of the twenty-one original participating health plans and performed audits of medical records using the HEDIS specifications for measures of the appropriate quality of care.

The National Committee for Quality Assurance, a not-for-profit organization, seeks to improve the quality of patient care and performance by health plans in partnership with plans offering managed care, purchasers, consumers, and the public sector. Efforts by NCQA in that regard are complementary: they evaluate the internal processes for quality assurance in health plans (through review of accreditations), and they develop measures of the performance of a plan. Currently, NCQA is developing standards for performance so that eventually health plans can better assess and compare themselves, and so that purchasers, consumers, and others can evaluate the performance of health plans.[3]

WHAT WILL TOMORROW BRING?

Trends

Current	*Future*
Treat Sickness	Wellness
Fee-for-Service	Capitation
Solo Practice	Group Practices
Insurance	Managed Care
Super Specialists	Primary Care
Inpatient Care	Ambulatory Care
The Hospital Building	The Continuum
Profit Centers	Cost Centers

Assess the current status of your group in each category, to determine where the practice stands. Determine the difference between what exists and what is desired. Define the differences and establish specific goals and objectives supported by the necessary human and fiscal resources. Develop work plans and divide responsibilities among members of the team. Begin implementation and monitor progress. Report results monthly, quarterly, and annually. Review strategy, progress, and desired outcomes on an annual basis.

What to Look for in Physicians' Partnerships

The following matrix is used by physicians to model the characteristics of success in the effective integrated organization. The guide is applied to help physicians examine weaknesses and strengths as it examines potential partners in building a comprehensive integrated system.

Decision Matrix for Integration

Presence of Essential Components for Hospitals	Potential Partners #1	#2	#3	#4

- Existing market presence
- Capital for development of network
- Inpatient hospital network
- Ancillary services
- Outpatient clinics
- Emergency services
- High-tech programs in tertiary care

Presence of Essential Components for Physicians	#1	#2	#3	#4

- Management information systems
- Nursing support staff
- Preventive/community education
- In-home services
- Utilization review/Quality assurance systems
- Patients
- Care management expertise
- Existing market presence
- Organized network of physicians, extenders, and outpatient services
- Primary care gatekeepers
- Physicians' leadership
- Direct patient care expertise
- Quality assurance, practice protocols, utilization management
- Prevention, education, and research
- Contracting of specialists

Presence of Essential Components
Potential Partners for Managed Care #1 #2 #3 #4

- Existing membership base
- Capital for development of network
- Expertise in managed care
- Database for identifying cost-efficient
  providers
- MIS systems for tracking costs
  and outcomes
- Employer/broker relationships
- Quality assurance/utilization management
  systems
- Health education and promotion
- Government relations
- Marketing
- Actuarial/underwriting
- Provider contracting

Presence of Essential Components
for Systems Integration #1 #2 #3 #4

- Coordinates entire continuum of care
- Eliminates redundant systems
- Eliminates fragmentation
- Capital for development of clinics
- Comprehensive medical record
- Single managerial structure

TOTALS =

The scores awarded to each partner are summed for purposes of comparison. The physicians can analyze each potential relationship in more detail following the initial matrix screening.

STAYING A LITTLE IN ADVANCE OF THE TIMES

Rapid change in medical technology makes it difficult to stay abreast of everything that could possibly influence the practice of medicine. The same holds true for the management of medical groups and the field of health care in general. It is, however, important to be aware of proven advancements in administrative leadership among medical and hospital practices and advances in managed care.

From the perspective of administrative leadership in medical and hospital groups and managed care, the following advances have received noteworthy attention, and although many have been identified in previous years, their consideration for implementation has been much greater recently. When the advances in administrative leadership are implemented in practice is an issue of timing for each medical group to consider—but the advances should not surprise the physicians, nor do they warrant "knee-jerk" plans for implementation. Nevertheless, just as clinical and scientific advances must be dealt with by the physicians in the practice,[4] these advances in administrative practice must be systematically dealt with in the operations of contemporary networks:

- Protocols and practice guidelines
- Sum-certain capitation-based reimbursement in managed care
- Disease state management, wellness, and prevention
- Integration of physicians, hospitals, and health plan services
- Reengineering and operational improvement of networks for the delivery of services
- CQI and outcome-focused standards applied to clinical practice, operating systems, and administrative governing structures

Protocols and Guidelines

Regardless of the size of the group, it is important to participate in the development of protocols and guidelines. Many purchasers currently require their providers to follow established guidelines. Thirty-one percent of medical groups had formal medical protocols or standards of care for physicians in 1993 (see Table 11.1). Over two-thirds of groups without protocols planned to implement them during the next two years (see Figure 11.5). Of groups with protocols, 74 percent were single-specialty and 26 percent were multispecialty groups. Sixty percent of groups with protocols said their standards applied to primary care.[5]

The largest medical groups, with more than one hundred physicians, were most likely to have developed formal treatment protocols and standards of care (64 percent), compared with only 28 percent of the smallest groups (see Table 11.2). The likelihood that protocols covered primary care increased with the size of the group as well. But about the same proportion of most sizes of groups had protocols covering specialty care (83 percent overall). Ninety-six percent of groups with formal protocols reported that their protocols were developed internally by the group practice. Generally, medical protocols came from more than one source.

Table 11.1. Medical Practice Guidelines

Medical Practice Guidelines/Treatment Protocols

	Ratio of Cap to Noncap*		Overall Average
	Low	High	
Hypertension	40%	40%	40%
Immunization	60	80	75
Diabetes	40	80	55
G.I. Disorders	20	40	30
Depression	20	20	20
Asthma	60	60	60
Respiratory Infections	—	40	20
Other	60	80	60

Effect of Medical Practice Guidelines on Group Practices

	Type of Medical Group		Percentage of Managed Care		Overall Average
	Single Spec.	Multi w/PC	<50%	>50%	
No Effect on Practice Patterns	—	—	—	9%	9%
Identified Areas for Quality Improvement	50%	89%	88%	82	85
Reduced Use of Diagnostic Tests	—	44	13	64	40
Reduced Variations in Practice Patterns	50	83	75	82	80
Improved Patient Outcomes	50	44	50	36	45
Improved Pharmaceutical Therapy	—	50	25	64	45

* Low and high ratios of cap to noncap represent treatment protocols for groups as a function of their revenues from prepaid/capitated managed care plans or noncapitated HMOs and PPOs. The low ratio includes groups with more noncapitated revenues, while the high ratio includes groups with a higher percentage of prepaid and capitated revenues. Respondents gave multiple answers, so totals exceed 100 percent.

Source: *Managed Care Digest, 1994: Medical Group Practice Edition. Hoechst Marion Roussel Managed Care Digest, 1994.* Data supplied by Medical Group Management Association (MGMA) Englewood, Colorado, and American Medical Group Association (AMGA), Alexandria, Virginia.

TABLE 11.2. Quality Assurance

	Percentage of Groups with Formal Treatment Protocols	Protocols Apply to Primary Care*	Protocols Apply to Specialty Care*
Size (# of FTE Physicians)			
10 or Fewer	28.2	52.6	83.4
11 - 25	41.4	52.9	86.7
26 - 50	32.9	95.7	70.8
51 - 100	29.2	100.0	83.3
101 or More	64.3	88.9	87.5
Specialty Composition			
Single Specialty	30.6	46.4	88.6
Multispecialty	32.4	88.4	67.2
All Groups	**31.0**	**60.3**	**82.6**
Sample Size	**860**	**209**	**242**

*Respondents gave multiple answers, and groups could have protocols that applied to primary and/or specialty care.

Source: Medical Group Management Association. Activities and Trends Survey: 1994 report based on 1993 data. Englewood, Colorado, 1994. Reprinted with permission.

FIGURE 11.5. Plan to Implement Treatment Protocols in Next Two Years*

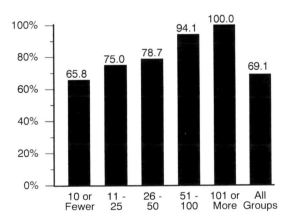

*Based on respondents that did not currently have protocols in place.

Source: Medical Group Management Association. Activities and Trends Survey: 1994 report based on 1993 data. Englewood, Colorado, 1994. Reprinted with permission.

Groups with protocols also reported that a medical specialty organization (28 percent), a hospital (25 percent), or an HMO/PPO (25 percent) helped develop their protocols.

Seventy-five percent of medical group practices had guidelines on immunizations. Groups were also likely to have practice guidelines and protocols in diabetes (55 percent) and asthma (60 percent). Thirty percent of groups had guidelines for medical practice on GI disorders, and 40 percent had them for hypertension. Groups were least likely to have protocols for depression (20 percent) and respiratory infections (20 percent).

The frequency with which guidelines were followed by the majority of MDs follows:

- Seldom (0-29 percent of the time) = 5 percent
- Occasionally (30 percent-60 percent) = 35 percent
- Frequently (70 percent-100 percent) = 60 percent

Groups with More Managed Care Follow Certain Protocols

Groups with a higher percentage of revenues from prepaid or capitated contracts were more likely to have practice guidelines for immunization, diabetes, GI disorders, and respiratory infections than groups whose revenues were seldom from managed care plans. Other protocols mentioned by some groups included back pain, sinusitis, estrogen replacement, HIV, depression, mammograms, Pap smears, and hysterectomies. Groups reported that medical practice guidelines helped them identify areas for quality improvement (85 percent). Between early 1993 and early 1994, medical practice guidelines helped 80 percent of groups reduce variations in practice patterns.

UNDERSTANDING TRENDS: HOW HEALTH PLANS VIEW PHYSICIAN SERVICES, MARKET-DRIVEN REFORM, AND PRACTICE SYSTEM OPTIONS

Tendencies

Positive	Negative
Physicians' commitment to guidelines	Too many guidelines and multiple work groups means changing and measuring complex work processes
Camaraderie between participating medical groups	Development of guidelines is far easier than implementation

Positive	Negative
A predictable system of care for customers	The ability to define and measure key variables in a process is difficult, particularly in groups with limited support from informational systems
Common elements in data and methods for informational system	The development, implementation, and measurement of guidelines requires extensive time of physicians, typically removed from their most important task, seeing patients
Measurement of public health and preventive outcomes across a broad network	

Sum-Certain, Capitation-Based Reimbursement for Managed Care

If your practice serves patients under Medicare/Medicaid, you may be asked in the near future to accept sum-certain (capitation) prepayment for the medical care and services provided. Capitated arrangements that foster more coordinated, efficient delivery systems will mandate team-based care. Your group must prepare for an increasing amount of capitated business. Overhead expenses need to be reduced as the capitated enrollment increases. Implications will be significant for providers and consumers.[6]

Physicians

Team-managed care will afford physicians greater support in meeting patients' needs through case management and linkages with other providers, such as mental health facilities and primary care clinics. Physicians will, however, need to develop skills in delegation, supervision, team development, and consensus building. Traditionally, physicians' competencies have been geared to approaches that are more directive and less team oriented.

Hospitals/Provider Organizations

Team-managed care will have significant implications for job design, organizational processes, and managerial hierarchies. Health care executives will have to redesign current systems, which focus on the individual provider. Developing team-based compensation, incentives, and performance systems will be critical, as will establishing appropriate strategies for using human resources and labor relations to help the organization manage the process of change.

Managed Care Organizations

Team-based care could result in lower-cost, high-quality care if it continues to drive some aspects of care to provision by nonphysicians. For example, patients may receive services from a physician's assistant rather than a physician when care is routine. For team-managed care to be effective, executives will need to allocate resources to train teams and develop skills.

Employers' Groups

With team-managed care, employers will see improvements in clinical outcomes and cost management, as well as increased employee satisfaction. Patients' health status will improve through partnerships between caregivers and well-informed patients.

Patients

Patients could have quicker access to care at lower costs, if well-trained ancillary personnel can deliver some services, rather than physicians. Team-managed care will, however, require shifts in patients' expectations. Some patients may prefer the traditional "Marcus Welby" model of care and may need to develop trust and appreciation for the improved range of services possible with team-based care.

With respect to the increasing number of patients under Medicare and Medicaid, the following implications are anticipated.

Physicians. Patients on Medicare are the keystone of many practices. If these patients sign up with managed care programs, it will mean reduced fees, increased capitation, and fewer patients for some physicians, which will have significant financial ramifications. Further, to control costs, physicians will need to manage the health of enrollees in Medicare and Medicaid, rather than provide episodic, as-needed care.

Hospitals/provider organizations. Active participation in managed care under Medicare and Medicaid could have a negative impact on many hospitals. As the population ages, inpatient services are covered primarily under Medicare. Significant dislocation of patients on Medicare could close down hospitals quickly, particularly in competitive markets. Growth in managed care on Medicaid has and will continue to have significant impact on municipal hospitals, so hospital executives will have to compete aggressively for market share.

Managed care organizations. Executives in managed care should be prepared to make major changes in strategies for marketing, since sales, especially in HMOs, will be made on a one-to-one basis, rather than in groups, by patients on Medicare being given a choice of plans. Patient satisfaction will also be an issue, if organizations want to maintain enrollment under Medicare. Further, with an increased number of patients on Medicare and Medicaid in managed care, executives are going to have to monitor expenses closely. Providing high-quality care at manageable cost will be an ongoing challenge.

Employers' groups. An increased enrollment of patients on Medicare in programs for managed care will enhance opportunities for retirees and make this type of coverage more affordable for employers.

Patients. For patients on Medicare, increased enrollment in programs for managed care will mean better benefits but more restrictions. For patients on Medicaid, it will provide better access and comprehensive services of higher quality.

At the Forty-Fifth Annual Conference of the American Group Practice Association in January 1995 in New Orleans, Louisiana, David Eddy, MD, PhD, summed up the harsh realities that practitioners must face.[7] Eddy related these as a series of principles that health care must ultimately live up to:

Principle #1: The financial resources available to provide health care to a population are limited.

Principle #2: Because financial resources are limited, when deciding about the appropriate use of treatments, it is both valid and important to consider the financial costs of the treatment.

Principle #3: Because resources are limited, it is necessary to set priorities.

Principle #4: A consequence of priority setting is that it will not be possible to adequately address the potential benefit every treatment might have for each patient.

Principle #5: The objective of health care is to maximize the health of the population served, subject to the available resources.

SURVIVAL TACTICS

"Seek first to understand—then to be understood" is sage advice from Stephen Covey, used in the initial remarks of this text to alert physicians about the sensitivity needed to succeed in the business of medicine.[8] To thrive in medical practice requires an understanding of the effects that change has brought to improve the health care marketplace. Once the effects and their causes are understood, it becomes a much easier task to position your group for success. The following trends are summations by physicians participating in an analysis of future trends sponsored by the Group Practice Association of America.[5]

- *Value of Satisfying Patients/Members:* Patient satisfaction will be a critically important component of health care delivery as a measure of quality. Groups will continuously assess and measure satisfaction. They will watch patient retention closely.
- *Standards of Care:* Medical directors of group practices believe medical practice guidelines and standards of care will be a high priority during the next five years. These groups view guidelines as important because within the cultures of their group practice, they live with such guidelines each day, without being told, as a result of close interactions of physicians and ongoing peer review.
- *Medical Guidelines:* Medical directors want to see the guidelines developed properly. Good guidelines will help focus the delivery of care in a standard manner. It is believed that quality of care will improve and that cost will decrease.
- *Medical Groups as Total Care Systems:* Medical groups want to view themselves as total care systems in their own right, not as components of existing systems for managed care. Medical groups will be risk-bearers, which provides physicians with the financial incentive of making the most revenue with the least expense. Group practices will bear risk through capitation for primary and specialty care. Medical groups see themselves as able to supplant today's managed care organizations by coordinating and delivering total care. Medical groups want to be able to contract directly with employers.
- *Survival Tactics for Small Groups:* Smaller medical group practices are expected to ally themselves with other small groups in confederations so they develop the critical mass and the interdependent physician culture necessary to deliver coordinated primary and specialty care successfully to defined patient populations. Physicians in small groups and in solo practices can no longer be independent, whether they like it or not. They must learn to work in interdependent teams.
- *Freeing Physicians to Care for Patients:* Medical groups will make more use of midlevel practitioners in coming years, to handle many routine aspects of patient care such as strep throat and other common illnesses. This will free physicians to spend more time with patients who need more attention and for whom diagnosis and treatment are more complex. Group practices who are already reengineering their

operations to accomplish this goal are finding that doctors like it, patients like it, and physicians are able to interact with patients much more effectively than before.

- *Helping Patients Make Good Medical Decisions:* Physicians in group practices will increasingly use tools for patient education, such as interactive videos, to inform patients about their conditions and the options for treatment available to them. These patient education devices are viewed as very helpful in supporting good decisions by patients about medical care and in enhancing patients' compliance with prescribed therapies.

APPLICATIONS

Targeted Goals

1. Describe your practice strategy for integration. What structure for governance balances leadership among physicians, hospitals, and health plan? What structure has the greatest potential for mutual success for the long term?
2. Why should members/patients select your physicians' group over others? How do you position the group's image, services, and outcomes? What most distinguishes your practice?
3. At what level of satisfaction should each of your services be rated, and why? How do you maintain effective communications with physicians who refer patients to your practice? How do you maintain contact with active and past patients and other purchasers of your services?

Objectives

1. How did you compare the characteristics of other organizations that might be potential partners in a merger to your own? What attributes above all others are most important to seek in a partner in long-term integration, and why? What are the least important attributes, and why?
2. How does your practice compare to the competition's? What will it take to become the provider of choice to members/patients in your area? Describe the differences, in rank order.
3. Define, from the customer's perspective, how each service provided should meet the customer's need. What questions will you use to assess consumer satisfaction?

Content

Long-standing and contemporary principles and strategies for businesses are combined to address the challenges of health care in the 1990s and past 2000. Each practice must assess its needs and match them with well-developed plans and services, to achieve desired outcomes. What are the characteristics of a thriving contemporary practice?

Evaluation

Measure progress toward desired outcomes after new strategies for positioning the practice have been fully implemented. How do results compare to those for similar practices on the local, regional, and national levels?

Continuous Quality Improvement

What ongoing process will be used to identify opportunities for refinements? How will refinements be implemented? Who will pay the costs? How will their success or failure be judged?

Chapter 12

Inferential Management

POINTS FOR FOCUS

Inferential management extends the decision-making process by providing the capability to predict and achieve predetermined outcomes. Inferences are drawn from existing data to optimize the matching of resources with desired results. Once targets have been identified, the model for inferential management systematically provides decision makers with the steps needed to achieve their targets successfully by focusing resources on the five or six most important activities responsible for the results.

Targeted Goals

1. To learn how to use inferential management to improve the success of your practice.
2. To understand the relationships between desired outcomes for the practice, planned goals/objectives, budgeted resources, and inferential management.
3. To apply the Inferential Management Model (IMM) to your practice/organization.

Objectives

1. Understand and apply each step of the IMM to your practice.
2. Describe desired outcomes for the practice within the strategic plan and budget.
3. Analyze results in the practice and compare to desired outcomes.

Content

The IMM is described and applied at various levels in medical managerial settings. Examples are used to illustrate its general applicability. Data required for application of the model currently exist in any medical practice or health care setting.

Evaluation

The model itself is an evaluative tool. Results in the practice are analyzed by comparing desired outcomes with actual findings. The discrepancy between desired and actual results is decreased and/or potentially eliminated by focusing activity and resources on the contributing elements responsible for the discrepancy.

Continuous Quality Improvement

At least annually, a comprehensive evaluation is conducted of progress in the practice and/or systemwide toward defined targets. Refinements are incorporated into those activities responsible for less-than-desired performance. Results from one year are compared to those for subsequent years to determine levels of success, complete with refinements, as needed.

A NEW WAY TO LOOK AT ACHIEVING SUCCESSFUL MEDICAL SERVICES

Survival in the contemporary practice of medicine will depend upon:

1. Physicians' ability to adapt to less reimbursement for services provided
2. Consideration of the need to develop an increasingly large base of patients served
3. The ability to remain or to become proactively customer oriented to attract and keep new patients
4. The development of strong linkages with sources who refer patients

Thriving will require all the things necessary for survival and then some. To thrive, physicians will need to:

1. Broaden their base of resources, both financial and programmatic
2. Reduce unnecessary expenses incurred by their practice
3. Avoid duplication of services and expenditures
4. Improve operations

Managers can provide an essential service by helping the medical staff orchestrate a contemporary practice. Such help will require minimizing the effect of adverse market conditions and maximizing the benefits of trends in reimbursement and in capabilities for delivering services, while adjusting to shifts in a practice's share of the potential market, and seeking out opportunities to provide new and/or expanded services to that market.

As resources continue to become even more scarce, managers must be able to conduct the business of medicine more proactively, with an eye on future requirements and probable changes in the market, while simultaneously taking advantage of current and past results associated with the practice. A solution to this complex problem does not exist in a vacuum, nor can it be identified by focusing independently on what are perceived to be the most important elements currently related to a successful medical practice. Instead, what is needed is a technology of evaluation for use by providers of medical services; such technology must consider appropriately the simultaneous effects of important indicators of success in the practice, including financial elements, enabling those providing the services to maximize their abilities to meet their current and future goals and missions.[1,2]

In the practical sense (operations), the role of evaluation in the process of management is a matter of technique. An event occurs, and a record is made of its effects. Careful study and statistical analysis of that record generates quantifiable statements that can serve as inferential indicators that can lead to explanations, interpretations, generalizations, predictions, and decisions. Statistical analysis is used to understand and reduce variation for purposes of improving performance.[3] In the theoretical sense (reasoning), evaluation is a matter of using concepts, conceptual systems, constructs, models, and theories. An event can be most accurately studied if those who manage can delineate questions meaningful to the practice as a business, in measurable terms and comprehensive enough to explore all plausible aspects of each problem, thoroughly. Such questions require the identification of key concepts or generative ideas that can lead and guide the techniques to be used. Thus, evaluation can be thought of as bringing together conceptual systems (at the theoretical level) and useful techniques (at the level of practical operations).[1]

Many factors may account for the theoretical relationships underlying the practical acts of doing something. To ask or answer questions involving complex relationships and numerous factors, however, necessitates an approach that is suited to considering simultaneously occurring events and activities. If one focuses on a specific relationship, it is apparent that many of the factors theoretically relevant to the concerns of a manager are randomized, when only one or two elements are examined. We may seem to recognize complexities regarding factors that affect the delivery of medical services and operations, but we often fail to conduct analyses that adequately reflect the combined effects of the many elements responsible for the complexities.

Where change in the targeted populations to be provided medical services is rapid and continuous, managers must apply cutting-edge technology to maximize the efficient and effective provision of services.[4] As one window of opportunity closes during turbulent times, others will be opening to those leaders in the provision of medical services who are ready to take advantage of the marketplace. The time has come to expand one's thinking about how to address the amalgamation of defined needs and the provision of services, proactively. The proactive thought process opens one's mind to the use of multivariate thinking and inferential technology, which can enhance the management of systems for the provision of medical services.[5] Survival and, more importantly, thriving as a contemporary provider of medical services will require continuous attention to the factors that account for change in systems for the delivery of health care. It will also require determination of how, when, and to what degree the effects of those changes will hinder and/or enhance their provision of these services.

WHY INFERENTIAL MANAGEMENT?

Since a successful medical practice is based upon the appropriate mix of elements of service and needs for health care in the market to which services are provided, it is necessary to determine both the influence of market conditions on the provision of medical services and the influence upon each other of interactive services and needs. The documented relationships found between and among activity indicators and outcomes are analyzed to determine the importance of the relationship.[6,7,8] Some relationships are more important than others in accounting for successful practices. Characteristics to be considered concurrently include, but need not be limited to, the following:

- Operational elements of the practice and services provided, for example:

    1. shifts in volume (number of patients seen)
    2. trends in types and timing of clinical activity
    3. systems for services providing information to management, medical records, functions of the business office, and communications with patients, to continuously improve quality of outcome
    4. ratings of consumer satisfaction, and other factors

- Changes in the market, for example, (to give only three examples among many):

  1. a competitor moves in across the street from your practice and your practice loses 10 percent of its patients seen for primary care
  2. a business for which your practice has been providing services related to workers' compensation leaves the area and your income from operations decreases 7 percent
  3. a health care purchasing alliance invites your group to bid on providing capitated health care to the companies the alliance represents (many of which reside in your area of patient catchment)

- Financial indicators, for example (three of many):

  1. a new 2 percent state tax is assessed against your net revenues
  2. your practice is asked by the HMO from which a majority of your patients come to accept bigger discounts (from 20 percent to 30 percent of billed charges)
  3. the resource-based relative value scale (RBRVS) and Medicare reimburse even less than what was in the budget (budget reflected a 13 percent decrease while actual is 18 percent)

- Longitudinal/historical trends and statistically significant changes associated with any important characteristic of your medical practice and/or the hospitals where the physicians admit patients
- demographic shifts within the area of patient catchment that change the composition of the basic population of patients for your primary and referral practice

Multivariate thinking provides managers with an opportunity to consider the role of many factors upon the success—or lack thereof—of the medical practice or of one or more medical services, and also the role of significant elements of the practice, for example:

1. Income from operations
2. Referrals
3. Visits for ambulatory care and admissions to the hospital
4. Overhead expenses
5. Customer satisfaction, and other quantifiable factors

Both descriptive and inferential statistics are helpful in illustrating results and relationships that help to understand and reduce variation for purposes of improving performance.[6,7] Descriptive statistics are typically utilized in charts and graphs and include discussion about measures of central tendency (e.g., mean, mode, and median), and about variability (e.g., range, standard deviation, and variance). Inferential statistics yield quantities that are interpreted along the baseline of a distribution of statistical probability. The findings allow for conclusions to be drawn from sampled data and generalized toward defined groups of the population. Inferential statistics are characterized by statistical significance, which illustrates (by a "level of probability") a significant departure from what might be expected by chance alone.[7]

An individual uses descriptive statistics to talk about the data he/she has. With inferential statistics, he/she can talk about data that he/she does not have, for example, "What do I need to know about today's practice that will enable me to plan for its future success?" Findings are generalizable (inferable) within "limits of probability" that permit the projection or prediction of results toward other, similar, populations. For example, a statistically significant finding at a probability level of 0.05 indicates that 95 times out of 100, the same results would predictably occur again (without attribution to chance).[6]

APPLICATION TO SYSTEMS
FOR DELIVERING MEDICAL SERVICES

Medicine is replete with information—to some degree, more information than is required to conduct an effective business. A process has been needed to enable medical managers to define, monitor, and influence changes in that information, to maximize the impact of the medical products and services they manage. That process is inferential management, used in conjunction with an established strategic plan (business plan). The plan, which represents a preset, agreed-upon direction for the organization, should be based on specific targets or goals in outcome (so you will know where the practice is meant to go), and on strategies with defined objectives, programs, and services that enable you to know how you plan to get there. The objective of inferential thinking is to take systematic advantage, by reasoning, of what is happening or has happened that is reflected in measurable evidence.

Members of the staff who are responsible for each aspect of the business need to develop related, quantifiable goals and objectives to facilitate the measurement of individual outcomes related to overall organizational efforts. Evaluations of performance, considerations of compensation (including incentives), and promotions of personnel should be based upon desired accomplishments of individuals and of the organization. Formation of the annual budget follows development of the strategic business plan, with rank-ordered consideration of financial support and the support of human resources for those programs, services, and activities identifiable in the strategic plan as priorities. Routine review of measurable (inferable) performance according to the plan is critical and necessitates at least quarterly assessment, with a comprehensive, in-depth analysis conducted annually.[2,5]

A dynamic business/strategic plan is one that is receptive to changing conditions in the marketplace and is updated at least annually. As discussed in Chapter 9, the plan remains in a "rolling," dynamic, fluid state that evolves proactively and moves in relationship to changing times. If the plan has embraced the organization's mission, it is likely to remain fairly stable, focusing on what your business expects to do over the long-term future. The mission would be supported by a vision statement outlining organizational hopes and dreams and how those who will benefit from the intended health care service will be affected. In order to write a statement of either mission or vision, those in management need to agree on values at the core of their understanding of the organization. A statement of core values would reflect expectations concerning the business: how individuals should consider their role, their style of practice or management as it relates within the organization.

As threats to progress and opportunities for development are identified, inferential evaluation is needed to consider the incorporation of such effects, positive and negative. Attentive management with the necessary tools to address change is important to a dynamic plan. It helps minimize the effects of adversity while maximizing proactive contributions (not reactive). The desired outcome is consensus (agreement within the group) on those strategies, defined by reasoning in association with presenting market conditions, that reflect the commitments of the organization aimed at attaining its desired mission and vision.

Strategies may take various forms and shapes. They need specific definition, in order to address issues concerning the medical practice as a business while emphasizing its reputation for service, its image, and its superior points of difference from the competition that need to be placed in the minds of its customers. Strategies provide direction for clinical and other revenue-producing supporting departments; they should be opportunistically oriented to take advantage of the marketplace. For example, "here is a specific opportunity; here is how we will use it." Since it is not possible to fund all strategic initiatives sufficiently, each service or program should be rank ordered on the basis of their measured impact and importance in helping the business achieve success in its overall mission and plan. Financial and human resources should be allocated more richly to the top 20 percent of rank-ordered programs that account for a majority of the success of the organization. Multivariate evaluation, specifically multiple linear regression analysis, is well suited to help rank order factors that are the most important predictors of defined success; this analysis helps determine what elements of service or what business activities account for a majority of the variance associated with indicators of business success.

Once the strategic initiatives and measurable objectives have been specified, inferential methodology can be used to facilitate planning and the alignment of resources with those plans. The method infers predictable outcomes within statistically significant parameters. Probability of a desired outcome is predicted by calculating the cumulative effects of important historical and financial factors and associated trends, with the desired business outcomes, through applied mathematics.

MODEL FOR INFERENTIAL MANAGEMENT

The model was initially designed, field tested, copyrighted, and published by the author in 1971[1] as an inferential evaluative method. Various applications over the years have demonstrated the utility of the inferential approach, as documented by the references at the end of the chapter. The following general structure illustrates how the model operates:

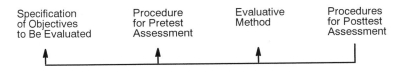

| Specification of Objectives to Be Evaluated | Procedure for Pretest Assessment | Evaluative Method | Procedures for Posttest Assessment |

Specification of Objectives to Be Evaluated

An essential step is the specification of objectives or targets your organization wants to achieve. The process requires a good deal of thought focusing on those elements that are indicators of business success. Often this is a multiphased process where it is necessary to understand surveys, studies, and/or financial and historical reviews in order to specify the objectives or targets of evaluation adequately. Since it is usually impractical and expensive to include in surveys and studies the entire population to be served, techniques for sampling the population and inferential statistics are used to provide results about the population in general. Such techniques are used routinely in political campaigns and election polls; they can accurately predict ultimate winners from rather small representative samples. If the study or survey identifies a need, managers must establish measurable objectives for exploring the opportunity to serve that need. It is at this point that relatively sophisticated inferential models are most helpful.

When the objectives to be evaluated are identified in quantifiable terms, they serve as benchmarks against which to compare future activity and results. To reduce the risk of a premature evaluation that might assess outcomes before the program has been given a chance to work, or to determine whether there are significant differences before implementing a new service or making changes in an existing program, it is necessary to collect baseline data in advance of introducing elements of change (interventive services or programs). Such information typically includes results of any sampling activity used to gather information about the population in general, and historical, financial, and operational data related to the activity or service under study.

Procedures for Pretest Assessment

Prior to instituting a new service or making changes in an existing program, it is important to know as much as possible about the conditions that may influence (or are influencing) success or failure. Steps taken during the pretesting phase include:

1. Review of proposed strategies by managers
2. Review of results of existing programs or servicess, including findings from other institutions that may be appropriate for consideration in current business efforts
3. Planning of specific procedures, time schedules, and monitoring necessary to implement the strategies

When a number of strategies are under consideration, multivariate analysis can be applied to illustrate the relative benefits of each, within the limits of probability. This information, in conjunction with data collected during the specification of objectives, is used by managers to select the most parsimonious set of predictors against which to measure the outcomes (achievements) of a program or service.

Information is collected and analyzed to demonstrate relationships between and among elements of the service or program and the objectives evaluated. The pretest findings are used to answer questions like these:

1. How much of what should be accomplished by the new service or with changes to an existing service is already known or desired by the targeted population?
2. Does the population for which the new service or change is intended have the prerequisite behavioral or physical capacity, and/or do they need to benefit from the activity?

Answers to such questions will help managers structure an evaluation that can focus on the service delivered or the change in a program or system, and help them understand the effects of preintervention differences in need or readiness between individuals served and groups served. Pretesting attempts to identify bias and other factors that can potentially influence posttest results. Once pretest influences have been identified, it is important to understand the potential problems they might cause and to eliminate those causes or control their impacts on outcomes. Most importantly, it is essential to identify and control each known biasing factor in advance of the introduction of a new service, program, or system (intervention), to promote a valid evaluative process. This step will keep a focus on the interventions being considered, not the patients or groups of patients.

Managers require accurate information about the state of affairs surrounding the objectives to be evaluated, prior to implementing a new or modified service. Following attention to adequate safeguards and the implementation of proposed changes, it is then important to monitor data reflecting the new outcomes. This type of information monitoring is essential as a base for decisions on the maintenance, further modification, or discontinuation of an ongoing program or service.

Evaluative Method

Inferential procedures can help reflect in statistics the complexities of systems for the provision of medical services that can benefit from data-based evaluation to provide reliable conclusions. A multifaceted question requires a multifaceted methodological approach to achieve an appropriate solution. Multivariate analysis was selected as the basic statistical method of this model of inferential evaluation. It enables managers to delineate, assess, and draw inferences from the conclusions about performance in the program or service from a multifaceted domain.

Multivariate analysis assumes that performance, behavior, or any desired outcome is subject to the influence of more than one variable or condition at a time and that adequate explanation involves more than a single variable or condition. If several variables are proposed as relevant to the outcome, it becomes necessary to measure both the influence of each variable on the targeted outcome or service, and their influence upon each other. Multivariate analysis allows administrators to reflect such complexities in the process of management, and adds the dimension of predicting future outcomes from past events. The power of prediction as a tool for management resides in the fact that such benchmarks enable rigorous testing of the adequacy of various trends in the business systems—historical, financial, and operational—affecting the outcome of programs and the results of delivery of services, while predicting the necessary combination of elements accounting for the achievement of predetermined targets (objectives) of the practice as a business.

Procedures for Posttest Assessment

Procedures for posttest assessment (assessment after the evaluative monitoring and predictions) are used to determine if, and to what extent, the specified objectives and targeted outcomes of the medical service have been reached. New business activity, and any service units with an increased allocation of financial and/or human resources, are assessed to determine whether there are any differences between relevant data collected from pretest assessments to posttest assessments. Posttest assessment measures progress toward achievement of defined objectives (the extent of difference within the limits of probability), direction and degree of inference, and predictability of results. Evidence is reviewed to determine whether the business components are performing as expected, and what refinements are needed.

It is important to screen the information being collected to detect defects in procedural design and in the process of implementing the service. The purpose of such exchange of information is to monitor the procedures for collecting data and to document the observable effects, not only at the end of the evaluative cycle but throughout the process, to identify potential problems and to correct the operation of systems for delivering the service, as needed. A dynamic, continuously self-improving business system is the desired outcome. The inferential evaluative approach embraces an outcome-based method for continuous enhancement of a medical practice, incorporating improvements when they are called for as a way of doing business. According to Balestracci W. Edwards Deming summed it up in the following:

> If I had to reduce my message for management about statistical analysis to just a few words, I'd say that it all has to do with reducing variation.[3]

In summary, the success of an effective business system will ultimately depend on:

1. Devising quantitative, operationally defined objectives to be evaluated
2. Before the intervention begins, establishing and measuring specific baseline criteria associated with the desired outcomes
3. After the intervention has occurred, comparing subsequent achievement with the predetermined expectations and standards of service
4. Drawing conclusions from the new outcomes that enable the organization to improve, expand, realign resources (financial, human), *or* terminate features of the new service or program, in part or totally

EXAMPLES OF APPLICATIONS: HOW TO IMPLEMENT, INTERPRET, AND DRAW CONCLUSIONS FROM INFERENTIAL MANAGEMENT

The following series of examples illustrates ways and means to apply multivariate and inferential management to the provision of medical services. The four stages of the Model of Inferential Evaluation (MIE) have been considered in each example:

1. Objectives evaluated (or, the intent of evaluation) have been specified in each case
2. The status of the environment or targeted population has been pre-assessed and defined by quantifiable targeted measures
3. Evaluative method has been selected, to measure outcomes and reflect the effects that the service or program will have on standards of targeted services, financial results, and/or groups of patients
4. Quantifiable results (achievements) have been determined and illustrated as conclusions leading to recommendations for improvement, expansion, and/or other changes

This section presents examples that illustrate the usefulness of the inferential approach and demonstrate the ease with which it can be applied to any defined medical service and/or program. The various examples illustrate different medical services and managerial settings where application of the procedures has proven its usefulness.

Points to Keep in Mind as Each Example Is Reviewed

What Is Inferential Evaluation?

It is a process used to evaluate sources of information and to determine their related values toward the accurate prediction of a defined target. The goal is to identify the most important predictors for each desired target. Resources are then applied to each of the predictors to enhance their impact while eliminating nonproductive and undesirable effects.

Example Definitions

Information	Outcome	Predictor	Resources
• volumes • perceptions • attitudes • demographics • financials • past trends	• new customers • return customers • net revenue • staff turnover • quality product • highly satisfactory service • exemplary experience	• motif • income level • age • sex • distance from service • perceptions • perceptual expectations • attitudes • feelings • habits	• human resources • capital • operations • cash

How Is Information Interpreted and Applied?

The method infers predictable outcomes within statistically significant parameters. The probability of achieving a desired target outcome is predicted by calculating the cumulative effects of information/factors important to the target.

What Are Expected Results?

Being able better to match desired outcomes to elements of the medical practice. Specific results will be reflected in:

a. Increased consumer satisfaction and net revenue, increased market share, increase in new customers, reduction in rate of turnover of customers, and so forth
b. Elimination of nonproductive/undesirable elements in the practice, with reallocation of expenses toward the creation of positive outcomes

Example 1

Marshfield Clinic, Marshfield, Wisconsin[9]
Number of Physicians: 400 (1993 MGMA Directory)
Number of Employees: 2,730 (1993 MGMA Directory)
Founded: 1916
Type of Group: Multispecialty

Objectives to Be Evaluated

Determine the level of consumer satisfaction among patients, parents, case coordinators, and sources who refer concerning the medical and health care services provided. Also, determine what factors were most important to their current satisfaction and predicted future satisfaction.

Procedures for Pretest Assessment

Baseline measurement of consumer satisfaction was documented after the first six months of service, and thereafter at six-month intervals throughout the cycle studied.

Evaluative Method

Multivariate analysis (specifically, multiple linear regression) was used to predict the importance to consumers of various activities of medical service provided them. Analysis of variance (ANOVA) was the inferential method used to describe statistical changes over the course of the study.

Procedures for Posttest Assessment

Longitudinal assessment was used to determine the stability of consumer satisfaction across multiple elements of service. Five evaluative intervals were measured between July 1, 1975 and February 1, 1978, with the total number of cases being 402. The most important factors related to overall satisfaction by parents (rank ordered) included: opportunity to ask questions, clarity of medical findings, ease of scheduling appointments, and progress made since medical intervention. Case coordinator results of most important factors related to overall satisfaction: how helpful medical findings were in determining specific educational activities for child; and how well medical staff answered questions based upon child's clinic visit.

Example 2

> Gundersen Clinic, LaCrosse, Wisconsin[10]
> Number of Physicians: 270 (1993 MGMA Directory)
> Number of Employees: 1,200 (1993 MGMA Directory')
> Founded: 1919
> Type of Group: Multispecialty

Objectives to Be Evaluated

Validate previous findings (Marshfield study) about consumer satisfaction among patients, parents, case coordinators, and sources who refer, concerning the medical and health care services provided them.

Procedures for Pretest Assessment

Baseline measurements were provided by the results of the 1980 study.

Evaluative Method

Findings from the previous study were validated and expanded. Inferential analyses included multiple linear regression analysis, analysis of variance, and a matched pair analysis of responses to similar questions on both questionnaires/surveys (to patients and parents, and to case coordinators and sources who refer).

Procedures for Posttest Assessment

The longitudinal study in Example 1 (Marshfield) was extended from February 1, 1978 to July 31, 1979, adding 152 to the number of cases studied (N). Results from the first analysis (N = 402, from July 1, 1975 to February 1, 1978) were included with the results of the second analysis (N = 152, from February 1, 1978 to July 31, 1979). Statistically significant findings were noted and, as a result of the findings illustrated in the 1980 study, were attributed to changes made in the system for delivering services. Positive gains related to overall satisfaction were noted in all of the case coordinator questions with statistical significance (p = .05) present in 8 of 10 questions due to focused attention by clinic staff or helping the case coordinators interpret and apply medical information to the child's classroom. A member of clinic staff traveled to child's school or day care program to complete conversion of medical data into the educational program. Parent results centered on two main factors accounting for overall satisfaction: how well medical findings focused on child's educational needs; and having a clinic staff member travel to child's school to implement medical findings into child's classroom program in conjunction with teachers.

Example 3

Ramsey Clinic, St. Paul, Minnesota[5]
Number of Physicians: 231
Number of Employees: 473
Founded: 1966
Type of Group: Multispecialty

Objectives to Be Evaluated

Consolidate services of a group of physicians and their hospital to achieve a vertically integrated network of health services. Primary interest was in eliminating duplicated overhead expenses and streamlining essential combined operations in the vertically integrated system.

Procedures for Pretest Assessment

Audited financial data, data from the business office, and data on patient volumes prior to consolidation in 1987 were used as baselines, except for measures of outcome (against which to compare performance), which were made from the onset of consolidation (1987). Data were taken from the physicians' group (Ramsey Clinic) and from the hospital (St. Paul-Ramsey Medical Center). The main focus was on the effects of intervention (planned change) measured throughout the five-year period ending in 1991.

Evaluative Method

Basic statistical and inferential longitudinal trend analysis was applied to the data. This included multiple statistical comparisons to analyze the predictability of the results, and tests to determine statistically significant trends.

Procedures for Posttest Assessment

Longitudinal assessment was used to determine the effects of consolidation on the group of physicians, the hospital, and the combined physician-hospital system over the five-year period. Results for the five-year period identified three main areas that were responsible for combined clinic-hospital financial success: overhead expense reduction related to the elimination of duplication of business office systems; increased efficiencies related to improved production of clinical staff; and increased decision-making due to integration of management systems.

Example 4

Ramsey Clinic, St. Paul, Minnesota[4]
Number of Physicians: 231
Number of Employees: 473
Founded: 1966
Type of Group: Multispecialty

Objectives to Be Evaluated

Physician-hospital organization established in 1987 and last measured through 1991 was updated through reevaluation after adding data from 1992 in a continuously refined process of management.

Procedures for Pretest Assessment

Results from 1992 compared to those from 1991 which, together with trends of previous four-year period, served as baseline.

Evaluative Method

Continuation of previously established longitudinal study. Methods for basic statistical and inferential longitudinal trend analysis were applied to the data. Best financial outcomes for physician group in its history as a group practice were documented. The hospital also had very good financial performance. The best predictors of combined net revenue included (rank ordered): inpatient days (although average length of stay decreased the number of patients increased); inpatient referrals (the number of referrals significantly increased ($p = .05$) leading to more hospital admissions of fee for service patients); outpatient clinic visits (number of outpatients increased expanding overall patient base); and physician compensation (compensation increased and physician turnover decreased due to joint clinic-hospital reduction in overhead).

Procedures for Posttest Assessment

Methodology for analysis of variance was used to determine statistical significance of data from 1992 when compared against points of previous data that comprised the longitudinal trend for each defined target in outcome.

Other Examples

Three additional examples follow, showing how inferential evaluation has been used to benefit management and/or to answer evaluative questions of a multidimensional nature.

Example 5

> Public Schools, Mound, Illinois
> Number of Children Studied: 52[11]
> Type of Service: Special Education District of Southern Illinois

Objectives to Be Evaluated

Determine whether a test of sensory motor abilities (the Kinesio-Perceptual Test Battery) could predict racial identity among black and white students classified as disadvantaged.

Procedures for Pretest Assessment

Random selection of fifty-two disadvantaged children (twenty-six black, twenty-six white) without severe emotional or neuromuscular problems was made from the population of a rural public special education district in southern Illinois, to determine whether there were differences, and to what extent, in sensory motor abilities.

Evaluative Method

Following completion of the Kinesio-Perceptual Test Battery by each participant in the study, basic descriptive and inferential statistical procedures were applied to the data. The means, standard deviations, and intercorrelations were obtained. Multiple linear regression analysis was used to predict racial identity.

Procedures for Posttest Assessment

Scores by black participants were compared to scores by white participants; findings reflected the predictability of race by the test battery in that black participants performed better ($p = .001$). The information could be further evaluated as an alternative diagnostic and training opportunity to improve the learning capabilities of black children. It should be noted, however, that the regression analysis was not cross-validated in this study; that would be required before results could be generalized to another population.

Example 6

Bowen Children's Center, Harrisburg, Illinois; Mound, Illinois Schools[12]
Number of Children Studied: 120
Type of Service: Residence for Mentally Retarded Children; Public Schools

Objectives to Be Evaluated

Determine whether a test of sensory motor abilities (the Kinesio-Perceptual Test Battery) could predict IQ among children in a residence for the mentally retarded.

Procedures for Pretest Assessment

To determine the usefulness of some commonly measured kinesio-perceptual abilities in IQ, 120 children (sixty-seven boys, fifty-three girls) were randomly selected from a total population of 230 at a state residential center for the mentally retarded in southern Illinois.

Evaluative Method

Following completion of the Kinesio-Perceptual Test Battery by each participant in the study, basic descriptive and inferential statistical procedures were applied to the data. Statistical estimates of objectivity, Hoyt's analysis of variance, and test/retest reliability were calculated. Multiple linear regression analysis was used to predict IQ.

Procedures for Posttest Assessment

Scores made by participants on selected items on the Kinesio-Perceptual Test were related to their IQ scores. This correlation was found to be statistically significant (p = .001). Unlike other perceptual motor tests reflecting developmental growth patterns, the selected KPT items appear to be indicators of intelligence within this group of retarded children. This information could be used to supplement a diagnostic battery, providing a different type of measure that might offer a direct remedial opportunity to help the retarded to learn. The regression analysis, however, was not cross-validated, which would be necessary before findings could be generalized to another population.

Example 7

Bowen Children's Center, Harrisburg, Illinois; Mound, Illinois Schools[13]
Number of Children Studied: 120
Type of Service: Residence for Mentally Retarded Children; Public
   Schools

Objectives to Be Evaluated

Determine whether a test of sensory-motor abilities (the Kinesio-Perceptual Test Battery) can reliably differentiate between those who need remediation and those who do not.

Procedures for Pretest Assessment

At a state residential center for the mentally retarded in southern Illinois, 120 randomly selected children were given the Kinesio-Perceptual Test Battery. A second random sample of 105 children from a public school was used to cross-validate the findings.

Evaluative Method

Descriptive and inferential statistical analyses were applied to the data. Measures of interobserver reliability and estimates of stability were obtained, in addition to predictive validity achieved by application of multiple linear regression analysis.

Procedures for Posttest Assessment

Cross-validation procedures were applied to the scores of both samples, from the state residential center and from the public school district. None of the cross-validated findings were determined to be significantly greater than zero. Such a result cautions against generalizing the findings beyond the parameters of the population on which the validity studies were conducted. Further application of the Kinesio Perceptual Test battery is required before more meaningful interpretations can be made of the data.

APPLICATIONS

Targeted Goals

Describe how the IM model was applied to your practice using each step of the model. How does your plan and budget directly support desired results? Can you identify and rank order resources (human and capital) for each activity in the practice? Describe and list how activities of your practice fit into the strategic plan and budget.

Objectives

Specify goals and objectives of the practice, describe procedure for pretest assessment, describe evaluative methodology, and describe procedures for posttest assessment. Are desired outcomes for the practice clearly represented in the strategic plan? Are resources appropriately budgeted to achieve targets realistically? How well did the practice achieve its predetermined results?

Content

The IM model needs to be put into operation in the way your practice does business. The process does not require data different from those currently available in any medical practice or health care organization.

Evaluations

Two forms of evaluation are required—evaluation of both programs/services and the system: (1) How did desired or expected results compare to actual results? (2) Were desired targets clearly represented in the strategic plan and adequately supported by essential resources (human and capital)?

Continuous Quality Improvement

How will you build the necessary refinements into both activities of the programs/services, and systems on an ongoing basis?

Notes

Introduction

1. Schuller RH. *Hour of Power.* Weekly television program. Crystal Cathedral Ministries, Garden Grove, CA, 1996.
2. Covey SR. *The Seven Habits of Highly Effective People.* Fifth habit: Simon and Schuster: New York, 1989.

Chapter 1

1. Kissick W. What Every Successful Group Practice Needs to Know. Closing speech of AGPA 45th Annual Conference on Quality-Change Management-Managed Care, January 18-21, New Orleans, LA, 1995.
2. Ladell, P. Physicians Are Increasingly Leading the Way in Shaping the Future of Healthcare: The State of Healthcare in America, Marion Merrell Dow, Inc., *Business and Health,* 13(3c), 1995.
3. Blair JD, Fottler MD, Paolino AR, Rotarius TM. *Medical Group Practices Face the Uncertain Future: Challenges, Opportunities and Strategies,* Center for Research in Ambulatory Health Care Administration (CRAHCA), Englewood, CO, 1995.
4. Ehlen JK, Sprenger G. RAINMAKERS. Allina Moves the Market: *Pacesetters—Hospitals and Health Networks,* American Hospital Association/American Hospital Publishing Inc., Chicago, 1995.
5. Wise T, White M. HealthPartners—Relevant Trends, Research, and Demographics. HealthPartners (internal study), Minneapolis, MN, 1995.
6. Brown A. *Research: Health Care, Likely Trends as the Health Care System Evolves.* A Brown & Sons: Baltimore, MD, January 3, 1995.
7. Davies S. *Future Perfect: A Startling Vision of the Future We Should Be Managing Now.* Addison-Wesley, Reading, MA: 1987, p. 240.
8. McMenamin B. "In Bed with the Devil." *Forbes,* September 12, 1994.
9. Ladell P, Koop CE. Challenges Facing the U.S.: The State of Health Care in America. Marion Merrell Dow, Inc. *Business and Health,* 12(3), Kansas City, MO, 1994.
10. Berwick DM. The Future of Health Care. *Quality Connection,* 3(3), Summer 1994.
11. Shoor R. Hospitals Forming Alliances with Other Providers. Shoor R. Managed Care Organizations. Both in *Business and Health,* 12(3), 1994.

12. Editors Note. Uses of Health Care Funds. *Medical Benefits,* 12(2), February 15, 1995.

13. Japsen B. An Off Year for Consolidation. *Modern Healthcare,* January 12, 1998.

14. Wetzel S. Applying Market Power: The BHCAG Is Flexing Its Muscle. *Minnesota Medicine,* 77, December, 1994.

15. Minnesota Department of Health. *Minnesota Health Care Report—1995, Health Policy and Systems.* Compliance Division: Health Economics Program, Minneapolis, MN, 1995.

16. Wetzell S, Hamacher F. Buyers Health Care Action Group (BHCAG) Request for Proposal for 1997. Distributed in December 1995. Bloomington, MN, 1995.

17. Manning J. "BHCAG Enrollees Opt for Lower Price, Higher Satisfaction." *City Business Magazine,* March 6, 1998.

18. Howatt G. "Cost Counts, Report from BHCAG Shows." *Minneapolis Star Tribune,* March 6, 1998.

19. Borger JY. "Viewing Buyers Group as Rival, HMO Opted to End Health Pact." *St. Paul Pioneer Press,* March 6, 1998.

20. National Committee for Quality Assurance. *NCQA Update,* 1(1), February 1998.

21. Rardin K. "Healthy Outcomes." Group Health Foundation Report. Minneapolis, MA, 1996.

22. HealthPartners. Health Plan Member Materials Related to Prevention of Disease and Healthy Lifestyle Development. *HealthPartners Today.* Minneapolis, MN, Fall 1997.

23. Joiner B. Quality Improvement. *Quality Connection,* 3(3), Summer 1994.

24. Sommers PA, Luxenberg MG, Sommers EP. CQI Longitudinally Applied to Integrated Service Outcomes. *Medical Group Management Journal* 42(2): 50-54, 56-58, 80-82, 1995.

25. Sommers PA. Malpractice Risk and Patient Relations. *The Journal of Family Practice,* 20(3): 299-301, 1985.

26. Sommers PA and Sommers EP. "Health Care Integration: A Greater Whole to Face Complex and Competitive Market." *HMO Magazine,* 45-48, September/October 1994.

27. Sommers PA. Longitudinal Analysis of a Physician Hospital Collaboration That Works: The Ramsey Model 1987-1991. *Group Practice Journal,* 43(3): 3,14,16-18,20,22-23,26,55, 1994.

28. Sommers PA. Preparing for 2000 and Beyond Through Physician Group Hospital and Health Plan Integration. *Group Practice Journal,* 43(6): 38-43, 1994.

29. Metropolitan Health Care Council, Minneapolis/St. Paul. *Health Care Cost Savings Shown in New Data.* Self-published: November 11, 1993.

Chapter 2

1. Sommers PA, Luxenberg MG, Sommers EP. Continuous Quality Improvement (CQI) Longitudinally Applied to Integrated Service Outcomes: An Inferen-

tial Evaluation Model (IEM) Approach. *Medical Group Management Journal,* 42(2): 50-54, 56-58, 80-82, 1995.

2. Sommers PA, Bartelma R, Whelan M. Marketing Medicine the Old-Fashioned Way: Consumer Satisfaction. *Strategic Health Care Marketing,* 8(7): 10-12, 1991.

3. Sommers PA. Malpractice Risk and Patient Relations. *Grand Rounds on Medical Malpractice.* American Medical Association/Harvard Medical Institutions, Inc.: Article 1.1, 20-22, 1990. (Originally published in *Journal of Family Practice,* 1985.)

4. Sommers, PA. Minimizing Malpractice Risk: A Patient Approach. *Group Practice Journal,* 36(5): 86-90, 1987.

5. Sommers PA. Getting the Most Out of Your Visit to the Doctor. *Executive Health Report,* 26(1): 1,4-5, 1989.

6. Sommers PA. What Physicians Should Know About Consumers' Satisfaction. *The American Journal of Medical Sciences,* 295(5): 415-417, 1988.

7. Sommers PA, Thompson MA. The Best Malpractice Insurance of Them All: Consumer Satisfaction. *Health Marketing Quarterly,* 1(1): 83-92, 1983; and in Winston W. (ed), *Marketing the Group Practice—Practical Methods for the Health Care Practitioner.* The Haworth Press: New York, 1983.

8. Sommers PA. Active Consumers' Participation in the Health Delivery System: An Evaluation of Patient Satisfaction. *Bulletin of the Pan American Health Organization,* 16(4): 367-383, 1982.

9. Sommers PA, Fuchs C. Pediatric Care for Exceptional Children: An Inferential Procedure Utilizing Consumer Satisfaction Information. *Medical Care,* 18(6): 657-667, 1980.

10. Sommers PA. Consumers Satisfaction with Medical Care. *Group Practice Journal,* 29(7): 5-8, 20, 1980.

11. Sommers PA. Consumer Satisfaction in Medical Practice. Commonwealth Press, Edmonton, Alberta Canada, 1998.

12. Sommers PA, Nycz G. A Procedure to Study the Efficiency of Clinical Services Provided to Children with Exceptional Health and Educational Needs: A Question of Consumer Satisfaction. *American Journal of Public Health,* 68(9): 903-905, 1978.

13. Sommers PA. Multivariate Analysis Applied to the Delivery of Medical Services: A Focus on Evaluation and Replication. *International Journal of Applied Psychology,* 34:203-224, 1985.

14. Nelson A. Consumer Satisfaction Evaluation Study of Ramsey Clinic Services. Internal study conducted by Nelson Research Services, Inc., Minneapolis/St. Paul, MN, 1987.

15. Kilmann RH. *Management of Corporate Culture.* John Wiley and Sons, New York, 1988.

16. Silversin J, Kornacki MJ. Employee Values and Commitment to Service, *Medical Group Management Journal,* 3, October 1989.

17. Hoxie L. Department of Ambulatory Healthcare—Accreditation Services Study, *Joint Commission on Accreditation of Healthcare Organizations,* Chicago, January/February 1991.

18. Accreditation Manual for Hospitals (AMH). *Joint Commission on Accreditation of Healthcare Organizations,* Chicago, August 1993.

Chapter 3

1. Batalden P. An Exercise in Quality Management, AGPA 45th Annual Conference on Quality Change Management—Managed Care, January 18-21, New Orleans, LA, 1995.
2. Skabelund H. Changing Physician Practice Style. Unpublished paper. University of Minnesota, 1996.
3. Eisenberg JD. *Doctor's Decisions and the Cost of Medical Care.* Health Administration Press: Ann Arbor, MI, 1986.
4. Soumerai SB, McLaughlin JT, Avorn J. Improving Drug Prescribing in Primary Care: A Critical Analysis of the Experimental Literature. *The Milbank Quarterly,* 67(2): 268-317.
5. Handley MR, Stuart ME, Kirz, HL. An Evidence-Based Approach to Evaluating and Improving Clinical Practice: Implementing Practice Guidelines. *HMO Practice,* 8(2): 75-83, June 1994.
6. Lomas J, Enkin M, Anderson GM, Hannah W, Vayda E, Singer J. Opinion Leaders vs. Audit and Feedback to Implement Practice Guidelines. *Journal of the American Medical Association,* 265(17): 2202-2207, May 1991.
7. Greco P, Eisenberg J. Changing Physicians' Practices. *New England Journal of Medicine,* 329(17): 1271-1274, October 21, 1993.
8. Schroeder SA. Strategies for Reducing Medical Costs by Changing Physicians' Behavior: Efficacy and Impact on Quality of Care. *International Journal of Technology Assessment in Health Care,* 3: 39-50, 1987.
9. Schoenbaum S. Feedback of Clinical Performance Information. *HMO Practice,* 7(1): 5-11, March 1993.
10. James BC. *Quality Management for Health Care Delivery.* Hospital Research and Educational Trust: Chicago, 1989.
11. Goldfield NI, Berman H, Collins A, Cooper R, Dragalin D, Kongstvedt P, Payson N, Siegel D, Southam A, Weis E. Methods of Compensating Physicians Contracting with Managed Care Organizations. *Journal of Ambulatory Care Management,* 15(4): 82-92, 1992.
12. Nelms RC. Medical Education and Health System Reform. *Minnesota Medicine,* 77, 1994.
13. Anders G. "Image of the HMO: Pioneer of the Species Has Hit a Rough Patch—Kaiser Permanente Can't Cut Prices as Much as Rivals That Lack Its Fixed Costs." *The Wall Street Journal,* p. 1, December 1, 1994.
14. Toubin FM. Bullish on Physician Opportunities (an interview with Dr. Andrew J.K. Smith, Incoming President of the Minnesota Medical Association). *Minnesota Medicine,* 77: 1994.
15. Mitka M. "Physicians Can Make Future Work for Them." *American Medical Association News,* January 17, 1994.
16. Byrd J. HealthPartners unpublished paper. Long-Range Planning Group—Attribute and Contact Alignment. Richard E. Byrd: Minneapolis, MN, 1995.

17. Sommers PA, Sommers EP. "Health Care Integration: A Greater Whole to Face a Complex and Competitive Market." *HMO Magazine,* September/October, 1994.

Chapter 4

1. Ellwood P, Kaiser L. *The Medical Organization of the Future.* American Group Practice Association: Alexandria, VA, 1985.
2. Halvorson GC. *Strong Medicine.* Random House: New York, 1993.
3. Kelly M. "You Can Prevent Your Own Heart Attack." *Discover Magazine,* HealthPartners, Summer 1994.
4. Howatt G. "HealthPartners to Emphasize Wellness in Goal-Setting Prevention Program." *Star Tribune,* Tuesday February 22, 1994.
5. Majeski T. "Largest HMO Bringing Bid for Wellness to Home, Office." *St. Paul Pioneer Press,* February 22, 1994.
6. Kelly M. "Here's Your Blueprint for Better Health." *Discover Magazine,* HealthPartners, Spring 1997.

Chapter 5

1. Covey SR. *The Seven Habits of Highly Effective People.* Simon and Schuster Inc: New York, 1989.
2. Fuchs VR. *Who Shall Live?* Basic Books: New York, 1974.
3. Colombotos J, Kirchner C. *Physicians and Social Change.* Oxford University Press: New York, 1986.
4. Hoffmann PB. Ethical Decision Making Requires Collaboration Between Administrators and Clinicians. *Frontiers of Health Services Management,* 8: 1, 1991.
5. Musfeldt CD. Ten Differences Between "Docs" and "Hocs." *Group Practice Journal,* 41-42, January/February 1996.

Chapter 6

1. Carlsson E, Sommers PA. Salary Administration Gundersen Clinic Style. *Group Practice Journal,* 3(3): 13-16, 1985.
2. HealthPartners. *Rightsizing Taskforce Report* (Internal Report). HealthPartners: Minneapolis, MN, 1994.
3. Hsiao WC, Braun P, Yntema D, Becker ER. Estimating Physicians' Work for a Resource-Based Relative-Value Scale. *New England Journal of Medicine,* 319(13): 835-841, 1988.
4. Miskowic A, McCally JF. Using RVUs and RBRVS to Improve Practice Management and Bottom Line Revenues. *Group Practice Journal,* 34-40, January/February 1996.
5. Hsiao WC. An Overview of the Development and Refinement of the Resource-Based Relative Value Scale. *Medical Care,* 30: 11, 1992.

6. Crossley K, Spurrier B. *Department of Medicine Compensation Plan* (Internal Report). Ramsey Clinic: St. Paul, MN, 1995.

7. Sommers PA. Managing Medical Service Outcomes by Predicting and Achieving Success: An Inferential Approach. *Group Practice Journal,* 44(3): 24, 26-28, 30, 1995.

8. Sommers PA. The Inferential Evaluation Model (IEM). *Journal of Educational Technology,* 65-67, May 1973.

9. Popham WJ. *Educational Statistics.* Harper and Row: New York, 1967.

10. Kelly FJ, Beggs DL, McNeil K, Eichelberger T, and Lyon J. *Multiple Regression Approach.* Southern Illinois University Press: Carbondale, IL, 1969.

11. Halvorson G. *Strong Medicine.* Random House: New York, 1993.

Chapter 7

1. Zirkle TE, Peters GR. *HealthCare Commentaries and Almanac of Essential Facts.* HealthCare Commentaries: Boulder, CO, 1993.

2. Sun-Tzu. *The Art of War* (translated by Ralph D. Sawyer). Westview Press: Boulder, CO, 1994.

3. Houle CO. *Governing Boards: Their Nature and Nurture.* Jossey-Bass: San Francisco, 1989.

4. Dayton K. *Governance Is Governance.* Keynote address for the Second Professional Forum presented by the Oakleaf Foundation, Independent Sector, May 7, 1985.

5. Wachel W. Managing the Board and Governing the Organization. *Healthcare Executive,* 7(5): 29-31, 1992.

6. Carver J. *Boards That Make a Difference: A New Design for Leadership in Non-Profit and Public Organizations.* Jossey-Bass: San Francisco, 1990.

Chapter 8

1. Medical Group Management Association. *MGMA Cost Survey: 1994 Report Based on 1993 Data.* MGMA: Englewood, CO, August 1994.

2. *Managed Care Digest, 1997: Medical Group Practice Edition, Hoechst Marion Roussel Managed Care Digest, Medical Group Practice Digest,* Kansas City, MO, 1997.

3. Meyer CR. Will Computers Become Tools of Our Trade? *Minnesota Medicine,* 77: 5, 1994.

4. Levitt JL. Why Physicians Continue to Reject the Computerized Medical Record. *Minnesota Medicine,* 77: 17-20, 1994.

5. Levitt JL. Quote from Why Physicians Continue to Reject the Computerized Medical Record. *Minnesota Medicine,* 77: 17-20, 1994.

6. Carpenter PC. The Computer-Based Patient Record Institute (CPRI). *Minnesota Medicine,* 77: 25-27, 1994.

7. Carpenter PC. Quote from the Computer-Based Patient Record Institute (CPRI). *Minnesota Medicine,* 77: 25-27, 1994.

8. Clement D. Medical Informatics. *Minnesota Medicine,* 77: 1994.

9. Meyer CR. The Computerized Medical Record in Action. *Minnesota Medicine,* 77: 8-14, 1994.

10. Fromberg R, Bader BS. Information Systems for Managed Care. *Health System Leader,* 1(8): 1994.

11. Hoehn B. Getting and Keeping Business. In Fromberg R and Bader BS article about Information Systems for Managed Care. *Health System Leader,* 1(8): 1994.

12. Lockridge RA, Minette HG. Ready, Set . . . Affiliate—Physicians, Networking and the Antitrust Laws. *Minnesota Physician,* 16, February 1995.

13. Waxman JM. The New Antitrust Guidelines—Encouraging Joint Arrangements and Market Competition. *Group Practice Journal,* January-February 1995.

14. Aaron HE. Application of the Medicare and Medicaid Anti-Kickback Statute to Business Arrangements Between Hospitals and Hospital-Based Physicians. *Annals of Health Law,* 1: 53-69, 1992.

15. Smith JH, Marx D. *Antitrust Overview: Challenges of the Health Care Field.* National Health Lawyers Association: Washington, DC, 1990.

16. Eggelston R. "Judge Keeps Verdict on Clinic Monopoly But Ruling Reduces Damages: Marshfield Must Pay Insurer." *St. Paul Pioneer Press,* Business, p. 1, March 17, 1995.

17. American Medical Association. *American Medical Association News* (AMA), 38(37): October 2, 1995.

18. Minnesota Medfax. "Supreme Court Denies Blue Cross' Request in Marshfield Clinic Case." Minnesota Physician Publishing, Inc. March 25, 1996.

19. Platt JB. Reducing Liability Risk in Managed Care. *Minnesota Medicine,* 77: December 1994.

20. Azedo D: Courts Let UR Firms Off the Hook—and Leave Doctors On. *Medical Economics,* 70(2): 30-44, 1993.

21. Pechette JMR. Computerized Patient Records: Avoiding the Pitfalls. *Group Practice Journal,* 44(1): 15-16,18, 1995.

22. Mills D, Lindgren OH, Brown DG. Maintaining an Effective Risk Management Program: Malpractice and Other Considerations. In Gitnick G, Rothenberg F, Weiner J (Eds.): *The Business of Medicine.* Elsevier Science: New York, 1991.

23. Sommers PA: Malpractice Risk and Patient Relations. *Journal of Family Practice,* 20(3): 299-301, 1985.

24. Sommers PA, Thompson M. The Best Malpractice Insurance of Them All: Consumer Satisfaction. In Winston WJ (Ed.), *Marketing the Group Practice.* The Haworth Press: New York, 1983.

25. Sommers PA, Luxenberg MG, Sommers EP. CQI Longitudinally Applied to Integrated Service Outcomes. *Medical Group Management Journal,* 42(2): 50-54, 56-58, 80-82, 1995.

26. Sommers PA. Longitudinal Analysis of a Physician Collaboration That Works: The Ramsey Model 1987-1991. *Group Practice Journal,* 43(3): 3, 14, 16-18, 20, 22-23, 26, 55, 1994.

27. Paulus K. Trauma Center Administration—1994 Continual Quality Improvement Project—Referring Providers Communication. Unpublished final report. Regions Hospital (formerly St. Paul-Ramsey Medical Center), St. Paul, MN, 1994.

28. MGMA. 1993 Cost Survey—1993 Report Based on 1992 Data. Medical Group Management Association Englewood, CO, 1993.

29. Center for Research in Ambulatory Health Care Administration. *CRAHCA Performance Efficiency Evaluation Report (PEER):* 1993, 1992 and 1991 Annual Reports, MGMA: Englewood, CO, 1993, 1992, 1991.

30. American Medical Association. *The Business Side of Medical Practice.* AMA: Chicago, 1989.

31. American Medical Association. *Buying and Selling Medical Practice: A Validation Guide.* AMA Financing and Practice Services Inc: Chicago, 1992.

32. *Managed Care Digest, 1994: Medical Group Practice Edition, Hoechst Marion Roussel Managed Care Digest, Medical Group Practice Digest,* Kansas City, MO, 1994. Data supplied by Medical Group Management Association (MGMA), Englewood, Colorado, and American Medical Group Association.

33. Center for Research in Ambulatory Health Care Administration. *CRAHCA Physician Services Practice Analysis Comparison (PSPA): 1993 Medians.* MGMA: Englewood, CO, 1994.

34. MGMA. *The Academic Practice Management Survey: 1994 Report Based on 1993 Data.* Medical Group Management Association: Englewood, CO, 1994.

35. American Group Practice Association. *AGPA 1994 Group Practice Activities and Trends Survey.* AGPA: Washington, DC, 1994.

Chapter 9

1. Cochrane JD. *Payor-Provider Partnership,* Integrated Healthcare Report. Integrated Healthcare Press: Lake Arrowhead, CA, February 1994.

2. Ottensmeyer DJ. The Lovelace Institutes. Presented at the Eastern Symposium on Integrated Healthcare—A Summit Meeting for Innovators, Amelia Island, Florida, November 7, 1994.

3. Sommers PA. Integration Outcomes—The Ramsey Model (1987-1994). Presented at the Symposium on Integrated Healthcare—A Summit Meeting for Innovators, Amelia Island, Florida, November 7, 1994.

4. Sommers PA. Managing Medical Service Outcomes by Predicting and Achieving Success: An Inferential Approach. *Group Practice Journal,* 44(3): 24, 26-28, 30, 1995.

Chapter 10

1. Medical Group Management Association. *Physician Compensation and Production Survey—1993 and 1992 Reports Based on 1992 and 1991 Data.* MGMA, Englewood, CO, 1994.

2. Barry MJ. Guidelines: Physicians in the Lead. *Health Management Quarterly,* 20-23, 1991.

3. HealthPartners. *The Institute for Clinical Systems Integration (ICSI).* HealthPartners: Minneapolis, MN, 1994 and 1996.

4. Grayson MA. Good News on Guidelines. *Hospitals and Health Networks,* 72(1): 12, January 5, 1998.

5. Sommers PA. Managing Medical Service Outcomes by Predicting and Achieving Success: An Inferential Approach. *Group Practice Journal.* 44(3): 24, 26-28, 30 1995.

6. Sommers PA. The Inferential Evaluation Model. *Journal of Educational Technology,* May 1973.

7. Brown, A. *Managed Care Overview.* Alex Brown and Sons Inc., Baltimore, MD, May 5, 1995.

8. Modaff JC. *Minnesota Health Care Costs: A Study of Minneapolis Area Relative Medical Care Costs.* Milliman and Robertson: Brookfield, WI, 1995.

9. *Managed Care Digest, 1994: Medical Group Practice Edition, Hoechst Marion Roussel Managed Care Digest, Medical Group Practice Digest,* Kansas City, MO, 1994. Data supplied by Medical Group Management Association (MGMA), Englewood, CO, and American Medical Group Association (AMGA), Alexandria, VA.

10. Medical Group Management Association. *Cost Survey: 1993 Report Based on 1992 Data.* MGMA: Englewood, CO, 1994.

11. Joint Commission on Accreditation of Healthcare Organizations. Accreditation Manual. Oakbrook Terrace, IL, 1997.

12. Kongstvedt PR. *The Managed Health Care Handbook.* Third Edition, Aspen Publishers, Inc.: Gaithersburg, MD, 1996.

13. National Committee for Quality Assurance. NCQA accredition process. Washington, DC, 1997.

14. Dacso ST and Dacso CC. *Managed Care Answer Book.* Second Edition. Aspen Publishers, Inc: New York, 1997.

15. Sommers PA. Getting the most out of your visit to the doctor. *Executive Health Report,* 26(1): 1, 4-5, 1989.

Chapter 11

1. Stromberg RE. Success Models for Integrated Health Systems Development. Presented to the Eastern Symposium on Integrated Healthcare, Amelia Island, Florida, November 7-8, 1994.

2. Sun-Tzu. *The Art of War* (translated by Ralph D. Sawyer). Westview Press: Boulder, CO, 1994.

3. National Committee for Quality Assurance (NCQA). *Health Plan Employer Data and Information Set (HEDIS).* NCQA: Washington, DC, 1994.

4. Thomas P. Top Ten Medical Advances of 1994: Scientific Progress. *Harvard Health Letter,* 20(5): 1995.

5. *Managed Care Digest, 1994: Medical Group Practice Edition, Hoechst Marion Roussel Managed Care Digest, Medical Group Practice Digest, 1994.* Data supplied by Medical Group Management Association (MGMA), Englewood, CO, and American Medical Group Association (AMBA), Alexandria, VA.

6. Bartling AC. Trends in Managed Care. *Health Care Executive*, March/April 1995.

7. Eddy D. The Harsh Realities That Practitioners Must Face. Proceedings of the American Group Practice Association's 45th Annual Conference on Quality-Change Management—Managed Care—What Every Successful Group Practice Needs to Know. January 18-21, New Orleans, LA, 1995.

8. Covey SR. *The Seven Habits of Highly Effective People.* Simon and Schuster: New York, 1989.

Chapter 12

1. Sommers PA. An Inferential Evaluation Model: Systematic Analysis to Hasten a Technology of Evaluation in the Behavioral Sciences. PhD dissertation. Southern Illinois University, Carbondale, IL. Copyright 1971.

2. Sommers PA. Managing Medical Services Outcomes by Predicting and Achieving Success: An Inferential Approach. *Group Practice Journal*, 44(3): 24, 26-28, 30, 1995.

3. Balestracci, D. Statistical Tools to Help Manage Utilization and Costs. AGPA 45th Annual Conference on Quality-Change Management—Managed Care, January 18-21, New Orleans, LA, 1995.

4. Sommers PA, Luxenberg MJ. Physician-Hospital Integration, Ramsey Style. *Minnesota Medicine,* 77: 22-25, 1994.

5. Sommers PA. Longitudinal Analysis of a Physician-Hospital Collaboration That Works: The Ramsey Model (1987-1991). *Group Practice Journal,* 43(3): 3,14,16-18,20,22-23,26,55, 1994.

6. Kelly FJ, Beggs DL, McNeil K, Eichelberger T, Lyon J. *Multiple Regression Approach.* Carbondale, IL: Southern Illinois University Press, 1969.

7. Popham WJ. *Educational Statistics.* Harper and Row: New York, 1967.

8. Sommers PA. The Inferential Evaluation Model. *Journal of Educational Technology,* May 65-67, 1973.

9. Sommers PA, Fuchs C. Pediatric Care for Exceptional Children: An Inferential Procedure Utilizing Consumer Satisfaction Information. *Medical Care,* 18(6): 657-667, 1980.

10. Sommers PA. Multivariate Analysis Applied to the Delivery of Medical Services: A Focus on Evaluation and Replication. *International Journal of Applied Psychology,* 34(2): 203-224, 1985.

11. Sommers PA, Holt LE, Joiner LM, Gross JC, Willis MA, Mainord JC. Kinesio-Perceptual Abilities as Predictors of Race: A Study of the Disadvantaged. *The Negro Educational Review,* XXI(4): October, 114-123, 1970.

12. Sommers PA, Joiner LM, Holt LE, Gross JC. Reaction Time, Agility, Equilibrium and Kinesio-Perceptual Matching as Predictors of Intelligence. *Journal of Perceptual and Motor Skills,* 31: 460-462, 1970.

13. Gross JC, Joiner LM, Holt LE, Sommers PA. A Kinesio-Perceptual Test's Reliability and Validity with Retarded Subjects. *The Journal of Special Education,* 6(2): 223-231, 1970.

Bibliography

Aaron HE. Application of the Medicare and Medicaid Anti-kickback Statute to Business Arrangements Between Hospitals and Hospital-Based Physicians. *Annals of Health Law,* 1: 53-69, 1992.

Accreditation Manual for Hospitals (AMH). Joint Commission on Accreditation of Healthcare Organizations. Chicago, August 1993.

American Medical Association. *American Medical Association News,* 38(37): October 1, 1995.

American Medical Association. *The Business Side of Medical Practice.* AMA Financing and Practice Services Inc.: Chicago, 1989.

American Medical Association. *Buying and Selling Medical Practice: A Validation Guide.* AMA Financing and Practice Services Inc.: Chicago, 1992.American Medical Association. *Medical Groups in the U.S.* AMA: Chicago, 1990, 1993.

American Medical Group Association. *1994 Group Practice Activities and Trends Survey.* AGPA: Washington, DC, 1994.

Anders G. "Image of the HMO: Pioneer of the Species Has Hit a Rough Patch—Kaiser Permanente Can't Cut Prices as Much as Rivals That Lack Its Fixed Costs." *The Wall Street Journal,* p. 1, Thursday, December 1, 1994.

Azedo D. Courts Let UR Firms Off the Hook—and Leave Doctors On. *Medical Economics,* 70(2): 30-44, 1993.

Balestracci D. Statistical Tools to Help Manage Utilization and Costs. AGPA 45th Annual Conference on Quality-Change Management—Managed Care, January 18-21, New Orleans, LA, 1995.

Barry MJ. Guidelines: Physicians in the Lead. *Health Management Quarterly,* 20-23, 1991.

Bartling AC. Trends in Managed Care. *Health Care Executive,* March/April 1995.

Batalden P. An Exercise in Quality Management. AGPA 45th Annual Conference on Quality-Change Management—Managed Care, January 18-21, New Orleans, LA, 1995.

Berwick DM. The Future of Health Care. *Quality Connection* 3(3), Summer 1994.

Blair JD, Fottler MD, Paolino AR, Rotarius TM. *Medical Group Practices Face the Uncertain Future: Challenges, Opportunities and Strategies.* Center for Research in Ambulatory Health Care Administration (CRAHCA): Englewood, CO, 1995.

Borger JY. "Viewing Buyers Group as Rival, HMO Opted to End Health Pact." *St. Paul Pioneer Press,* March 6, 1998.

Brown A. *Managed Care Overview.* Alex Brown & Sons: Baltimore, MD, May 5, 1995.

Brown A. *Research—Health care.* A. Brown and Sons. Baltimore, MD, January 3, 1995.

Byrd J. *HealthPartners—Long-Range Planning Group—Attribute and Contact Alignment.* Richard E. Byrd: Minneapolis, MN, 1995.

Carlsson E, Sommers PA. Salary Administration: Gundersen Clinic Style. *Group Practice Journal,* 3(3): 13-16, May/June 1985.

Carpenter, PC. The Computer-Based Patient Record Institute (CPRI), *Minnesota Medicine,* 77: 25-27, August 1994.

Carver J. *Boards That Make a Difference: A New Design for Leadership in Non-Profit and Public Organizations.* Jossey-Bass: San Francisco, 1990.

Center for Research in Ambulatory Health Care Administration. *CRAHCA Performance Efficiency Evaluation Report* (PEER): 1993, 1992, 1991 Annual Reports. MGMA: Englewood, CO, 1992, 1993, 1994.

Center for Research in Ambulatory Health Care Administration. *CRAHCA Physician Services Practice Analysis Comparison (PSPA): 1993 Medians.* MGMA: Englewood, CO, 1994.

Clement D. Medical Informatics. *Minnesota Medicine,* 77, August 1994.

Cochrane JD. Payor-Provider Partnership. Integrated Healthcare Report. Integrated Healthcare Press: Lake Arrowhead, CA, February 1994.

Covey SR. *The Seven Habits of Highly Effective People.* Simon and Schuster: New York, 1989.

Crossley K, Spurrier B. *Department of Medicine Compensation Plan—Internal Report.* Ramsey Clinic: St. Paul, MN, 1995.

Dasco ST and Dasco CC. *Managed Care Answer Book.* Second Edition. Aspen Publishers Inc.: New York, 1997.

Davies S. *Future Project: A Startling Vision of the Future We Should Be Managing Now.* Addison-Wesley: Reading, MA, 1987, p. 240.

Dayton K. Governance Is Governance. Keynote address May 7, 1985: Oakleaf Foundation, Independent Sector's 2nd Professional Forum.

Eddy D. The harsh realities that practitioners must face. Proceedings American Group Practice Association 45th Annual Conference on Quality-Change Management—Managed Care—What Every Successful Group Practice Needs To Know, January 18-21, 1995, New Orleans, LA.

Editors Note. Uses of Healthcare Funds. *Medical Benefits,* 12(2): February 15, 1995.

Eggelston R. "Judge Keeps Verdict on Clinic Monopoly: But Ruling Reduces Damages—Marshfield Must Pay Insurer." *St. Paul Pioneer Press,* p. 1, March 17, 1995.

Ehlen JA, Sprenger G. RAINMAKERS: Allina Moves the Market, *Pacesetters—Hospitals and Health Networks,* American Hospital Association/American Hospital Publishing: Chicago, 1995.

Eisenberg JM. *Doctor's Decisions and the Cost of Medical Care.* Ann Arbor, MI: Health Administration Press, 1986.

Ellwood P, Kaiser L. *The Medical Organization of the Future.* American Group Practice Association: Alexandria, VA, 1985.

Fromberg R, Bader BS. Information Systems for Managed Care. *Health System Leader,* 1(8): October 1994.

Fuchs VR. *Who Shall Live?* Basic Books: New York, 1974.

Goldfield NI, Berman H, Collins A, Cooper R, Dragalin D, Kongstevedt P, Payson N, Siegel D, Southam A, Weis E. Methods of Compensating Physicians Contracting with Managed Care Organizations. *Journal of Ambulatory Care Management,* 15(4): 82-92, 1992.

Grayson MA. Good News on Guidelines. *Hospital & Health Networks,* 72(1): p. 12, January 5, 1998.

Greco P, Eisenberg J. Changing Physicians' Practices. *New England Journal of Medicine,* 329(17): 1271-1274, October 21, 1993.

Gross JC, Joiner LM, Holt LE, Sommers PA. A kinesio-perceptual test's reliability and validity with retarded subjects. *Journal of Special Education,* 6(2): 223-231, 1970.

Halvorson GC. *Strong Medicine.* Random House: New York, 1993.

Handley MR, Stuart ME, Kirz HL. An Evidence-Based Approach to Evaluating and Improving Clinical Practice: Implementing Practice Guidelines. *HMO Practice,* 8(2): 75-83, June 1994.

HealthPartners. *The Institute for Clinical Systems Integration (ICSI).* HealthPartners: Minneapolis, MN, 1994.

HealthPartners. *Right-Sizing Taskforce Report.* HealthPartners (Internal Report): Minneapolis, MN, 1994.

HealthPartners. Health Plan Member Materials Related to Prevention of Disease and Healthy Lifestyle Development. *HealthPartners Today.* Minneapolis, MN, Fall 1997.

Houle CO. *Governing Boards: Their Nature and Nurture.* Jossey-Bass: San Francisco, 1989.

Howatt G. "HealthPartners to Emphasize Wellness in Goal-Setting Prevention Program." Minneapolis *Star Tribune,* Tuesday, February 22, 1994.

Hoxie L. *Department of Ambulatory Healthcare—Accreditation Services Study.* Joint Commission on Accreditation of Health Care Organizations, Chicago, January/February 1991.

Hsiao WC. An Overview of the Development and Refinement of the Resource-Based Relative-Value Scale. *Medical Care,* 30: 11, 1992.

Hsiao WC, Braun P, Yntema D, Becker ER. Estimating Physicians' Work for a Resource-Based Relative-Value Scale. *New England Journal of Medicine,* 319(13): 835-841, 1988.

James BC. *Quality Management for Health Care Delivery.* Hospital Research and Education Trust: Chicago, 1989.

Japsen B. "An Off Year for Consolidation." *Modern Healthcare,* January 12, 1998.

Joiner B. Quality Improvement. *Quality Connection,* 3(3): Summer 1994.

Joint Commission on Accreditation of Healthcare Organizations. Accreditation Manual. Oakbrook Terrace, IL, 1997.

Kelly FJ, Beggs DL, McNeil K, Eichelberger T, Lyon J. *Multiple Regression Approach.* Southern Illinois University Press: Carbondale, IL, 1969.

Kelly M. "You Can Prevent Your Own Heart Attack." *Discover Magazine,* Health-Partners, Summer 1994.

Kelly M. "Your Blueprint for Better Health." *Discover Magazine,* HealthPartners, Spring 1997.

Kilmann RH. *Management of Corporate Culture.* John Wiley and Sons: New York, 1988.

Kissick W. What Every Successful Group Practice Needs to Know. Closing speech of AGPA 45th Annual Conference on Quality-Change Management—Managed Care, January 18-21, New Orleans, LA, 1995.

Kongstvedt PR. *The Managed Care Handbook,* Third Edition, Aspen Publishers, Inc.: Gaithersburg, MD, 1996.

Ladell, P. Physicians Are Increasingly Leading the Way in Shaping the Future of Healthcare: The State of Healthcare in America, *Business and Health,* 13(3c): 1995.

Ladell P, Koop CE. Challenges Facing the U.S.: The State of Health Care in America. *Business and Health,* 12(3a): Marion Merrell Dow, Kansas City, MO, 1994.

Levitt J. Why Physicians Continue to Reject the Computerized Medical Record. *Minnesota Medicine,* 77: 17-20, August 1994.

Lockridge RA, Minette HG. Ready, Set . . . Affiliate—Physicians, Networking, and the Antitrust Laws. *Minnesota Physician,* 16, February 1995.

Lomas J, Enkin M, Anderson GM, Hannah W, Vayda E, Singer J. Opinion Leaders vs. Audit and Feedback to Implement Practice Guidelines. *Journal of the American Medical Association,* 265(17): 2202-2207, May 1, 1991.

Majeski T. Largest HMO Bringing Bid for Wellness to Home Office. *St. Paul Pioneer Press,* February 22, 1994.

Managed Care Digest, 1994: Medical Group Practice Edition, Hoechst Marion Roussel Managed Care Digest, Medical Group Practice Digest, Kansas City, MO, 1994. Data supplied by Medical Group Management Association (MGMA), Englewood, CO, and American Medical Group Association (AMGA), Alexandria, VA.

Managed Care Digest, 1997: Medical Group Practice Edition, Hoechst Marion Roussel Managed Care Digest, Medical Group Practice Digest, Kansas City, MO, 1997. Data supplied by Medical Group Management Association (MGMA), Englewood, CO, and American Medical Group Association (AMGA), Alexandria, VA.

Manning J. "BHCAG Enrollees Opt for Lower Price, Higher Satisfaction." *City Business Magazine,* March 6, 1998.

McMenamin B. "In Bed with the Devil." *Forbes,* September 12, 1994.

Medical Group Management Association. Robert Wood Johnson Foundation. *Considerations for Medical Group Formation.* Ballinger: Cambridge, MA, 1976.

Medical Group Management Association. *Cost Survey: 1993 Report Based on 1992 Data.* MGMA: Englewood CO, 1994.

Medical Group Management Association. *1994 Cost Survey: 1994 Report Based on 1993 Data.* MGMA: Englewood CO, 1994.

Medical Group Management Association. *The Academic Practice Management Survey: 1994 Report Based on 1993 Data.* MGMA: Englewood, CO, 1994.

Medical Group Management Association. Physical Compensation and Production Survey-1993 and 1992 reports based on 1992 and 1991 data. Englewood, CO, 1994.

Metropolitan Health Care Council. *Health Care Cost Savings Shown in New Data.* Self-published: Minneapolis/St. Paul MN, November 11, 1993.

Meyer CR. The Computerized Medical Record in Action. *Minnesota Medicine,* 77: 8-14, August 1994.

Meyer CR. Will Computers Become Tools of Our Trade? *Minnesota Medicine,* 77: 5, August 1994.

Mills D, Lindgren OH, Brown DG. Maintaining an Effective Risk Management Program: Malpractice and Other Considerations. In Gitnick G, Rothenberg F, Weiner J (Eds.), *The Business of Medicine,* Elsevier Science: New York, 1991.

Minnesota Department of Health. *Minnesota Health Care Report—1995, Health Policy and Systems.* Compliance Division: Health Economics Program, Minneapolis, MN, 1995.

Minnesota Medfax. "Supreme Court Denies Blue Cross Request in Marshfield Clinic Case." Minnesota Physician Publishing: March 25, 1996.

Miskowic A, McCally JF. Using RVUs and RBRVS to Improve Practice Management and Bottom Line Revenues. *Group Practice Journal,* 34-40, January/February 1996.

Mitka M. Physicians Can Make Future Work for Them. *American Medical Association News,* January 17, 1994.

Modaff JC. *Minnesota Health Care Costs: A Study of Minneapolis Area Relative Medical Care Costs.* Milliman and Robertson: Brookfield, WI, 1995.

National Committee for Quality Assurance (NCQA). *Health Plan Employer Data and Information Set* (HEDIS). Government Printing Office: Washington, DC, 1994.

National Committee for Quality Assurance. NCQA Accreditation Process. Washington, DC, 1997.

National Committee for Quality Assurance. *NCQA Update,* 1(1): February 1998.

Nelms RC. Medical Education and Health System Reform. *Minnesota Medicine,* 77: August 1994.

Nelson A. Consumer Satisfaction Evaluation Study of Ramsey Clinic Services. Internal study conducted by Nelson Research Services, Inc., Minneapolis/St. Paul, MN, 1987.

Ottensmeyer DJ. The Lovelace Institutes. Presented at the Eastern Symposium on Integrated Health Care: A Summit Meeting for Innovators. Amelia Island, FL, November 7, 1994.

Paulus K. Trauma Center Administration—1994 Continuous Quality Improvement Project—Referring Providers Communication. Unpublished final report, Regions Hospital (formerly St. Paul-Ramsey Medical Center) MN, 1994.

Pechette JMR. Computerized Patient Records: Avoiding the Pitfalls. *Group Practice Journal,* 44(1): 15,16,18, 1995.

Platt JB. Reducing Liability Risk in Managed Care. *Minnesota Medicine,* 77 (on law and policy): December 1994.

Popham WJ. *Educational Statistics.* Harper & Row: New York, 1967.

Rardin K. Healthy Outcomes. Group Health Foundation Report. Minneapolis, MN, 1996.

Schoenbaum S. Feedback of Clinical Performance Information. *HMO Practice,* 7(1): 5-11, March 1993.

Schroeder SA. Strategies for Reducing Medical Costs by Changing Physicians' Behavior: Efficacy and Impact on Quality of Care. *International Journal of Technology Assessment in Health Care,* 3: 39-50, 1987.

Shoor R. Hospitals Forming Alliances with Other Providers. *Business and Health,* 12(3): 1994.

Shoor R. Managed Care Organizations. *Business and Health,* 12(3): 1994.

Schuller RH. *Hour of Power.* Weekly television program, Crystal Cathedral Ministries, Garden Grove, CA, 1996.

Silversin J, Kornacki MJ. Employee Values and Commitment to Service, *Medical Group Management Journal,* Vol. 3, October 1989.

Skabelund H. Changing Physician Practice Style. Unpublished paper. University of Minnesota, 1996.

Smith JH, Marx D. *Antitrust Overview: Challenges of the Health Care Field.* National Health Lawyers Association: Washington, DC, 1990.

Sommers PA. An Inferential Evaluation Model: Systematic Analysis to Hasten a Technology of Evaluation in the Behavioral Sciences. PhD dissertation. Southern Illinois University, Carbondale, IL. Copyright 1971.

Sommers PA. The Inferential Evaluation Model. *Journal of Educational Technology,* 65-67, May 1973.

Sommers PA. Consumer Satisfaction with Medical Care. *Group Practice Journal,* 29(7): 5-8, 20, 1980.

Sommers PA. Active Consumer Participation in the Health Delivery System: An Evaluation of Patient Satisfaction. (In English) *Bulletin of the Pan American Health Organization,* 16(4): 367-383, 1982; (In Spanish) *Boletin de la Oficina Sanitaria Panamericana,* 94(1): Emero, 1983.

Sommers PA. Malpractice Risk and Patient Relations. *Grand Rounds on Medical Malpractice.* American Medical Association/Harvard Medical Institutions, Inc., Article 1.1, 20-22, 1990. *Journal of the National Medical Association,* 76(10): 953-956, 1984; and *Journal of Family Practice,* 20(3): 299-301, 1985.

Sommers PA. Multivariate Analysis Applied to the Delivery of Medical Services: A Focus on Evaluation and Replication. *International Journal of Applied Psychology,* 34(2): 203-224, 1985.

Sommers PA. Minimizing Malpractice Risk: A Patient Approach. *Group Practice Journal,* 36(5): 86-90, 1987.

Sommers PA. What Physicians Should Know About Consumer Satisfaction. *American Journal of Medical Science,* 295(5): 415-417, 1988.

Sommers PA. Getting the Most Out of Your Visit to the Doctor. *Executive Health Report,* 26(1): 1, 4-5, October 1989.

Sommers PA. Longitudinal Analysis of the Physician Hospital Collaboration That Works: The Ramsey Model 1987-1991. *Group Practice Journal,* 43(3): 14, 16-18,20,22-23,26,55, 1994.

Sommers PA. Integration Outcomes—The Ramsey Model (1987-1994). Presented at the Symposium on Integrated Healthcare: A Summit Meeting for Innovators. Amelia Island, FL, November 7, 1994.

Sommers PA. Preparing for 2000 and Beyond Through Physician Group, Hospital, and Health Plan Integration. *Group Practice Journal,* 43(6): 38-43, 1994.

Sommers PA. Managing Medical Service Outcomes by Predicting and Achieving Success: An Inferential Approach. *Group Practice Journal,* 44(3): 24,26-28,30, May/June 1995.

Sommers PA. *Consumer Satisfaction in Medical Practice.* Commonwealth Press: Edmonton, Alberta, Canada, 1998.

Sommers PA, Bartelma R, Whelan M. Marketing Medicine the Old-Fashioned Way: Consumer Satisfaction. *Strategic Health Care Marketing,* 8(7): 10-12, July 1991.

Sommers PA, Holt LE, Joiner LM, Gross JC, Willis MA, Mainord JC. Kinesio-Perceptual Abilities as Predictors of Race: A Study of the Disadvantaged. *The Negro Educational Review,* 114-123, 1970.

Sommers PA, Joiner LM, Holt LE, Gross JC. Reaction Time, Agility, Equilibrium and Kinesio-perceptual Matching as Predictors of Intelligence. *Journal of Perceptual Motor Skills* 31: 460-462, 1970.

Sommers PA, Fuchs C. Pediatric Care for Exceptional Children: An Inferential Procedure Utilizing Consumer Satisfaction Information. *Medical Care,* 18(6): 657-667, 1980.

Sommers PA, Luxenberg MG. Physician-Hospital Integration Ramsey Style. *Minnesota Medicine,* 77: 22-25, 1994.

Sommers PA, Luxenberg MG, Sommers EP. CQI Longitudinally Applied to Integrated Service Outcomes. *Medical Group Management Journal,* 42(2): 50-54, 56-58,80-82, March/April 1995.

Sommers PA, Nycz G. A Procedure to Study the Efficiency of Clinical Services Provided to Children with Exceptional Health and Educational Needs: A Question of Consumer Satisfaction. *American Journal of Public Health* 68(9): 903-905, 1978.

Sommers PA, Sommers EP. Health Care Integration: A Greater Whole to Face Complex and Competitive Market. *HMO Magazine:* 45-48, September/October 1994.

Sommers PA, Thompson MA. The Best Malpractice Insurance of Them All: Consumer Satisfaction. *Health Marketing Quarterly,* 1(1): 83-92, 1983; and in Winston W. (Ed.), *Marketing the Group Practice: Practical Methods for the Health Care Practitioner.* Haworth Press Inc: New York, 1983.

Soumerai SB, McLaughlin TJ, Avorn J. Improving Drug Prescribing in Primary Care: A Critical Analysis of the Experimental Literature, *The Millbank Quarterly,* 67(2): 268-317, 1997.

Stromberg RE. Success Models for Integrated Health Systems Development. Presented to the Eastern Symposium on Integrated Health Care, Amelia Island, FL, November 7-8, 1994.

Sun-Tzu. *The Art of War* (translated by Ralph D. Sawyer). Westview Press: Boulder, CO, 1994.

Thomas P. Top Ten Medical Advances of 1994: Scientific Progress. *Harvard Health Letter,* 20(5): March 1995.

Toubin FM. Bullish on Physician Opportunities, (An interview with Dr. Andrew JK Smith, incoming president of the Minnesota Medical Association). *Minnesota Medicine,* 77: September 1994.

Wachel W. Managing the Board and Governing the Organization. *Healthcare Executive,* 7(5): 29-31, 1992.

Waxman JM. The New Antitrust Guidelines—Encouraging Joint Arrangements and Market Competition. *Group Practice Journal,* January/February 1995.

Wetzel S. Applying Market Power: The BHCAG Is Flexing Its Muscle. *Minnesota Medicine,* 77: December 1994.

Wetzel S, Hamacher F. Buyers Health Care Action Group (BHCAG) Request for Proposal for 1997. Distributed in 1995, Bloomington, MN.

Wise T, White M. HealthPartners—Relevant Trends Research and Demographics. Internal HealthPartners study, Minneapolis, MN, 1995.

Zirkle TE, Peters GR. *HealthCare Commentaries and Almanac of Essential Facts.* HealthCare Commentaries: Boulder CO, 1993.

Index

Order Your Own Copy of
This Important Book for Your Personal Library!

MEDICAL GROUP MANAGEMENT IN TURBULENT TIMES

_____in hardbound at $79.95 (ISBN: 0–7890–0487– 9)

COST OF BOOKS_____

OUTSIDE USA/CANADA/
MEXICO: ADD 20%_____

POSTAGE & HANDLING_____
*(US: $3.00 for first book & $1.25
for each additional book)
Outside US: $4.75 for first book
& $1.75 for each additional book)*

SUBTOTAL_____

IN CANADA: ADD 7% GST_____

STATE TAX_____
*(NY, OH & MN residents, please
add appropriate local sales tax)*

FINAL TOTAL_____
*(If paying in Canadian funds,
convert using the current
exchange rate. UNESCO
coupons welcome.)*

☐ **BILL ME LATER:** (§5 service charge will be added)
(Bill-me option is good on US/Canada/Mexico orders only;
not good to jobbers, wholesalers, or subscription agencies.)

☐ Check here if billing address is different from
shipping address and attach purchase order and
billing address information.

Signature_____

☐ **PAYMENT ENCLOSED: $**_____

☐ **PLEASE CHARGE TO MY CREDIT CARD.**

☐ Visa   ☐ MasterCard   ☐ AmEx   ☐ Discover
☐ Diner's Club

Account # _____

Exp. Date _____

Signature _____

Prices in US dollars and subject to change without notice.

NAME _____

INSTITUTION _____

ADDRESS _____

CITY _____

STATE/ZIP _____

COUNTRY _____ COUNTY (NY residents only) _____

TEL _____ FAX _____

E-MAIL_____
May we use your e-mail address for confirmations and other types of information? ☐ Yes   ☐ No

Order From Your Local Bookstore or Directly From
The Haworth Press, Inc.
10 Alice Street, Binghamton, New York 13904-1580 • USA
TELEPHONE: 1-800-HAWORTH (1-800-429-6784) / Outside US/Canada: (607) 722-5857
FAX: 1-800-895-0582 / Outside US/Canada: (607) 772-6362
E-mail: getinfo@haworthpressinc.com
PLEASE PHOTOCOPY THIS FORM FOR YOUR PERSONAL USE.

BOF96